And Their Eyes Were Opened

And Their Eyes Were Opened

A Theological Analysis of Blindness in the Hebrew Scriptures

RAY McALLISTER

◆PICKWICK *Publications* • Eugene, Oregon

AND THEIR EYES WERE OPENED
A Theological Analysis of Blindness in the Hebrew Scriptures

Copyright © 2021 Ray McAllister. All rights reserved. Except for brief quotations in critical publications or reviews, no part of this book may be reproduced in any manner without prior written permission from the publisher. Write: Permissions, Wipf and Stock Publishers, 199 W. 8th Ave., Suite 3, Eugene, OR 97401.

Pickwick Publications
An Imprint of Wipf and Stock Publishers
199 W. 8th Ave., Suite 3
Eugene, OR 97401

www.wipfandstock.com

PAPERBACK ISBN: 978-1-6667-3052-4
HARDCOVER ISBN: 978-1-6667-2216-1
EBOOK ISBN: 978-1-6667-2217-8

Cataloguing-in-Publication data:

Names: McAllister, Ray [author]

Title: And their eyes were opened : a theological analysis of blindness in the Hebrew Scriptures / Ray McAllister.

Description: Eugene, OR: Pickwick Publications, 2021 | Includes bibliographical references.

Identifiers: ISBN 978-1-6667-3052-4 (paperback) | ISBN 978-1-6667-2216-1 (hardcover) | ISBN 978-1-6667-2217-8 (ebook)

Subjects: LCSH: Blindness in the Bible | Blindness—Religious aspects | Blind—History | Blind in literature | Blindness—History

Classification: BS680.B52 M33 2021 (paperback) | BS680.B52 (ebook)

10/27/21

The dedication shown by my wife, Sally Ann, in spending hundreds of hours reading technical literature to me, driving me to and from committee meetings, and providing constant emotional support most definitely warrants my dedication of this book to her.

Contents

Acknowledgments		ix
I	Introduction	1
II	Ancient Near Eastern Parallels	6
III	Biblical Hebrew Word Studies	48
IV	Blindness in the Torah	78
V	Blindness in the Prophets	158
VI	Blindness in the Writings	226
VII	Summary, Conclusions, and Implications	257
Bibliography		275

Acknowledgments

I first wish to acknowledge my dissertation committee for their constant supportiveness and guidance during this project. I also wish to acknowledge Camille Clayton and her father, Laren Kurtz, who have assisted me with the technical formatting and work with Hebrew fonts. I also must acknowledge my wife, Sally Ann, for the attributes and actions listed in the dedication section. Finally, I must acknowledge God, who, according to Dan 2:21, gives wisdom to the wise and understanding to the learned.

I

Introduction

BACKGROUND TO THE PROBLEM

A wide array of scholars have written on the topic of blindness as it occurs in the Hebrew Scriptures and other ancient Near Eastern documents.[1] R. K. Harrison, in a brief dictionary article on blindness in the Hebrew Scriptures, for example, notes how the Code of Hammurabi prescribes how doctors could appropriately charge for treating ophthalmic disorders. Some of the disorders encountered by these people were glaucoma and conjunctivitis.[2]

An encyclopedia article in *Encyclopedia Judaica* notes how a number of words were used in the Hebrew Scriptures to describe blindness and issues associated with blindness. One word, עִוֵּר, refers directly to a blind individual (Lev 19:14). Another word, סַנְוֵרִים (Gen 19:11; 2 Kgs 6:18), while being associated with blindness, may actually refer to a dazzling light that causes blindness.[3]

The same article discusses a number of causes given for blindness in the Hebrew Scriptures. Based on Exod 4:11, God is responsible for all blindness. Nonetheless, human agencies are also said to be involved in causing this condition. The removal of an eye was said to be a divinely ordained punishment for one's removing of the eye of his neighbor in ancient Israel

---

1. See the Bibliography for this dissertation.
2. R. K. Harrison, "Blindness," *IDB* (1962), 1:449.
3. *Encyclopaedia Judaica*, 1971 ed., s.v. "Blindness."

(Exod 21:21–24). This use of blinding was a result of the principle of *lex talionis* (law of retaliation) common to the Code of Hammurabi. Blindness was also seen as a simple affliction of the elderly. This form of the condition was not necessarily associated in the text with punishment (1 Kgs 14:4).[4] However the condition came about, ancient Israel was to treat all blind people with respect, not intentionally causing them to stumble (Lev 19:14). As Erhard S. Gerstenberger notes in his general commentary on the book of Leviticus, this law, being placed in the midst of holiness legislation, connects proper treatment of the disabled with holiness.[5]

Blindness also carried a number of symbolic meanings in the Hebrew Scriptures. One such meaning is expressed in Eccl 11:7, 8. There it is said that it is good for the eyes to see the sun while one must remember that days of darkness are coming. Roland E. Murphy, in his general commentary on the book of Ecclesiastes, notes that in this passage, the light refers to life, and the darkness refers to the trials associated with death.[6]

STATEMENT OF THE PROBLEM

A search through dissertation abstracts, books, and journal articles for material on blindness in the Hebrew Scriptures shows either thorough research on individual passages or broad, brief studies on the topic. There is not, though, a broad study of blindness as it is discussed throughout the entire Hebrew Scriptures. This book, then, seeks to answer the following question: "How can one understand the theological aspects of blindness in the Hebrew Scriptures?" This question can be further pursued through the following research questions. How does the treatment of the issue of blindness in ancient Israel compare with that in other ancient Near Eastern cultures? How can one best understand the Hebrew words used to describe blindness? How should one understand the limitations placed on the blind in the Hebrew Scriptures? How were God, himself, and society, as commanded by God, expected to accommodate the blind? What part does God play in the cause of blindness? What are the major symbolic meanings given to blindness? Finally, how was the issue of blindness to be treated in the Messianic era?

---

4. *Encyclopaedia Judaica*, 1971 ed., s.v. "Blindness."
5. Gerstenberger, *Leviticus*, 281.
6. Murphy, *Ecclesiastes*, 116.

STATEMENT OF PURPOSE

The purpose of this book is to provide an exegetical and theological analysis of blindness, with its physical, social, and spiritual ramifications, as discussed in the Hebrew Scriptures.

JUSTIFICATION

There are a number of reasons this study should be conducted. As noted above, such an undertaking has not been done in formal academia. The literature review in Felix Just's dissertation on blindness in the New Testament demonstrates how literature on disabilities has tended to not discuss matters concerning blindness in the Bible or ancient Near Eastern texts.[7] A number of scholarly books have even been written concerning disabilities as a whole in the Hebrew Bible.[8] While commentaries on books of the Hebrew Scriptures abound, they discuss blindness only as it occurs in the natural flow of the text and then move on to a different topic as that topic occurs. In reality, though, the insights gained from comparative studies of passages discussing blindness throughout the Hebrew Scriptures would be new to research.

As one who is blind, I understand in a special way the importance of increasing awareness of issues relating to disabilities. Because of this research, the actual and ideal positions of the blind in ancient Israel would be more clearly understood. This information could guide ethicists as they work to understand how to respond to more contemporary issues relating to blindness and the blind.

SCOPE AND DELIMITATIONS

A number of delimitations affect this study. This study concerns the theology of blindness, according to the Masoretic Text of the Hebrew Scriptures. First, blindness is to be understood as any weakening of the eyesight that tangibly affects the individual with such a condition. Partial and total blindness, then, are considered. This study is also centered on the theology of blindness. Issues relating to the sociology, physiology, or psychology of blindness are discussed only when they aid one's understanding of the theology of blindness. In addition, this study is limited to blindness in the Hebrew Scriptures. Blindness as discussed in the NT, rabbinic literature,

---

7. Just, "From Tobit to Bartimaeus, From Qumran to Siloam," 3–10.
8. Olyan, *Disability in the Hebrew Bible* and Raphael, *Biblical Corpora*.

and the writings of the church fathers is not considered unless insights are discovered that aid one's understanding of blindness in the Hebrew Scriptures. This study also concerns only the Masoretic Text of the Hebrew Scriptures. Thus, for example, the issue of blindness as it appears in Isa 61:1–2 in the LXX is not considered.

This study also analyzes only those passages that clearly concern blindness or visual impairment. Thus, for example, the opening of Balaam's eyes in Num 22:31 is not studied in depth as the word for "open" is not the usual word used for opening the eyes of the blind, חקפ, rather, הלג, the word used for uncovering or revealing, as in Dan 10:1. It may be simply said, then, that Balaam's gaze was opened by God to a new reality. This passage, though, is considered in the context of 2 Kgs 6:16–20 as a potential literary parallel. Numbers 33:55, with reference to the inhabitants being pricks in Israel's eyes, is also not considered. The concept of pricks in the eyes is set in parallel with that of thorns in the side, suggesting that the issue is pain rather than loss of sight.

ORGANIZATION OF STUDY

First, for comparative purposes, a study is presented in chapter 2 regarding how blindness was understood in other ancient Near Eastern cultures. Blindness is considered as it was understood in ancient Egypt, in Mesopotamia, and finally, in the Hittite Empire. In each culture, blindness is studied with reference to cultus and religious thought, causes, social justice, reversal, and meanings, in order. In considering causes of blindness, matters of theodicy in the cultures are analyzed where relevant. The study of meanings of blindness considers both meanings of physical blindness (how, for example, omen texts might affect the way one understands and relates to a blind individual) and meanings of symbolic blindness.

Chapter 3 involves word studies on the Hebrew words for "blind," "blindness," and related terms as found in the Hebrew Scriptures. Consideration of these words focuses first on their etymology and cognates in other ancient Near Eastern languages. The Hebrew words are then analyzed with reference to their usage, both literal and idiomatic, in the Hebrew Scriptures.

Chapters 4, 5, and 6 study the concept of blindness as it is discussed in the Hebrew Scriptures. The topic is analyzed exegetically with emphasis on studying the main passages in the Hebrew Scriptures that concern blindness. This aspect of the study is divided into three chapters. Chapter 4 considers blindness in the Torah; chapter 5, blindness in the Prophets; and chapter 6, blindness in the Writings. For each passage, issues of translation are discussed, followed by matters of exegesis including literary analysis, context within the Bible and the ancient Near East, and general concepts of intratextual interpretation. Each of these three chapters concludes with a brief theological synthesis of the findings in the study of the translation and exegesis of the passages. Consideration in these chapters focuses on the same five main issues concerning blindness as discussed in the chapter concerning blindness in the ancient Near East.

The dissertation concludes with chapter 7, which synthesizes the findings of the study. The same five issues of cultus, causation, social justice, reversal, and meanings are considered in order. The chapter concludes by offering possible suggestions for further study and the possible implications of this research in practical reality.

A number of presuppositions influence this study. First, the study is performed under the assumption that the writers of the Hebrew Scriptures intended that their writings be understood to have theological and historical validity. It is also assumed that methods of exegetical, contextual, structural, and linguistic analysis aid one's understanding of the Bible.

II

Ancient Near Eastern Parallels

In studying blindness in the Hebrew Scriptures, it is first necessary to examine the treatment of this topic in the writings of other ancient Near Eastern cultures of the same general time period. Establishing such context at the start of this study allows parallels with biblical passages to be observed clearly without the need of frequent and lengthy digressions. In this chapter, the ancient cultures of Egypt, Mesopotamia, and Hittite Anatolia are considered. Since religion held a central place in ancient Near Eastern thought and life, blindness in mythology and cultus is considered first. It would then be logical to start at the chronological origins and analyze the perceived causes of blindness as they relate to the religious context. Issues of social justice involving the presently blind are studied next, in the context of these causes and the ever-present religious background when relevant. The study then turns to a logical end in a chronological analysis and considers methods of healing: how blindness could be removed altogether. Finally, with an understanding of the views regarding physical blindness, symbolic uses of the subject are presented.

BLINDNESS IN ANCIENT EGYPT

This section considers a number of aspects of blindness as it was understood in ancient Egypt. The first section, in examining issues of mythology and religion, discusses the significance of the eye in Egyptian mythology, the wounding of Horus's eye, and the function of blind harpists. The second portion examines the factors that were understood as causing blindness, ranging from magic, to divine punishment, to simple old age. The third section focuses primarily on a passage in Egyptian Wisdom Literature concerning the proper treatment of the blind. Next, the concept of the reversal of blindness is presented with passages concerning healing, which discuss both magic and medicine. Finally, a number of passages are analyzed which show the positive and negative connotations of blindness to the Egyptians.

Mythology and Religion

The Wounded Eye

The eye held a significant place in Egyptian thought and mythology. Staring at someone was thought to invoke the power of the "evil eye." This evil eye could be used by the serpent Apophis, serpents in general, deities, the evil dead, or the eye itself as an independent agent. Texts designed to ward off this evil eye were often rolled up and worn about the neck. In mythology, in fact, Apophis was once commanded to cease from staring at the sun god, presumably because of the evil eye.[1] One wishing relief from nightmares would command the demon responsible to turn his face away.[2]

In addition, the sun and moon, for example, were understood respectively as the right and left eyes of Horus and were often called the "Sound Eyes."[3] The following excerpt discusses the power of these eyes, "O be fearful of him, O be afraid of him—this god who made your needs. Give adulation to his might and become content in the presence of his two sound eyes."[4]

Another passage discussing the awesome power of the sound eyes is known as the "Spell for Putting Incense on the Flame": "To the *ba*-soul of the East, to Horus of the East, to Kamutef within the solar disk, to the Terrible One who shines with his two Sound Eyes, to Re-harakhti, the great god, the winged power, foremost of the two southern conclaves of heaven."[5]

The wounding of such an eye, then, would necessarily hold deep importance in Egyptian thought. The following is an excerpt from the myth regarding the wounding of Horus's eye, out of which developed the cultic abomination of the pig in Egypt:

> Re then said: "Look at that black pig." Then Horus looked at that black pig. Then Horus cried out over the condition of his

---

1. Szpakowska, *Behind Closed Eyes*, 26.
2. Szpakowska, *Behind Closed Eyes*, 168.
3. James P. Allen, "From the Berlin 'Hymn to Ptah,'" 21.
4. James P. Allen, "From the Berlin 'Hymn to Ptah,'" 21.
5. Ritner, "Daily Ritual of the Temple of Amun-Re at Karnak," 55.

throbbing ("raging") eye, saying: "Behold, my eye feels as at that first wound which Seth inflicted against my eye."

Then Horus lost consciousness ("swallowed his heart") before him. Re then said: "Place him on his bed until he is well." It was the case that Seth made transformations against him as that black pig. Then he cast a wound into his eye. Re then said: "Abominate the pig for Horus." "Would that he be well," SO SAID THE GODS. THAT IS HOW THE ABOMINATION OF THE PIG CAME TO BE FOR HORUS BY THE GODS AND THEIR FOLLOWERS.[6]

According to this myth, Horus's brother, Seth, took the form of a pig in order to wound Horus's eye. The god Ptah was then said to be given to Horus in compensation.[7]

It is also noted in myth that Thoth put Horus's eye back together in parts. Later, doctors would use the names of these parts to refer to fractions as a form of shorthand for parts of a whole. Each part of the eye became a symbol for a certain fraction with a denominator of sixty-four (i.e., 1/64, 2/64). Horus's eye also became known as a symbol of unity, and so, wholeness and health. This eye, then, symbolized a doctor's desires for a patient's health.[8] In addition, from Horus's eye came symbols for volume measure.[9]

The healed eye of Horus is mentioned a number of times in liturgical texts. In the daily ritual of the temple of Amun-Re at Karnak in the twenty-second dynasty, it was said in the spell for the daily striking of the fire, "Come, come in peace, Eye of Horus, luminous, sound, rejuvenated in peace!"[10]

In this incantation, the struggle with Seth is mentioned in addition to the power of Horus's eye, in repelling Amun-Re's foes.[11]

The spell, recited when placing the incense bowl, notes that the one performing the act has been purified by the Eye of Horus.[12] The spell for unfastening the naos refers to Seth's being withdrawn from Horus's Eye and Amun-Re's being called to receive the white crown as the Eye of Horus.[13]

Finally, it must be noted that Horus was not the only deity to be described as having suffered a wound to the eye. Re, during the creation, was

---

6. Ritner, "Coffin Text 157, 'Cultic Abomination of the Pig,'" 30–31.
7. Ritner, "Coffin Text 157, 'Cultic Abomination of the Pig,'" 30.
8. Estes, *The Medical Skills of Ancient Egypt*, 95.
9. Estes, *The Medical Skills of Ancient Egypt*, 96.
10. Ritner, "Daily Ritual of the Temple of Amun-Re at Karnak," 55.
11. Ritner, "Daily Ritual of the Temple of Amun-Re at Karnak," 55.
12. Ritner, "Daily Ritual of the Temple of Amun-Re at Karnak," 55.
13. Ritner, "Daily Ritual of the Temple of Amun-Re at Karnak," 56.

said to have lost an eye. Humanity was then formed from the tears he cried after this event. This story makes use of a significant wordplay as "remy" means "tears," and "remet" means "humanity."[14]

Harpists

It is also necessary to consider the works and lives of the Egyptian harpists who are often depicted as blind. Egyptian royal harpists held a most honorable status in the land. Paintings depict them with bulging stomachs, evidence of excellent nourishment. They are also shown wearing fine clothing. Their heads are clean-shaven which indicates ritual purity.[15] Their songs would often be performed during funerary banquets, which would be held at cemeteries on festival days. Such works would discuss the inevitability of death and the afterlife.[16]

J. Worth Estes has noted, though, that these harpists may not necessarily have been blind. It may be possible, for example, that these individuals were shown as blind because they had no access to written music. Blindness would then have been merely a symbolic depiction.[17]

One must, then, analyze more carefully the depictions of these harpists. The Egyptian depictions of eyes are not always easy to interpret. The Egyptians had four main ways of showing a damaged eye in any of a number of states of deformity. They are discussed as follows: "(1) omission of the iris inside the outline of an otherwise normal eye; (2) representation of the eye as a narrow slit with an iris; (3) depiction of the eye as a narrow slit without an iris; and (4) a line drawn following the upper curve of the eye."[18]

These drawings, though, may simply show healthy, seeing eyes. An eye depicted as a narrow slit may simply be closed. A dot, which represents an iris, could easily disappear as paintings degrade through history. Because of this, out of approximately twenty possible depictions of damaged eyes at Thebes, only about four or five can be confirmed as actually describing genuine deformity.[19]

While the pictures at Thebes may be ambiguous, those at El-Amarna are plain and straightforward. These pictures clearly show eyeballs which are shrunken or destroyed. Artists of this period, the time of King

14. Sparks, *Ancient Texts for the Study of the Hebrew Bible*, 326.
15. Manniche, *Music and Musicians in Ancient Egypt*, 99.
16. Lichtheim, "Harpers' Songs," 48.
17. Estes, *The Medical Skills of Ancient Egypt*, 88.
18. Manniche, *Music and Musicians in Ancient Egypt*, 99.
19. Manniche, *Music and Musicians in Ancient Egypt*, 99.

Akhenaten, would exaggerate in their work to emphasize features for clarity and emphasis.[20]

In the Karnak Reliefs, though, musicians are depicted as performing in the palace while wearing white blindfolds over their eyes. After they perform, they bow to the king and remove their blindfolds.[21]

One may also consider the blindness of Raia, the chief singer of Ptah, in the nineteenth dynasty. When not shown as a harpist before the king, he is depicted as having healthy eyes. When he is shown as performing, though, each of his eyes is a "narrow slit with a prominent supra-orbital ridge."[22]

Apparently it was important, at least in cases such as this one, not that the performer actually be blind but that he simply be unable to see the king. The reason for this hiding of the eyes, according to Lise Manniche, may have stemmed from the understanding that the king of Egypt was a god. A god had the power to blind those who saw him. Thus, it would be to the advantage of a harpist either to be blind or to cover his eyes.

It is interesting, though, that this danger was not understood as applying to women. Manniche notes how the women may have been thought to occupy the position of consort of the gods. He notes how Pharaoh's consort would not need to hide her eyes when engaging in sexual relations with him as she was seen as the consort of Horus. Likewise, other women before such a king/deity could keep their eyes uncovered.[23]

Lise Manniche proposes another possible reason as to why harpists were expected to wear blindfolds. They may have functioned as anonymous substitutes for the king, standing in his place to perform their ceremonies. The blindfold, then, would not be to keep the harpist from seeing, but to keep him from being seen. Manniche discusses an ancient Egyptian picture showing a harp with a face of the king, not the face of the harpist.[24] One problem with this theory is that it does not allow for a satisfactory explanation of why women were not expected to wear the blindfold. If the purpose of the blindfold was to keep the focus on the king and away from the anonymous substitute, such should apply to anyone performing such a function, male or female. Thus, while this latter explanation may be sufficient in certain cases, Manniche's previously discussed explanation, then, is more logical since it takes into account both a male's vulnerability before a god and a female's special position as a potential consort of such a god.

---

20. Manniche, *Music and Musicians in Ancient Egypt*, 99.
21. Manniche, *Music and Musicians in Ancient Egypt*, 100.
22. Manniche, *Music and Musicians in Ancient Egypt*, 101.
23. Manniche, "Symbolic Blindness," 20.
24. Manniche, "Symbolic Blindness," 18.

As one can see, then, scholars on both sides of this debate may be correct in part. Some harpists, namely those depicted with shrunken, destroyed eyeballs, were most likely blind by disability and found this occupation a meaningful use of their abilities. Many other harpists, though, simply became temporarily blind to perform their ritual service. One who is blind by disability, however, would be at an advantage, in a way, since he could approach the deity/king without needing to be troubled with the blindfold.

Causes of Blindness

Blindness and Old Age

With an understanding of blindness in Egyptian mythology and religious life, one may now examine a number of major causes for blindness as understood by the Egyptians. The physical cause of old age is considered first. As is noted in the Instruction of Ptahhotep in the context of old age, "Eyes are dim, ears deaf, Strength is waning through weariness."[25]

Blindness as a Curse or Divine Punishment

One common way that gods would bring about blindness was through divine curses, often as a result of an individual's sins, and often invoked by other human beings.[26] Below are excerpts from Egyptian magical texts where blindness is described as a curse.

1. This text is a spell against those with the evil eye, that is, those who bring misfortune. One may note the reference to Horus, whose eye was once wounded, as a bringer of this curse on the eye:

   Sakhmet's arrow is in you, the magic (ḥkꜣ) of Thoth is in your body, Isis curses you, Nephthys punishes you, the lance of Horus is in your head. They treat you again and again, you who are in the furnace of Horus in Shenwet, the great god who sojourns in the House of Life! He blinds your eyes, oh all you people (rmṯ), all nobles (pʽ.t), all common people (rḫy.t), all the sun-folk (ḥnmm.t) and so on, who will cast an evil eye (ir.t bin.t) against Pediamunnebnesuttowi born of Mehtemweskhet.[27]

---

25. Estes, *The Medical Skills of Ancient Egypt*, 75.
26. Estes, *The Medical Skills of Ancient Egypt*, 88.
27. Van Voss et al., eds., *Ancient Egyptian Magical Texts*, 2.

2. The following is a curse against a poisonous snake that has stricken an individual. This spell would be uttered during a ritual to cure one of snake bite. Where "NN" appears, one was to supply the appropriate person's name. One may note how in this curse, blindness is one of the punishments that would befall the snake:

> "Break out, poison!—Seven times.—Horus has conjured (šnỉ) you, he has crushed (bḫn) you. He has spat on you. You will not rise upwards, you will be trampled down. You will be feeble, you will not be strong. You will be cowardly, you will not be brave. You will be blind, you will not see. You will go upside-down. . . . Turn yourself, venomous snake (bṯw), draw out (šdỉ) your poison which is in all the limbs of NN born of NN! See, the magic (ḥkꜣ) of Horus has gained the victory over you. Break out, poison, come to the earth!"[28]

3. The next passage to be considered in this section is a curse to invoke the sun god to act against a crocodile. Here the weeping Eye of Horus is specifically named as being threatened. Since, as noted above, such a weeping, tearing eye was thought to be involved in creation, an attack like this would seem to threaten the creative power of the god. In addition, part of this curse against this creature, which threatens a god's eye, involves blindness, an attack on the eye of the offending crocodile: "May the one who is on the water escape safely! If the one who is on the water is attacked, the weeping eye of Horus is attacked. . . . Oh you water-dwellers: your mouths are closed by Rēʿ, your throats are stopped up by Sakhmet, your tongues are cut out by Thoth, your eyes are blinded by Heka."[29]

4. One may next consider the story of the blinding of Pheros, son of Sesostris, king of Egypt. As Herodotus relates, Pheros cast his spear into a river in an emotional outburst after the river had flooded. This impiety, then, was punished immediately with blindness by the gods. For ten years, nothing he did could appease the gods and reverse the blindness. Finally, in the eleventh year, an oracle came to him regarding how his blindness could be healed. According to the oracle, if he washed his eyes in the urine of a woman who had known no man besides her husband, he would be cured. After trying several women, his wife first, he finally found one whose urine cured him. The king had all

---

28. Van Voss et al., eds., *Ancient Egyptian Magical Texts*, 75, 76.
29. Van Voss et al., eds., *Ancient Egyptian Magical Texts*, 85, 86.

the other woman burned and married the one who cured him.³⁰ One must note, though, that Diodorus of Sicily says that the account of the river curse is a myth. Pheros's blindness, then, came as a result of his inheriting a condition from his father.³¹

In this study, it is irrelevant whether or not the story actually took place, inasmuch as this book is concerned more with how such a story was understood and believed, and how these beliefs would have affected people's theology of blindness. This story, then, shows how people believed that the gods could and would smite one with blindness for several years because of a single act of impiety. No curse uttered by another human being was necessary to bring about this act from the gods. Such an individual would be at the mercy of the gods, waiting until a message came with instructions concerning how to be healed, however unusual such oracle might be.

Social Justice

Didactic Literature

The first text to be considered in this section is the Wisdom of Amenemopet. This document was a didactic text written by a high official to his son regarding Egyptian agriculture.³² One passage deals especially with the treatment of the disabled:

> Do not laugh at a blind man,
> Nor tease a dwarf,
> Nor cause hardship for the lame.
> Don't tease a man who is in the hand of the god,
> Nor be angry with him for his failings.
> Man is clay and straw,
> The god is his builder.
> He tears down, he builds up daily,
> He makes a thousand poor by his will,
> He makes a thousand men into chiefs,
> When he is in his hour of life.
> Happy is he who reaches the west,
> When he is safe in the hand of the god.³³

30. Herodotus, *The History*, 176, 2.111.

31. Diodorus of Sicily, *Diodorus of Sicily*, trans. Oldfather, 1:205, 1.59.2. One may also note from this account the idea of blindness being brought about by heredity.

32. *Ancient Egyptian Literature*, trans. Foster, 196.

33. Lichtheim, "Instruction of Amenemope," 121.

Clearly, this official desired to teach that it is improper to mock, or otherwise hinder, those with disabilities, including blindness. The reason is that the gods have created everyone, disabled or non-disabled. Poverty, success, and ability status are results of divine action. One, then, should not mistreat a person whom the gods have willed to be as he/she is.

The Blind and Employment

The blind were permitted to hold at least certain types of employment in ancient Egypt. One may recall the writings concerning the blind harpists. Also worthy of note is how Pheros, son of Sesostris, was apparently still able to rule Egypt, even while blind. He apparently maintained the authority to summon a number of women to try to cure him.

Reversal of Blindness

Visiting the Doctor

In addition to the story of Pheros, a number of other accounts of reversal, or at least attempted reversal, of blindness in ancient Egypt exist. A number of these stories of healing of blindness involve the Egyptian eye doctor. It must be noted how the Egyptian eye doctor, the *swnw irty*,[34] was well-respected in surrounding lands. Herodotus discusses how the Persian king Cyrus desired nothing greater from Pharaoh Arnasis than the best eye doctor to serve as medical counselor for the king.[35] This demonstrates the great importance Egyptians placed on the ability to treat eye diseases when possible. Apparently, the Egyptian doctors were respected enough that leaders from other lands would request their services.

The first selection to be considered in this section, then, is an ancient text describing such an Egyptian doctor's appointment. In this appointment, the premier Egyptian physician Inhotep visits the daughter of a prince. This daughter had recently changed her eye makeup and was suffering from ingrown eye lashes. In the end, the doctor used tweezers to remove the lashes, cleaned and massaged the area with a cream of frankincense, and placed a wet dressing over her eyes.[36] The following excerpts begin with the daughter's speech to the physician:

---

34. Nunn, *Ancient Egyptian Medicine*, 198.
35. Stetter, *The Secret Medicine of the Pharaohs*, 93.
36. Stetter, *The Secret Medicine of the Pharaohs*, 92–93.

"You will do everything to let me see again, won't you physician?" She took a step forward, without help, in her blindness.

The physician took a pouch with herbs from the basket, which he carried with him and ordered that hot water be brought. "Sit down," he said, "I will bring you to the seat, and then you can tell me of your eye pain. First, however, I will raise your lids and inflict pain?"

She said, "I know that it hurts, I already tried it myself, but the sun blinded me again."

Tears mixed with pus fell from her eyes. "Three days ago," she said, "it started as I was painting myself."

"Now courage. At the end of the pain is the cure."[37]

It is clear from the above passage that a doctor was understood to provide healing for at least some types of blindness. This doctor, though, at least at times, must inflict pain as part of the cure.

Magical Healing

A study of blindness in Egypt would not be complete without a look at the role of magic in healing. Illnesses were often understood to be healed by combining a ritual action with the saying of an incantation. The following paragraphs discuss a number of spells involved in treating blindness.

1. The first spell was to be repeated four times while placing a medicine over a patient's two eyes. In this spell, one finds frequent references to the great Eye of Horus previously discussed in this study:

   That Eye of Horus has come (ii) which the Souls of Heliopolis created.... What has been said about it: "how welcome is this Eye of Horus (and) the Noble One (šps.t) which is in the Eye of Horus!"—It is to do away with the influence (s.t-ꜥ) of a god, the influence of a goddess, a male opponent (ḏꜣy), a female opponent, a male dead (mt), a female dead, a male enemy (ḫfty), a female enemy who might oppose themselves (ḏꜣi) against these eyes of the man under my fingers that <I> have brought you. Protection (sꜣw) behind protection, protection has arrived![38]

2. The following is a headache spell where blindness is listed as one of many conditions that the patient could face. In this text, it is notable

---

37. Stetter, *The Secret Medicine of the Pharaohs*, 92.
38. *Ancient Egyptian Magical Texts*, 47–48.

that the individual with the headache is identified with Re, and that the eye of said god is to be involved in the healing:

> Backwards, enemy (ḫfty), fiend (pfty), male dead (mt), female dead, and so on who cause this suffering to NN born of NN. You have said that you would strike a blow in this head of his in order to force your entry into this vertex of his, to smash in these temples of his! . . . —from your desire to damage this body of his, these limbs of his, to weaken his vessel<s>, to blind his eyes. . . . Break out what you have taken in as all kinds of bad things of an enemy. . . . For it is NN born of NN that has arisen as Rēʿ; his safeguarding (mk.t) is this eye of his.[39]

3. The following spell, according to the Ebers medical Papyri, 1553–1550 B.C.E. during the reign of Amen-Hotep I,[40] was to be spoken over a mixture containing a number of chemicals including verdigris and beetle-wax. Reciting this incantation was to heal the patient of cataract. A reference to the Eye of Horus appears in this spell:[41]

> Come, Verdigris!
> Come, Verdigris!
> Come, Thou Fresh One!
> Come, Efflux from the Eye of the god Horus!
> It comes, That which issues forth from the Eye of Tum!
> Come, Juice that gushes from Osiris!
> He comes to him, he drives away from him Water,
> Matter, Blood, Inflammation of the Eyes,
> Mattery-discharge, Blindness, Dripping Eyes.
> This the God of Fever works all Deadly Arts, the uxedu of every kind, and all things evil of these eyes.[42]

4. Another cure for blindness is also described in the Ebers Papyri. Here, a spell was to be recited twice over a mixture containing, among a number of unique ingredients, wild honey and the crushed, dried eyes of a pig. Then the mixture was to be injected into the patient's ear. The spell reads, "I HAVE BROUGHT THIS THING AND PUT IT IN ITS PLACE. THE CROCODILE IS WEAK AND POWERLESS."[43]

---

39. *Ancient Egyptian Magical Texts*, 27, 28.
40. Bryan, *Ancient Egyptian Medicine*, 2.
41. Bryan, *Ancient Egyptian Medicine*, 99.
42. Bryan, *Ancient Egyptian Medicine*, 99–100.
43. Bryan, *Ancient Egyptian Medicine*, 104.

This use of an eye to heal an eye condition is an example of sympathetic magic, a system that uses an object similar to the diseased organ for the cure. In a similar use of sympathetic magic, fish head was to cure headache.[44]

It must also be noted that the Egyptians had gods that were to oversee various types of healings. One hymn refers to Amun as "the Doctor of Eye Illness."[45]

Then, one must consider this magical incantation, which would be spoken to provide protection for a child against a number of possible diseases: "Your vertex is Re, you healthy child, the back of your head is Osiris, your forehead is Satis, the mistress of Elephantine, your temple is Neith, your eyebrows are the master of the east, your eyes are the master of humanity, . . . no limb of yours is without a god, every god protects your name."[46]

As one can see, health to the eyes is one of many delights this individual shall experience, according to this text. In addition, as in the headache spell, the beneficiary of the incantation is identified with the gods.

Meanings of Blindness

Blindness in Egypt, both physical and symbolic, carried a number of meanings. This section briefly considers a sampling of passages discussing such.

Physical Blindness

1. While, as previously noted, physical blindness often carried the meaning of a curse, for some, such as the harpists, blindness held the meaning of freedom to approach and play for the king without any barriers over the eyes. The first passage to be considered in this section describes another positive aspect of physical blindness. In this passage, a blind man prays the following to Sopdu: "Address praises to Sopdu, prostrate for the Lord. O God beautiful, give me peace! See, you whose power is great, you have allowed that I do not cease to see the darkness which you created. Be gracious towards me! That I may always see you!"[47]

    In this prayer the blindness of the individual allows him to see the darkness which the god created, a darkness, which the individual, apparently, believes is good enough to praise the god for allowing him

---

44. Estes, *The Medical Skills of Ancient Egypt*, 106.
45. Stetter, *The Secret Medicine of the Pharaohs*, 102.
46. Stetter, *The Secret Medicine of the Pharaohs*, 104.
47. Barucq and Daumas, *Hymnes et Prières de L'Egypte Ancienne*, 479.

to see. In this darkness the individual seeks always to be able to see Sopdu who created it.

2. One may now consider this brief text by a man from Deir el Medineh. In this letter from this man to his son, he complains about his blindness and requests medicine. In this letter one finds this prayer to Chons, the moon god, "Behold: you cause me to see darkness of your making. Have mercy upon me, that I may proclaim it."[48]

This text would show a more negative aspect of blindness. This man, who dwells in darkness, the realm of the moon, seeks mercy from the moon god concerning such darkness. As a result, he would proclaim such mercy, praising that god for such an act. It is unclear from this passage whether or not this man is requesting full healing for his blindness or some other mercy that would aid him.

Figurative Blindness

Blindness of failing to act

The next passage to be analyzed, the first in a set of passages involving figurative blindness, is known as "The Eloquent Peasant," dating to the time of the twelfth and thirteenth dynasties. This passage contains a story of a peasant who is robbed and who does not find justice at the hands of the high steward, Ransi, son of Meru.[49] In the following excerpt, the peasant describes the steward's ineptitude by comparing him to people with various disabilities:

> The son of Meru goes on erring. His face is blind to what he
> sees, deaf to what he hears, forgetful about what he should have
> remembered.
> Behold, you are a town without a mayor,
> Like a group without its ruler,
> Like a ship without a captain,
> Like a band without a leader.[50]

According to the peasant, the steward has seen, heard, and understood the case. Since no action of justice was taken, the steward has metaphorically been blind, deaf, and forgetful. The leader's blindness of mind, lack of concern, compassion, and rightness made the city a town without a mayor, as a ship without a captain. Apparently, then, if one sees but does not act

---

48. Assmann, "Occular Desire in a Time of Darkness," 26.
49. Shupak, "The Eloquent Peasant," 98.
50. Shupak, "The Eloquent Peasant," 102.

accordingly, it is as if he/she were blind. This sets blindness, according to Egyptian thought, in the dimension of action, not merely perception.

Blindness of fear

In the Egyptian document known as DUA-KHETY OR THE SATIRE ON THE TRADES, it is discussed why the job of scribe is the best of the trades. To make this argument, other occupations are harshly criticized.[51] One may examine the following analysis of the job of fisherman where blindness is described as a dulling of the perception as a result of fear:

> I'll speak of the fisherman also,
> His is the worst of all the jobs;
> He labors on the river,
> Mingling with crocodiles.
> When the time of reckoning comes,
> He is full of lamentations;
> He does not say, "There's a crocodile,"
> Fear has made him blind.[52]

Blindness of ignorance

It is next important to consider a remark in the Egyptian text known as "Debate between a Man Tired of Life and His Soul." In this excerpt, blindness is connected with ignorance, which clearly places lack of sight as a state of the mind or intellect: "Who is there to talk to today? Emptiness in trusted friends; blind ignorance to life that brings wisdom."[53]

Blindness as a term of disgrace

The final quotation to be considered in this section is found in a text referred to as "THE TURIN JUDICIAL PAPYRUS." This excerpt was written after the failed Harem Conspiracy against Ramses III. It is mentioned in this passage that a conspirator previously known as "The Servant of Amon" would be renamed as "The blind servant."[54] This would be thought to have

---

51. Lichtheim, "Dua-Khety or the Satire on the Trades," 122.
52. Lichtheim, "Dua-Khety or the Satire on the Trades," 124.
53. *Ancient Egyptian Literature*, 62.
54. Ritner, "The Turin Judicial Papyrus (The Harem Conspiracy against Ramses III)," 27.

the effect of harming the individual in the afterlife.[55] Clearly, then, blindness carries strong pejorative connotations in this passage. Once this individual was understood to be a servant of a god. After his role in the conspiracy, he would be disgraced and shamed, compared to a blind man.

Summary

As has been noted, the eye held a highly important place in ancient Egyptian thought. The wounding of Horus's eye was discussed in a number of literary contexts, including even magical texts. The blind were to be treated with respect, some even being granted the opportunity to be royal harpists. While blindness was often understood as a curse, the Egyptians also realized that the elderly might face this condition simply as a result of growing old. Healing for blindness was obtained through a number of remedies involving medicine and forms of magic, the line between such being often difficult to place. Physical blindness, while at times, being understood to be a curse of the gods, also was understood to allow one better access to the divine reality. Figurative blindness contained a number of meanings including ignorance and lack of mental perceptiveness.

BLINDNESS IN ANCIENT MESOPOTAMIA

After considering blindness in ancient Egypt, the attention may be turned to its understanding in ancient Mesopotamia. This section opens with an analysis of the ancient Sumerian story of the origin of blindness. Afterward, the issue of blindness as it relates to ancient Mesopotamian cultus is considered. Then, blindness as a civil penalty, as a means of controlling prisoners of war, and as a curse/divine punishment is analyzed. Next is a discussion of ancient law codes and other texts regarding the treatment in the judicial system for those wrongly blinded by other people. Then, the focus is turned to the treatment of those who were already blind, how they were supported, and how it was to be understood if a blind individual was made to damage a property marker. After a study of magical texts regarding the healing of blindness, various meanings of blindness are considered.

---

55. Ritner, "The Turin Judicial Papyrus (The Harem Conspiracy against Ramses III)," 30.

Mythology and Cultus

Mythology

Enki and the Creation of the Blind

The first myth to be considered in this section is the myth of Enki and Ninmah. In this creation story, Enki, god of subterranean fresh waters, wisdom, and magic, creates humankind from pieces of clay. Humankind is to relieve gods of labor and perform agricultural labor. At a great feast, mother goddess Nimnah competes with Enki, making crippled versions of people for Enki to attempt to place in honorable positions in society. Enki succeeds every time and then creates a deformed creature, which Nimnah cannot place. Thus, Enki claims the victory, and Ninmah is confounded and angered.[56] The following is an excerpt from this tale: "Second—she fashioned from it one 'deprived of light,' a blind(?) man. Enki—upon seeing the one 'deprived of light,' the blind(?) man, decreed its fate: he allotted to it the musical art, and seated it (as) chief-[musician] in a place of honor, before the king."[57]

The term in this passage that refers to blindness literally means "a seeing man," according to Jacob Klein. This may be a use of a euphemism for a displeasing condition.[58]

In *Myths of Enki: The Crafty God*, by Samuel Noah Kramer and John Maier, a different position is taken. The reference to the blind man is translated as one "who could see though blind."[59] It is noted in an endnote that the Sumerian word for "blind" in this passage is "giš-nu11-gi4-gi4," which is approximated to mean, one "who turns back the light." Such an individual was thought to have inner sight. Thus, as one who could see inwardly, he would be an excellent choice for a court musician.[60] This individual would, therefore, parallel the blind harpist in Egypt whose blindness was also involved in qualifying him to perform music for the king.

Clearly, more study, which would reach beyond the scope of this dissertation, is required to understand this Sumerian story. What can be understood, though, is that the individual with the disability is physically blind, and that this blindness was created as part of a contest among the gods.

---

56. Klein, "Enki and Ninmaḫ," 516.
57. Klein, "Enki and Ninmaḫ," 518.
58. Klein, "Enki and Ninmaḫ," 518.
59. Kramer and Maier, *Myths of Enki*, 34.
60. Kramer and Maier, *Myths of Enki*, 213.

Eye disease in the Descent of Ishtar to the Underworld

The next text is a brief passage in "The Descent of Ishtar to the Underworld." The Akkadian version of this myth dates to the Late Bronze Age in Babylon and Assyria. After Ishtar enters this land deprived of light, punishment is pronounced against her.[61] The passage reads as follows:

> Send out against her sixty diseases Ishtar
> Disease of the eyes to her [eyes],
> Disease of the arms to her [arms],
> Disease of the feet to her [feet],
> Disease of the heart to her [heart].[62]

In this passage a number of various unfortunate conditions are called to be sent against the goddess. In this comprehensive list of ailments, eye disease is mentioned first. This may suggest the intensity of the concept of blindness, or, at least an eye disease of some sort. Such a condition was severe enough to place at the beginning of the list.

Cultus and Ritual

This section considers a brief passage from ancient Mesopotamia that lists requirements for a diviner. One who becomes a diviner must be without blemish, and so, for example, may not be "sharp of eye" or "chipped of tooth." Marten Stol suggests that the term "sharp of eye" refers to having "bad eyesight."[63]

The *Chicago Assyrian Dictionary*, though, argues that this term refers to being cross-eyed. This same Akkadian term, "*zaqta īnī*," is also found in the Akkadian quotation, "If an ox squints in such a way as to show (only) the whites (of his eyes)." The term must be translated as "squints" in this passage as it makes the most sense in the context of showing only the whites of the eyes. This leads *CAD* to note that the term actually means "cross-eyed."[64] One difficulty with this interpretation is that the showing of the whites of the eyes is not generally a result of squinting.

While it may be difficult to determine the exact meaning of "*zaqta īnī*," two points can still be considered. First, both conditions involve a weakening

---

61. Dalley, "The Descent of Ishtar to the Underworld," 382.
62. Dalley, "The Descent of Ishtar to the Underworld," 382.
63. Stol, "Blindness and Night-Blindness in Akkadian," 295.
64. *Assyrian Dictionary* (1956–61), s.v. "Zaqtu."

of the eye. Second, it seems reasonable to assume that if an individual was barred from being a diviner due to being cross-eyed, someone who was totally blind should not have expected any easier chance of obtaining the position.

One may next determine why one with a visual disability was barred from being a diviner. The following omen excerpts illustrate how one with any sort of visual disability would not be adequate for the task of diviner: (1) "If the 'rise of the head of the bird' is dark on the left and the right";[65] (2) "If there is an eclipse of the moon in Nisannu."[66]

A number of reasons may be suggested as to why one with weakened eyes would be forbidden from being a diviner. First, it could be suggested that limited eyesight could hinder ability to function. One might determine some attributes of an animal by touch, but the fingers are not able to discern the color of a head. In addition, while a blind man might feel the air cooling during a solar eclipse, there is no discernable temperature change with a lunar eclipse. A diviner must have fully functioning eyes in order to perform the tasks expected.

While impaired eyesight could interfere with one's work as a diviner, possessing a chipped tooth would not interfere with the work of either observing the sky or that of communicating, even verbally, what is observed. Since reduction of competence, then, cannot be understood as the basis for denying one with a chipped tooth from being a diviner, one must seek other explanations for the rationale for these restrictions. One may recall that the text above states that one with a blemish could not serve as a diviner. Apparently, then, while blindness would definitely hinder one's ability to function as a diviner, it was simply important that the diviners be physically whole and free from any blemish. The significance of parallels with the priesthood in the Hebrew Bible is considered later in this dissertation. One may consider, at present, the following diviners' prayer where the term "extispicy" refers to "divination by means of animal sacrifice."[67]

> O Shamash, I hold up to you the plentiful yield of
> the gods, the radiance of the grain goddess.
> O Shamash, lord of judgment, O Adad, lord of divination,
> In the ritual I perform, in the extispicy I perform,
> place the truth![68]

---

65. Guinan, "Divination," 423.
66. Guinan, "Divination," 423.
67. Guinan, "Divination," 422.
68. Foster, "Diurnal Prayers of Diviners," 417.

As noted above, those involved in such ritual animal sacrifice were to be free from physical blemish. This demonstrates that ancient Israel was not the only culture to connect cultic activity with physical holiness.

Causes of Blindness

Blindness as a State Punishment

1. The punishment of blinding in Mesopotamia could be administered by human agents. The following law, in the Code of Hammurabi, whose law code is studied in greater depth in the next section, names blinding as a punishment: "193. If the child of (i.e., reared by) a courtier ... identifies with his father's house and repudiates the father who raised him or the mother who raised him and departs for his father's house, they shall pluck out his eye."[69]

2. The next passage is from an eighth-century B.C.E. Aramaic treaty document written in the year Tiglath-pileser III conquered the region of Arpad.[70] This excerpt contains punishments that would be placed on Matiʻel, ruler of Arpad, if he should break this treaty: "And just as the man of wax is blinded, so may Matiʻel be blinded! [Just as] this calf is cut in two, so may Matiʻel be cut in two, and may his nobles be cut in two!"[71]

3. One may note this brief comment listed in the "Dialogue of Pessimism or the Obliging Slave," "No, slave, I will definitely not go in for skulduggery! The man who goes in for skulduggery is killed, flayed, blinded, arrested or thrown in jail."[72]

Here, the speaker expresses the concern that he may face blinding, among a number of possible penalties, as a result of crimes. This excerpt demonstrates that threats of blinding were not simply idle remarks made by rulers. People actually feared that such a penalty might befall them.

Blinding Prisoners of War

Prisoners of war may also have been blinded to hinder their mobility. The pre-Sargonic text, DP339, mentions twelve blind individuals of Uruaz who

---

69. Roth, "The Laws of Hammurabi," 348.
70. Fitzmyer, "The Inscriptions of Bar-Gaʼyah and Matiʻel from Sefire," 213.
71. Fitzmyer, "The Inscriptions of Bar-Gaʼyah and Matiʻel from Sefire," 214.
72. Livingstone, "Dialogue of Pessimism or the Obliging Slave," 496.

were captives from there.⁷³ Peter Machinist also notes an Assyrian text, which discusses fourteen thousand blinded captives from Ḫanigalbat who were relocated by Šalmaneser I. Machinist notes, though, how if these individuals were blinded in both eyes, that would greatly weaken their ability to perform labor, and so these people may have simply been blinded in one eye.⁷⁴

Blindness as a Curse or Divine Punishment

1. One can recall from the myth of Nimnah and Enki how blindness was said to have come into existence because of a contest between the gods. It was also thought possible for a curse of blindness to be placed on an individual. The following is a list of curses found at the end of a stele of the Assyrian king, Sinjar, ca. 800 B.C.E.⁷⁵ Anyone who damages, removes, or alters this stela was cursed. "May Marduk [. . .] overthrow his rule. May he give him up to be bound by the hands (and) over the eyes. May Šamaš, judge of heaven and earth, cause there to be darkness in his land so that no one can see the other."⁷⁶

    Being bound over the eyes and having a land darkened as described above would both prevent vision. It can be seen, then, that while blindness was not the only punishment, those who damaged the stele could expect a number of curses relating to vision.

2. One may consider the conclusion of a law code written by an unknown Sumerian king, circa 2050–1800 B.C.E. It is hypothesized that these curses make up the conclusion of the Laws of Ur-Nammu.⁷⁷ These curses would befall one who erases the inscription and/or writes his/her name in place of the king's: May his city be a city despised by the god Enlil; may the main gate of his city be left open (and undefended). May the young men of his city be blind; may the young maidens of his city be barren.⁷⁸

    One may note how these curses would all potentially weaken the defensibility of a city. If a city is despised by a god, the city could not expect assistance from such god. The main gate's being left open would

---

73. Gelb, "Prisoners of War in Early Mesopotamia," 87.

74. Machinist, "Provincial Governance in Middle Assyria and Some New Texts from Yale," 18 n. 41.

75. Younger, "Saba'a Stela," 274.

76. Younger, "Saba'a Stela," 275.

77. Roth, *Law Collections from Mesopotamia and Asia Minor*, 37.

78. Roth, *Law Collections from Mesopotamia and Asia Minor*, 39.

render the city vulnerable to invasion. Blind men would find it more difficult to see to fight. Barren women would not produce offspring who would become soldiers. Blindness, here, is the weakening and demoralizing condition threatened to smite the males.

3. Another noteworthy list of curses can be found in a treaty of Esarhaddon. The treaty notes that one who alters or destroys the document of the treaty would face a number of severe curses at the hands of the gods.[79] A curse of leprosy is named, after which follows this curse of blindness, found in lines 422–24, "[May Shamash, the light of the heavens and] earth [not] [judge] you justly (saying): 'May it be dark in your eyes, walk in darkness.'"[80] The text then says that the flesh of the violating party would be eaten by eagles and jackals. The wives of such violators would lie in the lap of enemies, and foreigners, rather than the sons, would possess the houses of the violators.[81]

4. One may next consider a prayer to Enki written by Sin-Shamuh, the Scribe, as he pondered his weakened condition:[82]

> "I [feared] you like a father. Never a theft at your sacrificial feasts, which I kept faithfully, did I commit.
>
> Now, no matter what it is I did, the verdict of my sin never ends.... [At night] I cannot sleep, my strength has been struck down, my life is ebbing away. The bright day is made a dark day for me. I have slipped into my own grave. I, a writer who knows many things, am made a fool. My hand has stopped writing. There is no talk in my mouth. I am not an old man, but my hearing is heavy, and my eyesight dim....
>
> Today I bring my sins to you....
>
> Look down into the place where I have been thrown. Take pity on me. Turn my dark places to sunlight. I want to live in your sin-absolving gate, I want to voice your glory."[83]

Among many maladies, this individual faces dim eyesight, which is, normally, a condition that he understands to affect the elderly. First, it can be noted how, just as in Egypt, ancient Sumerians understood that blindness was a common result of growing old. This man, though, suffered from this condition prematurely. Even though he believed he had followed his

---

79. Wiseman, *The Vassal-Treaties of Esarhaddon*, 58.
80. Wiseman, *The Vassal-Treaties of Esarhaddon*, 60.
81. Wiseman, *The Vassal-Treaties of Esarhaddon*, 60.
82. Kramer and Maier, *Myths of Enki*, 96.
83. Kramer and Maier, *Myths of Enki*, 96–98.

religion with reasonable uprightness, he thought his condition was somehow a result of sin he committed. He, therefore, pled for forgiveness. One, then, finds in this letter another example of one who believed blindness was a punishment of the gods, or at least, a consequence of being unfaithful to the gods.

Social Justice

Law Collections

LAW CODES BEFORE HAMMURABI

In a study of social justice as it relates to blindness in ancient Mesopotamia, one may first consider excerpts from law collections of the region. Such law collections show what justice those wrongly blinded by other people would expect in the judicial system, and thus, how such victims would be treated in the courts. The Laws of Lipit-Ishtar, a Sumerian king who ruled Isin from 1935–1925 B.C.E., contain one entry relating to blindness.[84] It reads, "If a man rents an ox and destroys its eye, he shall weigh and deliver one-half of its value (in silver)."[85] No entries are found concerning one who damages the eye of another human being.

One may next consider the Laws of Eshnunna, who lived shortly before Hammurabi.[86] One law in this collection is relevant to this discussion: "42 If a man bites the nose of another man and thus cuts it off, he shall weigh and deliver 60 shekels of silver; an eye—60 shekels; a tooth—30 shekels; an ear—30 shekels."[87]

It can be noted here how removing another individual's eye carries the same penalty as removing a nose, but twice the penalty as removing an ear or a tooth.

THE HAMMURABI LAWS

The Laws of Hammurabi, who ruled Sumer and Akkad between 1792–1750 B.C.E., list a significantly more severe penalty for the crime of blinding.[88] One may consider the following excerpts:

   84. Roth, *Law Collections from Mesopotamia and Asia Minor*, 23.
   85. Roth, *Law Collections from Mesopotamia and Asia Minor*, 33.
   86. Roth, "The Laws of Eshnunna," 332.
   87. Roth, "The Laws of Eshnunna," 334.
   88. Roth, "The Laws of Hammurabi," 335.

> 196 If an *awīlu* should blind the eye of another *awīlu*, they shall blind his eye.
> 198 If he should blind the eye of a commoner or break the bone of a commoner, he shall weigh and deliver 60 shekels of silver.
> 199 If he should blind the eye of an *awīlu*'s slave or break the bone of an *awīlu*'s slave, he shall weigh and deliver one-half of his value (in silver).[89]

It must be noted that when an awelum, or a gentleman,[90] blinds the eye of a commoner, the penalty is identical to that named in the Laws of Eshnunna. If a gentleman blinds the eye of an equal, though, that gentleman who committed the crime is to be blinded in one eye himself. In addition, Felix Just insightfully notes that since the penalty for blinding one eye of a gentleman's slave is payment of half the value of the slave, the penalty for blinding both eyes of a slave would logically be twice that, or the full value of a slave. This would, therefore, mean that a slave blinded in both eyes is as good as a dead slave and so would need to be replaced with a new slave.[91]

The following laws concern fees charged by physicians who treat eye conditions: "215 If a physician performs major surgery with a bronze lancet upon an *awīlu* and thus heals the *awīlu*, or opens an *awīlu*'s temple with a bronze lancet and thus heals the *awīlu*'s eye, he shall take 10 shekels of silver (as his fee)."[92]

According to Law 216, the fee for treating a commoner was 5 shekels. According to Law 217, the fee for treating a slave was 2 shekels paid by the master.[93]

The following laws concern the penalty for a physician who injures the eye of a patient:

> 218 If a physician performs major surgery with a bronze lancet upon an *awīlu* and thus causes the *awīlu*'s death, or opens an *awīlu*'s temple with a bronze lancet and thus blinds the *awīlu*'s eye, they shall cut off his hand.[94]
> 220 If he opens his (the commoner's slave's) temple with a bronze lancet and thus blinds his eye, he shall weigh and deliver silver equal to half his value.[95]

89. Roth, "The Laws of Hammurabi," 348.
90. Westbrook, "Mesopotamia: Old Babylonian Period," 377.
91. Just, "From Tobit to Bartimaeus, From Qumran to Siloam," 175.
92. Roth, "The Laws of Hammurabi," 348.
93. Roth, "The Laws of Hammurabi," 348.
94. Roth, "The Laws of Hammurabi," 348.
95. Roth, "The Laws of Hammurabi," 349.

It should be noted that the same Akkadian word "ḫuppudu," which refers to blinding in Laws 196–99 is used in the above laws to refer to a physician injuring an eye.[96] It should also be noted that the penalties in both sets of laws for blinding a gentleman both involve bodily harm to the offender. The penalties for injuring a slave are also both one half the value of the slave. Apparently Hammurabi made little or no distinction between a physician who causes injury and an individual who criminally assaults another.

The following law discusses one who rents an ox: "247 If a man rents an ox and blinds its eye, he shall give silver equal to half of its value to the owner of the ox."[97]

It is noteworthy that the same situation is described also in the Laws of Lipit-Ishtar with exactly the same penalty. When one also considers the similarities noted above between Hammurabi's Laws and the Laws of Eshnunna, it becomes clear how the Hammurabi laws were built on previous understandings.

When considering the Hammurabi laws as a whole, one can note Hammurabi's remark in the epilog that describes him as one to whom Shamash gave insight and truth.[98] This illustrates how it was desired that Hammurabi's writings would be understood as a religious effort whose ultimate origin was divine.

Nonetheless, it must also be understood that there is no evidence of Hammurabi's Laws actually being enforced. The only ancient literature describing his system refers to it as a guide.[99] Thus, Hammurabi's laws may have been more of a political statement than an actual law code he would enforce. It was understood in the ancient Near East that the gods demanded that the king enforce justice. Thus, a king such as Hammurabi would wish to appear worthy of divine blessings, and so produce an honorable code of laws.[100]

Welfare Systems

Recipients of barley rations

In addition to considering law codes about causing blindness, one may also study the treatment of those who were blind. The following is a list

---

96. *Assyrian Dictionary* (1956–61), s.v. "Ḫuppudu."
97. Roth, "The Laws of Hammurabi," 350.
98. Roth, "The Laws of Hammurabi," 352.
99. Bottero, *Mesopotamia*, 163.
100. Westbrook, "Mesopotamia: Old Babylonian Period," 364.

of recipients of barley rations under Queen Uru-KA-gina, a ruler's wife in pre-Sargonic Girsu:

> (1) (tentatively translated as) "barley rations to the men who get allotments";
> (2) "barley rations to blinded persons, carriers and those who are registered in individual lists";
> (3) "barley rations to women and (their) children";
> (4) "barley rations to those who are subordinate to the royal children."[101]

As one can see, the blind were grouped together with women, children, and those who did general service for the palace. In one count there were 750 people in the first three groups receiving barley rations.[102] Many of these blind individuals were purchased slaves, though.[103] Under supervision, they performed various tasks such as assisting the "gardener" with digging responsibilities.[104]

The Arua Institution

In pre-Sargonic Sumer, the temples were designed with orchards, gardens, and other places of labor. The Arua Institution, as this labor system became known, provided barley rations to such individuals as sterile women, widows, orphans, the elderly, the blind, the deaf, and female captives of war who had no male provider.[105] As I. J. Gelb describes this institution simply and plainly: "The over-all impression derived from the study of the *arua* texts is simply this: The rich gave away of their own free will anything they could afford, animals, objects, as well as humans out of their service personnel; while the poor, forced by economic stress, gave away other poor, unwanted people, mainly their women and children."[106]

One ancient list describes the people who labored in the Arua Institution, 1,741 children, babies, 604 men, and 180 blind.[107]

The Arua Institution, while providing food and shelter, was not a place of ease and comfort. One list from Lagash describes the experiences of a

---

101. Maekawa, "Collective Labor Service in Girsu-Lagash," 51.
102. Maekawa, "Collective Labor Service in Girsu-Lagash," 51.
103. Maekawa, "Collective Labor Service in Girsu-Lagash," 52.
104. Maekawa, "Collective Labor Service in Girsu-Lagash," 59.
105. Gelb, "The Arua Institution," 10.
106. Gelb, "The Arua Institution," 9.
107. Gelb, "The Arua Institution," 4.

group of individuals in the Arua during one year. Among seventeen women, four died, twelve became fugitives, and only one remained to receive her rations.[108]

Boundary Stones

One of the more unusual styles of literature that mentions blindness in Mesopotamia is the Babylonian boundary or memorial stone. The following paragraphs consider a sample of texts regarding three such stones that serve as representatives of a larger body of texts.

1. The first text to be considered was inscribed on a stele in the form of a Kudurru (boundary stone) and dates from the time of Nebuchadnezzar I:[109]

   > Whenever in after time one of the sons of Khabban, or any other man, who may be appointed as governor of Namar, or as prefect of Namar, be he small or great, whoever he may be, with regard to the cities of Bît-Karziabku, which the king has freed . . . shall obliterate the name of a god or of the king . . . and shall write another (in the place thereof), or shall employ a fool, or a deaf man, or a blind man, or a knave, and shall smash this memorial with a stone, or burn it in the fire, or put it in the river, or hide it in a field where it cannot be seen, may all the great gods, whose names are mentioned in heaven and earth, curse that man in wrath! May god and king look upon him in anger![110]

2. The next Kudurru to be considered here dates from the time of Marduk-nadin-akhê. This deed recorded a land grant from this ruler to Adad-zêr-iḳîsha:[111]

   > If he shall send a fool, or a man who is deaf, or blind, or an imbecile, or one without intelligence, and shall remove this memorial stone, or cast it into the water, or hide it in the ground, or destroy it with a stone, or burn it in the fire . . . may all the gods who are upon this stone (and) all whose names are mentioned curse him with a curse that cannot be loosened![112]

---

108. Gelb, "The Arua Institution," 12.
109. King, ed., *Babylonian Boundary-Stones and Memorial-Tablets*, 29.
110. King, ed., *Babylonian Boundary-Stones and Memorial-Tablets*, 35.
111. King, ed., *Babylonian Boundary-Stones and Memorial-Tablets*, 42.
112. King, ed., *Babylonian Boundary-Stones and Memorial-Tablets*, 48.

3. The final Kudurru discussed here is from the time of Meli-Shipak. It is a deed of gift recording a grant of corn land in the province of Bît-Pir'-Amurri, by Meli-Shipak to Khasardu, son of Sumê. This land was on the bank of the royal canal in the city of Shaluluni.[113] This quotation begins with the end of a sentence listing various defilements one might make against the boundary stone marking this territory:

> Or because of these curses shall fear and shall cause a fool or a deaf man or a blind man to take it up, and set it in a place where it cannot be seen, that man who shall take away the field, may Anu, the father of the gods, curse him as a foe! May Enlil, the king of all, inflict his punishment upon him! May Ea, the creator of men, give him an evil fate![114]

Apparently those laying boundary stones were concerned that an individual who might fear being caught defiling the stone himself might arrange for one with a disability to inflict the damage. One who witnesses a blind man damaging a boundary stone might be inclined to believe that such a one who cannot see would not perceive that the stone holds any importance. A deaf individual might also be assumed as ignorant if it is believed that such a one was unable to hear warnings about the treatment of boundary stones. One who is "stupid" would not be expected to be able to comprehend laws about damaging boundary stones. Whatever the disability of the one committing the vandalism, people might not necessarily connect such defilement with another party who arranged for one with a disability to commit the vandalism. Thus, a stone would be damaged, and no one would be punished. These rulers, then, wrote curses to ensure that the gods would punish, not the unknowing disabled individuals, but those who arranged for them to commit the defilement. The disabled, then, including the blind, would be protected from punishment, since, in a way, they were victims of the scheming of others.

Reversal of Blindness

1. This section, on healing of blindness in Mesopotamia, examines a sampling of magical texts describing spells that were to cure one with an eye disease or visual disability. This first spell was part of a ritual designed to heal one whose eyes were filled with blood:

---

113. King, ed., *Babylonian Boundary-Stones and Memorial-Tablets*, 19.
114. King, ed., *Babylonian Boundary-Stones and Memorial-Tablets*, 19.

> O clear eye, O doubly clear eye, O eye of clear sight! O darkened eye, O doubly darkened eye, O eye of darkened sight! O eye of sleepy (?) sight, O eye of . . . sight, O eye of evil sight! O failing eyes, O painful eyes, . . . eyes, like the slaughter of a sheep . . . like a cup of sour wine (vinegar) thrown away. . . . It is the charm of Ea [and Marduk] . . . [the charm of Nin-aḫa-kuddu] the mistress of charm; Gula, [quicken the] recovery, thy gift (?).[115]

The goddess, Gula, mentioned above, was often associated with healing in ancient Mesopotamia even as late as the Seleucid and Parthian periods. Her offspring, Damu, would often be named with her in such rituals.[116] In another ritual, these two deities were invoked to heal a baby from a worm that was said to be causing blindness.[117]

2. The following ritual would be performed for a sick eye:

> This (is) for red wool, a thread thou shalt spin, tie seven knots, as thou tiest (them) recite the charm, bind on his sick eye.
> Charm . . . O failing eyes, O painful eyes, O eyes sundered by a dam of blood! Why do ye fail, why do ye hurt? Why hath the dust of the river come nigh you, (or) the spathe of the date-palm whereof ye have chanced to catch the pollen which the fertilizer hath been shaking? Have I invited you, Come to me? I have not invited you, come not to me, or ever the first wind, the second wind, the third wind, the fourth wind cometh to you![118]

3. The following charm, spoken after again tying red and white wool, would be thought to heal a person for whom one eye is sick, but the other is whole:

> Of these twain, the daughter of Anu between them hath built a wall; the one will not move in accord with its fellow. Whom shall I send to the daughter of Anu of Heaven, that they may bring me their ewers of *ḫulalu*, their basins of bright lapis that they may gather (the waters) and bring (them) to the failing eyes, the painful and troubled eyes?[119]

4. This incantation designed to bring healing to one for whom eye disease was believed to be caused by wind such as that of a sand storm:

---

115. R. Campbell Thompson, "Assyrian Medical Texts," 29–30.
116. Avalos, *Illness and Health Care in the Ancient Near East*, 102–4.
117. Avalos, *Illness and Health Care in the Ancient Near East*, 107.
118. R. Campbell Thompson, "Assyrian Medical Texts," 31.
119. R. Campbell Thompson, "Assyrian Medical Texts," 31.

> In Heaven the wind blew and brought blindness to the eye of the man: from the distant heavens the wind blew and brought blindness to the eye of the man. Unto the sick eye it brought blindness; of this man his eye is troubled, his eye is pained. The man weepeth grievously for himself. Of this man, his sickness Ea hath espied and (said) "take pounded roses, perform the Charm of the Deep, and bind the eye of the man." When Ea toucheth the eye of the man with his holy hand, let the wind which hath brought woe to the eye of the man go forth![120]

According to these texts, a significant number of techniques were used to heal blindness in ancient Mesopotamia. Certain rituals involved objects such as red and white cords. Incantations may be addressed to specific deities or the wounded eye itself. An incantation may even be designed to resist the actions of an external agent such as the wind which could blow dust or pollen into the eyes. In all cases, though, the emphasis was on performing the actions of the ritual properly and saying the incantation accurately.

5. The final ritual to be considered was designed to heal one of night blindness:

> If a man's eyes suffer from "Sin-lurmâ" (night-blindness), thou shalt thread *makut* of the liver of an ass (and) flesh of its neck on a cord (and) put it on his neck. . . . A priest shall take seven (rounds of) bread; he whose eyes are sick shall take seven (rounds of) bread: [(then) the priest] shall say [to] the sick man, "Receive, O clear of eye:" [the si]ck man shall say to the priest, "Receive, O dim of eye" (Col. iii, 1). . . . Thou shalt chop up the *makut* of the liver . . . , assemble some children and they shall say thus: . . .
> [Charm:] . . . may Ea hear, may Ea receive . . . [Do not se]e, O clear of eye: see, O dim of eye. Recite the charm.[121]

Marten Stol notes that the charm listed above may mean that somehow the blindness would be transferred to the priest. The priest's sightedness would, then, be transferred to the individual with the eye disease.[122] One can assume that the priest must be immune, though, to such an eye condition, otherwise whenever a blind person came

---

120. R. Campbell Thompson, "Assyrian Medical Texts," 32.
121. R. Campbell Thompson, "Assyrian Medical Texts: II," 41.
122. Stol, "Blindness and Night-Blindness in Akkadian," 298.

for healing the priest would become permanently blind. The blindness would then transfer to the immune priest, and, thus, dissipate.[123]

It must be noted that magic, not use of natural remedies, is seen here as the agent for the cure of blindness. As Marten Stol rightly notes, if there were any actual natural, healing property in the above actions and/or objects, the healing would be attributed to the magic.[124]

Meanings of Blindness

Omen Texts

To understand more deeply the meanings of physical blindness, one may consider excerpts from the plethora of Mesopotamian omen texts. While blindness here is physical in nature, studying these texts helps one gain an understanding of the *meanings* that such physical blindness held in this ancient society.

BIRTH OMENS CONCERNING BLINDNESS IN BOTH EYES

The following are passages from birth omen texts of Kuyunjuk that discuss what would take place if both eyes were blind. It should be understood that the term "anomaly" refers to a creature that one is not able to identify.

1. If a woman gives birth to a blind child—the land will be disturbed; the house of the man will not prosper.[125]
2. If a woman gives birth, and (the child) has no eyes—the land will experience famine.[126]
3. If a ewe gives birth to a lion, and it has neither eye—that city will be taken by means of a breach.[127]

---

123. If this is so, a significant parallel would exist between this charm and Lev 10:16, 17. In Lev 10 Aaron is told that the priests, in eating the offerings, would bear the sin of the people. In Lev 10, though, it is sin which is born, not disease.
 124. Stol, "Blindness and Night-Blindness in Akkadian," 298.
 125. Leichty, *The Omen Series Summa Izbu*, 37.
 126. Leichty, *The Omen Series Summa Izbu*, 50.
 127. Leichty, *The Omen Series Summa Izbu*, 76.

4. If an anomaly's eyes are missing—the years of the reign of the king will come to an end.[128]

5. If an anomaly has no eyes—the days of the prince will be at an end; the prince will be imprisoned in his palace; famine and hard times will seize the land; there will be confusion; the kings will not agree; destruction will seize the land; the rains in the heavens and the floods in the *nagbu* will be late; the king will not grow old.[129]

6. If a mare gives birth to one (foal) and it has no eyes—Enlil will change the reign.[130]

Clearly, the birth of either a blind human or a blind animal was understood to signify that a time of bad fortune was coming. It would often be understood that the government would experience an untimely set-back. Birth omens concerning blindness in one eye

The interpretation is different if only one eye is missing. The following are birth omens, also from Kuyunjuk:

1. If a woman gives birth, and (the child) has no right eye—an enemy will dam up the canal of the prince, and the land will become waste.[131]

2. If a ewe gives birth to a lion, and it has no right eye—the city will be taken by means of a breach.[132]

3. If a ewe gives birth to a lion, and it has no left eye—the city of the enemy will be taken by means of a breach.[133]

4. If an anomaly has no right eye—a despotic king will dam up the river(s); the floods will be late in the *nagbu*.[134]

5. If an anomaly has no left eye—the man's adversary will die, and he will dig his canal; the flood will rise in the *nagbu*; the army of the prince will expand.[135]

According to these omens, a factor for interpretation stronger than the existence of eyes is their location. Dennis Pardee notes, in a discussion of Ugaritic omen texts, how the right side was understood to be good, while

---

128. Leichty, *The Omen Series Summa Izbu*, 123.
129. Leichty, *The Omen Series Summa Izbu*, 124.
130. Leichty, *The Omen Series Summa Izbu*, 183.
131. Leichty, *The Omen Series Summa Izbu*, 50.
132. Leichty, *The Omen Series Summa Izbu*, 76.
133. Leichty, *The Omen Series Summa Izbu*, 76.
134. Leichty, *The Omen Series Summa Izbu*, 122.
135. Leichty, *The Omen Series Summa Izbu*, 122.

the left side, evil. The lack of an eye on the right side, then, would suggest a lack of good fortune. The situation would be reversed on the left side. The lack of an eye on the left would signify a lack of bad fortune. The "evil" of the missing eye and the "evil" of leftness would cancel each other out. A good event would, then, take place.[136] The same principle holds true for the above omen texts, also. The lack of a right eye at birth was thought to bring bad fortune, while the lack of a left eye, good fortune.

BLINDNESS IN CITY OMENS

It is also necessary to consider a brief number of city omens. This is a sample: "94 If there are many deaf persons in a city, [the city] will be destroyed. 95 If there are many blind persons in a city, the city will fall. . . . 97 If there are many bleeding persons in a city, the city will fall."[137]

Based on these omens, blindness was not the only disability that would be understood to bring bad fortune. Nonetheless, such a finding does not change the fact that blindness was also understood as a bad omen. When one adds this information with the understanding that blindness was also seen as a curse in ancient Mesopotamia, it would be difficult to expect the blind to be received positively in that place and time. The blind would be understood as undesirable, suffering for wrong acts they had done, or bearers of bad luck to come. People would wonder what evil deed a blind individual had done and would worry about what sorts of harm would befall them because of the blind individual.[138]

Ignorance and Immaturity

In considering the figurative meanings of blindness in Mesopotamia, one may begin with a passage in "The Dialogue between a Supervisor and a Scribe":

> Again, do not put your trust in your own unopened eyes
> Thus you would greatly scorn obedience, which is the honor of humanity . . . .
> The learned scribe respectfully answered his master: . . .

---

136. Pardee, "Divination," 287.

137. Nissinen et al., *Prophets and Prophecy in the Ancient Near East*, 189.

138. One may consider John 9:1–3, in the story of the man born blind, in the NT. It is true that this story took place centuries after the Hebrew Bible was completed. Nonetheless, the question of the disciples regarding who had sinned (John 9:2) shows how the belief that blindness might be a divine punishment might affect one's behavior around an individual with such a condition.

Once a puppy, my eyes are wide open now, I act with humanity. So why is it that you keep setting up rules for me, as if I were a shirker?[139]

In this passage, blindness refers to a state of the mind. One who has unopened eyes, who, therefore, does not see, is one who is as an immature puppy, one who must be made to conform to strict rules. The learned scribe believes that his mental sight has developed enough to make him deserving of more freedom.

Summary

According to ancient Sumerian myth, the origin of blindness was effectively a contest in the realm of the gods. As in ancient Egypt, blindness was understood to be both a curse and a result of aging in ancient Mesopotamia. A number of crimes in Mesopotamia, though, were punishable with blinding. One who was blind, while not being permitted to serve as a diviner, was made to serve as a temple slave in certain situations. It was understood, though, that a blind man made to damage a boundary stone would not be held responsible by the gods. As a just treatment of the victim, one who blinds another would face severe penalties often blinding, according to ancient law codes. As in Egypt, blindness was frequently treated with magic. Some such magical rites involved the supposed transfer of the blindness to a priest. Any healing that would take place, then, would be attributed to the magic. In omen texts physical blindness would be a sign of coming misfortune.

Blindness often symbolically referred to ignorance or immaturity.

BLINDNESS IN ANCIENT HITTITE ANATOLIA

The final section of this chapter concerns blindness in ancient Hittite Anatolia. The first portion examines a myth of the storm god whose eyes were stolen. A number of texts are then analyzed that describe causes of blindness. Next, Hittite law codes are considered in the context of their Mesopotamian counterparts. Then, one finds a brief study of how blindness was thought to have been prevented. Blindness, with its meanings of ignorance and immaturity, is then studied.

---

139. Vanstiphout, "The Dialogue between a Supervisor and a Scribe," 591.

Mythology

The Hittite myth to be considered in this section is the story of the storm-god and the serpent, Illuyanka, from the second millennium B.C.E.[140] The following excerpt picks up as the storm-god addresses his son after the storm-god's eyes and heart were taken from him by the serpent:

> "When you go to the house of your wife, then demand from them (my) heart and eyes." When he went, he demanded from them the heart, and they gave it to him. Afterwards he demanded from them the eyes, and they gave these to him. And he carried them to the Storm-god, his father, and the Storm-god (thereby) took back his heart and his eyes.[141]

This story, like the story of the wounding of Horus's eye, also involves a god whose eyes are affected by another being's actions. In both stories the eyes are restored eventually. The main difference is that Horus's eye was wounded while the storm-god's eyes, along with his heart, were taken from him. Nonetheless, one finds a common theme in both tales of a god whose eyes are stricken and then restored.

The concept of the eye listed in conjunction with the heart is noteworthy. The eye is often understood as a physical organ while the heart, at least in ancient times, is often understood as a mental/emotional organ. Even in Num 15:39 the Israelites are warned against following their eyes and their hearts, noting the avenues, both physical and mental, whereby temptation reaches the soul. The mentioning of eyes and heart in this myth may also be thought of to refer to physical and mental domains. The exact nature of such a connection demands further research beyond the scope of this study.

Causes of Blindness

Blindness as a State Punishment

It is also important to consider a brief number of passages that discuss blindness as a penalty administered by the state. The first such passage is from a letter dating to the Middle Hittite Period. This text illustrates how disobeying a direct order from a ruler could have been punishable by blinding. It is thus noted, "As soon as this tablet reaches you, drive quickly before

---

140. Beckman, "The Storm-God and the Serpent (Illuyanka)," 150.
141. Beckman, "The Storm-God and the Serpent (Illuyanka)," 150.

My Majesty, and bring with you Maruwa, the ruler of the city of Kakattuwa. Otherwise they will proceed to blind you in that place (where you are)!"[142]

One may next consider the treaty between Hattusili III of Hatti and Ramses II of Egypt. In considering these excerpts, it must be understood that, as Gary Beckman notes, the use of three original languages, Hittite, Egyptian, and Akkadian, increases the difficulty of one's producing a completely accurate translation.[143] Nonetheless, according to the text as it stands, blinding is listed as one of a number of possible penalties that are not carried out:

> 18. [And if] a single man flees from [Hatti, or] two men, [or three men, and they come to] Ramses, Beloved [of Amon, Great King, King] of Egypt, his brother, [then Ramses], Beloved of Amon, Great King, [King of Egypt, must seize them and send them] to Hattusili, his brother [. . .]—for they are brothers. But [they shall not punish them for] their offenses. They shall [not] tear out [their tongues or their eyes]. And [they shall not mutilate(?)] their ears or [their] feet. [And they shall not destroy(?) their households, together with their wives] and their sons.
>
> 19. And if [a single man flees from Egypt, or] two men, or three men, and [they come to Hattusili, Great King], King of Hatti, my brother shall seize them and send [them to me, Ramses, Beloved of Amon, Great King, King] of Egypt—for Ramses, Great King, King [of Egypt, and Hattusili are brothers. But they shall not punish them for their offenses. They shall] not [tear out their tongues] or their eyes. And [they shall not mutilate(?) their ears or their feet. And they shall not destroy(?) their households], together with their wives and their sons.[144]

The above passage demonstrates that these rulers were concerned about the possibility that blinding would be the punishment for a slave who escapes to another country. These rulers, though, made a treaty to prevent this possibility from becoming reality.

As it is also noted regarding such slaves, "If ever a slave angers his master, they either put him to death or mutilate (*idālawaḫḫanzi*) his nose, eyes (or) ears."[145]

---

142. Hoffner, "Middle Hittite Period (ca. 1450–1350 BCE): The King to Kaššū in Tapikka 13," 49.

143. Beckman, *Hittite Diplomatic Texts*, 91.

144. Beckman, *Hittite Diplomatic Texts*, 99.

145. Hoffner, "The Disabled and Infirm in Hittite Society," 87.

This most likely refers to an intense type of angering, not simply causing slight frustration, since the penalty of death is also mentioned.[146] It must also be noted that blinding is seen here as an extremely serious penalty as it is placed alongside death in a list of possible options from which an owner may choose.

Blinding Prisoners of War

Captives of Tapikka (Maşat) and Šapinuwa (Ortaköy), like Samson, were blinded and made to labor in mills. Such treatment would prevent escape and reduce threat to the captors.[147]

The texts of Tapikka may be considered at this point. These documents contain letters written to the king of this city.[148] One such letter contains a list of captives held for ransom. In this list, a number of the captives are described as blinded and others are not:

> The ransom of Mr. Tamiti of Taggašta, who has not been blinded, is "two boy hostages and one man" (line 3). The ransom of Mr. Šunaili of Kaštaḫaruka, who has been blinded, is "one man, one woman, one child, eight oxen, and three goats" (lines 4–5). The ransom of Mr. Piḫina of Kutuptašša, who has been blinded, is "two men, and three oxen" (lines 6–7). The ransom of Mr. Ḫimuili of Kamamma, who has not been blinded, is "two hostage girls and one man."[149]

One may ask at this point why certain people are said to be blinded and others are not. Harry A. Hoffner notes that while accidental blinding in battle could be considered as a possibility, it seems unlikely, when one considers other accounts of prisoners taken by the Hittites, that such a great number of people would have this injury.[150] In addition, if accidental causes for injury were listed, one would ask why other accidental injuries were not. Thus, Hoffner logically reasons that it is more likely that these people

---

146. Hoffner, "The Disabled and Infirm in Hittite Society," 87.

147. Hoffner, "The Disabled and Infirm in Hittite Society," 86.

148. Hoffner, "The Treatment and Long-Term Use of Persons Captured in Battle According to the Maşat Texts," 66.

149. Hoffner, "The Treatment and Long-Term Use of Persons Captured in Battle According to the Maşat Texts," 67.

150. Hoffner, "The Treatment and Long-Term Use of Persons Captured in Battle According to the Maşat Texts," 68.

were blinded by their captors as a punishment and to reduce the threat of escape.[151]

It is also said in a letter in which Kikarša replies to his colleague Mr. Taḫazzili, who inquired regarding a blind man:

> I hope all is well with my dear brother and that the gods are lovingly protecting you. Concerning the matter of the blind men that you wrote me about: they have conducted all of the blind men up to the city Šapinuwa. They have left behind here ten blind men (to work) in the mill houses. I have inquired about them, and there is no one here by the name you wrote me.[152]

One may recall the story of Samson in Judg 16:21, as he was blinded and made to work. Other texts directly refer to blinded people in Šapinuwa working in mills as Samson did. It is said in one letter regarding such: "Thus says Šarpa: Speak to (Ḫimuili?), the provincial governor, and to Mr. Tarḫuni as follows: Blind men have fled from the mill house in Šapinuwa and have come (to you) there. As soon as this tablet reaches you, [seize the blind men] provisionally [and conduct them back here] safely."[153]

Hoffner notes that it may be assumed that such escaped blind men either had assistance from sighted individuals in their escape or they were blinded only in one eye.[154] In addition, women often worked in the mills. Thus, for a man to be made to do this would be a humiliation, forcing him to do what was once called "women's work."[155]

Blindness as a Curse

1. One may first consider a magical incantation, which was to be given regarding a vineyard that will not produce. This incantation was intended to release the field from a curse placed by the enemy of the previous owner. The woman set over the field would say, "Let the evil

---

151. Hoffner, "The Treatment and Long-Term Use of Persons Captured in Battle According to the Maşat Texts," 68.

152. Hoffner, "The Treatment and Long-Term Use of Persons Captured in Battle According to the Maşat Texts," 68, 69.

153. Hoffner, "The Treatment and Long-Term Use of Persons Captured in Battle According to the Maşat Texts," 69.

154. Hoffner, "The Treatment and Long-Term Use of Persons Captured in Battle According to the Maşat Texts," 69.

155. Hoffner, "The Treatment and Long-Term Use of Persons Captured in Battle According to the Maşat Texts," 69.

man, evil tongue (and) evil eyes be hammered down (in the ground) with the hatalkišna-branch."[156]

2. One of the more prominent Hittite texts in which blindness is described as a curse is the First Soldier's Oath, dating to the Middle Hittite Period, fifteenth century B.C.E. The following two excerpts describe the fate of one who becomes an enemy or transgresses against the king or queen of Hatti:[157]

> May these oath deities seize him and [may they] blind his army too, and further, may they deafen them. May comrade not see comrade. May this one not hear [that one]. May they give them a horrible d[eath]. May they fetter their feet with a wrapping below, and bind their hands above.[158]
>
> They lead before them a woman, a blind man and a deaf man and you say to them as follows: "Here (are) a woman, a blind man and a deaf man. Who takes part in evil against the king and queen, may the oath deities seize him and make (that) man (into) a woman. May they b[li]nd him like the blind man. May they d[eaf]en him like the deaf man. And may they utt[erly] destroy him, a mortal, together with his wives, his sons, and his clan."[159]

Clearly, both quotations indicate that the offenders would be made blind and deaf. The second excerpt is similar to the Aramaic treaty with the ruler of Arpad in that both documents emphasize the penalty with a tangible portrayal of such blindness.

3. A text may here be considered where a ruler believed that an enemy's troops were temporarily stricken with blindness by a deity, most likely to render them easier to conquer. As the king notes in the "Annals of Muršili II," "The mighty Stormgod, my lord, had summoned for me the god Ḫašammili, and he (i.e., Ḫašammili) kept me hidden, so that no one saw me (as I approached the land of Piggainarešša for battle)."[160]

---

156. Engelhard, "Hittite Magical Practices," 119.
157. Billie Jean Collins, "The First Soldiers' Oath," 165.
158. Billie Jean Collins, "The First Soldiers' Oath," 165.
159. Billie Jean Collins, "The First Soldiers' Oath," 166.
160. Hoffner, "The Disabled and Infirm in Hittite Society," 86.

Social Justice in Law Codes

Next one may consider the treatment in the courts of those wrongly blinded by other people. The Hittite law code to be considered dates from 1650 B.C.E., to 1500 B.C.E., thus, after Hammurabi but before Moses.[161] Following each of the first two of these laws below are later versions of the same laws:

> 7 If anyone blinds a free person or knocks out his tooth, they used to pay 40 shekels of silver. But now he shall pay 20 shekels of silver. He shall look to his house for it.
> (Late version of 7) If anyone blinds a free man in a quarrel, he shall pay 40 shekels of silver. If it is an accident, he shall pay 20 shekels of silver.
> 8 If anyone blinds a male or female slave or knocks out his tooth, he shall pay 10 shekels of silver. He shall look to his house for it.
> (Late version of 8) If anyone blinds a male slave in a quarrel, he shall pay 20 shekels of silver. If it is an accident, he shall pay 10 shekels of silver.[162]
> 77b If anyone blinds the eye of an ox or an ass, he shall pay 6 shekels of silver. He shall look to his house for it.[163]

Apparently, by the time of the later version of Laws 7 and 8 the law was changed so as the penalty was doubled if the blinding of a slave or a free man was not an accident. It can also be noted that the above laws are more similar to the laws of Eshnunna in the sense that the penalty for blinding in both cases is simply a fine. The Hammurabi laws stipulate blinding of the eye of one who blinds another gentleman. One may, then, recall that the Laws of Eshnunna said that one who blinds another must pay sixty shekels, while the Hittite code stipulated forty shekels, and that, only when one intentionally blinds a free man. Apparently, then, the Hittite laws regarding blinding were not necessarily as severe as their Mesopotamian counterparts.

Reversal of Blindness

While no Hittite texts concerning healing of blindness could be found for this study, one may consider a magical apotropaic incantation, which was to protect a Hittite king from a number of conditions, including blindness. The reference to absolving the eyes can be assumed to refer to protecting the eyes

---

161. Hoffner, "Hittite Laws," 106.
162. Hoffner, "Hittite Laws," 107.
163. Hoffner, "Hittite Laws," 113.

from possible harm. As it reads, "Absolve his eyes! Keep sickness from him! ... Keep head sickness (from him)! Keep the evil words of man (from him)!"[164]

Meanings of Blindness

Blindness as Immature Innocence

Hans G. Gueterbock discusses a Hittite ritual for the initiation of a prince. According to his research, this initiation would last several days and involve a number of ceremonies. After the prince was served by prostitutes, a goat would be killed. Then a blind man would be stripped naked, beaten, and led to the House of the Dead. There, feasting would be enjoyed. It is thought that the mistreating of the blind man would symbolize reaching maturity, in a way, throwing off one's blind innocence of youth.[165]

Blindness as Weakness

One may also consider the following Hittite incantation intended to protect one from words of sorcery: "In a meadow there stands a šišiyamma tree. Under it sit a blind man, a deaf man, and a lame man. The blind man doesn't see, the deaf man doesn't hear, and the lame man doesn't run. In the same way may the words of sorcery never see (this) client."[166]

Blindness, in the above incantation, refers to the inability of one's words of sorcery to hurt the individual protected. Words of sorcery, then, would be weak, as unable to find the protected client as would be a blind man. The type of magic employed in this sorcery defense, then, involves making an analogy between a literal condition, physical blindness, and the desired condition of symbolic blindness that would be placed on the words of sorcery. The magic, then, would be drawn to act in a manner similar, in a way, to physical blindness.

Summary

Like ancient Egyptian mythology with the story of the eye of Horus, ancient Hittite mythology contained the story of the storm-god whose eyes were assaulted and later returned to their original state of usefulness. Blindness

---

164. Engelhard, "Hittite Magical Practices," 91.
165. Güterbock, "An Initiation Rite for a Hittite Prince," 102.
166. Hoffner, "The Disabled and Infirm in Hittite Society," 86.

was understood as a civil penalty, means of controlling prisoners of war, and a curse. As in ancient Mesopotamia, penalties were to be imposed on one who blinds another. The reversal of blindness, as in the previously studied cultures, was held in the realm of magic. As a symbol, blindness referred to immaturity and weakness.

SUMMARY OF BLINDNESS IN THE ANCIENT NEAR EAST

In the above pages it has been shown that a number of writings from various ancient Near Eastern cultures discuss blindness. With reference to religion, a significant number of myths involve the blinding of a deity. One myth in Sumeria involves the creation of the blind as part of a contest between deities. In Egypt, a blind man could function as a harpist, while in Mesopotamia, one with an eye disease was forbidden to be a diviner.

A number of causes for blindness are discussed in ancient Near Eastern literature. Blindness, inflicted by the state, was understood as a punishment for crimes in all three regions. In Mesopotamia and the Hittite cultures, punishments were administered for blinding another individual. Nonetheless, a number of texts associate blindness with old age. Magic was often thought to be involved in causing as well as curing blindness in all cultures studied. Blindness was also understood to be brought about by curses or divine punishment.

With reference to social justice, the blind could occupy various roles in society ranging from that of an honored harper in Egypt to that of a temple slave in Sumeria. One with an eye disability was forbidden to be a diviner in Mesopotamia. Both Mesopotamian and Hittite law codes declared punishment for blinding another person, and in some cases, an animal. Egyptian Wisdom Literature counseled against mistreating one who is already blind.

Sources even discuss the reversal of blindness. In both Egypt and Mesopotamia magical texts would discuss cures for blindness. The Egyptian eye doctors were famous around the land for their ability to treat blindness.

Blindness also carried a number of meanings in the ancient Near East. In all three cultures, blindness, viewed as caused by a curse or divine punishment, would carry the meaning of such. In Egypt, physical blindness could be seen as a means to allow one to see the divine reality more clearly. Mesopotamian omen texts demonstrate how blindness in both eyes was seen as a sign of bad fortune. The blind in such a culture would ever be denied opportunities and rejected because of the stigmas placed on them by such superstitions. The blind, then, could be understood as either cursed for things they had done and/or as omens concerning bad things that would come to pass. When used figuratively, blindness was a universal symbol of weakness or ignorance in all three cultures.

III

Biblical Hebrew Word Studies

A number of words are used to refer to blindness, sight, and seeing in the Hebrew Scriptures. Before studying the passages that consider blindness, it is necessary to understand the meanings of these words, both the denotations, and, where possible, connotations. As a result, in the following paragraphs, a number of significant Hebrew words and terms relating to blindness are considered. First, the actual words for blindness are studied. Next, words often found in the context of blindness are analyzed. This would include words such as נָקַר, "he gouged out," or, משש, "he groped." Words for light and darkness, where relevant to this study, are also examined. Finally, words relating to seeing, such as עַיִן, "eye," and רָאָה, "he saw," are considered in contrast to blindness.

TERMINOLOGY FOR BLINDNESS

The first section of this chapter concerns words that directly refer to blindness in the Hebrew Scriptures. First, עור is considered with its related forms including עִוֵּר. After considering the meanings associated with these words, one finds a statistical study comparing the frequencies of use of such words with the frequencies of use of other words for significant disabilities in the Hebrew Bible. Then, סַנְוֵרִים is considered, followed by כהה and שעע.

עוֹר and Related Forms

Semitic Cognates

The first words to be studied in this section are עוֹר, "to blind," and all derived forms. This root has a number of cognates in other ancient Near Eastern languages. In Arabic, for example, *'awira* means to "be one-eyed." In Ethiopic, *'ōra* also refers to blindness. The stem is not clearly present in Akkadian.[1]

Biblical Usage

עוֹר

The word עוֹר occurs first in Exod 23:8. There it is said that pride blinds the eyes of those who see, or, literally, "those who are open." Deuteronomy 16:19 repeats this thought by saying that a bribe blinds the wise.

There are three instances in the Hebrew Scriptures where this word is used literally. In each of these three texts, 2 Kgs 25:7; Jer 39:7; and Jer 52:11, it is said that the Babylonians put out, or blinded, Zedekiah's eyes. As one can see, then, this word can be used both literally and figuratively. One may be blinded physically by having the eyes removed, and one may be blinded in a figurative sense, as when one's mental or spiritual judgment is clouded by means of a bribe.

עִוָּרוֹן AND עִוֶּרֶת

A number of words are derived from עוֹר. The first word to be considered here is עִוֶּרֶת, an adjective meaning "blind." This word occurs only once and is found in Lev 22:22 where it says that it is forbidden for one to offer a blind animal as a sacrifice. Most likely this is a literal usage of the word as other literal, physical disabilities such as being maimed (v. 22) and missing a bodily organ (v. 23). Since this is the only occurrence of this word in the Hebrew Scriptures, it is impossible to know if it was possible for such a word ever to be used figuratively. Since עוֹר, though, can be used literally and figuratively, it is logical to assume that its derived forms could be, at least, in theory.

The word עִוָּרוֹן, "blindness," occurs twice, both times with an unclear meaning. First, Deut 28:28 says that if Israel violates the covenant with God, the Lord would smite them with madness and blindness, mentioned among

---

1. Wächter, "'Iwwēr: Etymology," 575.

a number of curses in surrounding verses. Then, Zech 12:4, referring to the Day of the Lord, says that the Lord would open his eyes and smite the horses of Judah's enemies with blindness. Since these verses are discussing future events, it is impossible to be completely certain as to how this blindness is to be understood. One may consult the exegetical analysis of these passages in later chapters of this dissertation for a more thorough study of this word.

עִוֵּר

עִוֵּר used by itself

The word, which, by far, is found most commonly in the Hebrew Scriptures to refer to one who is blind is עִוֵּר. This word is first studied in passages that concern only blindness. Then, to discover unique idiomatic uses of this word, it is analyzed in passages that also discuss the other commonly mentioned physical disabilities in the Hebrew Scriptures: deafness, lameness, and muteness. The other, more seldomly discussed physical disabilities, such as being broken found in Lev 22:22–24, are not separately studied in the context of blindness because they occur only once or twice in the context of blindness. There is little one can conclude, then, concerning the literary use of these other disabilities in the context of blindness.

In Deut 27:18, it is said that one is cursed who makes the blind to stray. Then, Deut 28:29 says that the Israelites, if they violate God's covenant, would grope at noonday as the blind grope in the darkness.

In the Prophets, all but one of the occurrences are in the book of Isaiah. Isaiah 42:7 says that God would open the eyes of the blind and release prisoners who are in darkness in the dungeon. Isaiah 42:16 says that God would lead the blind on a way they do not know and turn their darkness into light before them. Isaiah 59:10 refers to those who grope like the blind, like those with no eyes, stumbling at noon as at twilight. Then, in Zeph 1:17, God says that he will bring distress on the people so they would walk like the blind.

This word also occurs a number of times in the Writings. Psalm 146:8 describes God as the one who opens (eyes, supplied) of the blind. Lamentations 4:14 discusses how the people go through the streets like the blind because they are defiled with blood. Clearly, blindness was an undesirable condition, one that limited one's abilities so he/she would need special protection even with a curse (Deut 27:18).

One may next consider the extent and nature of such blindness. First, Felix Just rightly observes how עִוֵּר is not used in the passages that refer to temporary or partial blindness, such as Gen 48:8–10 or 2 Kgs 6:17–20. Other words are used in those passages. In addition, he also notes certain passages, such as Isa 42:7, which refers to one's being a light to the blind, suggesting that such people cannot even see light. One must also note Isa 59:10, which discusses groping as the blind and as those with no eyes, placing עִוֵּר in parallel with "no eyes." It is reasonable, then, to assume that עִוֵּר refers to total blindness without even light perception.[2] In addition, Isa 29:18 refers to the blind being in a state of gloom and darkness, which would also suggest not simply weakened vision, but lack even of light perception. When one notes also how עוּר, in the physical sense, refers to the direct removal of the eye, it may be even understood that an עִוֵּר would often not even have any eyes at all. If such a one has eyes, the eyes would be so badly deformed that there would not even be light perception.

עִוֵּר in the context of other disabilities

First one may consider texts that concern both the blind and the deaf. In Lev 19:14, God says not to curse the deaf nor place a stumbling block before the blind. Only the disabilities of blindness and deafness are listed here. This appears to be a method of parallelism. One should respect the deaf, and one should respect the blind.

Blindness and deafness are also discussed together in the book of Isaiah. In Isa 29:18, it is said that the deaf would hear the words of a certain scroll and that the blind, out of their gloom and darkness, would see. Then, Isa 42:18 contains a command for the deaf to hear and for the blind to look and see. In Isa 42:19, God asks who is blind like his servant, deaf like his messenger. Then he repeats, asking two more times in that verse, who is blind. Finally, Isa 43:8 contains God's command to bring out the blind who have eyes and the deaf who have ears.

One can notice the poetic parallelism in the above verses. In Isa 42:18, the command for the deaf to hear is paralleled with the command for the blind to see. In Isa 43:8, the blind who have eyes are placed in a parallel relationship with the deaf who have ears.

In addition, blindness and deafness are often used symbolically in Isaiah. Isaiah 42:19, discusses the blind messenger. The following verse refers to how such a one sees but does not observe and has open ears but does not hear. This blindness and deafness must necessarily be deeper than lacking physical ability to see and hear.

---

2. Just, "From Tobit to Bartimaeus, From Qumran to Siloam," 32.

One may also note the intensity of language used to describe these disabilities. Isaiah 29:18 briefly mentions the deaf, but discusses in detail how the blind live in gloom and darkness. Isaiah 42:19 refers only once to the messenger being deaf, but three times to the messenger being blind. Apparently more intensity and emphasis was placed on the blindness than on the deafness. While the deaf would have experienced suffering, blindness, in its gloom and darkness, might have been seen as more intense and deserving of more attention, literally.

עִוֵּר can also appear in connection with פִּסֵּחַ, "lame." First, Lev 21:18 says that no priest who is blind, lame, or suffering from a number of other less common blemishes, shall draw near to the most sacred regions of the temple. In Deut 15:21, it is said that no lame or blind animal may be used as a sacrifice. In 2 Sam 5:6, it is stated by the Jebusites that the blind and lame of their city will repel David when he attacks them. Then, in 2 Sam 5:8, David orders his troops to attack the lame and the blind, whom David hates, of Jebus. David adds that the blind and lame shall not enter the house. Next, Jer 31:8 makes reference to bringing from the north country the blind and the lame, pregnant and in labor. Then, Mal 1:8 discusses those who offer the blind, lame, and sick of their animals for sacrifices. The people are asked if a governor would accept such an imperfect gift. Finally, on a more positive note, in Job 29:15, Job says he was eyes to the blind and feet to the lame.

A number of observations can be made at this time. First, one can note how עַוֶּרֶת is used in Lev 22:22 to refer to the blind animal that is not permitted to be used as a sacrifice. Then, Lev 21:18, forbids an עִוֵּר from officiating as a priest, and Deut 15:21 and Mal 1:8, which all prohibit a blind עִוֵּר animal from being offered as a sacrifice. No other word, besides those derived from עור, is used with reference to blindness and the cultus. The other words for blindness do not appear.

Next, one may consider the special use of "blind" and "lame" when the words appear in near proximity. While Job 29:15 employs a form of parallelism, the majority of the verses discussing blindness and lameness appear simply to be placing the conditions in the form of a list. One should, though, pay special attention to Deut 15:21. While this verse simply mentions animals that are blind, lame, or blemished, Lev 22:22 provides a more complete list of animals one may not bring as a sacrifice. This list mentions not only the blind, but also animals that are broken or maimed. In all, six disabling conditions are named. Deuteronomy 15:21 reduces the list to three, or two, if one considers "any harmful blemish" to be a general summary statement. This would lead one to suggest that the concepts of blindness and lameness, when used by themselves in a passage, comprise a merism. The eye is near the top of the body and is a sensory organ. The leg, located in the lower region of the body, is a motor organ. By referring, then, to the two opposite concepts of blindness and lameness, any other disability not disallowed by qualifiers in the context would be included as among them.

This means that while Job was eyes to the blind and feet to the lame, he also was ears to the deaf and a mouth to the mute. Since Deut 15:21, though, mentions specifically the blind and the lame, but places such a list between two general references to any blemish, the mentioning of "blemish" could be seen as limiting the merism in that verse. Only animals blind, lame, or with other disabilities also considered a blemish, based on the larger list of Lev 22:22, 23, would be included as banned. Since Lev 21:18–20 places blindness and lameness at the beginning of a sizable list of disabilities, a merism is not necessarily employed with reference to the statement of those two disabilities. The exact nature of what disabilities would be included in this list, as well as in the list in Deut 15:21, is considered in the next chapter.

It is interesting to note, though, that blindness, not deafness, was chosen as the representative for upper body sensory disabilities. In fact, lameness and deafness never appear by themselves in a passage. This adds support to the notion that blindness held a special place in Israelite culture as an extreme disability.

There is one text in the Hebrew Scriptures which mentions blindness and muteness, with אִלֵּם, as the word for "mute." Isaiah 56:10 discusses blind watchmen who are mute as dogs. As this is the only example of this literary combining, little can be assumed except that it appears to be an example of poetic parallelism.

The final group of texts to be considered in this section is those where blindness is mentioned with two or more of the other above-mentioned disabling conditions of deafness, lameness, and muteness. In the first text, Exod 4:11, God asks who made the mute, the deaf, the blind, and the seeing. In the second text, Isa 35:5–6, it is prophesied that one day the eyes of the blind would be opened, the ears of the deaf would be unstopped, the lame would leap, and the mute would sing. In both cases, it appears that this use of terms is simply to generate a list. God lists for Moses conditions he assumes responsibility for creating. Isaiah is given a list of disabilities that will one day be healed. Even Lev 21:18–20; 22:22; Deut 15:21; and Mal 1:8, which can be seen as discussing three or more disabling conditions, are all lists. Thus, when blindness is mentioned with two or more other disabling conditions, the purpose of such naming is simply to produce a list.

Statistical Analysis of Word Use Frequencies

One may also consider the number of times these words for physical disabilities are used in the Hebrew Scriptures. עִוֵּר is used twenty-six times,[3] פִּסֵחַ, fourteen times,[4] חֵרֵשׁ, nine times,[5] and אִלֵּם, six times.[6] One may consult figure 1. The word blind, there, occurs nearly twice as many times as the second-place word, lame.

One may also examine word use occurrences based on all forms of the Hebrew root words that concern said disabilities. With reference to עור, עִוֵּר, the verbal form, occurs five times,[7] עִוֶּרֶת, one time,[8] and עִוָּרוֹן, two times.[9] When one adds those eight occurrences to the twenty-six times עִוֵּר occurs, it is seen that עור, and all its derived forms, occur thirty-four times in the Hebrew Scriptures.

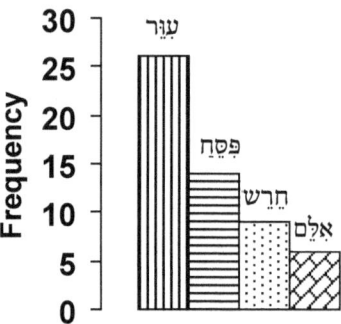

Figure 1. Terms for physical disabilities

The only instance where the verbal form of פסח, פִּסֵחַ, refers to lameness is 2 Sam 4:4 with reference to Mephibosheth. When one adds this to

---

3. Exod 4:11; Lev 19:14; 21:18; Deut 15:21; 27:18; 28:29; 2 Sam 5:6, 8 (twice); Isa 29:18; 35:5; 42:7, 16, 18, 19 (three times); 43:8; 56:10; 59:10; Jer 31:8; Zeph 1:17; Mal 1:8; Ps 146:8; Job 29:15; Lam 4:14.

4. Lev 21:18; Deut 15:21; 2 Sam 5:6; 5:8 (two times); 9:13; 19:27 (26, English); Isa 33:23; 35:6; Jer 31:8; Mal 1:8, 13; Job 29:15; Prov 26:7.

5. Exod 4:11; Lev 19:14; Isa 29:18; 35:5; 42:18, 19; 43:8; Ps 38:14 (13, English); 58:5; (4, English).

6. Exod 4:11; Isa 35:6; 56:10; Hab 2:18; Ps 38:14 (13, English); *1080; Prov 31:8.

7. Exod 23:8; Deut 16:19; 2 Kgs 25:7; Jer 39:7; 52:11.

8. Lev 22:22.

9. Deut 28:28; Zech 12:4.

the fourteen occurrences of פֶּסַח, one finds that פסח and its related form occur only fifteen times in the Hebrew Scriptures.

The other form of חֵרֵשׁ, deaf, in the Hebrew Scriptures is the verb חרשׁ. This word can also mean, "he was silent," though, as in Ps 28:1 where it is used in parallel with חשׁה, which also means, "he was silent." This makes it more difficult to determine the number of times the word for "to become deaf" is used. For the sake of this discussion, then, all occurrences of חרשׁ, which might refer to deafness but also might refer to silence, must be considered. These are Pss 35:22; 39:13 (12 in English); and 109:1, that all refer to the possible concept of God's not hearing, or being silent, to prayer. A fourth text, Mic 7:16, actually refers to ears being deaf, and so this one is a definite occurrence of חרשׁ meaning "he was deaf." Even with the three controversial occurrences of חרשׁ, though, the verbal form of חֵרֵשׁ occurs only four times in the Hebrew Scriptures. Added to the nine times חֵרֵשׁ occurs in the Hebrew Scriptures, one finds that there are, at most, twelve possible forms of חרשׁ that refer to deafness.

The verbal form of אלם, אִלֵּם, is used eight times in the Hebrew Scriptures to refer to muteness.[10] When one adds these occurrences to the six occurrences of the derived form אִלֵּם one sees that אלם and all relevant, related forms occur fourteen times, altogether in the Hebrew Scriptures. One may observe what is in figure 2.

One may note that עור and all derived forms occur more than two times more than the second-place term, פסח. In fact, while the other terms for disabilities hover around the thirteen to fifteen range, the related forms associated with blindness stand out far above at thirty-four. Even if one wished to include infertility, the disability most commonly associated with females, in the list of disabilities, the result of such a statistical analysis would not change as עָקָר (barren/infertile) occurs only twelve times in the Hebrew Bible, eleven of which refer to female infertility.[11] This is fewer times even than for חֵרֵשׁ "deaf" which ranked last in frequency of use. Again, the words for blindness occur significantly more often in the Hebrew Scriptures than words for other major physical disabilities.

---

10. Isa 53:7; Ezek 3:26; 24:27; 33:22; Pss 31:19 (18, English); 39:3 (2, English); 39:10 (9, English); Dan 10:15.

11. Gen 11:30; 25:21; 29:31; Exod 23:26; Deut 7:14 (twice, with the first occurrence referring to male infertility); Judg 13:2, 3; 1 Sam 2:5; Isa 54:1; Job 24:21; Ps 113:9.

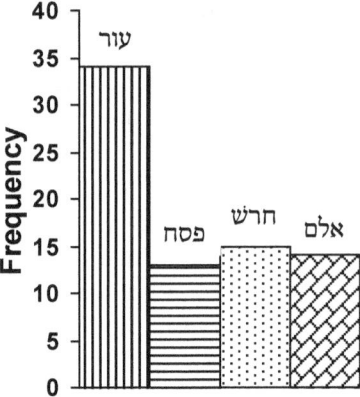

Figure 2. Root and derived forms of עור

This shows fairly conclusively that, at least linguistically, blindness, in its most total and permanent form, received more attention in the Hebrew Scriptures than other major physical disabilities. One may recall the previous discussion regarding the extremely graphic, repetitive, and intense language used to describe blindness that is not found for other physical disabilities mentioned in the same verse or passage. This shows the significance that blindness held as a disability of most troubling nature and implications and as a source for most intense metaphorical language regarding the spiritual realm.

סַנְוֵרִים

The Hebrew Bible employs a number of other words to describe blindness or blinding conditions. The first of these words considered here is סַנְוֵרִים.

Semitic Cognates

For this word, it is difficult to trace an etymology. In Akkadian, a similar-sounding term, *sillurmû*, with artificially constructed second form *Sîn-lurmá*, can mean "weak sighted" or "(severely) visually handicapped at night." This form, then, may have referred to "night blindness," a condition of temporary loss of vision. One may also note the approximate synonym, *sinnurbû(m)*, and secondary forms, *sinnūru* and *Sîn-nurmiātim*.[12] In addi-

---

12. von Soden, "'Iwwēr," 575.

tion, the Akkadian form, *šunwurum*, is similar in form to סַנְוֵרִים. This Akkadian adjective carries the connotation of intensity with its idea of a sudden stroke of blindness, possibly even that of a blinding light. For that reason, E. A. Speiser, in the Anchor Bible Commentary, suggests that the men of Sodom were described as having been blinded by a bright light from the angels when the men were smitten with סַנְוֵרִים (Gen 19:11).[13]

Biblical Usage

The word סַנְוֵרִים occurs only twice in the Hebrew Scriptures. In Gen 19:11 the angels smite the men of Sodom with blindness so they are unable to find the door to Lot's house. In 2 Kgs 6:18, as a result of Elisha's prayer, the Syrian army is also smitten with blindness, and they are unable to recognize Elisha. It is noteworthy that, in both cases, the blinding is caused by supernatural means. In both stories, also, the wicked are suddenly blinded so they are unable to harm the one who is righteous. In 2 Kgs 6:20, it is shown that such blindness can be temporary. There, God opens the eyes of the Syrians so they can see that they are in Sameria, surrounded by Israelite forces and unable to harm anyone. Temporary blindness would, of course, be the case with night blindness as discussed above with reference to possible Akkadian cognates.

כהה

Semitic Cognates

The next word to be considered is כהה which often refers to one's losing sight, especially due to age. The word more generally refers to growing weak. The Arabic cognate *kahiya* means "despair." The Ethiopian cognate *hakaya* means "be loose." The Tigre form, *hakka*, means "grow tired."[14]

Biblical Usage

כהה is first found in the Bible in Gen 27:1 with reference to Isaac's eyes that are said to have become dim. Then, in Deut 34:7, it is said that Moses' eyes were not dim at the time of his death. First Samuel 3:13 says that Eli did not restrain, כהה, his sons who were wicked. Isaiah 42:4 says that God shall not

---

13. Speiser, *Genesis*, 139, 140. This blindness caused by a bright flash of light is similar to what is described as happening to Saul on the way to Damascus in Acts 9:3–8.

14. Schunck, "Kāhâ," 58.

fail, כהה, till his purpose is accomplished. Next, Ezek 21:12 (21:7, English) refers to hands growing weak and spirits failing, כהה. Zechariah 11:17 refers to shepherds who abandon their flocks. It is said that such shepherds' right eyes would grow utterly dim, with an infinitive absolute/imperfect coupling employed. Finally, in Job 17:7 Job says his eye had become dim from sorrow. Clearly, then, this verb form refers to a weakening or failing. The eyes of one who is aged would weaken/fail, or, in practical language, become dim.

When one considers כֵּהֶה, כֵּהָה, the adjectival form of this root, the idea of dimming or becoming dark, grows even clearer. Leviticus 13:6 refers to a plague that is seen as dark, כֵּהָה, and is only a scab. Leviticus 13:21, 26, and 28 each discusses a spot having no white hairs, but seen as darkened by the priest. Leviticus 13:39 mentions a region that is darkish white. Then, Lev 13:56 describes a region inspected by a priest and found to be darkened. Next, 1 Sam 3:2 says that Eli's eyes had become darkened so he could not see. Isaiah 42:3 says that a darkened, or faintly burning, wick shall not be quenched. Finally, Isa 61:3 refers to one being given a garment of praise instead of a spirit that is faint/heavy/darkened. As one can see, then, the adjectival form of כהה most often refers to darkening or dimming. Thus, כהה is an excellent word to describe one whose eyes grow dim with age.

שעע

The final word to be considered in this section is שעע. This word in the hiph'il form means "to shut," and, thus, with reference to eyes, "to blind." In the hithpalpal form it simply refers to blinding. This word occurs in Isa 6:10 where it is commanded to shut (blind) the eyes of certain people so they cannot see. Then, Isa 29:9 uses the word twice as it refers to certain people who blind themselves and so, are blind and stagger but not from wine.[15]

One must be careful not to confuse the above word, שעע, with a different word spelled the same but clearly holding a different meaning. שעע, in Ps 119:16, clearly refers to rejoicing, not being blind. Nonetheless, the context of the above Isaian texts requires that one translate the word to suggest blindness. Isaiah 6:10 refers to how one should שעע the eye so one will not see. The same verse adds that one should make the ears heavy so this people would not hear and make the heart fat so the people could not understand. In addition, as John N. Oswalt rightly notes, the verse is in a chiastic form, with the eye and seeing in the center and climax, the impairing of the ear on the next level outward, and the impairing of the heart discussed on the two

---

15. Arnold, "שעע," 204.

ends.[16] The blinding of the eye would be the concept that best parallels the context of other related impairments.

The context also helps one identify the meaning of שָׁעַע in Isa 29:9. With reference to this verse, John D. W. Watts notes Ps 119:16 and recommends translating Isa 29:9 to read, "Delight yourselves and be delighted."[17] The unpleasant and negative concept of staggering but not from wine is paralleled with the clause containing שָׁעַע, though, suggesting that שָׁעַע would need to be understood as referring to the unpleasant concept of blindness rather than the positive concept of rejoicing. In addition, the surrounding verses consider blindness more clearly. Verse 10 says that God has closed the people's eyes and covered their prophets. Verse 18 says that the blind will see, using the more familiar word, עִוֵּר, for blind. Clearly, then, שָׁעַע, in these two places in Isaiah, can refer to blindness.

In both cases, though, this appears to be a spiritual form of blindness. Isaiah 6:9 says that the people see and do not perceive. Because of this lack of perception, God would simply have the people be blind. In addition, the heart, which understands spiritual matters, would be affected, according to v. 10. God would punish the people, according to v. 11, by laying their cities waste, a penalty more appropriate for spiritual blindness. Then, with reference to Isa 29:9, in v. 10, seeing is paralleled with prophecy, a spiritual event.

Summary

In this section עוּר and its related forms are shown to refer to total blindness in which no light is perceived. עִוֵּר often appears in parallelism with חֵרֵשׁ (deaf) and פִּסֵּחַ (lame). When עִוֵּר is listed alongside פִּסֵּחַ, they frequently comprise a merism. When עִוֵּר appears near the names for other disabilities, blindness is described with language either equally or more intense. עִוֵּר occurs significantly more times than the terms for other major disabilities. עוּר and its related forms also occur more frequently than each of the other respective sets of disability roots with related forms. This shows that blindness received more thought and attention in Hebrew literature than other disabilities.

Other words for blindness must also be considered. It is difficult to analyze סַנְוֵרִים in the context of other ancient Near Eastern languages. What is clear, though, is that when the word is used in the Hebrew Scriptures, it refers to a type of blindness, often temporary, inflicted on violent people in order to protect the innocent. כהה, when used in the context of eye conditions, refers to a weakening of the eyesight, often due to old age. Finally,

---

16. Oswalt, *The Book of Isaiah: Chapters 1–39*, 189.
17. Watts, *Isaiah 1–33*, 384.

שׁעע, in the context of the eye, refers to shutting the eye, effectively rendering one blind.

WORDS ASSOCIATED WITH BLINDNESS

In addition to analyzing words that directly refer to blindness, this study considers words and terms that are simply associated in some way with blindness. After studying נקר, the word often used with reference to the gouging out of an eye, משׁשׁ and גשׁשׁ, the two words that refer to groping, are studied. Then, מאוּם, blemish, analyzed as blindness, was listed as a blemish in a number of cultic texts. Next, פקח, "he opened," is analyzed, especially in how it often refers to the opening of blind eyes. Then, words for darkness, including and related to חֹשֶׁךְ and אֹפֶל, are studied. This section concludes with a consideration of ראה, "he saw," and עַיִן, "eye," especially with reference to how they are employed in discussions concerning matters relating to blindness. These words are simply considered in such a way as to deepen one's understanding of blindness, not to discuss all the intricacies of their use and connotations in every context.

נקר

Semitic Cognates

The first word to be analyzed in this section is נקר, which often refers to gouging, when in the context of the eye. The Old South Arabic cognate, *naqara*, means "hollow out, excavate." In Akkadian, *naqāru* means "scrape out."[18]

Biblical Usage

This word, in the qal form, means "pick out" or "hue out." In the pi'el form, it means "bore out, dig out, cut out." The derived word, נְקָרָה, refers to a cleft in the rock.[19]

This word first occurs in Num 16:14. There, Dathan and Abriam suggest that Moses might put out, נקר, the eyes of him and the rebels with him. Then, in Judg 16:21 it says that the Philistines put out Samson's eyes. In 1 Sam 11:2, Nahash says he would only make a covenant with Jabesh Gilead, which he was subjugating, if he would be allowed to put out the right eyes

---

18. Carpenter and Grisanti, "נקר," 158.
19. Carpenter and Grisanti, "נקר," 158.

of the men. Next, Isa 51:1 gives a command to look to the pit from where you were dug, נקר. The following verse refers to Israel's roots of Abraham and Sarah, out of which the nation came, or, figuratively, was dug. Job 30:17, instead of referring to an eye, discusses one whose bones are pierced, נקר. Finally, Prov 30:17 says that the eye that mocks one's father and despises one's mother shall be put out by ravens.

It is interesting to note that in all but two cases, נקר refers to the removal of an eye. It is also noteworthy that this removal of an eye is frequently a penalty for some form of rebellion. Dathan and Abiram, who had rebelled against Moses, were concerned about their eyes being removed. Samson's eyes were gouged out after he had repeatedly rebelled against the Philistines and was finally defeated. The mocking of father and mother in Prov 30:17 can also be seen as a form of rebellion against their authority. Even Nahash's demand to remove the right eye of the men of the city could be seen as involving the issue of rebellion. It would be more difficult to fight and rebel with one eye removed.

מששׁ

Semitic Cognates

The next word to be considered is מששׁ, which can refer in Hebrew to feeling (as with the hand, not the emotions), investigating, or, with reference to blindness, groping. In the Akkadian, *mašašu* means "to stroke, spread over." The cognate in Sabean, a dialect of Old South Arabic, is *mš*, which means to "touch." The Arabic equivalent, *masasa*, means to "feel, touch (with hand); strike, smite; afflict (with punishment, sickness, misfortune, insanity)." The Ethiopian form, *marsasa*, means to "feel, touch." In Syriac, *mewaš* and *maš* mean to "touch, feel." The Syriac word *mûšā* means "feeling." The Aramaic cognate, *mešaš* or *mûš*, means to "feel, touch, grope; test, examine, scrutinize, search, investigate." It is often understood that מששׁ in Hebrew is a secondary form of מושׁ, as in Aramaic and Sabean.[20]

Biblical Usage

This word occurs a number of times in the Hebrew Scriptures. First, in Gen 27:12, Jacob expresses the concern that his father who is blind might feel, מששׁ, him and know that he is Jacob pretending to be Esau. In Gen 27:21,

---

20. Johnston, "מששׁ," 1146.

Isaac does ask to feel, משש, Jacob, and in v. 22, he feels Jacob and exclaims that the voice is Jacob's, but the hands, Esau's.

Then, in Gen 31:34, Laban searches, משש, through the tent and does not find the idols. Jacob repeats this concept in v. 37 by explaining how Laban searched all Jacob's things and asks what was found. Exodus 10:21 discusses the plague of darkness that might be felt in Egypt. In Deut 28:29, one of the curses for violating the covenant between God and Israel would be that the people would grope at noonday like the blind in the darkness. In Job 5:14, Eliphaz says that God makes the crafty, who threaten the poor, to grope at noon as at night. This verse parallels Deut 28:29. In Job 12:24, 25, Job says that God makes the chief of the earth wander, grope in darkness (v. 25), and stagger as drunk.

It is noteworthy that the majority of the above passages concern blindness. Even if actual blindness is not concerned, the word still frequently refers to, at least, a state of temporary sightlessness caused by darkness or objects sought being rendered effectively invisible by being covered by fabrics. People in either situation are unable to see and so must rely on the sense of touch. Apparently, the concept of groping about became a common literary idea that would be associated in the context of these conditions.

גשש

Semitic Cognates

One must next consider the similar word, גשש, which also refers to groping in the one verse where it is found in the Hebrew Scriptures, Isa 59:10. The form in Arabic, *gassa*, means "feel, touch, spy out." *Gassa*, in the same language, means "feel, touch," and *gašaša*, "stroke, touch." In Ethiopian, *gasasa* means "feel, touch," and *gašaša*, "touch, stroke." The Syriac equivalents, *gšš* and *gš*, can be translated as "feel, touch." The Aramaic form, *gešaš*, means "touch, feel, grope." This form is especially interesting as in Targum Neofiti, Deut 28:29, *gšš* is used to translate the Hebrew term *mmšš*, discussed above as found in the MT.[21]

---

21. Johnston, "משש," 902.

Biblical Usage

This word in the qal means "to touch, feel," and in the pi'el, "to feel around, with the hand, grope about." In the hiph'il, it means "to feel out, investigate."[22]

In Isa 59:10 the Hebrew form, גשׁשׁ, refers to a people who grope as the blind. Then, again, using the same word the verse says that they grope as with no eyes. The context in both instances, again, is blindness.

מאוּם

This word in Hebrew means "blemish/spot/injury" and has cognates, מאוּם, in Aramaic Targum, Jonatan, MND, in Syriac, and mūm, in Arabic.[23] It first occurs in the Hebrew Scriptures in Lev 21:17, where it is said that no priest with a blemish may approach to offer the food of his God. Then, in vv. 18–20, there follows a list of such blemishes, beginning with blindness, and discussing conditions such as lameness, having a broken hand, and having a broken foot. One must first note that מאוּם occurs five times in this passage.[24] It is also noteworthy that every item in this list is potentially visible, at least, to someone inspecting. In addition, the terms for blindness due to old age, a blindness that does not involve as profound a visible deformity, are not listed as a blemish.

Jacob Milgrom, though, assumes that since a crushed testicle (Lev 21:20) is not regularly visible to the masses, the naming of such a condition in the list shows that non-visible defects such as deafness would be blemishes.[25] Even the testicles, though, while not visible to common view, would be seen by the priest's wife and by anyone in the priestly system designated to inspect people and/or animals. Thus, it should still stand that a physical מאוּם refers to a condition that is visible.

The next passage containing מאוּם is Lev 22:17–25 in the discourse concerning how blemished animals were not permitted to be offered as sacrifices in Israelite cultus. One must note, also, that the word מאוּם occurs three times in this passage (vv. 20, 21, and 25). Here, again, blindness is listed among these blemishes in v. 22. All these blemishes, such as brokenness, may also be understood as visible to one inspecting.

---

22. Johnston, "מששׁ," 902.

23. Koehler and Baumgartner, *The Hebrew and Aramaic Lexicon of the Old Testament*, 2:556.

24. Lev 21:17, 18, 21 (twice), and 23.

25. Milgrom, *Leviticus 17–22*, 1839.

This word also occurs in Lev 24:19–20, in the second talion discourse in the Torah. When מְאוּם "blemish" appears in Lev 24:19–20, again, issues concerning blindness are concerned (eye for eye, v. 20). Here, מְאוּם occurs twice (vv. 19–20). The other two ways a blemish could be placed in a human, according to v. 20, are by causing a break or wounding a tooth, two injuries that could be visually observed.

This word occurs five more times in the Torah, once in Num 19:3 and again in Deut 17:1, two texts that simply refer to an animal's being without a blemish. Deuteronomy 15:21, though, uses this word twice in referring to cultic restrictions on the offering of blemished animals with blindness and lameness as the only disabilities named. As in the list in Lev 21:18–20, both these conditions are visual in nature. Then, Deut 32:5 uses מְאוּם, apparently figuratively, inasmuch as the blemish of the Israelites is to result in great disasters as described throughout the rest of the chapter. Thus, in the Torah, passages that concern physical blemishes not only mention blindness, but repeat the word מְאוּם a number of times to emphasize the concept.

In 2 Sam 14:25, it is said that Absalom had no מְאוּם from the top of his head to the soul of his foot. Then, v. 26 describes how Absalom would remove his comely hair (an aspect of the top of his head) each year, and it would weigh two hundred shekels. Most likely the striking attribute of such hair, that would have made it worthy of mention in the text, would have been is stunning, visual beauty.

Two additional examples of the figurative use of מְאוּם may now be considered. In Job 11:14, 15 it is said that if Job rid himself of iniquity, he could lift his face without מְאוּם, blemish. Then, Prov 9:7 says that one who rebukes a wicked man will receive a מְאוּם, and this מְאוּם is set in parallelism with "shame," in the first half of the verse.

Next, this word is found in Song 4:1–7. In Song 4:1–5, it is first said twice that the bride was beautiful, יָפָה (Song 4:1). Then, a number of aspects of beauty, all visual, are described. Finally, in v. 7, it is said again that she is beautiful, using the same word as in v. 1, and then, that no מְאוּם is in her. It would be logical, then, to assume that מְאוּם continues in the same context as "beautiful" in v. 7, describing matters of visual appearance.

Even in Daniel, מְאוּם refers to visible defects when discussing the physical body. Erhard S. Gerstenberger notes, for example, how in Dan 1:3, 4, מְאוּם appears to refer to a blemish on the appearance.[26] This is reasonable, since the only reference to the physical body in v. 4 occurs immediately after it is said that no blemish was found and refers to the goodly appearance.

---

26. Gerstenberger, *Leviticus*, 316.

Nothing is said about how the people should have beautiful voices, soft skin, or hear well, for example.

As one can see, then, a physical מאום is that which is visible upon inspection. Blindness, then, is a מאום, inasmuch as it involves a visible deformity of the eye. The fact that מאום is also used to describe moral blemishes suggests that the banning of physical blemishes could have been seen as a symbol for the banning of moral blemishes.

פקח

Semitic Cognates

The word פקח (he opened) has a number of significant ancient Near Eastern cognate forms. In Aramaic, *pqh* (פקח) means "to open, make see." In Syriac, *pqh* actually means to "bloom." The Arabic equivalent, *faqaha*, means "open the eyes." In Old South Arabic, *pqh* means "open."[27]

Biblical Usage

Whereas פתח, "he opened," is the common word in Biblical Hebrew used to refer to opening the mouth, פקח, "he opened," often refers to opening the eye.[28] The first occurrence of פקח in the Hebrew Scriptures is found in Gen 3:5, before the fall of humanity. Here, the serpent tells the woman that if she would eat from the forbidden tree, her eyes would be opened, and she would be as God, knowing good and evil. In Gen 3:7, after she and her husband have eaten the fruit, their eyes are opened, and they see that they are naked. In Gen 21:19, God opens Hagar's eyes and she sees a well.

In 2 Kgs 4:35, a child, once dead, opens his eyes and sneezes. Then, in 2 Kgs 6:17, Elisha prays that God would open the eyes of his servant to see the flaming horses around the city. Next, in 2 Kgs 6:20, Elisha prays that God would open the eyes of the Syrians whom God had recently blinded, also upon Elisha's request. Then, in 2 Kgs 19:16, Hezekiah prays for God to open his eyes, so he would behold and respond to the actions of Senachareb. Next, in Isa 35:5, it is said that the eyes of the blind would be opened and the ears of the deaf unstopped in a great day of healing in the future to Isaiah. Isaiah 42:7 also refers to one's opening eyes that are blind and releasing prisoners from the dungeon. Isaiah 42:20 says, referring to the servant who

---

27. Hamilton, "פקח" 666.
28. Hamilton, "פקח" 666.

is blind (v. 19), that such a one opens his ears but does not hear. This is the only instance in the Hebrew Scriptures where פקח refers to another organ besides the eye.

In Jer 32:19 God's eyes are said to be opened to the ways of humanity, giving reward to all. Zech 12:4 says, regarding Judah, that God will open his eyes, when he strikes the horses with blindness.

Psalm 146:8 says that the Lord opens the eyes of the blind. The word "eyes" is not found in this verse, though, but is assumed. In Job 14:3, it is asked if God opens his eyes to bring one into judgment. Then, Job 27:19 says that the rich man opens his eyes and his wealth is gone, showing how fleeting wealth can be. Next, in Prov 20:13, it is commanded for one to open his/her eyes and have plenty. This concept is contrasted with "do not sleep," showing how opening the eyes is connected with being alert. The sense of sight, though, may still be concerned in this passage, at least, in a minor way, as the previous verse says God made the hearing ear and the seeing eye. One must wake up and open the eyes to see intelligently in order to have plenty. Finally, Dan 9:18 is a prayer that God open his eyes and see the desolation of Daniel's people and of the sanctuary.

A number of observations can be made based on this information. First, in nearly all the above texts, פקח refers to enabling one to see or to give attention. In Gen 21:19, the term is used literally as Hagar was enabled to see the well. In Gen 3:5, though, the word is used figuratively, as it appears in the context of becoming able to know good and evil. However the eyes would be opened, in order for such to happen, the eyes would have been closed, and often, then, previously blind.

It is also noteworthy that in all but one instance in the Bible in which someone's eyes are opened by another agent, named or unnamed, this opening of the eyes directly involves the healing of some type of blindness. The Lord's opening of the eyes of the Syrians in 2 Kgs 6:20 is an example of the ending of blindness by a named agent. Then, the opening of the eyes of the blind in Isa 35:5 is by an unnamed agent. When Hagar's eyes are said to be opened by God, in Gen 21:19, this would most likely be the reversal of a partial blindness, a blindness to the reality of the well. Finally, while Jer 32:19 involves a qal passive stem for פקח with reference to God's possessing opened eyes, the word functions adjectivally, describing how God's eyes function in a state of being open, not how someone, at one time, opened or will open them, as is the case with the passive forms in Gen 3:7 and Isa 35:5.

The word may have slightly different meanings when one is said to open his/her own eyes. When the word is used in the context of God's opening his own eyes, it refers to his giving attention and acting. Daniel and Hezekiah both wanted God not simply to see the trouble about them, but to act on it (2 Kgs 19:19; Dan 9:19). When the child opened his eyes, in 2 Kgs 4:35, the emphasis is on the regaining of life, rather than the regaining of sight. This may be assumed since the child was previously described as dead, not blind, and is said to sneeze, an action related to breathing, rather than behold anything after opening his eyes. Nonetheless, one who is dead is also unable to see.

Even the words derived from פקח often refer to matters related to sighted and blindness. The word פֶּקַח occurs in two passages. In Exod 4:11, when God lists the types of ability groups he creates, those contrasted with the blind are the פֶּקֵחַ, literally, the "open." It is assumed that this refers to those with open or seeing eyes. Then, Exod 23:8 says that a bribe blinds those who are פִּקְחִים, or, open. Again, it would be assumed that the eye is what would be open since a bribe would blind such an individual. The form פְּקַח occurs only once and concerns a separate issue. In Isa 61:1, this word is employed to discuss the opening of prisons for captives. A discussion on the relationship between prison and blindness occurs in a later chapter of this study.

Terms for Darkness

In studying words associated with blindness in the Hebrew Scriptures, one must necessarily analyze those concerning darkness. Not every word for darkness must be studied, however. This section considers only those words for darkness that occur in the various blindness passages in the Hebrew Scriptures.

This section first considers אֹפֶל and אֲפֵלָה and the verses that contain those words. Next, חשׁך is considered and its related forms, with verses containing such words noted. Finally, since a number of passages employ both אֹפֶל forms and חשׁך forms in close proximity, verses involving both words are considered. This eliminates unnecessary repetition and allows for consideration of how these words function when in close proximity.

הָלֵפָא and לְפָא

Semitic cognates

No verbal root form for these two words exists in the Hebrew Bible, though both words concern a type of darkness. Possible cognates in other languages include *apālu*, in Akkadian, which means "be late" and *'afala*, in Arabic, which means to "go under, sink."²⁹

Biblical usage

A study of these two Hebrew words yields a number of significant insights. Psalm 11:2 says that the wicked prepare to shoot the upright in the darkness. Psalm 91:6 refers to the plague in the darkness. In Job 3:6, Job, amid his distress, pleads that the night he was born would be seized by darkness. Then, Job 28:3 parallels a stone of darkness with the shadow of death, the latter, clearly a gloomy concept. In Job 30:26, Job says he looked for good and evil came, for light, and there was darkness, paralleling אֹפֶל with evil. Clearly, then, אֹפֶל, used by itself, refers to a distressing form of darkness, never with any positive connotations.

אֲפֵלָה also often refers to darkness or gloom. Deuteronomy 28:29 says that the rebellious Israelites would grope as the blind in the אֲפֵלָה, darkness, but at noonday. In Isa 58:10, a reversal of Deut 28:29 is promised. If one would help the needy, אֲפֵלָה darkness shall be as noonday. Isaiah 59:9 says that one waits for light, but walks in darkness. Jeremiah 23:12 says that the way of certain people shall be slippery, darkness, where they shall fall. Proverbs 4:19, using a figurative meaning, says that the way of the wicked is as אֲפֵלָה, darkness, as they do not know where they stumble. Then, Prov 7:9 says that the loose woman meets the foolish man at night in the darkness where she causes him harm. This darkness could refer to both physical night and the man's foolishness. Clearly, אֲפֵלָה refers to a distressing darkness. Thus, any form related to אֹפֶל carries only negative connotations, connotations which are most likely intended also when אֹפֶל is used in the context of blindness.

חשׁך

Semitic cognates

A number of significant Hebrew words for darkness stem from the verbal root חשׁך, to become dark, or be darkened. This word has cognate forms in a number of ancient Near Eastern languages. In Aramaic, *ḥᵃšôk* (חֲשׁוֹךְ) means "darkness" (Dan 2:22). In Syriac, *ḥešûk* also means "darkness." The Arabic word *suḥkûkun* means "very dark."³⁰

---

29. Price, "אֹפֶל (ōpel)," 479.
30. Price, "חשׁך," 312.

BIBLICAL USAGE

חֹשֶׁךְ. חֹשֶׁךְ appears a number of times in the Hebrew Scriptures, some of which concern blindness directly. In the first text, Exod 10:15, it is noted that the land was darkened because of the plague of locusts. Then, in Isa 5:30, in the context of sorrow, one is commanded to look and see how the light is darkened. Then, Isa 13:10 says that the sun shall be darkened. The following verse discusses the context of punishing the wicked for their evil. Jeremiah 13:16 says one should give glory to God before he makes darkness and causes the feet to stumble. Amos 5:8 says that God turns the shadow of death into morning and darkens the day, showing how God can bring about both positive and negative outcomes. Amos 8:9 says that God will darken the earth. The following verse parallels this idea with that of turning feasts into mourning. Then, Mic 3:6 discusses a night with no vision, darkened, so none can divine. In Job 3:9, Job, amid his distress, pleads for the stars to become dark. According to Job 18:6, the light of the wicked shall be darkened. Then, in Job 38:2, God asks Job concerning his darkening council with words without knowledge. Next, Ps 69:24 (23, English) suggests blindness in how it contains a plea that the eyes of the psalmist's enemies be darkened and their loins made to shake. Then, Ps 105:28 says that God made Egypt dark. Psalm 139:12 says, literally, that the darkness does not darken before God. According to Eccl 12:2, the sun, moon, and stars are one day to be darkened. During this time, according to Eccl 12:3, those who look out the windows would be darkened. Lamentations 4:8 says that those said to be white in the previous verse would have their appearance darkened more than that of a coal. Lamentations 5:17 says that because of disasters previously mentioned, the heart is faint, the eyes, darkened/dim. Clearly, nearly every occurrence of חֹשֶׁךְ necessarily carries distressing connotations. These connotations would also become associated with blindness when blindness appears in the context of such distressing words.

מַחְשָׁךְ. The next word to be studied is מַחְשָׁךְ, "a place of darkness," which is derived from חֹשֶׁךְ. Isaiah 29:15 pronounces woe on the one who hides his counsel and whose works are in the darkness. In Isa 42:16, God says he will make the darkness light for the blind. This word next occurs in Ps 74:20; there it is said that the dark places of the earth are full of the dwellings of cruelty. In Ps 88:7 (6, English), it is said that God has laid the psalmist in the lowest place, the place of darkness. Then, in Ps 88:19 (18, English), the psalmist adds that his friends have been set far from him, his acquaintance, in the darkness where such cannot be seen. In Ps 143:3, the psalmist says that his enemy made him dwell in darkness as those who are dead. Finally, Lam 3:6 says God has set the author in dark places as those dead for a long time. As with חשׁך, this word appears in a context of trouble and distress. This type of darkness and its mysteriousness is never positive, but consistently either a punishment or simply the abode of the wicked.

חֹשֶׁךְ

One must next analyze חֹשֶׁךְ. In Gen 1:2, darkness was said to be upon the face of the deep as God's Spirit hovers over the waters. God, though, limits the realm of this darkness, creating light in vv. 3–5, showing that total darkness was not a desired environment for the earth. Nonetheless, darkness in this form cannot be understood as evil since it still existed as night (Gen 1:5) and God is said to have seen everything he had made as very good, according to Gen 1:31.

In Exod 10:22, חֹשֶׁךְ is used to describe the plague of darkness that fell upon Egypt, a distressing situation. In Deut 5:23, it was through a voice heard in the darkness that God gave the Ten Commandments. This darkness, though associated with God's Presence, was still understood as an aspect of a most distressing and terrifying event as the people afterward requested that God henceforth speak indirectly to them through Moses (Deut 5:23–26).

One can then study חֹשֶׁךְ as it appears in the Prophets. Isaiah 5:20 says woe to those who call good, evil, and evil, good, who put darkness for light and vice versa. Here, darkness and light are symbols of evil and good, respectively. Isaiah 5:30 says if one looks at the land, he will see darkness and distress. Then, Isa 9:1 (9:2, English) says in a hopeful context that the people who walk in darkness have seen a great light. Isaiah 42:7, again referring to blindness, discusses the opening of the eyes of the blind and the releasing from the dungeon those who sit in darkness. In Isa 45:3, God tells Cyrus that he will give him the treasures of darkness, riches in secret places. Here, חֹשֶׁךְ is less negative, being paralleled simply with secret places. The word, though, still refers to the unknown. In Isa 45:7, God says he makes light and darkness, wealth and calamity, paralleling light with wealth, and darkness with calamity. Then, in Isa 45:19, God says he did not speak in secret, in the land of darkness. Again, one finds a less negative use of חֹשֶׁךְ, while it still refers to the unknown. Isaiah 47:5 says that the daughter of the Chaldeans would sit in silence and go into darkness. This, again, shows a more negative connotation for the word.

חֹשֶׁךְ also occurs in the other later prophets. In Ezek 8:12, God ask if Ezekiel sees what the people are doing in the darkness as they say the Lord does not see them. Darkness is associated with evil here as it is where the people do their own way, thinking that God is not watching. In Ezek 32:8, God says he will bring darkness over the land and darken the bright lights in the sky, another negative usage of חֹשֶׁךְ. Joel 3:4 (2:31, English) refers to the sun's being turned to darkness, the moon, to blood, among the signs on this dreadful day. Amos 5:18 asks why the people desire the day of the Lord as it is darkness, not light. Darkness, here, is clearly not something positive that one would desire. Finally, in Mic 7:8, the prophet says that when he falls, he shall rise; when he sits in darkness, the Lord shall be his light. Again, light is desired more strongly than darkness.

חֹשֶׁךְ, then, like the previously studied words for "darkness," describes an undesirable state of existence. Often, but not always, חֹשֶׁךְ is associated with evil. The student of Scripture must keep these connotations in mind when analyzing texts where these words are employed concerning the darkened world of blindness.

אֹפֶל Forms and חֹשֶׁךְ Forms Together

First, Exod 10:22 says that a חֹשֶׁךְ, darkness of, אֲפֵלָה, gloom/darkness, came over Egypt as the ninth plague. Next, in Isa 8:22, amid a list of calamities, it is said that the people would find the earth as trouble and darkness, חֲשֵׁכָה, and be driven to אֲפֵלָה, darkness/gloom. Then, Isa 29:18 says that the blind will see out of their אֹפֶל, gloom/darkness, and חֹשֶׁךְ, darkness. Next, Joel 2:2 describes the day of the Lord for which an alarm should be sounded (v. 1) as a day of חֹשֶׁךְ and אֲפֵלָה. Then, Zeph 1:15 says also that the Day of the Lord would be a day of wrath, trouble, distress, a day of חֹשֶׁךְ and אֲפֵלָה. In the latter two instances, these words appear to be used as a hendiadys, since they both refer to darkness and appear adjacent to each other.

A number of occurrences of these words used together exist in the book of Job. The first is Job 10:22. In v. 20, Job asks to be left alone to take comfort. In v. 21, he refers to going into a land of darkness, חֹשֶׁךְ. Then, in v. 22, he refers to this land again as a land as darkness, אֹפֶל, and then says the light has become as darkness, אֹפֶל. Finally, in Job 23:17, Job says that he has not been cut off from before darkness, חֹשֶׁךְ, and darkness, אֹפֶל, covers his face. Though the conclusion of this verse is difficult to translate, what must be noted is that this אֹפֶל, darkness, is clearly gloomy because of the context in v. 15, which discusses how Job was troubled at God's presence. It is also clear how these two words for darkness appear in separate clauses of parallelism. Both clauses concern Job's existence in a realm of darkness, but each clause uses a different word for darkness.

Thus, when these אֹפֶל forms and חֹשֶׁךְ forms appear together, they can stand as a hendiadys or in parallel clauses. One blindness text, Isa 29:18, employs both types of forms in the same verse. Using these types of forms together in the Hebrew Scriptures may intensify the concentration on the idea of darkness, since such is repeated. Such usage may also allow for variety in words so that the different words with their special connotations may be considered.

Seeing and the Eye

The last section in this chapter on word studies is devoted to analyzing words that concern sight, רָאָה, he saw, and, עַיִן, eye. It is necessary to study these words, in brief, in order to understand the meaning of the absence of seeing or an eye. This study, though, primarily focuses on occurrences of these words in a context either of blindness or one that at least assists one in understanding blindness more fully.

As in the above section, a number of verses contain both these words in near proximity. Thus, after considering texts that involve each word individually, the texts involving both words in near proximity are studied. This shows how closely related these concepts were in Hebrew thinking.

ראה

SEMITIC COGNATES

The first word to be studied in this section is ראה, "he saw." A number of cognate forms in other ancient Near Eastern languages are considered briefly. Words for "to see" include *rʾy*, in Old South Arabic, *rĕĕya*, in Ethiopian, *raʾā*, in Arabic, and *rʾy*, in Canaanite as found in Moabite. The Aramaic form, *rēw(ā)*, means "appearance."[31]

BIBLICAL USAGE

The first occurrence of ראה in the Hebrew Bible is Gen 1:4 where God is said to have seen the light that it was good. Genesis 1:10, 12, 18, 21, 25, and 31 repeat this idea. ראה, here, not only involves seeing but perceiving. God saw the light clearly enough to know that it was good. In Gen 2:19, God brings the animals to Adam to see what he would name them. This form of seeing

---

31. Fuhs, "Rāʾâ," 210.

is clearly a more intellectual type, as a name that is called would be heard by God, not seen. God brought the animals to Adam to observe/notice what he would call them.

ראה, at times, appears in the context of יָרֵא, "he feared/reverenced." In Gen 22:12, the angel says that Abraham fears God. In v. 14, Abraham names the mountain יְהוָה יִרְאֶה, and, according to the text, it is said that in the mountain of the Lord it shall be provided/seen, יֵרָאֶה, with ראה as the root for provided/seen. One may note the wordplay of the י, the ר, and the א with reference to יִרְאֶה יָרֵא and יֵרָאֶה. The concepts of seeing and fearing, then, are joined, at least literarily, in this passage. A similar wordplay between these two words occurs in Ps 119:74, which says that those who fear, יָרֵא, God see, ראה, the psalmist and rejoice. According to H. F. Fuhs, in the *Theological Dictionary of the Old Testament*, it is unclear whether or not there is a linguistic connection between these two words.[32]

Concerning ראה in the rest of the Bible, in Deut 4:28, it is noted that idols are unable to see. Since a human-fashioned idol cannot see physically or spiritually, this seeing could refer to either or both. In 1 Sam 9:9, a prophet is said to have once been called a seer, רֹאֶה. This type of seeing would be primarily spiritual rather than physical since it refers to a prophet. Then, Isa 6:9 says that the people see and do not perceive. It has already been noted how this seeing is most likely spiritual since the context is judgment (v. 11). Psalm 10:14 says that God sees affliction, referring to his active response to it. Psalm 31:8 (7, in English) refers also to God's seeing human trials.

Clearly, then, ראה can refer to both physical and figurative, often spiritual, sight. One who is said to be without sight, then, could be one who is physically blind or one who is spiritually blind.

עַיִן

SEMITIC COGNATES

The last word to be analyzed in this chapter is עַיִן, "eye." The word עַיִן, in Hebrew, is a rare instance of a noun out of which is derived a verb, עין. This verb found in the qal participle form in 1 Sam 18:9 means "to look with suspicion." עַיִן has a number of cognates in other ancient Near Eastern languages such as ʿn, in Ugaritic, īnu/ēnu, in Akkadian, ḫinaia, in Canaanite, Phoenician, ʿn, in Aramaic according to Dan 7:8, 20, ʿēnā, in Arabic, ʿayn,

---

32. Fuhs, "Yārē," 291.

Ethiopian, and *'yn*, in Egyptian. This latter Egyptian form is found only in non-hieroglyphic written characters as the usual word is *ỉr.t*.[33]

Biblical Usage[34]

The first occurrence of עַיִן in the Hebrew Bible is Gen 3:5, which has previously been noted to discuss the opening of Adam's and Eve's eyes when they would eat of the forbidden tree. Both Gen 6:8 and 19:19 refer to one's finding favor in the Lord's eyes, showing how the eye is an instrument of favor. Then, referring to the penalty in the Torah for damaging another human's eye, Exod 21:24 says "eye for eye." The eye was, then, understood as important enough for the Torah to prescribe a serious penalty for its damage. Numbers 15:39 says that the people should not wander after their hearts and eyes, again, showing the eye as an instrument of favor or desire, often covetous. Similarly, Ezek 6:9 says the people's eyes wander after idols. Next, regarding the eye as an instrument of judgment, 2 Kgs 3:2; 8:18; 8:27; and 13:2, all say that a king did evil in the eyes of the Lord. Second Kings 12:3 (12:2, English) and 18:3 are two examples of texts that say a king did what was right in the eyes of the Lord. Then, in Ezek 5:11; 7:4 and 9, God says his eye shall not spare, nor shall he pity. This shows the eye as an instrument of showing mercy. Next, Zech 14:12 says that the eyes of those who are against Jerusalem will consume away in their sockets. Psalm 38:11 (10, English) says that the light of the psalmist's eyes is no longer with him. Then, concerning how the eye is often a symbol of beauty, in Song 1:15 and 5:12 each partner in the couple says the other's eyes are doves. Thus, עַיִן can be used in a number of different contexts, both physical and spiritual, and can refer to judgment, beauty, and the power to show mercy. One lacking eyes, then, might be seen as devoid of these attributes, at least, in some way.

ראה *and* עַיִן *Together*

Both ראה and עַיִן appear together in a number of passages. First, Gen 13:14 and Gen 22:13, refer to Abraham's lifting up of his eyes and literally seeing the land in Gen 13:14 and a ram in Gen 22:13. Then, in Gen 27:1, Isaac's eyes are said to be dim so he could not see. In Gen 48:10, it is said that

---

33. Stendebach, "'Ayin," 29.
34. This word has already been considered in a number of other contexts. In studying עור, for example, it is noted that Zedekiah's eyes were blinded. In the context of נקר, it is noted that eyes may be forcibly removed. When studying פקח it is understood how eyes, physically or spiritually, may be opened.

Jacob's eyes were heavy so he could not see. While כהה is employed in Gen 27:1 to describe Isaac's failing eyesight, כבד "to be heavy" is used in Gen 48:10 to describe Jacob's failing eyesight. Both verses use ראה for "see," and not another word such as חזה. Apparently, ראה was frequently the word of choice for such expressions.

It is also interesting to note that while Gen 48:10 says that Jacob's eyes were heavy so he could not see, Gen 48:8 says that Jacob saw Joseph's sons. H. C. Leupold rightly resolves this apparent contradiction by noting that this inability to see, according to Gen 48:10, must have been only partial since he was able to see his grandsons.[35] This means that idiomatically, כבד used with עֵינַיִם simply refers to a weakening of the eyesight, not an absolute blinding. Here one finds two different uses of ראה in the same passage. Jacob is able to see Joseph's sons partially, but not necessarily well enough for him to make any practical use of his seeing. Then, in 1 Sam 4:15, Eli's eyes are said to be set so he could not see. Eli is described as suffering from failing eyesight due to age, according to 1 Sam 3:2. Then, 1 Kgs 14:4 says that Ahijah's eyes were set so he could not see because of his advanced age. The verb used for "set" in both these passages is קום. This suggests that these verses demonstrate an idiomatic use of this verb in the context of the eye. In addition, just as in Genesis, when someone's vision is compromised, the word used is ראה, not נבט, חזה, or any other word that refers to sight.

It is unclear how much partial vision such an individual such as Eli or Ahijah would have. Felix Just notes that when Eli's eyes were set, קום, he was still able to watch by the roadside (1 Sam 4:13) though his vision was weak enough so he would need to ask one nearby to describe the scene.[36] Felix Just also suggests that קום may refer to a more profound loss of vision than כהה since 1 Sam 4:15 is set some time after 1 Sam 3:2, presumably after Eli's vision would have deteriorated more.[37] In reality, though, it is unclear which word describes the more intense form of blindness, since 1 Sam 3:2 says only that Eli's eyes were beginning to קום. כהה, blindness, in 1 Sam 4:15, then, is only compared with the beginning of כהה, blindness, not the consummation of כהה, blindness. Compared with Ahijah, who experienced קום, vision loss, Isaac, who experienced כהה, blindness, is not shown to be any less physically vulnerable to deception from one pretending to be another. Ahijah simply had assistance from God concerning the nature of the deceit as Isaac did not. Thus, it is impossible to precisely determine which word describes a more profound type of vision loss.

---

35. Leupold, *Exposition of Genesis*, 2:1150.
36. Just, "From Tobit to Bartimaeus, From Qumran to Siloam," 38.
37. Just, "From Tobit to Bartimaeus, From Qumran to Siloam," 38.

Then, Jer 5:21, refers to those who have eyes, but do not see, ears, but do not hear. Ezekiel 12:2 says again that the people have eyes to see but do not see, ears to hear but do not hear. This theme of lacking spiritual sight is common in the Prophets.

These words appear a number of times in the Writings. Psalm 69:24 (23, English) is a plea that the eyes of the psalmist's enemies be darkened so they cannot see. Psalm 94:9, then, asks rhetorically if the One who made the eye cannot see. Both Pss 115:5 and 135:16 say that idols have eyes but do not see. Apparently idols are described as blind the same way people are described as blind. Again, the verb of choice for describing eyes that do not see is ראה. The other words for seeing simply do not appear in this context of describing failing vision in the Hebrew Bible.

Two more instances exist where these two words are used together in the Writings. Ecclesiastes 11:7, for example, says that it is good for the eyes to see the sun. The goodness of eyes, literally seeing the physical sun, is presented here as a metaphor for a reality discussed later in this dissertation. In addition, Dan 9:18 is a prayer for God to open his eyes and see the desolations of the people. This seeing would involve an active response, as the next verse is a plea that God would forgive and not delay. This passage also shows how God could be understood, in at least a symbolic sense, to see with eyes.

It is clear, then, that a number of blindness passages in the Bible employ both ראה and עַיִן in close proximity. These two words also appear in close proximity in a number of other contexts, such as that of gazing across a land, or desiring God to act concerning affliction. These words, when used together, may also refer to physical or spiritual vision.

Summary

In this section it is noted how a number of Hebrew words, while not directly meaning "blind" or "blindness, refer to issues that are related to blindness. נקר nearly always refers to the gouging out of an eye, and, in such cases, refers to a consequence of rebellion. Both משש and גשש refer to groping about with the hands, often by the blind. מאום, when referring to a physical blemish, concerns one that is visible in nature. This word may also refer to a moral blemish. פקח nearly always refers to the opening of blind eyes, especially when such is done by another agent. Forms of אֹפֶל and חֹשֶׁךְ are used to refer to darkness, often a distressing darkness in which the blind live. These words are often together as a hendiadys or in parallelism. ראה and עַיִן are often used respectively with reference to seeing and the eye. These words can refer to literal or figurative sight, or the lack thereof. When referring to the lack of vision, the verb of choice is ראה.

SUMMARY OF BIBLICAL HEBREW WORD STUDIES

A number of words concerning blindness are analyzed in this chapter. When referring to prohibitions concerning the blind in the cultus, עור forms are the only blindness terms used. These forms refer directly to blindness with no light perception and, often, to the lack of eyes altogether. This type of extreme blindness is a significant enough deformity for it to be listed as a מאום, which is a visible physical blemish.

A number of words discuss causes of blindness. One cause is the smiting with such by God to defend the innocent, סַנְוֵרִים. Old age, as shown by כבד, כהה, and קום, is also understood to cause blindness, though blindness described by these words is generally not complete. Blindness may also be caused by the gouging out of an eye, נקר, an action often understood as a penalty for rebellion. However blindness was caused, the only word meaning "he saw" used with a negation with reference to the inability to see is ראה.

Blindness was often described as a profound condition, with those having it being made to live in gloomy darkness and to grope about משש or גשש. Thus, a type of severe "eye for eye" penalty is prescribed for damaging another's eye. The term used with reference to the reversal of blindness was פקח, which referred frequently to the opening of the eyes of the blind.

With reference to the meanings of blindness, a number of terms such as עַיִן, "eye," and ראה, "he saw," are employed to refer to both physical and spiritual blindness. The intense language used to describe blindness, combined with the fact that blindness is discussed more often than other disabilities, shows the severity this condition was understood to have. In the Torah עור is used twice to refer to the blinding nature of a bribe. A word used three times by Isaiah to discuss spiritual blindness is שעע, which refers to the shutting of an eye.

IV

Blindness in the Torah

With an understanding of blindness in the ancient Near East and the words often associated with blindness in the Hebrew Scriptures, one may now analyze blindness as a topic developed throughout relevant passages in the Hebrew Bible. This chapter considers how blindness is addressed in the Torah, Genesis through Deuteronomy. Each section of this chapter focuses on blindness within each of the five books of the Torah, moving through each book from beginning to end as the passages appear. For each passage, matters of translation and exegesis are considered. At the conclusion of the chapter, there is a synthesis of the material in this chapter showing how the Torah discusses blindness as it relates to cultus, causation, social justice, reversal, and meanings.

GENESIS

This first section of this chapter concerns the book of Genesis. One first finds a brief analysis of issues in the creation story that are relevant to a study on blindness. After analyzing blindness in Gen 3:5–7, the blindness of the men of Sodom, Gen 19:11, is considered. Next, the opening of Hagar's eyes to the reality of the well in Gen 29:19 is examined. Then, the story in Gen 27 of Jacob's deceiving his father, blinded by age, is studied. Finally, the story of Jacob, blinded by age, blessing Ephraim and Menasseh (Gen 48:8–20) is examined.

Introductory Remarks on Creation

A study of blindness in the Torah must necessarily begin with an analysis of issues relating to sight and blindness in the creation stories of Gen 1 and 2. While blindness is not addressed in either account of the creation story, there are a number of facts one can assume about the condition from the text. Such are discussed below.

First, it must be understood that sight was important in creation. Genesis 1:4, 10, 12, 18, 21, 25, and 31 all say that God saw an aspect of creation as good. It is difficult to understand exactly what it means when the Bible says that the transcendent and unique God *saw*. One can recall from the previous chapter that ראה, the word for "he saw" in Gen 1, can refer to both perception of the physical realm and perception of the spiritual realm. The woman in Gen 3:6 even saw, ראה, the forbidden tree as both pleasant to the eyes, a physical perception, and desirable for gaining wisdom, a non-physical, mental perception. It may also be noted that טוב, "good," in Gen 2, refers to matters in the physical realm as well as the non-physical realm. The trees are said to be good, טוב, for food, a physical aspect (Gen 2:9). Then, in Gen 2:18, God says that it is not good, טוב, for man to be alone, a matter that reaches beyond the physical into the realm of the relational. Since both Gen 2:9 and Gen 2:18 are set before the creation of the female, Eve (Gen 2:21, 22), and since God said everything was very good, טוב, only after he had made humanity both male and female (Gen 1:27, 31), it may be assumed that the physical goodness of a pleasant tree and the relational goodness of a man's not being alone were aspects of what God saw. Possibly, then, God's seeing could have involved analysis of the aesthetic beauty and spiritual reality, but it is impossible to determine precisely what God would have observed. God would not necessarily see the world in exactly the same physical manner that humans do.

It must also be understood that humanity was originally intended to be able to see. In Gen 2:8, 9 God is said to have planted a garden in which he placed the man he created. In this garden grew every tree that was pleasant to the sight and good for food. For a tree pleasant to the sight to be enjoyed, one must be able to see it physically. It can, therefore, be assumed that Adam and Eve were able to see this tree. Then, Gen 3:6 says that the woman saw the forbidden tree as pleasant to the eyes. This seeing took place before she took the forbidden fruit and fell. Apparently her eyes functioned at a level so that she could see the tree, and her mind, at a level, so she could discern whether or not it was beautiful.

One can, therefore, assume that humanity, from the beginning, is understood from Scripture to have sight. Blindness was not part of the original plan for this species. One may contrast this, for example, with the Sumerian creation story in which certain human beings are created blind as part of a contest among the gods. According to Genesis, all was created by God to be very good (Gen 1:31) and "very good" meant, for humanity, that among many gifts they would possess sight.

Blindness and the Fall, Genesis 3:4–7

Translation

THE TEXT

The first possible reference to blindness in the Hebrew Scriptures is Gen 3:4–7. The text is translated below:

וַיֹּאמֶר הַנָּחָשׁ אֶל־הָאִשָּׁה לֹא־מוֹת תְּמֻתוּן:
כִּי יֹדֵעַ אֱלֹהִים כִּי בְּיוֹם אֲכָלְכֶם מִמֶּנּוּ וְנִפְקְחוּ עֵינֵיכֶם וִהְיִיתֶם כֵּאלֹהִים יֹדְעֵי טוֹב וָרָע:
וַתֵּרֶא הָאִשָּׁה כִּי טוֹב הָעֵץ לְמַאֲכָל וְכִי תַאֲוָה־הוּא לָעֵינַיִם וְנֶחְמָד הָעֵץ לְהַשְׂכִּיל וַתִּקַּח מִפִּרְיוֹ וַתֹּאכַל וַתִּתֵּן גַּם־לְאִישָׁהּ עִמָּהּ וַיֹּאכַל:
וַתִּפָּקַחְנָה עֵינֵי שְׁנֵיהֶם וַיֵּדְעוּ כִּי עֵירֻמִּם הֵם וַיִּתְפְּרוּ עֲלֵה תְאֵנָה וַיַּעֲשׂוּ לָהֶם חֲגֹרֹת:

> 4. But the serpent said to the woman, "You will not die;
> 5. for God knows that when you eat of it your eyes will be opened, and you will be like God, knowing good and evil."
> 6. So when the woman saw that the tree was good for food, and that it was a delight to the eyes, and that the tree was to be desired to make one wise, she took of its fruit and ate; and she also gave some to her husband, who was with her, and he ate.
> 7. Then the eyes of both were opened, and they knew that they were naked; and they sewed fig leaves together and made loincloths for themselves. (NRSV)

NOTES

It must be noted that the second-person forms in v. 5 are plural in the Hebrew. This means that the serpent was speaking of both Adam and Eve when referring to eyes being opened.

Exegesis

Context

Immediate biblical context

One may consider Gen 3:6 in the context of Gen 1 and 2. It is noteworthy that the verse opens by saying, "And the woman saw the tree that it was good." The words for "saw," "that," and "good," commonly appear in the same order in Gen 1 with reference to God's evaluation of his creation (Gen 1:4, 10, 12, 18, 21, 25, 31). Eve, already possessing God's image (Gen 1:26–28), is able to recognize objects as good, too.

One may next consider the attributes of the forbidden tree in the context of Gen 2:9. In Gen 2:9, when all the trees of the garden are described, they, too, are said to be good for food. Both verses describe their respective trees as visually appealing. This, in a sense, means that Eve was longing after a visual appearance she already could enjoy from the other trees.[1] Genesis 2:9, though, says that all the trees were pleasant to the sight, מַרְאֶה, but Gen 3:6 says that the woman saw the tree as pleasant to the eyes, עֵינַיִם. This break from a complete parallel may be for a significant reason. This use of עֵינַיִם appears a short space after the serpent used the same word in saying her eyes would be opened.

The author, then, intended to note that Eve's eyes already functioned sufficiently. She was able to see the tree and make a value judgment regarding whether or not it was attractive. She could even see that one could gain wisdom from such a tree. This type of non-visual perception shows that her eyes, in a figurative sense, also functioned adequately.

Intertextual connection

In Gen 3:4–7 the serpent tells Eve that if she would eat of the forbidden fruit, her eyes would be opened and she would be like God, knowing good and evil. It has already been noted in the preceding chapter that the opening of one's eyes, when employing the Hebrew words פקח and עַיִן, refers frequently to the giving of sight to one lacking such, or, in some sense, blind. The serpent, then, would be asserting that Eve was blind and accusing God of having created her to be blind. God who could see, then, was accused of creating Eve so she could not see, and by eating the forbidden fruit, this gift of sight into good and evil, jealously guarded by God, would become hers.

---

1. Kissling, *Genesis*, 192.

As noted in the *Seventh-day Adventist Bible Commentary*, "The promise, 'Your eyes shall be opened,' implied a present limitation of sight that could be removed by following the serpent's advice."[2] The eating of the forbidden fruit, though, would be the giving of special sight to them, sight that God did not desire them to possess.

General analysis

It has now been shown how Adam and Eve, whose eyes originally functioned adequately, had their eyes opened by eating the forbidden fruit. The nature of this opening may now be examined. When her eyes and the eyes of her husband were finally opened in v. 7, their new perception only gave them the ability to know that they had a nakedness that needed to be covered and that such nakedness could bring them fear (Gen 3:7, 10). In fact, as Victor P. Hamilton notes, the word for naked in vv. 7, 10, and 11, עֵירֹם, is slightly different from the form used in Gen 2:25, עָרוֹם, in saying that the man and his wife were naked and unashamed. This shows that not only were their eyes opened to a new reality, but this reality contained shameful elements that they would also now freely see.[3] While the exact nature of the nakedness before and after the fall is beyond the scope of this study—this study concerns how Adam and Eve *saw*, not how they looked—it is enough to note this. Before the fall, the unique word for nakedness is used in a context of a shameless, fearless existence, but after the fall, the different word used for nakedness is associated in each mentioning with shame and fear. Their new perception only made them want to hide from God.

In addition, after this point, no reference is made to Adam's and Eve's seeing anything. In Gen 3:7, when their eyes were opened, they knew יָדַע, not saw רָאָה, that they were naked. In vv. 8, 10 mention is made to hearing God's voice, but, again, nothing is said about anything being seen. Generally, when someone's eyes are opened, they are said to see something (Gen 21:19; 2 Kgs 16:18, 20). Strangely, in Gen 3, the references to sight occur only before the eyes are opened. Thus, in one sense, while Adam and Eve's eyes were opened to a negative form of seeing, in another sense, it could be said that the opening of their eyes resulted in their blindness, or, at least, blindness to what mattered the most.

A deeper analysis of the text yields a more complete understanding of the extent of this blindness. Most likely they would have seen God before

---

2. "Gen 3:5. Your Eyes Shall Be Opened," 230.

3. Hamilton, *The Book of Genesis: Chapters 1–17*, 191. See also Davidson, *Flame of Yahweh*, 56–57.

the fall if Adam was brought to life by God's blowing into his nostrils (Gen 2:7). In Gen 3:8, when they do hear God, they hide, hoping, in a sense, that God would not see them. God, though, calls forth and begins the dialogue whose conclusion means the expulsion of Adam and Eve from Eden. Thus, the opening of their eyes forbade them from seeing God and, in the end, all the beauties of Eden. Most troubling, then, Adam and Eve became blind to that which was most important to them.

Even if one does not consider Adam and Eve blind after their eyes were opened, the path of rebellion they started on eventually resulted in blindness, both physical and spiritual for the human race (Exod 4:11; Isa 35:5, 6; 42:7, 18–20). This is because, as noted previously, blindness of those types did not exist before sin. Thus, when Adam's and Eve's eyes were opened, a course of events was started that would eventually result in blindness among their descendants.

Blindness at Sodom, Genesis 19:11

Translation

THE TEXT

The next occurrence of blindness in Genesis is Gen 19:11 in the story of the destruction of Sodom and Gomorrah. This verse describes what the heavenly visitors to Sodom did to the wicked men of the city after Lot was rescued:

> וְאֶת־הָאֲנָשִׁים אֲשֶׁר־פֶּתַח הַבַּיִת הִכּוּ בַּסַּנְוֵרִים מִקָּטֹן וְעַד־גָּדוֹל וַיִּלְאוּ לִמְצֹא הַפָּתַח׃

> 11. And they struck with blindness the men who were at the door of the house, both small and great, so that they were unable to find the door. (NRSV)

NOTES

One must pay close attention to the Hebrew word order in the first clause of this verse. Literally, it reads, "And the men who were at the door of the house, they smote with blindness." The verb, which often comes at or near the beginning of Hebrew clauses, is near the end, with the object at the beginning. This word order places emphasis on the wicked men of Sodom rather than on the smiting with blindness. It, then, is those wicked men, not anyone else, who were blinded.

Exegesis

CONTEXT

Ancient Near Eastern context

It must next be noted that this blinding took place around nightfall, after evening (Gen 19:1–4). This would support, at least loosely, linguistic connections with סַנְוֵרִים and night blindness discussed in the previous chapter. The blinding, though, still could have involved a bright light.

Immediate biblical context

The lack of perception on the part of the men of Sodom can be compared with that shown in the immediate context of the book of Genesis. Terence E. Fretheim rightly notes how in Gen 18:21 God says that he would go down and see if the citizens of Sodom have acted as wickedly as the cry of them that went up to heaven. God, then, is shown to have his perceptive powers intact, while the men of Sodom, in Gen 19:11, lose theirs.[4] When one adds the notion that according to Gen 19:1 Lot saw the angels who visited Sodom, it can be said that God and Lot, both, are shown as having clear abilities of perception in contrast to the wicked men of Sodom. As unwise as Lot was to pitch his tents toward Sodom (Gen 13:13) even he appears still to possess more sight than the men of Sodom who are altogether wicked.

GENERAL ANALYSIS

A number of observations can now be made about this incident of blinding. First, it was miraculously instigated as an act of defense of one who was being attacked. The attackers, then, were rendered unable to carry out their mischief. In addition, this blinding could be seen as a further disorientation of the mob. From the outset, they needed to inquire as to the exact location of Lot's visitors (Gen 19:5). The partial inability to ascertain the angels' location was compounded by the blinding of the mob so they could not even find the door.

---

4. Fretheim, "The Book of Genesis," 374.

In addition, Victor P. Hamilton insightfully notes that this blinding, though, might have involved more than a simple interruption of the sense of vision. It would seem that one of the men should still have touched the door by accident and recognized it. The mob, then, would have been not only blind, but in such a confused, chaotic state that they simply had to disburse.[5]

Finally, one must recall how Lot said to the mob in v. 8 that he permitted them to do to his daughters whatever seemed good in their eyes as long as they did not harm his guests. The mob ignored this offer, however appropriate or inappropriate it was, and in attempting to move by force against Lot, lost the use, at least temporarily, of those eyes. Gordon J. Wenham, then, rightly notes that the men of Sodom suffered from both spiritual and physical blindness.[6] This is reasonable, as the men of Sodom on the one hand did not perceive spiritually the reality of their moral decay and the presence of angels. They also lost the ability to perceive physically the location of Lot.

Hagar's Blindness, Genesis 21:19

Translation

THE TEXT

The next instance of blindness in the Hebrew Scriptures is Gen 21:19 when Hagar's eyes must be opened for her to see a well. The text is considered in translation:

וַיִּפְקַח אֱלֹהִים אֶת־עֵינֶיהָ וַתֵּרֶא בְּאֵר מָיִם וַתֵּלֶךְ וַתְּמַלֵּא אֶת־הַחֵמֶת מַיִם וַתַּשְׁקְ אֶת־הַנָּעַר׃

> 19. Then God opened her eyes and she saw a well of water. She went, and filled the skin with water, and gave the boy a drink. (NRSV)

---

5. Hamilton, *The Book of Genesis: Chapters 18–50*, 38.
6. Wenham, *Genesis 16–50*, 56.

Exegesis

CONTEXT

Immediate biblical context

The wordplay regarding the word ראה, "see," is abundant in this Hagar narrative. After Sarah sees, ראה, Hagar's son mocking Isaac (Gen 21:9), a course of events is set into motion that results in the expulsion of Hagar and Ishmael from Abraham's house. When their water runs out, Hagar removes herself from the lad as she does not desire to "see" ראה (Gen 21:16) the death of the child. God, though, hears the voice of the child (Gen 21:17) and comes to Hagar to assist her. After commanding her to arise and lift up the child (Gen 21:18), God opens Hagar's eyes, and she sees ראה a well of water (Gen 21:19). Thus, "the God who sees me," ראה, for "see" in Gen 16:13, returns in Gen 21 to give a form of sight to Hagar. Apparently, while not necessarily blind to all physical reality, she was blind to the existence of this well, needing her eyes to be opened so she could see it.

Intertextual connection

It is noteworthy that the previous time the Hebrew Scriptures refers to opening of eyes using the same words is in the fall story when, too, a woman sees, takes sustenance by mouth, and assists another in the process. The difference literarily between these two stories is that at the fall, as noted previously, the woman sees and handles sustenance only before her eyes are opened. With Hagar, the opening of her eyes precipitated the seeing and handling of sustenance. In addition, in Gen 3, the opening of eyes was the result of humans taking initiative and resulted in hardship. With Hagar the opening of eyes was initiated by God and resulted in sight, not only in an immediate physical sense, but spiritually in how she saw directly God's providence for her and the child.

Terence E. Fretheim insightfully notes how Gen 21:8–21 also is paralleled in the Aqadah (Gen 22:1–19). In both stories one of Abraham's children's lives is threatened. An act is performed involving the parents' eyes, עֵינַיִם, and, in both cases, they see, ראה, what would be the salvation of the child (Gen 21:19; 22:13).[7] While the cause of Abraham's seeing of the ram may have been different from the cause of Hagar's seeing of the well, both individuals did not see the means of their salvation until God willed them to

---

7. Fretheim, "The Book of Genesis," 489.

see such. Both stories, then, show how God, who sees all, controls the sight and the destiny of all flesh.

General analysis

This section examines why the well was previously invisible to Hagar. It must first be noted that no reason is presented in the text as to why she could not see it. One possibility is that the well was miraculously dug by God who then showed her. It is also possible that the well was present but hidden from sight before God revealed it to her. A number of controversies did surround wells dug in the region of Beer Sheba where she was (Gen 21:14). Regarding one well, Abraham even said Abimelek's servants stole it, and as a result of the oath taken by Abraham concerning his ownership of said well, the well was called Beer Sheba (Gen 21:25–31). It is possible that the well from which Hagar was sustained was this well that Abraham dug. In reality, though, all these ideas fall into the category of speculation as the text is silent concerning how the well became visible. It is certain only that Hagar was once blind to its existence and then made able to see by miraculous intervention. As soon as she saw it, she gave her son water, and he lived.

Jacob and the Blessing, Genesis 27

Translation

The text

The next occurrence of blindness in the Hebrew Scriptures is found in Gen 27. Verse 1 is translated below:

וַיְהִי כִּי־זָקֵן יִצְחָק וַתִּכְהֶיןָ עֵינָיו מֵרְאֹת וַיִּקְרָא אֶת־עֵשָׂו בְּנוֹ הַגָּדֹל וַיֹּאמֶר אֵלָיו בְּנִי וַיֹּאמֶר אֵלָיו הִנֵּנִי׃

> 1. When Isaac was old and his eyes were dim so that he could not see, he called his elder son Esau and said to him, "My son"; and he answered, "Here I am." (NRSV)

Exegesis

Context

In this story, Isaac asks Esau, the eldest son, to hunt game and cook it for him, and then Isaac would bless him. One must recall, though, that the Lord had told Rebekah that the older would serve the younger (Gen 25:23). Rebekah, then, must have felt the need to devise a plan to accomplish God's will, whether or not the plan was according to God's ways.

Next, even though no direct penalty is named for Jacob's deception in Gen 27, Gen 29 may indicate that Jacob was rewarded quite negatively for his acts. After having been forced to flee from his angry brother (Gen 27:41–44), Jacob resides with his uncle Laban. There, regarding the acquisition of a wife, Jacob experiences at Laban's hand nearly exactly the same deception that Jacob once used against his father. First, both deceptions involve the presenting of the wrong sibling. Jacob comes instead of Esau in Gen 27 and Leah comes instead of Rachel in Gen 29:23, 24. Second, birth order is at issue. Jacob steals the blessing intended for the firstborn, and Leah, as the firstborn, claims marriage first. Third, lack of sight is involved in both deceptions. Isaac is literally blind in Gen 27. Jacob is as good as blind in Gen 29:23, 24 as Leah wore a veil to hide her face, and their intimate encounter took place at night, before the morning (Gen 29:25). Finally, both deceptions produced irreversible results. Jacob maintained the blessing (Gen 27:36, 37), and he also continued to be married to Leah (Gen 29:27). If Jacob had attempted to argue that Laban's deception invalidated his marriage to Leah, he would have also rendered his blessing from Isaac invalid. Thus, a providential form of divine *lex talionis* may be at work, allowing Jacob, who had deceptively stolen the blessing, to inadvertently have sexual relations with the wrong woman.[8]

---

8. The RSV says of Leah in Gen 29:17 that her eyes were weak. This could be understood as suggesting poor vision. Nahum M. Sarna, though, suggests that the word at issue, רכות, should be translated to mean "lacking in luster." Sarna, *Genesis*, 204. The NRSV says that Leah's eyes were lovely. One must consider how the last half of this verse discusses Rachel's beauty, how she was beautiful in shape and sight, מראה, a word derived from ראה, and used to describe the appearance of someone or something (Gen 2:9). It is logical, then, to conclude that the focus in Gen 29:17 is on how one looks to someone else's eyes, not how one sees with her own eyes. Thus, either the second and third translation option is preferred since, compared with a reference to how well Leah's eyes may have functioned, a reference to the beauty, or lack thereof, in her eyes provides a better literary balance to the clear reference to Rachel's beauty. Even if Gen 29:17 is suggesting that Leah had poor vision, there is so little data about this condition in the text that no useful conclusion could be drawn concerning blindness in the Hebrew Scriptures based on this text.

One may next briefly consider Gen 37:31:32. Terence E. Fretheim insightfully notes how, as clothing was involved in Jacob's deception of his father, clothing was involved in Joseph's brothers' deception of Jacob. Thus, Jacob would reap the results of his deception for many years.[9]

General Analysis

J. Gerald Janzen rightly discusses how concepts of sight and blindness are deeply woven into the literary fabric of Gen 27, in passages other than Gen 27:1. In v. 12, for example, Jacob notes how he would be perceived in his father's "eyes" after being subjected to tactile examination. The physical eyes were not functional for literal seeing. Nonetheless, the mental "eyes" of perception and discernment via resourceful analysis by other senses and reasoning were available for those tasks. In addition, the root of the word "deceiver," which Jacob fears being seen as by his father, is תעה, which refers to going astray (Ps 119:176). Jacob, then, would be suggesting leading his blind father astray. This whole scenario is foreshadowed in v. 11 that says that Jacob was a smooth, חלק, man. Not only would this refer to his physical smoothness, but based on other uses of this word in the Hebrew Scriptures (i.e., Dan 11:34), the word can also be associated with deceptiveness.[10]

A number of assumptions are made in this story that bear relevance. First, Kerry H. Wynn rightly observes that the loss of vision was assumed in the text *not* to lessen one's authority to pronounce a blessing. Isaac was still the father, and he still held all rights and privileges thereto.[11] It can be noted that nowhere in Gen 27 is there any discussion concerning Isaac's authority and capability to bless being questioned because of his disability, even though such disability contributed to his deception by Jacob.

Next, it is assumed that the blind father would be permitted to perform tests to determine if it is actually Esau visiting him (Gen 27:11, 12). Terence E. Fretheim rightly notes that such test would not simply involve listening to a voice, but also feeling the skin to determine if such feels hairy as Esau (Gen 27:21, 22). In reality, throughout Gen 27, hearing, touch, smell, and taste are all employed as tests by Isaac, with smell being the final and definitive (Gen 27:29).[12] This is very reasonable as voices can be difficult for a blind person to recognize, even among family. Anything from the father's being slightly

---

9. Fretheim, "The Book of Genesis," 535.

10. Janzen, *Abraham and All the Families of the Earth*, 104.

11. Wynn, "The Normate Hermeneutic and Interpretations of Disability within the Yahwistic Narratives," 95.

12. Fretheim, "The Book of Genesis," 535.

hard of hearing to a son's having a cold could make it difficult to be certain whose voice is being heard. Most people in twenty-first-century society have even answered the telephone when a close relative calls but fail to recognize who is calling. Thus, as Robert Alter logically concludes, Isaac would have assumed, then, that the hairiness of Esau's skin, the unique taste of the food, and the scent of Esau's clothing would be more difficult to counterfeit and more distinct to recognize than a simple voice.[13]

It is also assumed in this story that Jacob believed such an attempt at deceit would result in a curse (Gen 27:12). Jacob, as he noted to his mother in pretending to be Esau, understood that he would risk receiving a curse rather than a blessing. What is noteworthy, though, is that it is also assumed that the curse would only be effective if Jacob was discovered to be a deceiver. If he could perform a perfect deception and actually receive a blessing, the blessing would be binding. Thus, Rebekah and Jacob reasoned that if they could do the deception well enough, punishment would be avoided.

One can determine from this, as David Cotter rightly notes, that Jacob and his mother were more interested in avoiding curses and punishments than in doing what is right. It was acceptable in their eyes to commit deceit as long as the penalty was avoided.[14]

Jacob's Blessing Joseph's Sons, Genesis 48:8–10

Translation

THE TEXT

The next blindness passage in the Torah is found in the story of Jacob's blessing Joseph's sons. A translation of Gen 48:8–10 appears below:

וַיַּרְא יִשְׂרָאֵל אֶת־בְּנֵי יוֹסֵף וַיֹּאמֶר מִי־אֵלֶּה׃
וַיֹּאמֶר יוֹסֵף אֶל־אָבִיו בָּנַי הֵם אֲשֶׁר־נָתַן־לִי אֱלֹהִים בָּזֶה וַיֹּאמַר קָחֶם־נָא אֵלַי וַאֲבָרֲכֵם׃
וְעֵינֵי יִשְׂרָאֵל כָּבְדוּ מִזֹּקֶן לֹא יוּכַל לִרְאוֹת וַיַּגֵּשׁ אֹתָם אֵלָיו וַיִּשַּׁק לָהֶם וַיְחַבֵּק לָהֶם׃

8. When Israel saw Joseph's sons, he said, "Who are these?"
9. Joseph said to his father, "They are my sons, whom God has given me here." And he said, "Bring them to me, please, that I may bless them."

---

13. Alter, *Genesis*, 137.
14. Cotter, *Genesis*, 201.

10. Now the eyes of Israel were dim with age, and he could not see well. So Joseph brought them near him; and he kissed them and embraced them. (NRSV)

Notes

The word "well" is added in the translation of v. 10 after the word "see." "Well" does not appear in the Hebrew. One may consult the previous chapter in this study, the section concerning ראה and עַיִן together, for an explanation of this and for the justification for saying that Jacob had *limited* vision when the text simply appears to say, literally, that he could not see.

Exegesis

Context

One finds significant parallels and contrasts between this blessing and that of Gen 27. In both passages a father, blinded by age, is said to bless his sons (Gen 27:1; 48:8–10). In addition, as Derek Kidner rightly notes, both passages include the father's asking who is present before him in the blessing ceremony (Gen 27:18; 48:8).[15] In addition, Gordon J. Wenham correctly observes that, as Esau unsuccessfully protests the blessing being given to one other than expected, Joseph unsuccessfully protests the blessing being given to another than expected (Gen 27:36, 37; 48:18, 19).[16]

When one considers Gen 27, though, it appears that Joseph learned from the misfortunes of his father. One can recall how Joseph had set his two sons in front of Jacob, just the way they should be placed for the blessing, Ephraim to Jacob's left, and Manasseh, the firstborn, to Jacob's right (Gen 48:13). Jacob, though, crossed his arms, so the blessing of the right hand, assumed to be greater (Gen 48:17–19), would fall on Ephraim. Joseph, however, did not allow this perceived mistake to continue. As Nahum Sarna rightly notes, where Jacob worked to deceive his blind father into blessing the wrong son, Joseph, in v. 18 moves to switch his blind father's hands, preventing what would seem like even an accidental misdirected blessing.[17] In v. 19 Jacob notes how he is aware who is the firstborn, but the greater blessing would still fall upon Ephraim.

---

15. Kidner, *Genesis*, 213.
16. Wenham, *Genesis 16–50*, 466.
17. Sarna, *Genesis*, 329.

In this story, then, it becomes clear to the reader how foolishly Jacob is said to have behaved in Gen 27. Genesis 48 teaches that if God intends for a certain individual to be blessed, he does not need anyone on earth to deceive one who cannot see. It would be reasonable, then, to assume that God could have easily devised a way for the blessing to be given to Jacob without any deception. Maybe, at the last moment, Isaac would have received special instruction from God regarding whom to bless. However the story would have been told had Jacob not practiced deception, it is likely that Jacob and Esau could have enjoyed the freedom from strife known by Joseph's sons who are never shown to fight against each other anywhere in the Torah.

General Analysis

H. C. Leupold rightly observes that words referring to matters of sight and the eye are employed strategically in Gen 48:8–20. Genesis 48:17 says that Joseph saw, רָאָה, his father crossing his hands and such was displeasing in Joseph's eyes, עֵינָיִם. These words are employed here to describe how well Joseph sees physically, but in vv. 8–10 they show how poorly his father saw.[18] E. A. Speiser, then, rightly observes that Jacob, though physically seeing less clearly than Joseph, seemed to possess inner vision regarding the way in which he should bless his sons. This inner vision even would have led him to place his hands as he did and as he wished.[19]

Next, one can consider how Jacob, though blind, appears to have uttered insights concerning the future. Jacob notes in Gen 48:19, 20 that Ephraim would become greater than his brother. Other texts in the rest of the Hebrew Scriptures show the accuracy of these prophecies, at least according to the Bible writers. By the time of the days of Isaiah, Ephraim, not Manasseh, became powerful enough to be named as a force against Judah. The names Ephraim and Israel appear to be used interchangeably regarding the invasion force of the northern kingdom (Isa 7:1, 2). Manasseh is never described as enjoying such prominence. In Jer 31:9, God calls Ephraim, not Manasseh, his firstborn, even though Manasseh, the individual, was born first. In Ezek 37:16–19, Ephraim, not Manasseh, is the son of Joseph named with reference to the stick representing the northern kingdom of Israel. Thus, it can be seen that God used Jacob, blinded by old age, to utter prophecies concerning his descendants, prophecies confirmed by biblical accounts of history and future prophecies.

---

18. Leupold, *Exposition of Genesis*, 1155.
19. Speiser, 360.

Summary

In this section it is first noted how sight is deeply involved in the creation story. Not only is God described as seeing, but humanity was created to see the trees of the garden. Such seeing could have been both physical and spiritual in nature.

The first passage to concern blindness is Gen 3:5–7. There, Eve is described by the serpent as blind. In a sense, though, Adam and Eve lost access to God, their most beautiful object of vision, after they fell, and the human race has been subjected to various types of blindness ever since.

One can, then, consider blindness in the rest of Genesis. In Gen 19:11, it is noted how the blindness that struck the men of Sodom came about to protect the innocent, who could see reality more clearly, even before the men of Sodom were blinded. Hagar's partial blindness concerning the well was resolved by God's opening her eyes, using the same language for such opening as in Gen 3:5, 7, but with God clearly listed as the agent. Finally, one may recall the stories of Jacob and Joseph and how they responded to their father's blindness. While Jacob resorted to deception to control who received the blessing, Joseph remained honest, even offering to correct his father when Jacob seemed in error.

EXODUS

This section concerns blindness as discussed in the book of Exodus. First, God's statement that he creates the blind and the seeing (Exod 4:11) is studied. Next, Exod 21:23–26 is considered, examining the penalties, according to Torah, for one's damaging another's eye. Finally, Exod 23:8 and the blinding nature of bribes is considered.

God, Creator of the Blind and the Seeing, Exodus 4:11

Translation

THE TEXT

The first text, Exod 4:11, appears translated below:

וַיֹּאמֶר יְהוָה אֵלָיו מִי שָׂם פֶּה לָאָדָם אוֹ מִי־יָשׂוּם אִלֵּם אוֹ חֵרֵשׁ אוֹ פִקֵּחַ
אוֹ עִוֵּר הֲלֹא אָנֹכִי יְהוָה:

Exod 4:11. Then the LORD said to him, "Who gives speech to mortals? Who makes them mute or deaf, seeing or blind? Is it not I, the LORD?" (NRSV).

Notes

The beginning words of God's speech literally read, "Who makes a mouth for humankind." The NRSV often translates אָדָם as "mortals," rather than "humankind," which is a more precise designation of the species since animals are also mortal and humankind was mortal only after the fall (Gen 3:22–24). Further instances where the NRSV translates אָדָם as "mortals," or "mortal," are not noted in this manner.

Exegesis

Literary Analysis

When one considers Exod 4:11–12, a simple chiasm/inclusio structure emerges. Exodus 4:11 and Exod 4:12 begin and end the inclusio by referring to the mouth and God's dealings concerning such. The center and climax of this chiasm is the list of disabilities the bearers of which are created by God. In addition, Peter Enns insightfully notes that both Moses and God use the pronoun אָנֹכִי in their speeches, Moses first, and then God in his rebuttal.[20] These literary techniques emphasize how God who made everything is able to strengthen anyone to overcome anything.

Context

This verse stands in sharp contrast to the Sumerian creation myth in which people with disabilities are said to have been created by another deity wishing to see if Enki could find placement for such individuals. In Exod 4:11, though, God says he has made all people of all ability status, and because of this, in v. 12, he can empower anyone to do his will.

---

20. Enns, *Exodus*, 111.

General Analysis

The actual message of Exodus 4:11

While one may seek to use this passage as an explanation for the origin of disabilities, it must be noted that such is not the intent here. The issue to be discussed is whether or not God can provide power for Moses, who feels inadequate, so he can successfully speak before Pharaoh. God assures Moses that since he can create all types of people, including even the mute, those more seriously speech impaired than slow-of-speech Moses, he would be able to create (enable) Moses to say what needed to be said. God, according to this passage, then, assumes power over all disabling conditions. If God calls someone, blindness, deafness, muteness, or any other disabling condition are immaterial before the Almighty. God can and will use anyone with any disability as long as such a one is willing to be used. In addition, Douglas K. Stuart rightly notes that since a number of other disabilities are named besides muteness, this speech by God can be seen as more than simply a rebuttal to Moses' statement about being slow of speech in Exod 4:10. God is offering general encouragement, expanding the message to refer to any condition or situation Moses might face.[21] It is reasonable, then, to say that the list of other disabilities could be a rhetorical device to provide emphasis to the idea that God can overcome any situation however impossible it may seem.

Theodicy and Exodus 4:11

With the message of this passage understood, one may explore what is implied regarding the issue of theodicy. One may recall how according to Gen 1 and 2, God, before the fall, created Adam and Eve to be "very good," and both able to see clearly, as noted earlier in this chapter. Now one finds a verse discussing the existence of total blindness, noted by עִוֵּר in Exod 4:11. In addition, in Gen 27 and 48, people blind, at least partially, because of age are also mentioned. One can suggest, then, that something at the fall changed the human condition to allow disabilities to exist. It is true that Gen 3:14–19 lists curses that would befall humanity. While the curses of Gen 3 do not discuss future disabilities, such conditions, which never existed before sin, could have arisen. Sometime after the fall, then, and before Moses, there began to be people with disabilities, such as total blindness.

---

21. Stuart, *Exodus*, 135.

Nonetheless, according to Exod 4:11, whatever the role is that sin played in the origin of disabilities, God is still saying that he is Creator. Thus, whether one believes that demons, bad health practices, accidents, faulty genetics, aging, or simply the existence of sin causes disabilities such as blindness, God still says he creates all such people. No one else can claim the position as Creator of life except God. The same, one Creator God makes all, both the able and the disabled.

This creates a most difficult apparent contradiction. On the one hand, God says he creates those with disabilities. On the other hand, since all such disabling conditions do occur in the Bible after Gen 3, the consequences of sin still cannot be removed as a cause. One possible way to reconcile these two concepts follows: While it may be assumed that sin may affect the genetic material (the clay of the ground) available for God to use, he still oversees and directs the creation and development of all life. God, then, is the perfect Creator, but sometimes the clay from which a human is formed may be imperfect. Everyone, whatever the disability, even Moses, could rejoice in God as his/her Creator and Provider.

In addition, if God were not the One who creates those with disabilities, the question would follow, "Who then is?" An evil being such as the devil is never shown in the Bible to have the power to create, and the negative theological and ethical implications to having a separate creator for the able and the disabled are profoundly dangerous. One could say, for example, that the disabled, made by some other Creator, are no longer brothers and sisters of the able, and so may be fit for removal from society. Instead, all people have one Creator, one God fully able to assign work and power to complete it.

One may also study Exod 4:11 in conjunction with Deborah Creamer's concept of limitness.[22] This term, which she invented, draws one to consider how every human being has limitations, whether it be near-sightedness, inability to walk as a newborn, or inability to fly without artificial technology for all human beings. The term *limitness* is preferred over "limitedness" or "limitations" as the latter terms often carry negative connotations. While Creamer is careful not to minimize the suffering disabilities may cause, and while she recognizes that the limits caused by such are more severe than those caused by a cold or near-sightedness, she notes how limits, all limits, show God's creativity in designing people to live in diversity. She notes, then, how God empathizes with all human beings in their limits and is transcendently available to reach beyond such situations.[23]

---

22. Creamer, "Including All Bodies in the Body of God," 63–65.
23. Creamer, "Including All Bodies in the Body of God," 67.

This is a helpful model to consider when studying Exod 4:11. It must be noted, though, that the fall of humanity definitely intensified human limitations, seen, for example, in how women would no more look forward to easy, pain-free child-bearing (Gen 3:16). The disabilities such as blindness, which were not discussed in Gen 3, would not necessarily need to be understood as designed by God. Nevertheless, God can still be seen to work within the present limitations of this world when creating people in diversity. In addition, as previously noted, the message of Exod 4:11 is not that the disabled are imperfect and helpless, created to be disabled and then abandoned to fend for themselves in their disabilities. Rather, God accepts responsibility as the one Creator, for the existence of all life, however limited. He is able and willing to help all human beings overcome and transcend their limitations, whatever they are, as he did for limited Moses. This way all human beings, whatever their perceived ability status, can accomplish his plans. Thus, Exod 4:11 should offer hope, not despair, to the blind.

Blinding as a Crime or Punishment, Exodus 21:23–26

Translation

THE TEXT

One must now consider Exod 21:24, 26. These verses are considered together because of their similar theme and context. They appear translated as follows:

עַיִן תַּחַת עַיִן שֵׁן תַּחַת שֵׁן יָד תַּחַת יָד רֶגֶל תַּחַת רָגֶל׃
וְכִי־יַכֶּה אִישׁ אֶת־עֵין עַבְדּוֹ אוֹ־אֶת־עֵין אֲמָתוֹ וְשִׁחֲתָהּ לַחָפְשִׁי יְשַׁלְּחֶנּוּ
תַּחַת עֵינוֹ׃

> 24. eye for eye, tooth for tooth, hand for hand, foot for foot. . . .
> 26. When a slave-owner strikes the eye of a male or female slave, destroying it, the owner shall let the slave go, a free person, to compensate for the eye. (NRSV)

NOTES

According to the literal word order at the conclusion of v. 26, the text reads, "a free person you shall release him for the eye." The same word תַּחַ appears before "eye," in v. 26 as does in "eye for eye," in v. 24.

Exegesis

CONTEXT

Ancient Near Eastern context

One may compare these laws, now, with other ancient Near Eastern law codes discussed previously in chapter 2 of this study. One can recall how the Hittite codes list only monetary fines for blinding, a greater fine if a free person is blinded than if a slave is blinded. In Mesopotamia, the laws of Eshnunna list only fines for blinding another person. The Akkadian law code that commands more than simply fines for blinding is the code of Hammurabi. One may recall Law 196 that says that one who blinds a gentleman forfeits his/her own eye. According to Law 199, though, the punishment for blinding a slave is a fine of half the value of the slave.

One may make observations based on these data. No distinction is made in Torah regarding how penalties would be administered differently depending on the social status of the person blinded. While other ancient Near Eastern codes may have placed more grievous penalties for injuring one of higher status, one in ancient Israel would receive the same penalty if he blinded a noble or a commoner. If one blinded a servant, then, only for his/her own servant in Israel (Exod 21:26), the servant must be set free, not simply learn that half his/her value has been paid, as in other ancient Near Eastern systems. Another difference between Israel's law codes and those in surrounding nations is that the Torah states no law regarding the penalty for blinding the eye of an animal while the code of Lipit-Ishtar and the Hittite codes did. In comparison, though, it must be noted that, just as in Babylon, with the Code of Hammurabi, there are no case examples of these laws being enforced in ancient Israel. In addition, Randall C. Bailey notes that nowhere in ancient Near Eastern law codes does one find a penalty given for one who blinds his/her own slave as one finds in Exod 21:26.[24]

As one can see, then, the laws of Moses may show evidence of being influenced by or, at least parallel to, other ancient Near Eastern law codes. Moses' laws, though, bear unique essence regarding equality of the victims that sets them apart as having their own special character.

---

24. Bailey, *Exodus*, 237.

Immediate biblical context

Exodus 21:24, 26 immediately follow the discussion of how punishment is to be carried out if men who are fighting smite a pregnant woman so that she goes into premature labor. The issue of whether or not punishment is carried out, eye for eye, if the child is injured is not considered here because the broader context of this passage suggests a more inclusive meaning for "eye for eye." Exodus 21:23 ends with the note "life for life," beginning the litany of *lex talionis* directives. Both Exod 21:12 and 14 say that if one slays another, the slayer shall be put to death. This can be seen as a form of "life for life," even though those words are not used. As one who takes a life would forfeit his/her life, according to Exod 21:12–14, one who takes a life would forfeit his/her life (life for/instead of life), according to Exod 21:23–25. This would suggest that the principle of *lex talionis* applies to more situations than simply when a pregnant woman is injured. In addition, Douglas K. Stuart rightly notes that the mentioning of "burn for burn" in Exod 21:25 logically extends the focus of the *lex talionis* laws beyond simply that of striking a pregnant woman in a fight so that she goes into labor.[25] Unless one considers the possibilities of two men hurling fire brands at each other or striking the woman so she falls into fire, two ideas that are less likely, these verses must be understood to state general laws of *lex talionis* that would, then, be applied to injuring a pregnant woman as an example.

GENERAL ANALYSIS

General analysis of Exodus 21:23–26

It must first be noted that among the specific injuries listed after "life for life" in Exod 21:23–25, blinding is the first in a list of injuries. In Exod 21:26, the crime of blinding one's servant is mentioned first. This shows the intensity surrounding the concept of blinding in ancient Israel.

One may also consider the concepts of the eye and the tooth as placed in parallel in Exod 21:26. C. F. Keil notes that the eye can be seen as a most important organ and the tooth as less important. Since something as great as the eye and something as small as a tooth are mentioned, every possible organ in between must also be considered.[26] While the tooth is still useful for eating, one at least has more teeth to spare if he/she loses one or two. Thus, it is reasonable to see the references to the eye and the tooth as

---

25. Stuart, *Exodus*, 492.
26. Keil and Delitzsch, *Exodus*, 135.

comprising a merism. Placing the eye as the important organ in this structure further illustrates the significant position the eye and its loss held in ancient Israelite thought.

Lex Talionis, literal or figurative

One may now examine the issue of whether or not these *lex talionis* commands in Exod 21:23–25 were intended to have been understood literally or figuratively. Two main points, though, must be understood at the outset of such an examination. First, this subject is extremely vast and complex in nature, and so a study like this is permitted only to touch on this topic briefly. In reality, whole dissertations could be written on it. It must also be noted that Exod 21:23–25 is only one of three passages in the Torah that contain such *lex talionis* language. Each passage, then, must be analyzed individually as each may have separate contexts and circumstances.

In addition, however Exod 21:23–25 is to be understood, a number of points can be agreed upon by all sides. First, R. Alan Cole rightly notes that this passage is definitely providing, at least, an *upper limit* on the intensity of retribution. One could not, as was assumed in Gen 4:23, 24, say that it was fair and proper to kill someone in revenge for an injury. The punishment must be equivalent, in some way, to the crime.[27] Finally, whether the blinding is to be understood as literal blinding or a payment of an equivalent, scholars on both sides could agree that the language of "eye for eye" would have necessarily placed, at least briefly, the thought in the reader's mind that the blinding of another human being would carry grievous penalties serious enough to cause fear equivalent to that of losing an eye. The thought of literally losing one's eye as a result of blinding another, even if one did not expect it to be carried out, would still linger in the mind of one reading those strong words.

A number of evidences exist for understanding Exod 21:23–25 literally. One strong evidence is that the surrounding verses of context are also literal. The killer was to be literally put to death, according to Exod 21:12, 14, and the freedom given to the blinded slave in Exod 21:26 is not a mystical figurative freedom but a literal freedom. As one can recall, the Hebrew word תחת even appears before the word "eye" at the end of v. 26 as it does in "eye for eye" in v. 24. It is logical to assume, then, that that which is literal in v. 26 should be literal when the same language appears in v. 24. Thus, the blinding of one who blinds could be understood as literal also based on the context.

27. Cole, *Exodus*, 169.

In addition, other forms of compensation are specifically and literally listed in Exod 21 when the author intended such to be understood. Exodus 21:19 says that one who injures another in a fight, if the injury is not permanent, must compensate the injured for his/her time. If a similar type of compensation had been intended in Exod 21:23–25, one would expect such to be stated as plainly.

David Daube also insightfully considers "eye for eye" in the context of "life for life" in Exod 21:23. "Life for life" is clearly to be understood literally as Num 35:31 commands the death penalty, and the death penalty only, for murder. Since the same pattern of "____ תַּחַת ____" is employed with reference to the eye in Exod 21:23, one must expect a literal interpretation also for "eye for eye."[28] These evidences place the burden of proof on those arguing figurative interpretation.

Finally, William H. C. Propp insightfully remarks how the Hebrew Scriptures also note specific instances when forms of *lex talionis* were employed. Judges 1:6–7 refers to a king whose thumbs and big toes were cut off in retaliation for his performing—or, at least, commanding—the same action against his enemies. In 1 Kgs 21:19 the dogs would lick up the blood of the one who caused Naboth's blood to be licked up by dogs. In Ezek 16:59, it is said that the woman would experience having done to her the things she had done. Finally, in Obad 15, 16 it is said that it would be done to Edom as Edom did to Israel. Thus, *lex talionis* is not an idea foreign to ancient Hebrew thought.[29]

A number of arguments against a literal understanding of these *lex talionis* laws must now be considered. One argument for interpreting the *lex talionis* passages to refer to financial compensation rather than literal blinding or maiming concerns the unusual case of one without eyes blinding another. The School of Hizkaiah in the Talmud noted that if one has no eyes, it would be impossible to remove any eyes. Thus, one should place fines on such offenders to avoid such inconsistencies.[30]

It could be said in response, though, that one may find the same problem arising with placing fines if the individual to be fined has no money and is disabled and so cannot be practically made to labor to pay the fine. The treatment of such a case discussed by the rabbis might be analogous to that of one where an individual commits more than one capital crime or who commits a capital crime but dies accidentally by a means other than

---

28. Daube, *Studies in Biblical Law*, 107.

29. Propp, *Exodus 19–40*, 230.

30. *Babylonian Talmud Baba Qama*, 84A, quoted in Milgrom, "*Lex Talionis* and the Rabbis," 16.

what the state would demand. Such a capital crime may be leading others astray into idolatry, where the penalty is stoning (Deut 13:7–11 [English, 6–10]), or murder as described in Num 35:31 where no ransom may be allowed instead. Since an offender cannot die more than once, the practical manifestation of the penalty would be seen as different from the legislated one. Nonetheless, the law still must stand with that unusual case seen as an obvious exception where the judges would be required to devise an alternative penalty, if possible. The fact that such an exception might exist does not rule out the possibility that the law, in most situations, would still apply, as one can always devise exceptional situations where any law would need to be reinterpreted.

The same rabbinic school also notes how other physical maladies besides those legislated may afflict one who is blinded. Since the law says only "eye for eye," and does not say "eye and life for eye," one must administer a different penalty besides literal blinding so as not to cause the offender to be punished also with death if death results from the blinding.[31]

In response it may first be noted that other laws that more clearly command physical mutilation do not consider unforeseen consequences. It is possible for a woman to suffer and possibly die from great blood loss if her hand would be cut off as Deut 25:12 legislates, but that law does not take such a possibility into consideration. In addition, since a possible consequence of the offender's blinding an innocent victim is also death to the victim, it could be said that subjecting the offender to the same risk of death is talionic justice.

Another argument set forth by those who interpret Exod 21:23–25 figuratively concerns Num 35:31. Here it is said that no ransom shall be accepted for a murderer. He must be put to death. According to Baruch A. Levine, this suggests that there were crimes where monetary compensation could be accepted as the penalty. One could, then, suggest that monetary compensation would have been accepted for inflicting bodily harm, but only the death penalty would be allowed as a punishment for murder.[32]

Jeffrey H. Tigay, though, logically notes that, as shown above, crimes did exist where financial compensation was allowed as the penalty, and so it could be those crimes to which Num 35:31 applies. It may also simply be that, at times, a judge could allow the payment of a fine according to the value of the eye rather than literal blinding.[33] It might be that if, as in a

---

31. *Babylonian Talmud Baba Qama*, 84A, quoted in Milgrom, "*Lex Talionis* and the Rabbis," 16.

32. Levine, *Leviticus*, 268. See also *Babylonian Talmud Baba Qama*, 83B, quoted in Milgrom, "*Lex Talionis* and the Rabbis," 16.

33. Tigay, *Deuteronomy*, 185.

theoretical case previously discussed, one already blinded destroys the eye of another, clearly, some other penalty would need to be devised for the already blinded criminal. Since one already dead cannot commit murder, this situation would not arise in a case where Num 35:31 would be applied. A similar situation might involve one who blinds both eyes of more than one person. One may only literally surrender over two eyes.

It is also argued by Gordon J. Wenham that this law is not to refer to literal blinding because of the exception in Exod 21:26. Since the freeing of a slave would not be literal blinding of the master, the penalty for any other type of blinding could also be other than literal.[34]

One could first say in response that the reason Exod 21:26 is in the text is that it is an exception. If usually *lex talionis* was to be enforced literally, any exception would need to be noted. Exodus 21:20–21 says that one who strikes his servant so that the servant dies must be punished. This verse, though, does not say that the one who struck the servant should be put to death, as "life for life." Numbers 35:31, as noted above, though, says that "life for life" is still to be taken literally. Thus, if the case of the slaying of one's servant allows an exception to that which is indisputably literal "life for life," even by those noted above who understand "eye for eye" as figurative, then, the case of the destroying of the eye of one's servant would be an exception to "eye for eye" (Exod 21:23–25), and not a precedent for how *lex talionis* should be enforced in all situations. One may recall that according to the Code of Hammurabi, Laws 196 and 199, the blinding of a slave was also met with a different penalty than the blinding of one in the upper class.

One must also consider the arguments set forth by J. K. Mikliszanski. He argues that since the injury in Exod 21:22–25 is accidental, men fighting among themselves who happen to strike a pregnant woman, literal death could not be a just penalty according to the Torah.[35] His arguments, most likely, would be based on the precedent set by the cities of refuge (Num 35:11).

The actual case, though, in Exod 21:22–25 concerns negligence, and not simply accidental killing. Two men who are fighting could, and should, exercise enough restraint to keep themselves away from a pregnant woman, or, simply, exercise enough restraint not to fight. Thus, the injury could be preventable. The Torah does allow death in cases of extreme negligence. Exodus 21:29, a few verses later, says that if a bull has a nature of goring people and nothing is done to remedy the situation, both the bull and the owner are to be put to death. Thus, while the owner of the bull might not

---

34. Wenham, *The Book of Leviticus*, 312.
35. Mikliszanski, "The Law of Retaliation and the Pentateuch," 296.

necessarily conspire to raise an animal that would commit murder, the negligence of the owner is still cause for the death penalty.

Mikliszanski also notes how contrary to Hammurabi, as in Law 196, Exod 21:23–25 does not say, in so many words, that one should be blinded. In Hammurabi Law 196, it says that one who destroys another's eye would lose his eye, not that simply "eye for eye" should be enforced.[36] One may respond to this argument by first recalling the discussion of the comments by Daube previously analyzed in this study concerning "life for life" in Exod 21:23. As noted, explicit contextual evidence from Num 35:31 and elsewhere in Exod 21 exists to demonstrate that "life for life" refers to literal killing of the murderer and not the demand of payment equal to the value of a life. Thus, "eye for eye" must refer to literal eye-destroying of the eye of an eye-destroyer, even if such is not as explicitly discussed elsewhere. One would simply apply the principle clearly set forth concerning one who takes another's life.

Mikliszanski also notes how not all acts of violence would be punished with literal talion. According to Exod 21:18, one who injures another who subsequently recovers after a day or two must simply compensate the injured for the loss of his/her time. Mikliszanski acknowledges that it can be argued that the reason literal talion is not enforced here is that the injury is not permanent. He responds by noting how some of the talion laws such as "burn for burn," or "stripe for stripe," in Exod 21:23–25 also concern possible temporary conditions. Thus, if justice is served by paying a fine in the situation of Exod 21:18, justice might also be served by paying a fine after committing a crime listed in Exod 21:23–25.[37]

One might respond to this argument by noting that financial compensation is also discussed in Exod 21:22–25. It is said that if no mischief or harm follows the premature birth, a fine is to be paid according to what the woman's husband demands. If harm follows, then "eye for eye" is to be enforced. David Daube rightly notes that if harm follows, the penalty must be greater than any fine a husband could impose when harm does not follow. Such a penalty would involve literal "eye for eye" justice.[38] This argument is reasonable since the same text that clearly commanded that the offender pay a fine when no harm followed could have clearly stated that a specific fine according to the assumed value of an eye or a tooth should be commanded when harm followed. Instead, if harm follows, the text says simply, "eye for eye."

36. Mikliszanski, "The Law of Retaliation and the Pentateuch," 297.
37. Mikliszanski, "The Law of Retaliation and the Pentateuch," 298.
38. Daube, *Studies in Biblical Law*, 108.

One might also say that a woman's prematurely giving birth with no harm following might be analogous to a man's recovering two days after an assault, in Exod 21:18. In both cases, pain and inconvenience result and are to be compensated. When harm follows, such a case might be more analogous to that of murder as also previously discussed in Exod 21, when talion must be enforced strictly. Thus, literal talion would still be enforceable in cases where great injury, not necessarily permanent, is inflicted.

Another explanation of Exod 21:23–25 is discussed by Raymond Westbrook. He notes how the only other place אָסוֹן (mischief/harm) appears in the Hebrew Bible is in the Joseph story, Gen 42:4, 38; 44:29. In the case of the Joseph story, such harm is not stated as coming from a known assailant; it simply happens. Thus, Westbrook says that the harm caused to the pregnant woman in Exod 21:22–25 is caused by an unknown assailant. The men are fighting, but it is unknown as to which of them struck the woman.[39] Westbrook then summarizes a number of ancient Near Eastern laws in which the community pays compensation when a crime is committed but the precise assailant is unknown. The paying of "a life," in these ancient Near Eastern sources, is the payment of the monetary value of a life.[40] Westbrook applies this concept to Exod 21:23–25, suggesting that such harm caused by an unknown assailant would be answered by the state by having the community pay the monetary value for the eye, tooth, or life. He even notes Deut 21:1–9, which discusses a case where one is found slain by an unknown assailant, and the community must perform a ritual to remove the blood-guilt.[41] Westbrook, though, notes that in the *lex talionis* case in Lev 24, talion would be enforced literally even though the language of "eye for eye" is identical. Westbrook resolves this inconsistency by noting the concept that these two passages have separate authors for each, and each author seeks to use a different interpretation of "eye for eye."[42]

This theory contains a number of weaknesses that at least remove it from serious consideration in this study. First, while as far as Jacob was concerned, Joseph was presumed slain by an unknown assailant, a wild beast (Gen 37:33), it is unclear whether or not Jacob, when speaking of Benjamin, assumes that he might also be slain by an unknown assailant. In Gen 42:4, 38; 44:29, Jacob simply worries that mischief/harm might befall Benjamin. Such could have involved an unknown assailant, or it could also have involved a known assailant whom the brothers were powerless to resist. Since

---

39. Westbrook, "*Lex Talionis* and Ex 21:22–25," 56.
40. Westbrook, "*Lex Talionis* and Ex 21:22–25," 63.
41. Westbrook, "*Lex Talionis* and Ex 21:22–25," 64.
42. Westbrook, "*Lex Talionis* and Ex 21:22–25," 68.

the matter of how known the assailant might have been is unclear in Gen 42–44, these verses may not be used as justification for the idea that an unknown assailant is necessarily in mind in Exod 21. Next, in the three verses in Gen 42–44, אָסוֹן is accompanied by either the verb קרא, as in Gen 42:4, 38, or קרה, as in Gen 44:29. These are two similar forms whose appearance may set up a possible idiomatic structure for expressing the idea of harm without a known assailant. The verb accompanying אָסוֹן in Exod 21:23–25 is היה, a form not at all similar to those in Gen 42–44. This means that even if it were certain that an unknown assailant was in mind in Jacob's comments in Gen 42–44, with a different idiomatic expression used in Exod 21, the meaning could be different.

Westbrook also discusses how other nations addressed situations in which a crime was committed by an unknown assailant. In reality, if the assailant were unknown in the case discussed in Exod 21:23–25, the crime would necessarily need to be answered differently by the community. Possibly, the payment of a fine by the community could be a reasonable option. As noted above, though, it is unclear that Exod 21:23–25 refers to an unknown assailant. In addition, the fact that other nations followed a certain tradition does not mean that Israel necessarily did, too. These other nations also did not practice monotheism while Exod 20:3 insists that Israel was to do so.

Westbrook's reference to Deut 21:1–9 also contains a number of weaknesses. First, no monetary payment is expected of the community who performs the ritual in Deut 21:1–9. The people simply kill a heifer and wash their hands over it, declaring their innocence. No restitution of any other type is commanded.

In addition, while the man was slain by a completely unknown assailant in Deut 21:1–9, the assailant in Exod 21:23–25 may be partially known. Even if it is unknown exactly which of the men fighting directly struck the pregnant woman, one could, at least, reduce the circle of blame to those people who were fighting. In reality, then, a case such as that could be treated as one in which there were multiple assailants, all acting irresponsibly, not completely unknown assailants. Even if one of the men fighting did not directly strike the woman, he may have pushed the other man in such a way so as to cause him to strike the woman. One may recall the above remarks concerning negligence with reference to the owner of a violent bull to see how all the men fighting, then, could have been considered responsible for gross negligence that led to the injury. When multiple assailants were involved in the rebellion of Korah, Dathan, and Abiram, all were punished corporally together by the Lord in Num 16:30–31. All those fighting, then, could have been subject to talionic punishment if harm followed in Exod 21:23–25.

Finally, one must consider the comment that the inconsistency between Exod 21 and Lev 24 is resolved by saying a different person wrote each passage. First, the concept that a complex idiomatic expression "eye for eye, tooth for tooth" could have two separate meanings in two separate places, while possible, needs defense with clear examples elsewhere in the Hebrew Scriptures, and such defense is not presented in Westbrook's article. Next, one could say that any apparent inconsistency between two texts, even two texts near each other, is due to the possibility of a different author writing each passage and easily remove himself/herself from having to resolve such a conflict. The challenge is to find a literarily consistent and logical way to interpret seemingly contradictory passages that maintains unity of the text as a whole, however many people one believes were involved in writing and editing it. In addition, those believing that one main individual wrote the Torah would find Westbrook's stance difficult to adopt, as it would first need to be proven that different authors wrote each passage before one could make Westbrook's assumption. Thus, as with the previous arguments against a literal interpretation of "eye for eye" in Exod 21:23–25, Westbrook's theory cannot be employed in this study as a satisfactorily convincing explanation.

A literal understanding of this law would have significant implications. It is true that the victim would not expect anything in compensation. Nonetheless, Cornelis Houtman rightly notes that one, however rich or poor, who might consider injuring another would expect the same injury in return. One could not expect simply to be able to buy his/her way out of such a punishment. Both rich and poor could not replace an eye, and the fear of being blinded would be just as terrifying, however wealthy one is.[43]

Another implication of this interpretation pertains to the positioning of the Torah's talion laws in the context of similar laws in surrounding cultures. A. S. Diamond notes how Akkadian and Sumerian law codes moved from less to more corporal punishments as time progressed. He notes how the Laws of Eshnuna and Lipit-Ishtar prescribe monetary penalties for certain crimes where Hammurabi, nearly two centuries later, prescribes mutilation as a penalty for the same. Both Hammurabi and Lipit-Ishtar were written for Akkadian and Sumerian audiences, based on the languages used. The Middle Assyrian Laws, three centuries after Hammurabi, also prescribe corporal punishments. Diamond concludes, then, that civilization moved from fewer to more corporal penalties as history advanced, thus, showing that prescribing literal talion may actually be a sign of a more developed society.[44]

---

43. Houtman, *Exodus*, 167.
44. Diamond, "An Eye for an Eye (Part 2)," 151–53.

The reason that specific examples from these laws as given by Diamond are not presented here is that more recent translations of these ancient law codes contain more examples of specific stipulations concerning the injury to an eye. Diamond's quoted sources discuss only breaks and other similar assaults. The new data actually strengthen his case. One may recall, for example, in the chapter on blindness in ancient Near Eastern cultures, how it was noted that Hammurabi prescribed the mutilation of an eye as a penalty for one's mutilating the eye of an Awilum. Lipit-Ishtar and Eshnuna only prescribe financial penalties for such crimes. Thus, Diamond's theory holds true for the case specifically discussed in Exod 21. Exodus 21:23–25, then, in its literal "eye for eye" language, may actually be echoing a more socially developed way of thinking in the context of ancient Near Eastern cultures. It may be anachronistic, then, to impose twenty-first-century displeasures concerning physical mutilation on people of ancient cultures who lived in different times and different situations.

Blinding a slave

The exception to this precise *lex talionis* principle in Exod 21 is found in Exod 21:26. Here it is said that if one injures the eye of his/her servant, male or female, that person shall be set free in compensation. Shalom Paul rightly emphasizes that male and female slaves were regarded equally in this respect. Either gender would gain freedom as a result of his/her eye being destroyed by the master.[45] Whatever the reason for the slavery, however great the debt, if such was owed, the servant must be set free if so injured. Walter C. Kaiser rightly observes that this would necessarily reinforce the notion that even a slave is to be treated as a human being, not just as a piece of property that could be destroyed or thrown away at whim.[46] The cycle of physical abuse would then be permanently broken by the slave's no longer being required to be in the presence of such a brutal master who would inflict permanent injury.

---

45. Paul, *Studies in the Book of the Covenant*, 78.
46. Walter C. Kaiser, "Exodus," 434.

The Blinding Effect of a Bribe, Exodus 23:8

Translation

The text

The final passage in Exodus to be considered here is Exod 23:8. It is translated below:

וְשֹׁ֖חַד לֹ֣א תִקָּ֑ח כִּ֤י הַשֹּׁ֙חַד֙ יְעַוֵּ֣ר פִּקְחִ֔ים וִֽיסַלֵּ֖ף דִּבְרֵ֥י צַדִּיקִֽים׃

> 8 You shall take no bribe, for a bribe blinds the officials, and subverts the cause of those who are in the right. (NRSV)

Notes

The literal word order of this verse begins, "And a bribe, you shall not take," showing emphasis on the idea of the bribe. Literally, the verse also says that such a bribe "blinds the open" (presumably, those with open eyes), not necessarily "the officials." The meaning of "open" is examined below in greater detail.

Exegesis

Context

Ancient Near Eastern context

One may briefly consider the Mesopotamian "The Dialogue between a Supervisor and a Scribe," noted in chapter 2 of this study. There, the metaphor of opened eyes refers to a form of intellectual maturity and awareness of reality. As unopened eyes in the dialogue refer to immaturity, blindness, a similar concept, refers to hindered judgment capacity in Exod 23:8. While not enough common words exist to say that Exod 23:8 and this text parallel each other, it is noteworthy that the idea of open eyes is understood to refer to intellectual powers elsewhere in the ancient Near East.

Immediate biblical context

The immediate context of this passage involves issues relating to justice and judgment. Verse 6 says not to interfere with the judgment of the poor. Verse 7 says to avoid words of falsehood and to not slay the innocent and the righteous.

Intertextual connection

Another meaning arises when one compares Exod 23:8 with Exod 4:11. These are the only two verses in the Hebrew Scriptures that use the word פִּקֵחַ, literally "open," understood to mean, "with open eyes." While Exod 4:11 mentions the noun form for "blind," the related verb form is employed in Exod 23:8. Both passages also make reference to speech. Exodus 23:8 refers to the corrupting of the words, דְּבָרִים, of the righteous, and in Exod 4:10 Moses says he is slow of speech, literally, דְּבָרִים, "words." In Exod 4:12, God says he would teach Moses what to say, דבר, the verbal form of "words."

These parallels may suggest that the blinding of the eyes due to receiving a bribe is a direct interfering with the power of God. Moses was instructed in Exod 4:11, 12 not to interfere with the power of God that makes the blind, the seeing, the dumb, and the deaf, and so would also make him able to speak. A bribe interferes with the power of God to create those who can have clear, open-eyed judgment. The blinding of this judgment, and the corrupting of right speech, then, reverses the creative power of God. Those created to see would suddenly be blinded, and those with right words would have such gift polluted. This intensifies the command not to take bribes.

The broader context of the rest of the Hebrew Scriptures shows the seriousness and magnitude of the problem of receiving bribes in ancient Israel, as illustrated by the following texts: Deut 16:19; 27:25; Isa 1:23; 5:23; 33:15; Mic 3:11; Ps 15:5; and Prov 17:23; most notably, 1 Sam 8:3, 12:3. In 1 Sam 8:3, it says that Samuel's children received bribes and perverted justice. In 1 Sam 12:3, Samuel says that he did not hide his eyes by receiving bribes. While the KJV says "blind" here, the Hebrew texts suggests hiding rather than blinding. Nonetheless, this Exodus command can still be seen as alluded to in 1 Sam 12 with the similar words and meaning.

General analysis

This text describes a bribe as a probable way that the poor might be oppressed, falsehood might be heeded, and the righteous might be slain. If one receives a bribe, he/she is more likely to be biased in favor of the side on which the giver of the bribe stands. Such a judge would also feel obligated to side with the giver to fulfill the evil pact made with such a one. Thus, Douglas K. Stuart rightly notes that the discerning ability of a potentially righteous judge would be weakened, in effect, blinded, by a bribe.[47]

---

47. Stuart, *Exodus*, 528.

A bribe might even literally blind a judge, in a way. The eye may not be as inclined to notice important evidence keenly if the mind is distracted by the thought of a gift and does not wish to find evidence that would change the verdict. One who repeatedly receives bribes would become less and less able to observe rightly and discern over time as those powers would go unused.

In addition, John I. Durham rightly observes that this command is not specifically addressed to judges. Thus, one may assume that while judges may have been in the mind of the writer, anyone who may need to practice discernment could be understood as the audience.[48] A master, for example, might need to settle a dispute between two slaves, or a father, a dispute between two children. In these and other cases, a bribe would interfere with the process of judgment as it would in a court of law.

Summary

In Exod 4:11 God describes himself as the Creator of all, disabled and non-disabled. This does not mean that God schemes regarding how much disability to force one to endure, but, instead, that God, the Creator, works within the limits of present reality when forming life. The actual message of Exod 4:11, though, is that God takes responsibility for being the Creator of all, and so, no matter how disabled one is, God can, and will, use that individual in his service.

In Exod 21:24-26, one finds penalties listed for injuring another's eye. One who blinds his/her own slave, male or female, would be required to set the individual free. One who injures any other person's eye would expect the same done to him/her by the judicial system.

Finally, a bribe is described as blinding one making judgments. Those who receive bribes would find their powers of judgment, their mental sight, weakened. Their own powers of physical observation might even be blinded, as such individuals would be less likely to notice certain types of unwanted evidence.

LEVITICUS

Four passages are considered in depth in this section on Leviticus. First, Lev 19:14 is studied with reference to how the Israelites were commanded not to place stumbling blocks before the blind. Then, the restrictions placed upon a blind priest in Lev 21:16-24 is considered. Next, the laws concerning

---

48. Durham, *Exodus*, 331.

offering blind sacrifices in Lev 22:17–25 are analyzed. Finally, the *lex talionis* passage in Lev 24:19–20 is studied.

A Stumbling Block before the Blind, Leviticus 19:14

Translation

The text

The first blindness passage in Leviticus is in Lev 19:14. It appears below:

לֹא־תְקַלֵּל חֵרֵשׁ וְלִפְנֵי עִוֵּר לֹא תִתֵּן מִכְשֹׁל וְיָרֵאתָ מֵּאֱלֹהֶיךָ אֲנִי יְהוָה׃

> 14. You shall not revile the deaf or put a stumbling block before the blind; you shall fear your God: I am the LORD. (NRSV)

Notes

The second clause of this verse uses different word order in the Hebrew than appears above. Literally it reads, "And before the blind, you shall not set a stumbling block."

Exegesis

Literary analysis

Erhard S. Gerstenberger insightfully notes how Lev 19:14 begins with two brief, but thematically related, commands with chiastic syntactical structure. The verb "curse" begins the first command, while the verb "place" comes near the end of the second command. The first command ends and the second command begins with the object.[49] This structure sets the opening portion of this verse apart as a unit.

In addition, John E. Hartley rightly notes that when one considers the remainder of this verse, one may also understand this verse to be structured with two specific commands followed by a general directive to fear God. This means that fearing God was seen as a continuation of the command. Charitable acts such as showing kindness to the blind, then, were part of proper reverence to God.[50]

---

49. Gerstenberger, *Leviticus*, 268.
50. Hartley, *Leviticus*, 315.

Context

Ancient Near Eastern context

One may now re-consider the Egyptian Wisdom of Amenemopet, mentioned in chapter 2 of this study. It can be recalled that this passage says that one must not laugh at a blind man or tease a dwarf. While Amenemopet discusses the divine cause for hardships and thus argues that one should not mistreat one the gods have weakened, this passage is simply wisdom advice from an elder. The need to follow the command as a direct aspect of showing reverence does not appear in the Egyptian text. In addition, cursing, in the Bible, can be seen as much more serious than simply ridiculing in the similar Egyptian text. One may recall Egyptian curse texts regarding blindness discussed in a previous chapter of this study and compare them with biblical curses such as Gen 8:21 and Gen 9:25-27. In both cases, a curse is believed to result in negative consequences against the one cursed. Ridiculing simply involves insulting and using cruel speech.

Immediate biblical context

Lev 19:13 says that one should not withhold the wages of a hired worker. Such would necessarily increase the vulnerability of one who must depend on another for support. Thus, proper instruction is given regarding how to treat those who are economically vulnerable, and then instruction is given regarding how to treat those who are physically vulnerable. Then, Lev 19:2 proclaims the theme of all these verses, saying that one should be holy as God is holy. Apparently, charity to the disadvantaged is an important aspect of holiness.

Intertextual connection

One must also consider the broader context of these verses. After the command to be holy as God is holy (Lev 19:2), one finds commands regarding a number of issues in the Decalogue. These issues include respecting father and mother (Lev 19:3; Exod 20:12), keeping the Sabbath (Lev 19:3; Exod 20:8-11), abstaining from idol worship (Lev 19:4; Exod 20:3-6), not stealing (Lev 19:11; Exod 20:15), and not speaking falsely (Lev 19:11; Exod 20:16). Among these parallels, the words for "father, mother, Sabbath, steal," and "deal falsely," are the same in both passages.

Apparently, then, honorably treating the disabled was to be understood as an element of holiness, no less important than how one should regard the Sabbath, or even, how one should offer a peace offering (Lev 19:5–8). Proper respect for the disabled was to be regarded as a sacred duty, like keeping the Decalogue, if not included, at least, in principle within the Decalogue. In the Wisdom of Amenemopet, nothing is said about kindness toward the disabled being part of holiness or on a level of importance akin to that of offering proper sacrifices.

In addition, the creation story also mentions "father" and "mother" (Gen 2:24), and the Sabbath and holiness are also discussed (Gen 2:1–3). This suggests a creation background to this command. Proper treatment of the disabled is necessary because such are also created by God. Mistreating the disabled, then, becomes as an attack on the Creator. Those created by God should act in a godly manner toward all others created by the same God.

One may finally consider the use of the command "fear your God" as it appears in the book of Leviticus. In Lev 19:32, this command follows a directive regarding showing respect to the aged, who would be weaker. In Lev 25:17, 36, and 43, this command appears in the context of how one should treat the economically disadvantaged. This command does not appear anywhere else in the book of Leviticus. Thus, whenever Leviticus discusses proper treatment of the disadvantaged, disabled or non-disabled, such commands are presented in the context of fearing God.

In addition, Jacob Milgrom rightly observes that the ו before "fear your God" in Lev 19:14 may be understood adverbially, introducing the answer to the question of why and how one should properly treat this group of disadvantaged people. As a result, one must see the command to fear God as not simply a miscellaneous additional law but a reminder that the blind and the deaf, just as other groups of disadvantaged people, should be treated fairly as an aspect of fearing the Lord. The Lord watches over all disadvantaged people, and desires that they all be treated fairly.[51]

General analysis

This is a relevant command as the deaf would not be able to hear a curse to defend themselves, and the blind would not see the object that might make them stumble. Felix Just incorrectly concludes from this verse that in order for the blind to trip over a stumbling block, they must have often walked away from their homes and without assistance in ancient Israel.[52] In reality,

---

51. Milgrom, *Leviticus 17–22*, 1641. See also, Gane, *Leviticus, Numbers*, 336.
52. Just, "From Tobit to Bartimaeus, From Qumran to Siloam," 84.

a family member of a blind person could leave an object out of place in the home and so cause the blind individual to trip over such a stumbling block. In addition, it is possible for a blind person to trip even if being guided by another if the stumbling block is unavoidable and/or comes as a complete surprise to the blind individual.[53]

Immediately after this command comes the reminder to fear God, placing this command in the context of reverence. It is noteworthy that this verse ends with God's saying, "I am the LORD." The sacred name, יהוה, is then stamped upon this command, as it is upon the command to abstain from idol worship (v. 4) and to fear one's parents and keep the Sabbath (v. 3). This, therefore, shows the significance and intensity of the command to treat the disabled properly.

In addition, John W. Kleinig rightly states that the One who places his name on this command defends the blind and those with other disabilities. He will see when one unseen by humans and the blind seeks to place a stumbling block. God will then judge accordingly.[54] In contrast, the Egyptian literature discussed here does not directly invoke the name of a deity for authority for the command. Leviticus 19:14, then, reaches beyond the reasoning in the Wisdom of Amenemopet to lift kindness for the blind and deaf to the level of holiness and worship.

The blind and the deaf in Lev 19:14 may be representative of all those with disabilities as a whole. While these other disabilities are not directly mentioned, a consideration of the context sheds light in a unique manner. Leviticus 19:9-10 refers to how one should leave remnants in the field after the harvest for the poor to glean. In Deut 24:19-22, though, not merely the field is mentioned but also the vineyard. If Lev 19:9-10 can be applied to other similar situations of harvesting, Lev 19:14 may also be applied to refer to other situations of disability. One, then, would also be forbidden to abandon a paraplegic so he/she could not maneuver out of a situation.

The word מִכְשׁוֹל can be used both literally and figuratively in the Hebrew Bible. Clearly, a literal interpretation is most obviously visible in Lev 19:14. Nonetheless, Jacob Milgrom insightfully draws attention to Ezek 7:19 that refers to silver and gold being the stumbling block of iniquity and how Ps 119:165 says those who love God's Torah will not find a stumbling block. These latter uses are most likely symbolic. If one keeps these more symbolic meanings of "stumbling block" in mind when reading Lev 19:14, the verse

---

53. The blind author of this dissertation has experienced both of these here-described situations in real life.

54. Kleinig, *Leviticus*, 396.

could be applied to concern any form of harmful or deceptive practice designed to harm the blind or deaf.[55]

One issue that is often overlooked in a study of this passage concerns the matter of intent. It is fairly simple for one to say that it is wrong to take advantage of another's disability intentionally, as Jacob did in Gen 27. It is much more complex, though, to consider whether or not this passage condemns the unintentional placing of stumbling blocks before the blind. One might, for example, not directly set a stone in front of a blind man, but that same person could unknowingly have a pit dug into which the blind man could accidentally fall. One may note that Joseph, in Gen 48:17–19, was not content to let the wrong son be blessed accidentally until he knew that Jacob understood which son was which. In addition, Lev 4:2 begins a discussion regarding offerings given for sins committed in ignorance that are later discovered. Clearly, those sins would not be committed with intent to commit them. Then, Deut 22:8 says that one should build a rim around the roof of his house so not to bring upon himself blood-guilt should one accidentally fall off the roof. The builder of a house, most likely, would not plan for a roof not properly constructed to be a "death trap." Nonetheless, the failure to build the rim around the roof could still bring blood-guilt consequences. Thus, within reason, Lev 19:14 should be interpreted to include a prohibition against accidentally cursing the deaf or tripping the blind. Ethicists, then, would wish to ponder whether or not this command applies to cities that do actions such as leaving man-hole covers open with no cordoning off around them.

The Blind Priest, Leviticus 21:16–24

Translation

The Text

One must next consider Lev 21:16–24. Here a number of disabilities are stated that could limit a priest's functioning in the sanctuary. Verses 17–20 appear translated below. When considering this translation it should be noted that the majority of the difficult words refer to disabilities that are beyond the scope of this dissertation, and, thus, no attempt is made to seek their precise meanings.

---

55. Milgrom, *Leviticus 17–22*, 1641.

דַּבֵּר אֶל־אַהֲרֹן לֵאמֹר אִישׁ מִזַּרְעֲךָ לְדֹרֹתָם אֲשֶׁר יִהְיֶה בוֹ מוּם לֹא יִקְרַב
דַּבֵּר אֶל־אַהֲרֹן לֵאמֹר אִישׁ מִזַּרְעֲךָ לְדֹרֹתָם אֲשֶׁר יִהְיֶה בוֹ מוּם לֹא יִקְרַב
לְהַקְרִיב לֶחֶם אֱלֹהָיו:
כִּי כָל־אִישׁ אֲשֶׁר־בּוֹ מוּם לֹא יִקְרָב אִישׁ עִוֵּר אוֹ פִסֵּחַ אוֹ חָרֻם אוֹ שָׂרוּעַ:
אוֹ אִישׁ אֲשֶׁר־יִהְיֶה בוֹ שֶׁבֶר רָגֶל אוֹ שֶׁבֶר יָד:
אוֹ־גִבֵּן אוֹ־דַק אוֹ תְּבַלֻּל בְּעֵינוֹ אוֹ גָרָב אוֹ יַלֶּפֶת אוֹ מְרוֹחַ אָשֶׁךְ:

Lev 21:17. Speak to Aaron and say: No one of your offspring throughout their generations who has a blemish may approach to offer the food of his God.
18. For no one who has a blemish shall draw near, one who is blind or lame, or one who has a mutilated face or a limb too long,
19. or one who has a broken foot or a broken hand,
20. or a hunchback, or a dwarf, or a man with a blemish in his eyes or an itching disease or scabs or crushed testicles. (NRSV)

Notes

The above translation must be compared with that of Jacob Milgrom:

> 17. Speak to Aaron and say, "A man of your offspring in any generation who has a blemish shall not be qualified to offer the food of his God.
> 18. No one at all who has a blemish shall be qualified: a man who is blind, lame, disfigured, or deformed.
> 19. A man who has a broken leg or broken arm,
> 20. Or who is a hunchback, or a dwarf, or has a discoloration of the eye, a scar, a lichen, or a crushed testicle."[56]

The difference between these two translations that is most relevant to a study of blindness is that found in the general remarks in v. 17. While the NRSV says that one with these conditions may not approach to offer the food of his God, Milgrom above says that such a one is not qualified to offer. The following word study on קרב explains the reasoning behind this translation.

---

56. Milgrom, *Leviticus 17–22*, 1792.

Word study on קרב

Semitic cognates

To understand this passage most clearly, a word study on קרב, shown in the qal and hiph'il stems in Lev 21:16–24, must be conducted. This word has a number of cognates in ancient Near Eastern languages, all of which carry the meaning of coming near. In Akkadian, *qere-bu* can refer to approaching as an aspect of sexual intercourse among its wide range of meanings. The D-stem refers to offering a sacrifice or serving a meal to the gods. The noun, *taqribtu*, refers to an offering in a religious sense. *Qere-bu* can also be used in a prohibitive context as when one may be told to not approach certain fields or houses and violate property rights. In Old Assyrian, *Awa-tam qarabun* would mean "bring a word near." In Old South Arabic, the cognate form, a non-cultic term, refers to sexual intercourse. The form, *qrbn*, though, refers to an offering, a religious sacrifice. The Ugaritic causative form refers to an offering or sacrifice. In Elephantine Aramaic, the non-cultic term קרב refers to asserting a claim legally. The pa'el of the Syriac, *qerēb*, though, means to offer a sacrifice, utter request, or give advice.[57]

Biblical usage

In Hebrew, קרב means "he drew near" in the qal stem and "bring near" in the pi'el and hiph'il. For the sake of this study, the uses most related to a religious context are considered. First, significant qal uses are concerned. Joshua 3:4 uses this word to refer to the limitations placed on the people's physical nearness to God. Exodus 3:5 expresses a similar idea with reference to Moses' approaching God. In Lev 9:5 lay people approach God in the sanctuary. The term refers to offering sacrifices in the court in Lev 1:3. In Lev 10:4, 5, the term refers to simply approaching to remove the corpses of the slain sons of Aaron.[58]

This word may also refer to having cultic access. According to Num 18:3, only the priests were permitted to approach to minister. The ordinary Levites would not have such access. The meaning carries the sense of being ritually qualified in Exod 12:48 that says that an alien must be circumcised to approach to celebrate Passover. Leviticus 21:17–18 says that a priest with a blemish may not approach to offer.[59]

---

57. Gane and Milgrom, "קרב," 136.
58. Gane and Milgrom, "קרב," 137–38.
59. Gane and Milgrom, "קרב," 140.

The common term for bringing something to God is the hiph'il stem of קרב, bring. The hiph'il of קרב is used in cultic contexts 156 times in all. This term refers only to the bringing of offerings and not to the whole Sanctuary system. Leviticus 1:15; 7:38; and 17:4 are examples.[60] One may even recall Lev 21:17, 18 where the qal stem refers to the priests' approaching, but the hiph'il stem refers to the bringing of an offering of the food of God.

The word קרב can also be used as a modal auxiliary verb, as "have," "could," and "shall" in English. In Lev 21:16–24, for example, קרב is frequently used followed by an infinitive, for example, "to offer," as in v. 17. קרב, then, explains how the offering would be accomplished. One draws near to offer. Thus, drawing near must mean more than simply approaching or touching in a basic, common sense. Instead, קרב must refer to officiating in a ceremonial way.[61] A blind priest, then, who accidentally bumped an altar would be in no danger of punishment.

Clearly, then, the word קרב holds important meanings when employed in a cultic context. Leviticus 21:16–24, then, forbids a priest from the specific actions that would involve directly approaching God's Presence and causing any object to do the same. Any other function of a priest could be acceptable.

Exegesis

Literary analysis

Jacob Milgrom rightly observes the presence of twelve blemishes in vv. 17–20 surrounded by twelve clauses concerning these blemishes. This suggests that the list of blemishes is a representative list. Other blemishes might also disqualify a priest.[62]

In addition, Mark F. Rooker correctly notes that Lev 21:17–20 contains the most comprehensive list of disabilities in the Hebrew Scriptures.[63] When considering the size of this list of disabilities, it is even more significant that blindness is placed at the head of this list. Apparently, even compared with all those other conditions, blindness was still the disability to be given attention first.

It is also important to consider repeated words and phrases in Lev 21:17–23. Milgrom notes that the term "seed" appears in vv. 17 and 21 with

---

60. Gane and Milgrom, "קרב," 141–42.
61. Milgrom, *Studies in Levitical Terminology*, 41, 42.
62. Milgrom, *Leviticus 17–22*, 1837.
63. Rooker, *Leviticus*, 276.

the context in both cases being the seed of Aaron. The word "blemish" appears five times, once in v. 17, once in v. 18, twice in v. 21, and once in v. 23.[64] The word קרב appears twice in v. 17, once in the qal and once in the hiph'il. The same word occurs in the qal once in v. 18 and twice in the hiph'il in v. 21. Other words for "approach/enter" such as נגש and בוא appear frequently in vv. 21–23. Thus, one can see the importance of this passage being addressed to Aaron's offspring and the extreme importance placed on the ideas of blemishes and approaching.

The order of the blemishes may even be significant. Moses Maimonides insightfully noted how as one reads through the list, blemishes become less and less severe.[65] Maimonides may be at least partially correct. The first disability mentioned is blindness, and toward the end of the list one finds mention of a type of discoloration of the eye that could not be as serious as blindness. Lameness is mentioned second in the list, while the brokenness of a leg, or what may be partial lameness, is discussed later in the list. The only problem with Maimonides' theory is that a number of men, most likely, would not rank having a crushed testicle in last place among disabilities even though it appears as the last disabling condition mentioned in Lev 21. Nonetheless, if Maimonides' observation is correct, at least in part, the placing of blindness as the first item in the list emphasizes the extreme severity of such a condition. In reality, whether or not there is a precise descending order of intensity for disabilities, the placement of blindness at the top of the list still can be seen as emphasizing that disability as highly noteworthy.

Ancient Near Eastern context

A number of passages similar in theme and concept to Lev 21:16–24 have been noted previously in ancient Near Eastern literature. In ancient Babylon a blind man was forbidden from being a diviner, and the reason for such forbidding was most importantly that such a person was blemished. One may also remember how in ancient Sumer, the blind as well as those with other disabilities were often made to function as temple slaves in the Arua Institution. In Egypt the blind could perform the sacred duty of being harpists.

---

64. Rooker, *Leviticus*, 276.

65. Moses Maimonides, *Temple Service*, Temple Entry 8:17, quoted in Milgrom, *Leviticus 17–22*, 1825.

General Analysis

Priests with any blemish were said not to be permitted to approach to offer the food of their God, a term described in Lev 22:19–25 (emphasis on vv. 20, 25) and Num 28:2 to refer to animal sacrifices. A number of observations can be made regarding blindness in the cultus based on this passage. First, Felix Just rightly notes that nowhere does this text say that a blind descendent of Aaron is not a priest or not to be considered as a priest. Such a one simply must recognize certain limitations placed on his functioning in the cultus.[66]

One may, then, analyze the nature of such a blemish of blindness. According to chapter 3 of this study, a מום is a visible, physical condition. This means, then, that the emphasis is on the existence of *a physical malformation*, not the severity of a disability. This may be why deafness is not mentioned in Lev 21, since one can appear physically intact while being unable to hear. This may also explain why the terms used to refer to blindness due to old age do not appear in Lev 21:16–24 since such blindness may not necessarily result in a significant physical deformation. Thus, it is not as much the inability to see that is the issue, but the physical deformity in the eyes.

It must also be understood that while one who was blind could not approach to offer the sacred food, he could still eat of the sacred food (Lev 21:22). In fact, in v. 22, the first word is לֶחֶם, "food," and the reference to eating appears afterward, showing the emphasis on the holy and most holy food. This means that a blind man could still receive sustenance. The amount of labor a blind priest was permitted to do, then, would have no bearing on the amount of food he was permitted to eat and take home to his family.

In practical terms, as John W. Kleinig logically notes, then, a blind priest was not permitted to enact the sacrificial ritual by officiation (Lev 21:22–23). He could not approach the altar with offerings to present before the Lord or enter the holy place to burn incense or sprinkle blood at the curtain.[67]

The blemished priest could eat the most holy food, which necessarily must be eaten in holy precincts (Lev 21:22; 10:12). He could eat the holy food taken from the offerings, sin offerings, and reparation offerings (Lev 7:6). He could eat God's food at the sanctuary where the other priests were permitted to do so. A blind priest was to eat of the grain offerings (Lev 2:3, 10; 6:9 [16, English]). The eating and touching of such would make even the blemished priest holy (Lev 6:11 [18, English]). Both blemished and unblemished priests, then, were as guests seated at God's holy table. No priest was

---

66. Just, "From Tobit to Bartimaeus, From Qumran to Siloam," 161.
67. Kleinig, *Leviticus*, 458.

to be deprived of livelihood based on a physical blemish.[68] As Kleinig also insightfully notes, the blemished priest, though, would receive that which makes holy because of the workings of the unblemished priests who could approach God's Presence.[69]

These statements are reasonable, with one exception. The blemished priest could eat of the offerings, except for certain cases such as with the sin offering when the eater of the food must also be the specific officiant of the ritual (Lev 6:16 [26, English]). Nonetheless, the idea of disabled priests still being guests at God's table draws one to recall Mephibosheth in 2 Sam 9, who, though crippled, was allowed to eat at David's royal table. Mephibosheth, whatever his physical condition, was still in the family of Saul, and, so, one David wished to honor. The blemished priests, like Mephibosheth, would be subject to an existence of limited activity, but still treated with the dignity and respect their positions deserved.

Other activities were allowable for a blind priest. The blemished priest, also, as long as he was ceremonially clean, would have been permitted to eat of the portion of the offerings designated for priests, their wives, and children (Lev 10:14), as wives, like the blemished priests, would never be officiants but would still eat of the food. In addition, there is nothing in the Hebrew Scriptures to say that a blind priest would be forbidden from singing in the Levitical choirs.

While a blind person of priestly heritage could still be a priest, it would be impossible for an עִוֵּר to be a high priest. Certain activities only the high priest could do, such as officiating in the rituals for the Day of Atonement in Lev 16 (Lev 16:32). Since only the high priest could officiate in those rituals, and since an עִוֵּר was forbidden to approach to officiate, which a high priest did throughout the day on the Day of Atonement (Lev 16), such a person must be blemish-free. An עִוֵּר in line to be high priest, then, must have needed to yield the position to the next in line. A high priest that, by some tragedy, became an עִוֵּר would be forced to resign and yield the position to his successor so the high priestly rituals could still be done.

One may then ask why a blind priest should not approach God's Presence. It might be suggested that blindness would hinder one's effectiveness in performing the rituals. If this were the case, though, the terms for blindness due to aging would also appear in this passage, as one blind by age would have similar difficulties. In addition, not all the disabilities mentioned in Lev 21:16–24 would affect one's ability physically to perform temple ritual. One with crushed testicles would not have any difficulty in presenting bread,

---

68. Kleinig, *Leviticus*, 458, 459.
69. Kleinig, *Leviticus*, 500.

offering incense, or even offering the blood on the Day of Atonement (Lev 16). It must be assumed, then, that the prohibition concerning a blind man's being a priest is not connected in the slightest with the physical ability to perform rituals.

One must, then, simply use the reason the text gives: that such a one has a blemish, repeating the same word, מום, five times in the passage. This is the same reason that a blind Babylonian was forbidden to be a diviner, as previously noted in this study. A priest was expected to be blemish-free, appearing spotless physically, to do God's perfect work. As Roy Gane notes, physical condition for a priest was not merely a qualification, such as tall height for a basketball player. Being free from blemish made one fit to do God's perfect work of holiness, however detrimental such a blemish would or would not have been concerning the performance of priestly tasks.[70] In addition, the word study on מום in chapter 3, shows that this word can also refer to a moral blemish. According to this logic, blindness becomes *a symbol for imperfection*, and its placement at the head of this list of disabilities emphasizes the intensity of such meaning. In addition, in Babylon, while a number of practical reasons could be presented for why a blind man would be forbidden from serving as a diviner, the need for such an individual to be blemish-free may have been more important.

This understood, though, the physical blemishes are mentioned after a list of spiritual and social imperfections a priest could bear. Nobuyoshi Kiuchi rightly notes that while only vv. 16–24 are devoted to the physical defects, vv. 1–15 are devoted to spiritual imperfections. While the possession of a physical blemish is said to not shut a priest away from eating of the sacred food, no such allowance is stated in Lev 21:1–15 to apply to a priest with a non-physical fault.[71] This argument is strengthened by the note that those non-physical blemishes in vv. 1–15 are not described with the word מום as the physical blemishes in vv. 16–24 are. Thus, a special word is used for the physical blemishes, physical blemishes that do not have as severe an effect on a priest as the spiritual faults listed earlier in the chapter. Milgrom also contrasts the treatment of the blemished priest with the treatment of the priest barred from serving because of extremely poor judgment in conduct. Some actions, such as being drunk in the sanctuary (Lev 10:9), being improperly dressed (Exod 28:43), or offering of unauthorized fire (Lev 10:1, 2) could cause a priest to be barred altogether from the sanctuary. Therefore, God's deepest concern in this case is for the spiritual blemishes to be avoided. Permanent physical blemishes are not treated as seriously,

---

70. Gane, *Leviticus, Numbers*, 374.
71. Kiuchi, *Leviticus*, 398.

and, in fact, God even provides accommodation for such so those with such blemishes would not starve. God, then, would not permit a simple, physical condition to interfere with the livelihood of a priest.[72] It may even be noted that those acts of poor judgment previously named, all behaviors that one can control, are also said to be punishable by death. One with a potentially unavoidable blemish such as blindness would not face any treatment even resembling such severity, but instead, would be allowed to function in a limited capacity and even to eat of the holy food. Clearly, God is seen in this passage to have mercy on at least some of those who cannot control the difficult situations in which they exist. A priest, though, might be conscious to take special care not to incur accidentally an injury such as blindness, and thus impair his ministry.

It is noteworthy, though, that Lev 22:1–16 says how one who is not a priest or one who is a priest but ceremonially unclean may not eat of the holy food. This means that blindness, although a serious physical blemish, would not bar a priest from certain actions that other disqualifications might.

The Blind Sacrifice, Leviticus 22:17–25

Translation

The text

The next passage to be considered is Lev 22:17–25. Verses 21 and 22, a central portion, are translated below.

וְאִישׁ כִּי־יַקְרִיב זֶבַח־שְׁלָמִים לַיהוָה לְפַלֵּא־נֶדֶר אוֹ לִנְדָבָה בַּבָּקָר אוֹ בַצֹּאן
תָּמִים יִהְיֶה לְרָצוֹן כָּל־מוּם לֹא יִהְיֶה־בּוֹ:
עַוֶּרֶת אוֹ שָׁבוּר אוֹ־חָרוּץ אוֹ־יַבֶּלֶת אוֹ גָרָב אוֹ יַלֶּפֶת לֹא־תַקְרִיבוּ אֵלֶּה
לַיהוָה וְאִשֶּׁה לֹא־תִתְּנוּ מֵהֶם עַל־הַמִּזְבֵּחַ לַיהוָה:

> 21. When anyone offers a sacrifice of well-being to the LORD, in fulfillment of a vow or as a freewill offering, from the herd or from the flock, to be acceptable it must be perfect; there shall be no blemish in it.
> 22. Anything blind, or injured, or maimed, or having a discharge or an itch or scabs—these you shall not offer to the LORD or put any of them on the altar as offerings by fire to the LORD. (NRSV)

---

72. Milgrom, *Studies in Levitical Terminology*, 41.

Exegesis

Context

One may compare Lev 22:17–25 with Lev 21:16–24. Both passages refer to blindness and other disabilities in a cultic context. Next, one may note the repetition of מוּם, "blemish," in the Hebrew of Lev 21:16–24. As noted in the previous chapter, this same word occurs three times in Lev 22:17–25, in vv. 20, 21, and 25. In addition, it is said in Lev 21:18 that a blind priest must not approach, קרב (qal form), the Lord. In Lev 22:20, it is said that one may not offer קרב (hiph'il/causative) a disabled sacrifice. In both cases the disabled were forbidden from coming near the sanctuary. The ritual act of approaching, then, is emphasized. It must be noted, though, that Lev 21:16–24 is only addressed to the priests, while Lev 22:17–25 is addressed to the entire Israelite assembly, most likely because the entire assembly would find Lev 22:17–25 more directly relevant to them as anyone could bring a freewill offering. Nonetheless, the linguistic and thematic parallels connect these two passages closely and help build an even stronger case that it was the blemish, not the incompetence, that was the issue of concern. In addition, because of the similarities between these passages, much information applicable to Lev 21:16–24 and this present passage, such as the word study on קרב, is not repeated here.

It is also necessary to compare and contrast the order of disabilities in the list of those barring one from priesthood and the list of disabilities barring an animal from eligibility as a sacrifice. This is significant because, if the same items are mentioned first, they probably hold equal significance. In this study, care is not taken to translate precisely the rare and confusing terms for disabilities other than blindness or lameness in these passages. Approximations are given due to the fact that they do not directly concern blindness which is all that is relevant to this study.

It is first noteworthy that the first disability mentioned in both lists is blindness, while a masculine noun עִוֵּר is named in Lev 21:18 and a feminine adjective עִוֶּרֶת is employed in Lev 22:22. Lameness is mentioned only in the list of restrictions on the priest in Lev 21, but not in the restrictions on sacrifices in Lev 22. While brokenness is mentioned near the beginning of both lists, the specific terms for "broken-handed" and "broken-footed" occur only in Lev 21:18. Leviticus 22:22 mentions the general term "broken," using the same linguistic root שבר, but a different form. It is said that a priest may not have a חָרֻם, flat nose, but this is not said of an animal. Instead, near the beginning of the list regarding animals, it is said that an animal may not be חָרוּץ, maimed. It is said, in Lev 21:21, that a priest may not serve if his testicles are crushed, but this is not stated regarding animals. Both were not to be scurvy, גָרָב, or scabbed, יַלֶּפֶת, terms said in the same order, according to Lev 21:20 and Lev 22:22.

What one may learn from the above information is that blindness held a special place of significance as a disability; in both lists it is mentioned first. Other disabilities, such as lameness, do not even occur in both these lists, though lameness appears in the list of restrictions on animal offerings in Deut 15:21. This further strengthens the argument that blindness bore a certain intensity not placed on other disabilities.

In addition, a logical order of thought moves through the text in Lev 21 and 22. Leviticus 21:1–15 contains a list of commands concerning how a priest and his family should live. Leviticus 21:16–24 concerns the limitations placed upon a blemished priest and a discussion of how such could still eat the food of his God. Leviticus 22:1–16 discusses who may and may not eat such food. Leviticus 22:17–25, then, considers how such food may not be blemished. Leviticus 22:26, then, begins a discussion of other restrictions placed on the use of animals. Thus, Lev 21:16–24 and Lev 22:17–25 are strategically placed in this discourse.

General analysis

In this passage it is said that animals with various disabling conditions and/or physical blemishes may not be offered as sacrifices. Blindness is also not one of the conditions allowable for freewill offerings but not votive offerings according to Lev 22:23. Both priest and lay person were to abide by these rules.

Jacob Milgrom insightfully notes that these restrictions apply to the four-legged animals that were the only kinds of animals allowed for freewill offerings, according to Lev 22:18. Nowhere in Leviticus are restrictions given for imperfect birds that might be offered. The reasons for both of these, he notes, may be that the freewill and votive offerings were optional. The bird offerings were allowed for the poor, according to Lev 5:7–10, who would not be able or expected to bring a freewill offering. The four-legged animal offerings, for the financially able, were to be "unblemished" because one wealthy enough to give such an offering could afford to offer the best (Lev 1:3, 10; and 4:3).[73] One too poor to fulfill a vow would obviously not be encouraged to make a vow, or at least a vow whose fulfillment would not come to pass before the resources were available to fulfill it. Thus, the poor, the ones who would not bring a four-legged animal, but a bird, instead,

---

73. Milgrom, *Leviticus 17–22*, 1874.

according to the principle of Lev 5:7–10, would not be concerned in Lev 22:17–25.

One may, then, determine if, in general, bird offerings by the poor were held to the same standards as four-legged offerings of those who were not poor. Deuteronomy 17:1, when saying that offerings in general must be without blemish, names only four-legged creatures, bulls and sheep, as examples. Next, in Lev 5:7–10, it is not said that a bird offered by a poor person must be blemish-free, with either מוּם, blemish, or תָּמִים, complete, as possible words to suggest such purity. This is said even though certain blemishes such as the existence of a misshapen wing or the lack of an eye could be easily observable upon inspection. In Lev 4:3, 23, 28, and 32, though, offerings with four-legged animals must be given with תָּמִים animals. In reality, anywhere in Leviticus when bird offerings are discussed, even for one not necessarily poor, being cleansed of a discharge, the bird offerings are not expected to be blemish-free. It may be possible, then, that since bird offerings were often associated with the poor, in their precarious position in society (Lev 5:7–10; 12:8; and 14:22), the offerings often associated with them were exempted from the requirement to be blemish-free. One too poor to offer a four-legged animal might not even have the resources to obtain and offer a blemish-free bird, and so such a person might be required to offer a blind bird as a sin offering if that were the best the individual could do. Nonetheless, one who was poor would understand the principle concerning offering blemish-free offerings and could still be encouraged to offer the best he/she could offer.

A disability in an animal would seldom make it more physically difficult to offer such as a sacrifice. A blind animal could be simply led, and a crippled animal would actually be less of an escape risk. The reason, then, for such animals to be forbidden must simply be, as stated in vv. 19, 25, that such a disability would be a blemish. A sacrifice must be ceremonially blemish-free to be acceptable. One, then, could not take a weakened animal that would not otherwise be put to service and devote it to the sanctuary. A sacrifice must truly be a sacrifice, a gift of something one could actually use and maybe even need. This reasoning regarding why blind animals were not to be offered also adds support to the argument that the reason a blind person could not serve as a priest was that he was blemished, not that he would be unable to perform the function.

It may be assumed that the priest would inspect each offering to ensure its validity. A precedent for this notion, as logically noted by Richard A. Taylor and E. Ray Clendenen, is Lev 27:11–12, in which certain types of offerings made to fulfill a vow were to be inspected for value by the priests.

It would be logical to assume that the same priests would inspect the validity of other animals offered at the sanctuary.[74]

Eye for Eye in Leviticus, Leviticus 24:19–20

Translation

THE TEXT

One must now consider the second occurrence of the "eye for eye" command in the Torah: Lev 24:19–20. A translation follows.

וְאִישׁ כִּי־יִתֵּן מוּם בַּעֲמִיתוֹ כַּאֲשֶׁר עָשָׂה כֵּן יֵעָשֶׂה לּוֹ:
שֶׁבֶר תַּחַת שֶׁבֶר עַיִן תַּחַת עַיִן שֵׁן תַּחַת שֵׁן כַּאֲשֶׁר יִתֵּן מוּם בָּאָדָם כֵּן יִנָּתֶן בּוֹ:

> 19. Anyone who maims another shall suffer the same injury in return:
> 20. fracture for fracture, eye for eye, tooth for tooth; the injury inflicted is the injury to be suffered. (NRSV)

Notes

One may wish to consult Jacob Milgrom's more accurate translation of this passage as follows:

> 19. If anyone maims another, as he has done so shall it be done to him:
> 20. Fracture for fracture, eye for eye, tooth for tooth. The injury that he has inflicted on the person shall be inflicted on him.[75]

Much has been read into the NRSV's rendering of these verses in the translation above. Milgrom rightly stays faithful to the Hebrew text in saying, for example, in the conclusion of v. 19, that it shall be done to the perpetrator as he did. This translation allows for the possibility that the courts would administer, or at least oversee, the punishment.

Milgrom also more accurately renders the conclusion of v. 20. The NRSV makes no mention of the agent's receiving the wrongful injury, while Milgrom states how the one who afflicts injury in "the person" would be punished. The NRSV also translates נתן differently in each of the two places

---

74. Taylor and Clendenen, *Malachi*, 269.
75. Milgrom, *Leviticus 23–27*, 2081.

where it appears in v. 20, using English words, "afflicted" and "suffered," respectively, and both English forms, passive. Milgrom, on the other hand, stays more faithful to the text in rendering both Hebrew occurrences as English forms of "afflict," and places an active form for the first and a passive form for the second.

The usage of מוּם in these verses is also significant. It may be noted that the term translated above by Milgrom as "maim," in the Hebrew of v. 19, contains the words, נתן (give/put) and מוּם, "blemish." Then, מוּם also appears in the conclusion of v. 20, translated as "injury" by Milgrom. Finally, the word אָדָם, for Adam/humankind, appears in this verse as the agent wrongly receiving the blemish/injury.

Exegesis

Literary Analysis

Gordon J. Wenham rightly notes that these verses are set at the center of a chiasm, illustrated by the following chart:

> A. alien and native together. v. 16.
> > B. taking man's life. 17.
> > > C. taking animal's life. 18.
> > > > D. what you do must be done to you. 19.
> > > > D'. whatever you do must be done to you. 20.
> > > C'. killing animals. 21a.
> > B'. killing human. 21B.
> A'. alien and Israelite. 22.[76]

It must also be noted that on either side of this chiasm reference is made to cursing God. As one can see, the concept of *lex talionis* with reference to injuring a human is central in this passage. Even though the broader context is that of a man who is to be stoned for blaspheming God, the center of this chiasm illustrates the general principle that what one does to harm another, any other, is to be repaid.

Context

As this passage is similar in a number of ways to Exod 21:23–25, comments applicable to both appear *only* in the discussion of Exod 21:23–25. For

---

76. Wenham, *The Book of Leviticus*, 312.

connections to other ancient Near Eastern law codes, then, one may simply see the section on Exod 21:23–25.

One difference between Lev 24 and Exod 21, with reference to their respective *lex talionis* commands, concerns the context of each command. Exodus 21:23–25 is set in the context of two men who are fighting but who accidentally strike a pregnant woman. The context of the command in Lev 24 is two men fighting, and so, assaulting each other, but not necessarily accidentally harming anyone. Instead, one of these people blasphemes God, and it is that blasphemy that results in the offender's stoning.

One may next compare Lev 24:18–21 with Lev 21 and 22 with reference to the discussion of blemishes. Both מוּם, "blemish," and שֶׁבֶר, "break," occur in Lev 21:16–24; 22:17–25; and 24:19–20. All three passages also concern matters relating to the eye. In the previous two passages, such blemishes could keep a priest or animal from being viable for use in direct service to approach God's Presence in the sanctuary. Leviticus 24:20, then, connects injuring another person with lessening the person's holiness. Israel was to be a kingdom of priests, according to Exod 19:6, and a people holy as God is holy, according to Lev 19:2. Any injury inflicted on a person would blemish and damage the holiness of the people just as the bringing of a blemished sacrifice or the officiating of a blemished priest.

General analysis

A number of observations can be made at this time. First, the injuring of a neighbor's eye carries the same penalty for a native offender as for a foreign offender. All humans in Israel were equally forbidden from wounding one another. It is noteworthy also that such a blemish of wounding another is said to be placed in humanity as a species, אָדָם, not merely in one man. This draws one's thoughts back to creation when God made humanity to be very good, thus, without blemish. One who injures the eye of another, then, blemishes all God-created humanity, not simply the one person injured.

As with Exod 21:23–25, one may ask if "eye for eye" is to be taken literally or figuratively. Much of the discussion on the general issue has already been stated regarding Exod 21:23–25, but a number of new issues arising in this passage are considered here.

Roy Gane insightfully notes how the simple language of Lev 24:19 suggests a literal understanding. The statement that one should do to the criminal as he has done suggests a literal doing. Making one pay a fine would only be doing as was done if the criminal was a thief. This, then, places consistency between killing a person and injuring a person. Both such offenses carry literal retribution as the penalty. An animal is not a human being, and so the destroying of such could be answered with the repaying of a live animal as a transfer of property. Genesis 9:6 says that one should not murder as humankind is made in God's image, suggesting that murder is an attack on God. The murder of an eye, then, would be a partial murder, a partial attack on the image of God, and so a partial attack on God. Such, then, would be punishable by a partial killing, the killing of an eye. Blasphemy, as the central theme of this passage, is also an attack on God, and so, like murder, it carries the death penalty. One, then, finds how three different types of crimes are addressed: attacking God, attacking humankind, and attacking an animal.[77]

Then, Jacob Milgrom insightfully brings the statement made by Samson in Judg 15:11 into the discussion. After the Philistines burned his wife and her father, he burned their grain, saying that he did to them as they did to him. While both acts were different, they both involved burning and destruction. Samson did not simply demand the Philistines pay a monetary fine and say that was doing to them as they did to him. Thus, while Samson's statement, in its boastfulness, might not be an exact example of this verbal formula, it can be considered as close and noteworthy in this discussion.[78]

Mark F. Rooker sets forth one argument against the literal understanding of Lev 24:19–20 by analyzing v. 18. There it is said that one who smites another's animal must make it good by replacing the animal, using the piel of שלם for "make good." "Life for life" is then used with the same structural formula as "eye for eye." Since "life for life" here is not literal killing of the offender's animal, "eye for eye" could refer to a punishment other than the removal of an offender's eye.[79]

In response to this, it could be said that שלם informs the reader as to the meaning of "life for life." The term, שלם, sets the context as one of repaying. Verse 19, though, starts a new thought and a new list of Talionic rules. This list begins by saying that one should do to the offender as was done in the crime. This is the context of equal retribution, not restitution. Thus, "eye for eye," here, is literal physical punishment. "Do to him as he did," then, is a formula for literal, physical talion.

One may next ask why a passage whose primary focus is the punishment of a blasphemer should concern itself with killing beasts and wounding eyes. It may be that God is seen as using this situation as an opportunity

---

77. Gane, *Leviticus, Numbers*, 426.

78. Milgrom, *Leviticus 23–27*, 2125.

79. Rooker, *Leviticus*, 298. (For more discussion concerning שלם in the context of *lex talionis*, see Daube, *Studies in Biblical Law*, 130–47.)

to compare and contrast different types of crimes. Murder, the attack on another's life, and blasphemy, the attack on the Name of God, are listed as carrying similar penalties, showing their similar intensity. Partial murder would then be discussed as a logical next step in a flow of thought in this argumentation. The killing of an eye, being placed in this discussion, was set apart by the author as an example, showing the significance of such a crime. In this list, though, blinding an eye is second after wounding by breaking, possibly because of the context of brawling.

The implications of a study of this passage in the context of Lev 21 are significant, since, as noted, the same word for "blemish" appears in both passages. If a blemish in a human is also a blemish in the image of God, a blemish in a priest is also a blemish in the image of God in Lev 21. If a blemish in an ordinary human is a serious matter, a blemish in a holy priest would be even more serious. A priest, who actively stands before God in the sanctuary, must be most careful to make sure he rightly displays God's image in both body and spirit. Any blemish weakens that holy image. In addition, if one keeps Lev 24 in mind when studying Lev 21, a priest could be barred from officiating if he becomes blemished as the result of a crime by another human since the same word for "blemish" occurs in both passages. Thus, a priest blinded by a crime, not just by a birth defect, would be blemished, and so unfit to officiate at the sanctuary.

Summary

Blindness is discussed four times in Leviticus. In Lev 19:14 the prohibition against setting a stumbling block before the blind is placed in the context of holiness and honoring the Ten Commandments. In Lev 21:16–24, it is said that a blind priest may not officiate in the sanctuary, though he could still eat of the sacred offerings. This means that he and his family could still be supported. In Lev 22:17–25, it is noted that blind animals were unfit to be used as sacrifices because they were blemished. Finally, in Lev 24:19–20, talionic justice is commanded against one who inflicts such a blemish in another human.

NUMBERS AND DEUTERONOMY

There is only one reference to blindness in Numbers considered here, and a number of the references to blindness in Deuteronomy are repetitions of previous references. For these reasons, these two books are studied together in this section.

First, blindness, as discussed by Dathan and Abiram in Num 16:14, is considered. Then, the blindness of idols is analyzed, according to Deut 4:28. After examining how Deuteronomy discusses blind offerings and blinding bribes (Deut 15:21; 16:19, respectively) the talion passage in Deut 19:20–21 is studied. The curse on those who lead the blind astray in Deut 27:18 is next considered. Then, blindness as it appears in the curses of the covenant, in Deut 28:28–29, is studied. Finally, Moses' lack of blindness due to old age, according to Deut 34:7, is analyzed.

The Blinding of Dathan and Abiram, Numbers 16:14

Translation

THE TEXT

The single reference to blindness in Numbers is Num 16:14. The text appears translated below:

אַף לֹא אֶל־אֶרֶץ זָבַת חָלָב וּדְבַשׁ הֲבִיאֹתָנוּ וַתִּתֶּן־לָנוּ נַחֲלַת שָׂדֶה וָכָרֶם הַעֵינֵי הָאֲנָשִׁים הָהֵם תְּנַקֵּר לֹא נַעֲלֶה׃

> 14. It is clear you have not brought us into a land flowing with milk and honey, or given us an inheritance of fields and vineyards. Would you put out the eyes of these men? We will not come! (NRSV)

Notes

The word order of the clause regarding the gouging is noteworthy. Literally it reads, "The eyes of these men, will you gouge out?" This shows emphasis on the eyes rather than the gouging. This means that the men were especially concerned about an attack on their eyes.

Exegesis

LITERARY ANALYSIS

Timothy Ashley insightfully notes how Egypt, called by Dathan and Abiram as a land of milk and honey, is paralleled with Canaan, which Moses referred to as such. In addition, structurally, the question about blinding parallels the question about being taken from a good land.⁸⁰ One may use this information to construct a chiasm chart of Num 16:12–14 with v. 14 at the end of this chiasm of argumentation by Dathan and Abiram. The outline follows below, with the issue of the rulership of Moses standing at the center and climax of this chiasm:

> A. We will not go up. (v. 12)
>   B. Question starting with interrogative ה. (Num 16:13)
>   C. A land flowing with milk and honey. (Num 16:13)
>   D. Moses being a prince over them. (Num 16:13)
>   C'. A land flowing with milk and honey. (Num 16:14)
>   B'. Question with interrogative ה. (Num 16:14)
> A'. We will not go up. (Num 16:14)

Context

One may consider the contextual background to the concept of a land flowing with milk and honey. In Exod 3:8, and again in v. 17, God says that he would take Israel up out of Egypt and bring them to a land flowing with milk and honey. Then, in Exod 13:5, Moses tells the Israelites how they would be going to a land flowing with milk and honey. In Num 16:13, though, Dathan and Abiram say that the Israelites had been brought up out of a land flowing with milk and honey. Dathan and Abiram, then, were saying that Moses had removed Israel from a good land with the promise of bringing them to a better land.

General analysis

One must first note the expression, "the eyes of these men," in Num 16:14. Baruch K. Levine suggests that this is an idiomatic expression referring to "our eyes," but the emotional intensity of the latter expression would have been too strong for one to say it so plainly. Another example of this literary concept is 1 Sam 29:4 with reference to the expression, "the heads of these men."⁸¹ It is also possible, though, that the eyes to be gouged out would be those of Dathan and Abiram, who seek to separate themselves from Korah so as not to be punished with him. As far as the theology of blindness is concerned, whoever among them was to be blinded is not significantly relevant to the study. All these people were rebels against Moses.

---

80. Ashley, *The Book of Numbers*, 310.
81. Levine, *Numbers 1–20*, 414.

Next, one must determine whether or not this reference to blinding is literal or figurative. If one takes the reference figuratively, as Philip J. Budd notes, it could be seen as an allusion to Exod 23:8 regarding the blinding nature of a bribe, previously discussed in this study.[82] "Exodus-Ruth" in *The Bible Commentary on the Old Testament* insightfully adds that Moses would, then, further deceive Dathan, Abiram, and their men with more empty promises of a better land, more bribes for the men's obedience.[83] When one considers the references to the land flowing with milk and honey, as previously noted, the men could truly be seen as accusing Moses of using deceptive bribes. Moses used the attractiveness of a new, great land, flowing with milk and honey to draw the Israelites away from Egypt, their land flowing with milk and honey so he could do with them as he pleased.

Arguments also exist in favor of literally interpreting this reference to blinding. First, the language and context is completely different from that of Exod 23:8 where blinding is used figuratively. In Exod 23:8, עור is the Hebrew word for "blind," in the context of how a bribe blinds those with open eyes. The verb in Num 16:14 is נקר, which, as Stephen K. Sherwood rightly notes, is shown to be used in the context of other literal eye-gougings such as Samson's and that threatened against the men of Jabesh Gilead in 1 Sam 11:2. This verb is to be understood literally in all other cases.[84] One may consult the previous chapter of this study, under "נָקַר," for a more detailed list of these literal occurrences. It may also be noted that these rebels were rebels who were attempting to threaten Moses' authority (Num 16:1–3). One may recall quotations such as the treaty between Hattusili III of Hatti and Ramses II of Egypt concerning escaped slaves, previously noted in chapter 2 of this study, and the stories of Samson and Zedekiah. These all show how blinding was used, or feared to be possibly used, as a penalty for certain crimes often involving the challenging of assumed authority in the ancient Near East. The burden of proof, then, appears to be on those interpreting the statement figuratively.

Ronald B. Allen takes a sensible position half-way between these in suggesting that Dathan and Abiram were exaggerating by suggesting that Moses would further blind the people regarding the dangerous outcome of their journeys. The reference to gouging out the eyes would be an extreme way of expressing the point.[85] This is a possible interpretation of this passage; however, the fact that these rebels show such reluctance to the idea of

---

82. Budd, *Numbers*, 187.
83. Cook, ed., *The Bible Commentary: Exodus-Ruth*, 218.
84. Sherwood, *Leviticus, Numbers, Deuteronomy*, 165.
85. Allen, "Numbers," 838.

appearing before Moses, and the fact that Moses insisted on a literal, physical penalty carried out only by God (Num 16:30, 31), suggests that these remarks were made regarding a real fear, however justified, of having bodily harm inflicted. However the rebels' words were meant, it is clear that they wished to portray Moses as a domineering tyrant intent only on oppressive rulership, a tyrant willing to use blinding as a tactic to increase his power.

Blind Idols, Deuteronomy 4:28

Translation

THE TEXT

The first passage to be considered in Deuteronomy is Deut 4:28, which introduces a theme revisited frequently in the Hebrew Scriptures. One may consider the following translation:

וַעֲבַדְתֶּם־שָׁם אֱלֹהִים מַעֲשֵׂה יְדֵי אָדָם עֵץ וָאֶבֶן אֲשֶׁר לֹא־יִרְאוּן וְלֹא יִשְׁמְעוּן וְלֹא יֹאכְלוּן וְלֹא יְרִיחֻן׃

> 28. There you will serve other gods made by human hands, objects of wood and stone that neither see, nor hear, nor eat, nor smell. (NRSV)

Exegesis

CONTEXT

Eugene H. Merrill rightly notes how the Israelites, as a result of their idolatry, would be carried into exile where they would then live out the idolatrous lives they desired to have, worshipping the strange gods that they desired to worship in the lands of the strange gods (Deut 4:25), gods that have no senses.[86] One may next consider how the gods of the pagan nations do not see, nor hear, nor smell, according to Deut 4:28. Richard D. Nelson insightfully contrasts this with the idea that, according to the Torah, Israel's God, though, does all three, in order (Gen 1:4; 20:17; and 8:21). No mention is made though of Israel's God eating. Comparing Deut 4:28 with Deut 34:7, one finds reference made to God's receiving petitions, petitions no pagan idol could observe by sight or hearing.[87]

---

86. Merrill, *Deuteronomy*, 128.
87. Nelson, *Deuteronomy*, 68.

General Analysis

It must be noted that in the list of senses in Deuteronomy, sight is mentioned first, showing the great importance placed on eyesight. It is stressed, then, that idols are blind, unable to see. All Israel could hope for, in rejecting God, is worshipping blind idols.

The Blind Firstling, Deuteronomy 15:21

Translation

The text

The next three passages considered are all near repetitions of previously analyzed texts. Thus, the primary focus may center on those similarities and differences with reference to corresponding passages and how the unique context of the Deuteronomy passages may influence the interpretation.

One must now consider Deut 15:21, translated below:

וְכִי־יִהְיֶה בוֹ מוּם פִּסֵּחַ אוֹ עִוֵּר כֹּל מוּם רָע לֹא תִזְבָּחֶנּוּ לַיהוָה אֱלֹהֶיךָ:

> 21. But if it has any defect—any serious defect, such as lameness or blindness—you shall not sacrifice it to the LORD your God. (NRSV)

Notes

This verse literally begins, "And if it has a blemish in it, lame or blind, any bad blemish." One may note the word מוּם, the cultic term for a disqualifying blemish. It may also be noted how the terms for disability, in the Hebrew, are placed between the references to the blemish, suggesting an inclusio.

Exegesis

Contextual analysis

One may briefly compare and contrast this passage with Lev 22:17–25, which also discusses the bringing of disabled offerings. In Deut 15:19–21, it is said that one may not offer a lame, blind, or ill-blemished animal as a firstborn offering. Where the animals would be potentially offered on the alter, in Lev 22:22, the offerings, in Deut 15:19, 20, would be brought to the tabernacle and eaten before the Lord by the people. In both passages, animals with disabilities were prohibited from use as offerings in the respective services and situations. Deuteronomy 15, though, adds how disabled animals may still be used. Animals with disabilities, according to Deut 15:22, however, could be eaten in one's gates, presumably as one would eat any clean animal. In addition, in Deut 15:21, as well as in Lev 22:22, mention is made only of the idea of being blemished and not on functional ability. The list of disabilities is considerably shorter in Deut 15:21 and has been noted in the previous chapter possibly to involve a merism. Blindness, though, is not mentioned first in the list in Deut 15:21, though it is so mentioned in a significant number of times, previously. It is noteworthy, though, that in Leviticus, where the emphasis is primarily on the priestly cultus, the disabled offerings are said not to be offered on the altar, where the priests serve (Lev 22:22). In Deut 15:19–21, where the context is Moses' final speech to the entire Israelite camp, disabled animals are said not to be permitted for offerings in a great assembly of the people. The warning against offering blind animals, then, was applied to the larger audience of the entire camp, showing God's great displeasure with the offering of blemished sacrifices. This shows God's general displeasure with offering blemished animals as a whole.

It must next be noted that such blemished animals could still be eaten in a general context of common consumption of food, according to Deut 15:22. Both clean and unclean could eat of this. Earl S. Kalland, then, rightly notes that God sets himself above the people by saying that he may not be given to ordinary religious life. One's gifts to God must be seen as higher than one's gifts to self or to other people. The people were to participate, one and all, in an existence of holy living, separating treatment of God and holy things from treatment of people and common things.[88] In addition, Lev 22 makes no mention of blemished animals' being put to common use. Deuteronomy 15, though, as part of an address to the people, could contain such material.

The Blinding Bribe, Deuteronomy 16:19

Translation

THE TEXT

In Deut 16:19 one finds a near direct quotation of Exod 23:8. A translation follows:

---

88. Kalland, "Deuteronomy," 108.

לֹא־תַטֶּה מִשְׁפָּט לֹא תַכִּיר פָּנִים וְלֹא־תִקַּח שֹׁחַד כִּי הַשֹּׁחַד יְעַוֵּר עֵינֵי חֲכָמִים וִיסַלֵּף דִּבְרֵי צַדִּיקִם׃

19. You must not distort justice; you must not show partiality; and you must not accept bribes, for a bribe blinds the eyes of the wise and subverts the cause of those who are in the right. (NRSV)

Exegesis

LITERARY ANALYSIS

J. A. Thompson rightly comments that Deut 16:19 contains apodictic legislation followed by a general statement of wisdom about bribes blinding the wise. The wisdom statement serves to justify and explain the laws, showing what might interfere with justice.[89] Such a change in style would accentuate the proverb, calling the reader's attention to the message of such.

CONTEXT

Deuteronomy 16:19 says that a bribe blinds the eyes of the wise and perverts the words of the righteous. While Exod 23:8 contains essentially the same message, a number of differences must be noted. First, the word order in Deut 16:19 differs slightly. While Exod 23:8 literally says, "and a bribe, you shall not take," Deut 16:19 says in usual Hebrew grammar, "you shall not take a bribe," showing less emphasis on the idea of the bribe in Deuteronomy. In addition, Deut 16:19 uses "wise" rather than "open," with reference to the type of person blinded by a gift. Exodus 23:8 notes how a bribe interferes with the gift of clear and open-eyed insight. According to Deut 16:19, then, a bribe interferes with the work of the similar attribute of wisdom. While the context of Exod 23:8 discusses proper treatment of the less fortunate, the context of Deut 16:19 discusses just judgment. Verse 18 contains the command for the Israelites to place just judges over themselves so that righteous judgment may take place. This bribe, then, that interferes with wisdom would also interfere with just judgment. In addition, Peter C. Craigie rightly notes that Deut 16:18 defines the relevant audience for v. 19 as primarily judges and officers while such a context is not as explicitly

---

89. J. A. Thompson, *Deuteronomy*, 200.

named in Exod 23.⁹⁰ Nonetheless, Nelson insightfully comments that the entire assembly may still be addressed, in a sense, in Deut 16:19, as both that v. 18 and v. 19 are in the second person. Those addressed as "you" in both vv. 18 and 19 are to set up just judges and not take bribes.⁹¹

Eye for Eye in Deuteronomy 19:21

Translation

THE TEXT

The *lex talionis* principle was apparently understood to be significant enough to have it mentioned three times in the Torah. This, the third and final instance, concerning the unique situation of breaking the ninth commandment (Exod 20:16), is translated below.

וְלֹא תָחוֹס עֵינֶךָ נֶפֶשׁ בְּנֶפֶשׁ עַיִן בְּעַיִן שֵׁן בְּשֵׁן יָד בְּיָד רֶגֶל בְּרָגֶל׃

> 21. Show no pity: life for life, eye for eye, tooth for tooth, hand for hand, foot for foot. (NRSV)

NOTES

Literally the first clause of the Hebrew of this verse reads, "Your eye shall not pity." In addition, the Hebrew for the *lex talionis* formulas in this verse differs slightly when compared with Exod 21:24, 25 and Lev 24:20. While Exodus and Leviticus use תַּחַת as the Hebrew preposition between the pairs of identical words, Deuteronomy uses בְּ. Koehler and Baumgartner observe how בְ and תַּחַת appear to be used interchangeably in these passages. בְּ in Deut 19 is compared with תַּחַת in Exod 21 and Lev 24. Both words are described as having similar meanings concerning repayment.⁹²

While this may be essentially true, one notable difference exists between these two passages with reference to the context. Both the passages in Exodus and Leviticus which employ תַּחַת concern judgment after a crime has actually been committed. Deuteronomy 19, though, which employs בְּ, discusses the case of a penalty applied, not after a victim's eye or tooth is

---

90. Craigie, *The Book of Deuteronomy*, 247.
91. Nelson, *Deuteronomy*, 218.
92. Koehler and Baumgartner, *The Hebrew and Aramaic Lexicon of the Old Testament*, 1:105.

wrongly removed, but while the criminal, a false witness, is yet seeking for such an act to take place. Thus, the actual blinding of the victim does not necessarily need to take place at all in Deut 19. The punishment is applied to a false witness who seeks to have the courts wrongly blind another. This difference between these cases may have necessitated the use of a different preposition in Deut 19.

Exegesis

CONTEXT

Immediate biblical context

The immediate context of Deut 19:21 is noteworthy. Deuteronomy 19:16–20 contains the law concerning the malicious witness. In vv. 16–19, it is said that one who falsely accuses another of wrongdoing shall, himself/herself, bear the penalty of said wrong. Verse 20 says that the people would fear as a result of such judgment. It is immediately following this statement that the *lex talionis* commands appear, setting forth examples for how punishment would be administered when one falsely accuses another.

It must, then, be understood that "eye for eye" was to be ordered by the courts. J. G. McConville rightly notes that the false witness who would testify in court would then find the decision made by the court that he/she would be punished. This removes "eye for eye" from the realm of personal vengeance where one would simply injure another for hurting him/her.[93]

Intertextual connection

One must first study Deut 19:21 in the context of Exod 21:23–25. It is noteworthy that the list of *lex talionis* commands in Deut 19 stops here, not continuing to include references to wounds and burns as it does in Exod 21:23–25. This list, then, must be seen as a brief statement of representative examples as in Deut 15:21.

Deuteronomy 19:21, though, instead of concerning judgment against a physical act that has already been committed, discusses the retaliation against a physical act that one intends to have committed. As one who wounds another would be wounded by the court, according to Exod 21:23–25 and Lev 24:19–20, one who seeks to have the court wound another would have such wounding done to him/her, according to Deut 19:16–21.

---

93. McConville, *Deuteronomy*, 314.

Lex talionis, then, applies also to situations where punishment could be dealt out for intentionally and actively seeking harm against another. Thus, one who falsely seeks to have another blinded by the courts must himself/ herself face such punishment. This also shows how the principle for *lex talionis* extends to more situations than that of one smiting a pregnant woman (Exod 21:22–23).

Deuteronomy 19:16–21 also contains an allusion to the Decalogue. Jeffrey H. Tigay rightly notes that the reference to a false witness draws one's attention to the ninth commandment in Exod 20:17.[94] The crime of falsely accusing, important enough to be addressed in the Ten Commandments, must carry serious consequences.

One may also consider 1 Kgs 21, the story of Naboth, previously noted in this study in the context of *lex talionis*. McConville insightfully observes that those who arranged for the false witnesses to testify against Naboth were prophesied to receive the same shame of having the dogs lick up their blood (1 Kgs 21:19, 23).[95]

General analysis

The repetition of the concept of the eye must first be noted in this verse. The eye that shall not pity would oversee the removal of an eye, the first specific bodily organ named in the *lex talionis* list after "life for life." This shows the literary and social significance placed on the eye. That which was capable of judgment and pity might be removed from a criminal.

Then, one may confront the interpretive issue yet to be discussed regarding this passage: whether or not "eye for eye" is to be taken literally. While one may refer to the comments on Exod 21:23–25 and Lev 24:19–20 in this study for a general discussion of *lex talionis*, a new argument for literal interpretation of Deut 19:20–21 must be discussed. One may recall how the text says that the eye should not pity. It must be noted how this exact idiom, with the same words for "eye," "not," and "pity" occurs elsewhere in the Torah. One finds precisely four other uses of this idiom, all also only in Deuteronomy. Deuteronomy 7:16 employs this idiom when discussing how the Israelites should consume and destroy the pagan nations in Canaan. Deuteronomy 13:9 (8, English) employs this idiom concerning the literal putting to death of one who attempts to lead the people after other gods. Deuteronomy 19:13, a few verses before the talion passage concerned in this section, employs the same expression with reference to the killing of

---

94. Tigay, *Deuteronomy*, 184.
95. McConville, *Deuteronomy*, 313.

a murderer, which Num 35:31 says must be literal with no possibility for ransom. Deuteronomy 25:12 uses this expression in the context of cutting off the hand of a woman who attempts to deliver her husband in a fight by seizing an assailant by the private parts. In none of these cases is financial compensation suggested as a possible alternative punishment of physical mutilation. In fact, the use of such an idiom concerning pity may have been to emphasize that in these situations the radical penalty of physical mutilation was to be administered. It would be logical to assume that since such an expression concerning pitying is linked with literal physical mutilation in these other cases, Deut 19:20–21, which also contains the same expression concerning pity, is also to be understood as referring to a literal physical mutilation and not the placing of a fine. Thus, Deut 19:20–21 is to be understood as referring to literal talion.

This argument also strengthens the case for literal talion in Exod 21 and Lev 24. The destroying of another's eye is the only crime in Torah that is described as being punished "eye for eye." There is, then, only one way a false witness could be punished by literal, physical blinding, in Deut 19: Such would be the case if he/she accused another of the only crime for which blinding was the penalty and if that crime carried the penalty of literal blinding. If "eye for eye" in Exod 21 and Lev 24 referred only to financial compensation, there would be no possibility for a penalty of physical mutilation to be sought falsely through the courts and so enforced on the false witness in Deut 19 with no pity shown.

Leading the Blind Astray, Deuteronomy 27:18

Translation

The text

The next passage to be considered is Deut 27:18, translated below:

אָר֗וּר מַשְׁגֶּ֥ה עִוֵּ֖ר בַּדָּ֑רֶךְ וְאָמַ֥ר כָּל־הָעָ֖ם אָמֵֽן׃

> 18. "Cursed be anyone who misleads a blind person on the road." All the people shall say, "Amen!" (NRSV)

Exegesis

CONTEXT

Ancient Near Eastern context

As with Lev 19:14, this style of addressing right treatment of the disabled is unprecedented elsewhere in the ancient Near East. One finds wisdom literature, such as that of Egypt mentioned above, but not a direct and general curse on one who commits this wrong.

When one considers Deut 27:17, though, a possible parallel with other ancient Near Eastern sources emerges. Deuteronomy 27:17 says that one would be cursed for removing a neighbor's boundary stone. One can recall in chapter 2 how one who caused a blind individual to damage or remove a boundary stone would be cursed, according to inscriptions on ancient Babylonian boundary stones. It is noteworthy how the commands regarding removing a boundary stone and leading the blind astray are consecutive in Deut 27. This raises the question as to whether or not they might be, in some way, related. While Deut 27:18 is still a general command regarding right treatment of the disabled, something still not seen even in the boundary stone texts, the context of moving boundary stones would have been clear to an audience accustomed to living in a world where such were common. Thus, the juxtaposition of these two laws in Deuteronomy may not have been accidental. Deuteronomy 27:17, 18, interpreted as a unit based on these similarities to other ancient Near Eastern laws, may be suggesting that one should not remove a neighbor's boundary stone nor mislead a blind person so he/she could do it either. Of course, this interpretation does not rule out the possibility that Deut 27:18 should be applied to any situation involving leading a blind person astray since these are two separate curses. Nonetheless, the fact that these two curses are juxtaposed draws one to examine possible parallels with boundary stone texts that proclaim curses on those who cause the blind to damage or remove them.

Immediate biblical context

Exodus–Ruth, The Bible Commentary on the Old Testament, notes that Deut 27:18 stands in the midst of twelve covenantal curses. The first eleven concern specific sins while the last is a general curse regarding the breaking of God's commandments.[96] Nelson, then, rightly discusses how these first eleven

---

96. Cook, *The Bible Commentary: Exodus–Ruth*, 322.

curses can be further subdivided. Both vv. 16, 17 concern issues of family relationships. Then, both vv. 18 and 19 concern oppression of the disadvantaged. Vv. 20–23 concern matters of sexuality. The final couplet of curses is found in vv. 24 and 25, both of which deal with murder.[97] This would mean that the curse regarding mistreatment of the blind, then, is logically placed in the context of mistreatment of all with disadvantages. Next, Christopher J. H. Wright insightfully writes that none of these curses is specific. No mention is made among these curses as to what types of harm would befall one who committed these sins.[98] As with Lev 19:14, then, these wrongs that are often hidden from humans would be punished by God who sees all.

Intertextual connection

One may note the strong parallels with Lev 18–19 in the Holiness Code to examine more deeply the relationship between proper treatment of the blind and holiness. The sexuality code in Lev 18 lists the same abominations as Deut 27:20–23 such as bestiality (Lev 18:23) and various forms of incest (Lev 18:6–18). Both passages refer to making graven images (Lev 19:4; Deut 27:15) and dishonoring father and mother (Lev 19:3; Deut 27:16). Deuteronomy 27, though, does not make reference to treatment of the deaf as in Lev 19:14. Clearly, the deaf would not suddenly be removed from consideration. One can assume that right treatment of all people with disabilities would be under the principle of Deut 27, but only treatment of the blind is directly concerned. Blindness, then, being the only disability mentioned, would likely be a representative of the others. Thus, the curses of Deut 27 can be understood to concern the same practical issues of holiness discussed in Lev 18 and 19. According to Deut 27:18, then, deceiving the blind so that they are led astray is a most serious offense, listed along with incest, bestiality, and idolatry. Proper treatment of the blind, then, is an issue of extreme holiness, the neglect of which not only distances one from the fear of God (Lev 19:14), but places him/her in danger of receiving covenantal curses.

The curses of Deut 27 contain a number of similarities with the Ten Commandments. It must be noted that similar parallels between Lev 19 and the Ten Commandments have already been noted. Both Deut 27 and the Decalogue concern graven images with the same words for "make" and "graven image" used (Exod 20:4–6 and Deut 27:15). Both lists also concern the treatment of father and mother, with the same words for "father" and "mother" employed (Exod 20:12 and Deut 27:16). The sexuality curses in

97. Nelson, *Deuteronomy*, 320.
98. Christopher J. H. Wright, *Deuteronomy*, 277.

Deut 27:20–23 might be, in a way, parallel with the commandment concerning adultery, Exod 20:14. Both passages also concern murder (Exod 20:12 and Deut 27:24, 25). No literary parallels exist concerning murder and adultery between these two passages, though. Thus, the curses of Deut 27 are not simply arbitrary curses placed on a few randomly chosen acts. Instead, a number of these are acts condemned even in the Ten Commandments. Leading the blind astray is listed right alongside these other acts, more explicitly condemned in the Decalogue. Possibly, though, leading the blind astray could be considered under the principle of bearing false witness (Exod 20:16), which also concerns deception at the heart, though no literary parallel exists between these two texts.

General analysis

The obvious and literal interpretation of this curse is plain. If one leads the blind astray, such a leader is in danger of divine judgment. Felix Just, though, incorrectly assumes from this verse that a blind person must be walking alone in order to be misguided in the path.[99] It is possible for one to be leading a blind person and deceive him/her by guiding him/her astray to go somewhere else than the blind person believes he/she is going.

Earl S. Kalland, though, insightfully applies this verse to other situations. Proverbs 28:10 uses the verb שגה to also refer to a righteous man's being led astray. Since this word can be used figuratively and literally, it is not unreasonable to apply this curse to any situation where one is, as blind, led astray into deception.[100] In addition, Tigay helpfully notes that leading the blind astray can refer to misleading anyone with faulty information.[101]

Nelson explains how the fact that the people said "amen" after each curse is also significant. This shows the people's agreement to the curses, in a way, their conditional cursing of themselves. Numbers 5:22 and Neh 5:13 are similar examples. Since the sins of Deut 27, such as leading the blind astray and sexual misconduct, may be difficult to witness, and so, to try in court, God must be the judge who would administer punishment. The people, then, would be agreeing that they allow God to act in such a manner.[102] The people, then, would be agreeing to honor God's covenant with God as the superior party.

---

99. Just, "From Tobit to Bartimaeus, From Qumran to Siloam," 84.
100. Kalland, "Deuteronomy," 165.
101. Tigay, *Deuteronomy*, 255.
102. Nelson, *Deuteronomy*, 319.

The Curse of Blindness, Deuteronomy 28:28–29

Translation

THE TEXT

What follows is a translation of Deut 28:28–29. This passage lists curses that would befall Israel should they violate God's covenant with them.

יַכְּכָה יְהוָה בְּשִׁגָּעוֹן וּבְעִוָּרוֹן וּבְתִמְהוֹן לֵבָב:
וְהָיִיתָ מְמַשֵּׁשׁ בַּצָּהֳרַיִם כַּאֲשֶׁר יְמַשֵּׁשׁ הָעִוֵּר בָּאֲפֵלָה וְלֹא תַצְלִיחַ אֶת־דְּרָכֶיךָ וְהָיִיתָ אַךְ עָשׁוּק וְגָזוּל כָּל־הַיָּמִים וְאֵין מוֹשִׁיעַ:

> 28. The LORD will afflict you with madness, blindness, and confusion of mind;
> 29. you shall grope about at noon as blind people grope in darkness, but you shall be unable to find your way; and you shall be continually abused and robbed, without anyone to help. (NRSV)[103]

Exegesis

CONTEXT

Ancient Near Eastern context

One must now recall the numerous texts previously noted in chapter 2 of this study that describe curses of blindness, most notably the treaty text of Esarhaddon. Moshe Weinfelt rightly observes how both this text and Deut 28 concern similar penalties for failure to honor the agreement properly (Deut 28:15). Both passages list, in the same order, curses of grave illness (Deut 28:22, 27), blindness (Deut 28:28–29), sexual violation of wives (Deut 28:30), and seizure of house by another. Both passages also discuss unburied corpses being eaten by birds (Deut 28:26) though each passage places this curse in a different position in the list.[104] Clearly, then, these ideas were understood in the ancient Near East as curses that could be placed on rebellious vassals. God, then, in Deut 28, as the superior party, is shown applying them on the national level.

---

103. This verse and Isa 59:10, not the ones noted by Felix Just, discuss the blind moving independently. In this case, they are described as groping about, which would be more necessary when such people are away from the familiar surroundings of their homes.

104. Weinfeld, *Deuteronomy and the Deuteronomic School*, 118.

Intertextual connection

One may compare the curses of Deut 28 with the plagues in the Exodus story. Deuteronomy 28:27 says that God would smite the people with the boils of Egypt, using the same word for "boils" as Exod 9:9 when referring to the sixth plague of Egypt in the Exodus narrative. Deuteronomy 28:38 says that the locust would consume the fields of the wayward people, the same word for "locusts" appearing in Deut 28:38 and Exod 10:12, there, again, in the context of the Exodus narrative. One may also note how the ninth plague of Egypt, though not directly referring to blindness, involved darkness that could be felt (Exod 10:21) and that kept the Egyptians from seeing one another (Exod 10:23). The same word for darkness, אֲפֵלָה, is used to describe the darkness in Egypt (Exod 10:22) and the darkness in which the blind grope (Deut 28:29). This suggests that this blinding darkness that would smite Israel for their rebellion would be part of a series of plagues designed to parallel the plagues of Egypt, which also came because of rebellion against God. The Israelites, then, would receive the same judgments that once rescued them from bondage. Blinding darkness was clearly to be understood as one of them. Finally, while blindness is not mentioned in Exod 10 in the context of the ninth plague, the fact that such darkness is associated with blindness in Deut 28:28–29 suggests that one may, at least, in a figurative sense, understand the nation of Egypt as having been smitten with blindness. Such parallels further reinforce the unfavorable position the blind were understood to occupy and how blindness was not viewed as desirable.

GENERAL ANALYSIS

Since this passage is a conditional curse that would be fulfilled possibly at some time in the future, it is difficult to know whether or not this blindness is literal. When the Israelites were taken into exile, there is no mention made of boils, locusts, and darkness at midday, though Zedekiah was blinded (2 Kgs 25:7). In addition, Samson was blinded (Judg 16:21), and the entire northern kingdom was carried into exile (2 Kgs 16). Merrill, though, logically notes that since the blindness discussed in Deut 28:28 is set directly between two clearly psychological states, madness and astonishment of heart, it is logical also to understand the blindness as mental as well, referring to a state of disorientation or confusion.[105]

---

105. Merrill, *Deuteronomy*, 361.

The blindness of Deut 28:29 is also difficult to understand concerning the degree of literalness one must understand it to bear. It can be certain, though, as Nelson observes, that the language of groping at midday is the language of disability such as blindness, not the language of absence of light, as when it is night.[106] Even if the passage predicts a solar eclipse that would make it dark at midday, the references to groping and the blind still draws one to consider the image of disability. However this blindness is to be understood, then, Deut 28:28–29 uses such language with strong negative connotations, describing great calamities and not pleasures.

Moses' Lack of Blindness in Old Age, Deuteronomy 34:7

Translation

The text

The first reference to matters of sight in the Torah is Gen 1, the first chapter of the Torah. The final reference to blindness in the Torah is in Deut 34, the last chapter of the Torah. Deuteronomy 34:7 is translated below.

וּמֹשֶׁה בֶּן־מֵאָה וְעֶשְׂרִים שָׁנָה בְּמֹתוֹ לֹא־כָהֲתָה עֵינוֹ וְלֹא־נָס לֵחֹה׃

> 7. Moses was one hundred twenty years old when he died; his sight was unimpaired and his vigor had not abated.

Notes

Literally the clause concerning Moses' sight reads, "Not dimmed was his eye." This allows the verse to be contrasted effectively with Gen 27:1 and 48:10 that also refers directly to the condition of the eye.

Exegesis

Context

One may recall Isaac in Gen 27 and Jacob in Gen 48, both of whom were blind in old age. Genesis 27:1 even uses the same verb, כהה, to describe the weakening of the eyes and the same word for "eye." Genesis 48:10, while using a different word to describe the weakening, still uses the same word for

---

106. Nelson, *Deuteronomy*, 325.

"eye," in the Hebrew. One may also note the numerous ancient Near Eastern passages discussing this condition. Such is not the case for Moses, however.

General analysis

Moses remained strong until the moment of his death at the age of 120 years as eyesight was only one in a list of attributes not weakened in Moses, according to v. 7. Tigay rightly notes how the good strength of Moses' eyesight and physical vigor set him apart from most elderly people of his day who would have suffered from weakening in both eyesight and vigor. While his strength may have been slightly weakened, with reference to going out and coming in, or leading the people, according to Deut 31:2, he still maintained the appearance and form of one with great ability.[107] It can even be noted that Moses is said to have possessed enough vigor to climb Mt. Nebo. This shows the unusual circumstances of his death and suggests that his years might have been miraculously cut short to keep him from entering Canaan as a result of striking the rock (Num 20:12). One may also understand Moses' remaining strong as a manifestation of God's providence in allowing him to lead the Israelites most effectively.

What is certain is that Moses saw clearly enough to climb Mt. Nebo. Then, as described in Deut 34:4, he would see the land of Canaan from afar, which he would not be able to do with weakened vision, or even, standard vision. God, then, strengthened Moses' eyesight to behold a land vast enough not to be visible even to one with standard eyesight. Moses, then, did not suffer the usual maladies associated with growing old. Nelson helpfully comments that, as was the case with his birth, Moses experienced an unusual and miraculous death.[108]

Summary

One may first recall blindness in Numbers. While it is difficult to determine whether or not Dathan and Abiram were speaking of literal blindness in Num 16:14, it is clear that they were expressing, in their rebellion, disapproval with how Moses was leading the people. These men even thought that Moses had taken them out of the land of milk and honey simply to dominate them.

---

107. Tigay, *Deuteronomy*, 338.
108. Nelson, *Deuteronomy*, 396.

Blindness is mentioned in seven passages in Deuteronomy. First, idols are said to be blind, according to Deut 4:28. It is noteworthy, though, that God is described as seeing throughout the Torah. Deuteronomy 15:21 contains a command not to offer disabled animals as firstling sacrifices. Such animals, though, may be eaten as regular food. Deuteronomy 16:19 reminds the people that a bribe blinds those who judge. Deuteronomy 16, though, says it is the wise who are blinded instead of the open-eyed, as expressed in Exod 23:8. In Deut 19:21, it is said that anyone who attempts to have the courts wrongly blind another will face literal blinding by those courts. The reference to eyes not pitying strongly suggests literal, physical mutilation. Deuteronomy 27:18 contains a curse against anyone who leads the blind astray. This passage strongly parallels Lev 19:14, which is set in a context of holiness. Deuteronomy 28:28–29 warns the Israelites concerning blinding consequences for dishonoring the Covenant with God. It is difficult to know how literal such blindness would be. Finally, in Deut 34:7, it is said that Moses retained excellent eyesight until the day of his death. In reality, though, God gave him even stronger eyesight than most mortals would possess when he showed Moses the promised land from afar.

THEOLOGICAL SYNTHESIS AND SUMMARY

General Remarks

Before considering the Torah's treatment of blindness with reference to cultus, causation, social justice, reversal, and meanings, one must consider a few brief remarks on blindness in general in the Torah. It is first necessary to note that, according to the Torah, God is always shown as able to see clearly. One may recall Gen 1 that frequently says how God saw creation, that it was good, and Gen 16:13 where Hagar calls God, "You, God, see me." It is the idols of the pagan nations, according to Deut 4:28, that are blind.

One must next recall how God originally designed the human race to have excellent vision (Gen 2:9). Since God designed Adam and Eve with the ability to see the goodness of the trees of Eden (Gen 2:9; 3:6) it would be understandable that blindness could be called a blemish in Lev 21:16–24.

The Cultus

With reference to the sanctuary, neither blind priests nor blind animals were regarded as their sighted counterparts in the Israelite cultus. In Israel, the reason according to Torah for restricting the blind, both priest and animal, is simply that the blind are blemished. A blind priest's or animal's ability to function is not considered. The priest was forbidden to officiate directly in the sanctuary while still encouraged to eat of the holy food. This, then, would restrict his powers, but not his opportunity to support himself and his family. The blind animal was forbidden from use as a religious offering, according to both Lev 22:16–24 and Deut 15:21, while the subsequent verses in Deut 15 allow for such an animal to be consumed as food for general purposes. Such prohibitions did not necessarily spread to ordinary religious life. As illustrated by Isaac and Jacob, a father, blinded by old age, was still understood as possessing authority to bless his children (Gen 27, 48). In addition, never does the Torah say that a blind individual could not be a Nazirite. Thus, only with reference to cultus proper was blindness a factor to bar one from participating.

Causes of Blindness

Physical Causes

The causes of blindness, according to the Torah, can be divided into two main categories, physical and spiritual. The first, and most prevalent, physical cause of blindness in the Torah is old age. Isaac and Jacob are examples. Moses, though, according to Deut 34:6, 7, did not face this difficulty of old age. This form of blindness, also, as noted in the study of Gen 48, is not necessarily complete. One may still have limited vision. As noted previously, gouging out of an eye was often a punishment for rebellion, though a master was forbidden to do such to a slave, according to Exod 21:26. One who wrongly destroyed the eye of another could face the penalty of his/her own eye being destroyed, according to Exod 21:23–25 and Lev 24:19–20. Even attempting to arrange, by false accusations, a situation where the courts might wrongly destroy another's eye would be just cause for the offender's own eye to be destroyed, according to Deut 19:20–21.

Spiritual Causes

With reference to spiritual causes of blindness, one must first note how, in Exod 4:11, God says that he makes the blind and the seeing. Previously, it was noted how human agencies such as the state or a criminal can perform blindings. Thus, God could not be the only agent involved in causing blindness. As noted previously in this study, God, in this verse, is actually taking responsibility for being the Creator of all life, and, as the Creator, he holds authority and power to enable anyone to serve him regardless of a disability. It would be theologically and morally unthinkable to say a blind person has a different creator. In addition, Exod 4:11 does not say that God makes blindness, though according to such verses as Gen 19:11, he does hold that power. God makes the blind, not necessarily their disabling conditions. Those could be a result of sin and nature.

One must then recall how blindness does not appear for the first time until several chapters after the fall of humanity in Gen 3. Thus, it is logical to assume the entrance of sin as an agent that eventually brought about the existence of disabling conditions such as blindness. Originally humankind was to see the trees that were pleasant to the sight (Gen 2:9).

God can, though, directly bring about blindness, as in Gen 19:11. In this case, the blinding was performed to protect innocent servants of God from attacks by evil people. The cases where blinding was administered as a state penalty involve strong spiritual roots also, since God is listed as the One who gave these commands (Exod 20–23; Lev 24). Those who would face blinding as a penalty would have broken God's law, disregarding their responsibility to submit to their Creator.

One must also note that the fact that God lists blinding as a penalty for one who blinds another or attempts to wrongly convince the courts to blind another suggests that such wrong acts might actually take place. These wrong acts would not be the plan of God, as God commanded that they should not happen.

Social Justice

God's Commands Concerning Treatment of the Blind

With reference to social justice, the first command that God gave concerning the treatment of the blind is in Lev 19:14. It has been noted that this command, not to cause the blind to stumble, is set in a context of charity to the disadvantaged and in the context of holiness. It has also been shown how this command refers both to intentional and unintentional methods of causing the blind to stumble. It is also noteworthy that no comment is given regarding how the individual became blind. Thus, if one was blinded as a result of enforcing talion law, such an individual would be entitled to the same respect as one born blind. One would be forbidden from further harming the one blinded by the state by causing such a one to stumble. The Hebrew Scriptures, then, consider it a matter of holiness to do whatever is possible to keep the blind, all blind, from stumbling and injuring or inconveniencing themselves. The similar command by Moses in Deut 27:18 places a curse on anyone who leads the blind astray. God would protect those who cannot protect themselves in society.

One may next consider the commands concerning the treatment of the blind priest. While a blind priest was forbidden to officiate in the sanctuary, he was expected to eat of the holy offerings. This meant that the blind priest could be fed and provide for the feeding of his family. Priests with temporary disqualifying conditions or disqualifying conditions brought on by improper conduct would not necessarily receive such positive treatment.

God's talion and talion-related laws in Exod 21:23–26 may now be considered. God's desire to prevent the unjust blinding of other people is shown in the laws that one who blinds another must face a similar penalty of blinding. If such a crime took place, the blinded individual would be given respect in the courts and a chance to obtain justice. According to Lev 24:19–20, such a crime was an assault on humanity as a whole, an act of partial murder. According to Deut 19:20–21, even attempting to cause the judicial system to blind another wrongly is punishable by the destruction of the eye or eyes of the offender.

A servant, male or female, in Israel, who was blinded by his/her master would receive freedom. Thus, a cruel master would be discouraged from seeking retribution. This would discourage masters from cruelly oppressing slaves as such masters would be hurt financially where it often mattered the most. Then, it could be deduced that if the freed servant's other eye were destroyed, he/she would be regarded as a free person and talion would be enforced.

The Actual Treatment of the Blind

One may also consider accounts of the actual treatment of the blind by other human beings. The first story one may consider here is Jacob's deception of his blind father in Gen 27. It has been noted how Jacob showed no regard for the potential immorality of his act, except that he might be punished. Jacob, however, faced a similar type of deceit at the hands of his uncle in

Gen 29. Thus, Jacob learned by experience the evil of deceiving his blind father. Joseph, in Gen 48, apparently, learned from Jacob's experience, and so worked to ensure that Jacob was blessing Ephraim and Menasseh in the proper manner. Though Jacob was not accidently offering the greater blessing to the wrong child, Joseph desired to make sure such a mistake was not unintentional, and attempted to move Jacob's hands.

The Reversal of Blindness

There is little in the Torah regarding the reversal of blindness. Nowhere, for example, is anyone healed who was born blind. With reference, though, to preventing blindness, one must recall Deut 34:7 and how it has already been discussed that righteous Moses, who spoke with God face to face, was spared the debilitation of blindness as he aged. No actual description of precisely how or why Moses was spared such difficulties is given in the text. Then, in Gen 21:19 God, the One who opens פקח the eyes, opens Hagar's eyes so she may see a well. This would be a case of healing a form of partial blindness. Even if her inability to see was merely a result of her teary eyes, such inability was remedied by God.

Meanings of Blindness

To examine the various meanings associated with blindness in the Torah, and, ultimately, in the Hebrew Scriptures as a whole, one must consider two main aspects. First, one must study the meanings attached to literal blindness and the connotations associated with the concept. Then, one can analyze how blindness was employed as a symbol for an invisible spiritual reality.

Meanings of Physical Blindness

With reference to the meanings of blindness, one may first consider the meanings of literal blindness, how it was understood in society. As with Isaac and Jacob, blindness became a symbol of the weakness of old age. With Moses, then, the lack of blindness in his old age was an evidence of his retention of strength and vigor. In addition, various texts that speak of kindness toward the disabled, such as Lev 19:14 and Deut 27:18, are placed in the context of proper treatment of widows and orphans, two other vulnerable groups in society. This further develops the understanding of blindness being associated with weakness.

One may also analyze the meanings of male blindness when compared with female infertility especially in the book of Genesis. Rebecca Raphael notes how in Genesis, while the primary disabling condition to afflict women is infertility (Sarah, Rebekah, Rachel, and the women of Abimelech's house, according to Gen 20:18), the primary disability to afflict men is blindness (Isaac, Jacob, and the men of Sodom).[109] Not only does blindness smite patriarchs and infertility matriarchs, but both conditions are also used as methods of defense by God as he offers protection in Gen 19 and 20. Then, Raphael notes how, with reference to the patriarchs and matriarchs, God must work through disabled individuals to accomplish his goals, through barren women to produce children, and through blind men to discern which child should be blessed and bless the right one.[110] It is necessary only to review briefly the story of Isaac to see how such blindness made the father potentially vulnerable to mistaking his sons. One may conclude, then, that male blindness, as with female infertility, meant, especially in Genesis, a weakness that could interfere with God's plans, but that God could and would overcome to accomplish his plans.

Blindness in the sanctuary system held the meaning of being a blemish, according to Lev 21:16–24 with reference to the priests, and Lev 22:17–25 and Deut 15:21, with reference to sacrifices. Such state of being blemished would render such a person or animal unacceptable for a number of types of service. Even Num 16:14, which may have involved an incorrect assumption that blinding would be the fate of the rebels, still demonstrates how people believed that such a penalty could befall those who defy authority.

Meanings of Spiritual Blindness

When blindness was employed as a spiritual symbol, the meaning was often associated with lack of perception. One may recall both Exod 23:8 and Deut 16:19 that say that a bribe blinds the eyes of those who should normally perceive clearly. The ability to see right from wrong would be weakened by a bribe. Then, in Gen 3, one may recall how Adam and Eve were said by the serpent to be blind to special knowledge. Their perception of such a reality might be enhanced by eating the forbidden fruit. In reality, though, humanity's ability to perceive God face to face was lost when Adam's and Eve's eyes were opened.

---

109. Raphael, *Biblical Corpora*, 54, 58, 60, 63.
110. Raphael, *Biblical Corpora*, 132.

Such loss of perception is often associated with rebellion against God. One may recall Deut 28:28–29, which lists blindness as a penalty for Israel's violating God's covenant (Deut 28:15).

V

Blindness in the Prophets

After analyzing blindness in the Torah, it is necessary to study the concept in the Prophets. This chapter employs a similar method of organization as the previous. Occurrences of blindness are listed in order, according to how they appear in the Hebrew Bible, from first to last. Passages are analyzed with reference to issues of translation and exegesis. Attention is given to issues of cultus, theodicy, social justice, healing, and symbolic usage, especially in the theological synthesis at the end of the chapter.

BLINDNESS IN THE FORMER PROPHETS

A number of blindness passages are considered in this section. First, Samson's blinding in Judg 16 is studied. Then, attention is turned to 1 and 2 Samuel. Eli's blindness in 1 Sam 3–4 is analyzed followed by the threatening blinding of the right eyes of all the men of Jabesh Gilead in 1 Sam 11:2. Then, the discussion of the blind and the lame at Jebus, in 2 Sam 5:6–8, is considered.

The focus then turns to the three blindness passages in 1 and 2 Kings. Ahijah's blindness due to old age in 1 Kgs 14:4–6 is first considered. Then, the matters of sight and blindness in the story of Elisha and the Syrian army, 2 Kgs 6:16–21, are analyzed. Finally, the blinding of Zedekiah in 2 Kgs 25 is examined.

Samson's Blindness, Judges 16:21

Translation

THE TEXT

The first instance of blindness in the Prophets is Judg 16:21, the blinding of Samson. Judges 16:21 is translated below with subsequent relevant verses summarized as needed.

> וַיֹּאחֲזוּהוּ פְלִשְׁתִּים וַיְנַקְּרוּ אֶת־עֵינָיו וַיּוֹרִידוּ אוֹתוֹ עַזָּתָה וַיַּאַסְרוּהוּ בַּנְחֻשְׁתַּיִם וַיְהִי טוֹחֵן בְּבֵית הָאֲסִירִים [הָ][אֲסוּרִים]:

> 21. So the Philistines seized him and gouged out his eyes. They brought him down to Gaza and bound him with bronze shackles; and he ground at the mill in the prison. (NRSV)

Exegesis

CONTEXT

Ancient Near Eastern context

One may recall earlier in chapter 2 of this study how the Hittites would blind prisoners of war and make them work in mills to do "women's work" to shame the captives. Other cultures would blind run-away slaves, or at least, feared that other people might. Judges 16, though, is a most striking example of a blinded captive getting revenge in the end, as he pulled down the Philistine temple after praying to be avenged for his blinding (Judg 16:28–29).

Immediate biblical context

One must consider the previous references to Samson's sight. K. Lawson Younger, Jr., notes how in Judg 14:1 and Judg 16:1 Samson is said to have "seen" Philistine women with whom he would have scandalous intimate relationships. Judges 14:7, in fact, says that he saw a Philistine woman as right in his eyes.[1] One may note how weak Samson's spiritual sight was before losing his physical sight because he was not even aware that his strength had left him (Judg 16:20). Lawson shows how the irony is further developed in the Samson narrative. Samson was made to grind in the mill, doing the

---

1. Younger, *Judges and Ruth*, 321.

work of women (Exod 11:5). Samson, then, without eyes, was made to do the work of those who once seemed good in his eyes.[2]

Intertextual connection

Since Samson was a Nazirite (Judg 13:5), one must also consider the laws of the Nazirite, according to Num 6:1–11 and how they compare to the laws of the priests and high priest. Jacob Milgrom notes a number of significant parallels. First, both the priest and the Nazirite were required to observe certain rules concerning the use of wine. While for the priests, wine was forbidden only within the sacred precincts (Lev 10:9), the Nazirite was never to consume anything from the grape, even the seeds (Num 6:4). Regarding corpse contamination, the Nazirite may have been more similar to the high priest. The Nazirite was forbidden to have physical contact with the dead, even for a member of the immediate family (Num 6:6). While the high priest was not permitted to be contaminated even for a member of his immediate family (Lev 21:11), a regular priest could, but only for the immediate family (Lev 21:1–3). The head was also important to both high priest and Nazirite as the Nazirite was not permitted to shave his/her head (Num 6:5), and the high priest was anointed on the head (Exod 29:7).[3]

Clear similarities even exist between the inscription on the miter of the high priest (holiness to the Lord, קֹדֶשׁ לַיהוָה, Exod 28:36) and the remark that the Nazirite should be "holy to the LORD," קָדֹשׁ הוּא לַיהוָה (Num 6:7). The root, קדשׁ, holy, and the phrase, לַיהוָה, to the LORD, appear in the same order in both expressions. In addition, as Num 6 lists no command forbidding a blind individual from being a Nazirite, Lev 21:16–24 lists no command removing a blind man from the priesthood (as noted before, the blind priest was barred only from officiating). Clearly, then, a Nazirite such as Samson held an extreme position of holiness in ancient Israel, similar in some ways to the regular priest and in some ways to the high priest.

This information aids one's understanding of the Samson narrative in a number of ways. The severity of the desecration that Samson allowed to fall upon him when his head was shaven is now most clear. Not only did he neglect his vows, but he completely disregarded the great holiness he was to bear. In addition, while Num 6 does not say that one who was blind was forbidden to be a Nazirite, Samson, as one who was to be a holy man, surely would have felt a certain sense of spiritual shame because of the blemish of his blindness. God, though, showed great mercy in returning his strength.

2. Younger, *Judges and Ruth*, 321.
3. Milgrom, *Numbers*, 316.

General Analysis

One must first note a possible use of wordplay in this passage. Tammi J. Schneider insightfully comments how the name Samson can be interpreted to mean "little sun" from שֶׁמֶשׁ, which means "sun." Thus, Samson, the little sun, lost his eyes, and so, his brightness.[4] Daniel I. Block rightly describes the extent of this loss of brightness by noting that Samson showed significant loss of independence as he needed a young boy to lead him to the pillars.[5]

Next, physical sight was clearly of extreme importance to Samson. In Judg 16:28 he pleads that God give him strength to obtain revenge on the Philistines for his two eyes. In v. 30, when he collapses the temple, he exclaims, "Let me die with the Philistines." He is choosing to die rather than to continue living blinded where he would be treated as a prisoner. He saw death, then, as a superior option when compared with his situation of blindness.[6]

In addition, it must be noted that God does not reject Samson after his blinding. Even though Samson dishonored his Nazirite vows in revealing his secret when he knew such revealing would cause his hair to be cut, God enables the judge to perform his mightiest act in his weakened condition. Samson's disability did not keep him from service to God and availability to be a channel of his power. God was able and willing to provide opportunities and means for work for the judge whatever his physical condition.

Samson's status as a Nazirite was also not affected after he lost his vision. In v. 22, immediately after the text says Samson's eyes were gouged out, it is said that Samson's hair (so important to a Nazirite) began to grow again. With this growing of the hair came the renewed strength, shown later in the chapter. Thus, Samson's position as a Nazirite was confirmed in God's providing new strength to Samson as his hair grew again.

Then, in Judg 16:28, Samson prays to God, after losing his eyesight, as he seeks strength to perform his final military feat. It is only then that he

---

4. Schneider, *Judges*, 219.
5. Block, *Judges, Ruth*, 466.
6. In this verse, Samson could either be praying for revenge for one of his two eyes (RSV), or for one revenge for his two eyes (NRSV). This confusion is most likely because of the enigmatic construction: נקם־אחת. The maqef joining these two words draws one to see them as one unit, "one revenge." Nonetheless, נקם is in a construct form, and masculine, while אחת is feminine, matching gender, then, with feminine עין, "eyes," and not with נקם. This reasoning would suggest a translation, "revenge of one of two of my eyes." Felix Just rightly notes, though, how this difficulty in translating v. 28 is irrelevant to this discussion. Since in either case Samson notes having lost both his eyes, it makes little difference how many eyes Samson was seeking revenge concerning. The end result was still one act destroying the entire temple in revenge by one blinded in both eyes. Just, "From Tobit to Bartimaeus, From Qumran to Siloam," 80.

collapses the temple of Dagon, killing more when he died than when he was alive (Judg 16:30). Apparently his loss of physical sight caused him to see more clearly spiritually. He realized that it was not simply his hair that gave him his strength, but his reliance on God.

Nonetheless, Block rightly notes that Samson, even in his final prayer, shows limited spiritual growth. He asks to get revenge on the Philistines because of his two eyes, which, in reality, generally served the purpose of getting him in trouble. Nothing is mentioned about God's name being glorified or anyone else being delivered. Samson uses first-person-singular language five times during his prayer.[7] Nonetheless, Samson apparently showed growth enough in spiritual vision after losing his physical vision for God to use him for this feat. His spiritual vision, at least, improved enough for him to see God, reached by prayer, as the source of his strength.

Eli's Blindness, 2 Samuel 3:2; 4:15

Translation

THE TEXT

In 1 Sam 3–4, Eli's failing eyesight holds a prominent position. Two texts bear notable importance in this study. First Samuel 3:2 and 1 Sam 4:15 are translated below.

וַיְהִי בַּיּוֹם הַהוּא וְעֵלִי שֹׁכֵב בִּמְקֹמוֹ (וְעֵינוֹ) [וְעֵינָיו] הֵחֵלּוּ כֵהוֹת לֹא יוּכַל לִרְאוֹת׃

3:2. At that time Eli, whose eyesight had begun to grow dim so that he could not see, was lying down in his room. (NRSV)

וְעֵלִי בֶּן־תִּשְׁעִים וּשְׁמֹנֶה שָׁנָה וְעֵינָיו קָמָה וְלֹא יָכוֹל לִרְאוֹת׃

4:15. Now Eli was ninety-eight years old and his eyes were set, so that he could not see. (NRSV)

Notes

The sentence order of 1 Sam 3:2 is different in the Hebrew. The clause concerning Eli's eyes beginning to grow dim occurs immediately after a complete clause about Eli's lying down in his place. The method used in the

---

7. Block, *Judges, Ruth*, 468.

Hebrew Bible further sets off the note about his blindness as a parenthetical statement interrupting the story.

Exegesis

LITERARY ANALYSIS

Both these discussions of Eli's failing eyesight are followed by information regarding judgment placed upon him. In 1 Sam 3, this judgment comes in the form of an oracle given through the young boy, Samuel, who predicts in Eli's hearing that judgment would come upon the priest's house because of wickedness. In 1 Sam 4:16–17, this judgment is described to Eli again by speech, telling that his sons had been killed and the Ark of the Covenant captured. One may assume a literary pattern of parallelism in these two chapters.

CONTEXT

The emphasis on Eli's failing physical vision is noteworthy in light of the context concerning spiritual well-being in 1 Sam 2:32–33. There, in another oracle against Eli's house, it is predicted that there would no more be any elderly men after the destruction, for example. Then, in v. 33, it is said that whoever is not cut off would consume Eli's eyes and bring him grief. The idiom in Hebrew, עינים כלה, is commonly used in the Psalms to refer to great distress. In Ps 119:82, for example, the psalmists eyes are said to be consumed as he asks when God would comfort him. Then, in v. 123 he follows a verse pleading for relief from oppression with the statement that his eyes have been consumed for God's salvation. In both these verses, the consuming of the eye appears to refer to a form of great distress. Eli, then, was told he would receive great distress, and even those left alive would cause him pain. It is noteworthy, though, that the idiom used refers to the eyes. Then, in 1 Sam 3–4, repeated references are made to the priests' failing eyesight. One may then assume that the references to Eli's weakening eyesight might hold a deeper meaning than simply that of reporting events as they happen. Eli's failing vision became a symbol of the grief he would undergo, a physical expression of an inner reality of mental eyes being consumed in great distress as God predicted.

General Analysis

Eli is said to have been the priest of the Lord (1 Sam 1:9), yet he is also said to have defective eyes (1 Sam 3:2; 4:15). One can recall how Lev 21:16–24 says that a blind priest was barred from approaching the Lord. Hector Avalos notes, then, that Eli's functioning as a priest was contrary to the Levitical commands. The shrine at Shiloh must have functioned in a manner different from a shrine operating in accordance with Lev 21:16–24.[8]

It must be noted, though, that the word עִוֵּר, which occurs in Lev 21 for "blind" does not occur in 1 Sam 3 or 4 to describe Eli. Eli's eyes were said to have begun to grow dim, כהה, according to 1 Sam 3:2, and to be set, קום, according to 1 Sam 4:15. As noted in chapter 3, these terms do not appear to refer to the profound level of vision loss suffered by an עִוֵּר. Thus, based on careful linguistic study, Eli is not to be understood as being in one of the groups barred from ministering before the Lord.

One must next study the nature and meaning of Eli's blindness. It must be noted that Eli's failing vision is mentioned twice in 1 Samuel. A close look at the two passages, though, sheds light on the nature of his failing eyesight. David Tsunuria rightly observes that while both verses say that Eli was unable to see, 1 Sam 3:2 uses an imperfect form of יכל, "he was able," showing incomplete action, while 1 Sam 4:15 uses a perfect form, showing completed action.[9] This already suggests a progression in the weakening of Eli's eyesight from an incomplete stage to a more complete stage. In addition, in 1 Sam 3:2 it is said that his eyes were beginning to fail him. Then, in 1 Sam 4:15, it is simply said that his eyes were dim. This reinforces the notion that in 1 Sam 3, Eli's vision had only begun to fail, and then, in 1 Sam 4, it had more completely left him. However weak his eyesight was, he still plays a significant role in this story. As the situation for Israel grows more and more grim, so does the situation of Eli's eyesight. One must wonder, then, if Israel possessed weakening spiritual eyesight as they considered sending the Ark of the Covenant into battle.

This loss of vision for Eli, though, was never described as complete for him. In 1 Sam 4:13 it refers to Eli's watching. Bruce C. Birch logically reasons that while Eli may have had the ability to vaguely recognize images, his eyesight was not strong enough for him to recognize the torn clothing of the messenger or any other useful details without needing to be told.[10] In addition, Birch also rightly notes that while Eli's physical vision was weak,

---

8. Avalos, *Illness and Health Care in the Ancient Near East*, 334, 335.
9. Tsumura, *The First Book of Samuel*, 175.
10. Birch, "The First and Second Books of Samuel," 1002.

he still maintained the discernment to know that it was the Lord repeatedly calling Samuel in 1 Sam 3.[11]

Eyes to Be Removed at Jabesh-Giliad, 1 Samuel 11:2

Translation

THE TEXT

The next occurrence of blindness in the Prophets is found in 1 Sam 11:2. The text appears below.

וַיֹּאמֶר אֲלֵיהֶם נָחָשׁ הָעַמּוֹנִי בְּזֹאת אֶכְרֹת לָכֶם בִּנְקוֹר לָכֶם כָּל־עֵין יָמִין
וְשַׂמְתִּיהָ חֶרְפָּה עַל־כָּל־יִשְׂרָאֵל׃

> 2. But Nahash the Ammonite said to them, "On this condition I will make a treaty with you, namely that I gouge out everyone's right eye, and thus put disgrace upon all Israel." (NRSV)

Exegesis

Gouging out the right eye would naturally weaken the people, making it more difficult for them to resist him. Arnold observes that one who is lacking the right eye would find it more difficult to aim when using a bow and arrow.[12] Robert D. Bergen also correctly notes that the loss of an eye would also hinder depth perception and range of vision.[13]

Such an act would also be greatly humiliating and painful to them. Henry Preserved Smith observes that while such an act would hinder the people's fighting ability, it would, more importantly, bring a reproach on Israel. Since the text itself does not discuss how the removal of an eye would hinder fighting ability, but does mention how it would bring reproach, one must understand the concept of reproach as the central reason for this act.[14] Tsunuria rightly notes that this word for "reproach," חֶרְפָּה, is used for other most serious disgraces such as the rape of Tamar in 2 Sam 13:13.[15] Weakening the soldiers would possibly be an aspect of this reproach.

---

11. Birch, "The First and Second Books of Samuel," 992.
12. Arnold, *1 & 2 Samuel*, 177.
13. Bergen, *1, 2 Samuel*, 135.
14. Henry Preserved Smith, *A Critical and Exegetical Commentary on the Books of Samuel*, 77.
15. Tsumura, *The First Book of Samuel*, 305.

When the men of Jabesh-Gilead cry to the rest of Israel for help, King Saul musters the people together, commanding them to fight or be like oxen that he cuts asunder (1 Sam 11:6, 7). The men of Jabesh-Giliad remember the successful brave rescue for many years. In fact, when King Saul dies, and the Philistines proudly display his body in dishonor, the men of Jabesh-Giliad daringly enter Philistine territory and retrieve his body for proper burial. This shows how grateful these men were for the deliverance that Saul gave them. The threat of having everyone in the entire town blinded in one eye was so grave that rescue from this demanded nothing less than a return retrieval of the dead body of the one who saved them. This shows plainly the intensity of the threat of losing an eye.

The Blind and the Lame in the House, 2 Samuel 5:6–8

Translation

THE TEXT

The text of 2 Sam 5:6–8 appears below.

וַיֵּלֶךְ הַמֶּלֶךְ וַאֲנָשָׁיו יְרוּשָׁלַם אֶל־הַיְבֻסִי יוֹשֵׁב הָאָרֶץ וַיֹּאמֶר לְדָוִד לֵאמֹר
לֹא־תָבוֹא הֵנָּה כִּי אִם־הֱסִירְךָ הַעִוְרִים וְהַפִּסְחִים לֵאמֹר לֹא־יָבוֹא דָוִד
הֵנָּה׃
וַיִּלְכֹּד דָּוִד אֵת מְצֻדַת צִיּוֹן הִיא עִיר דָּוִד׃
וַיֹּאמֶר דָּוִד בַּיּוֹם הַהוּא כָּל־מַכֵּה יְבֻסִי וְיִגַּע בַּצִּנּוֹר וְאֶת־הַפִּסְחִים וְאֶת־
הַעִוְרִים שָׂנְאוּ [שְׂנֻאֵי] נֶפֶשׁ דָּוִד עַל־כֵּן יֹאמְרוּ עִוֵּר וּפִסֵּחַ לֹא יָבוֹא
אֶל־הַבָּיִת׃

6. The king and his men marched to Jerusalem against the Jebusites, the inhabitants of the land, who said to David, "You will not come in here, even the blind and the lame will turn you back"—thinking, "David cannot come in here."
7. Nevertheless David took the stronghold of Zion, which is now the city of David.
8. David had said on that day, "Whoever would strike down the Jebusites, let him get up the water shaft to attack the lame and the blind, those whom David hates." Therefore it is said, "The blind and the lame shall not come into the house." (NRSV)[16]

---

16. It should be noted that in the parallel passage in 1 Chr 11:4–7, there is no discussion concerning the matter of the blind and the lame.

Exegesis

Literary Analysis

James E. Smith rightly notes that the text of 2 Sam 5:6 can be seen as fitting in the genre of pre-battle taunting. Another example of this is 2 Kgs 18:19–24 when Assyria taunts Hezekiah's forces.[17] This would place the statements less in the realm of reality and more in the realm of talk designed to lower morale.

Context

A possible notable parallel to this passage is the Hittite First Soldier's Oath, discussed in chapter 2. One may recall how disabled people, including one who is blind, are paraded before a soldier. The soldier is told that violating his oath of service would bring upon him the curse of those disabilities. Yigael Yadin notes that the Jebusites may have had the idea of a curse in mind. Those who fight against the city would become as the lame and the blind in the city.[18]

The main weakness of this theory is the lack of substantial textual parallels in 2 Sam 5:6–8 besides the mentioning of the blind. Nothing is said in 2 Sam 5:6–8 of a curse, a treaty, or an oath. The Jebusites do not speak of the blind and the lame in terms of threatening that one could become like them. The biblical passage of Lev 19:14 and Deut 27:18 may bear more relevance. David's soldiers might have become afraid to attack those the Torah commanded should be protected.

General Analysis

First, it can be understood, as noted previously, how mentioning blindness and lameness together is most likely a merism. Jebusites with other disabilities might have been sent out against David also. Second, these disabilities appear to be named as symbols of David's weakness. Keil and Delitzsch note that the Jebusite fortress was so naturally strong that David could not conquer it. Even the blind and the lame could resist him.[19] The Jebusites, previously, had been difficult to conquer as Joshua's forces were unable to drive them out, according to Josh 15:63. The Jebusites, aware of their strength,

---

17. James E. Smith, *1 & 2 Samuel*, 374.
18. Yadin, *The Art of Warfare in Biblical Lands*, 269.
19. Keil, and Delitzsch, *Biblical Commentary on the Books of Samuel*, 315.

may have been boasting to David that anyone, however weak, could defend against David. David's hatred of such people stems more from the remarks of Jebus than from prejudice.

In addition, Ronald F. Youngblood rightly analyzes the situation by noting that in 2 Sam 9:5–13, David invites lame Mephibosheth to eat at the royal table. David, then, clearly did not hate all people with disabilities. He may have used the references to the lame and the blind to refer to the Jebusites as a whole. The Jebusites would send out the lame and blind to fight David, and so David, then, would destroy Jebusites of all ability status, which were seen in his eyes as weak as the lame and the blind.[20]

One must, then, examine the meaning of "the house." As Birch insightfully notes, the building of the temple would not even be proposed until 2 Sam 7, and the blind and the lame were already barred from service near the Presence of God (Lev 21:16–24). There is also no direct evidence anywhere else that the lame and blind were excluded from the palace.[21] In addition, since Jebus had not yet been conquered in 2 Sam 5:6 and named as Jerusalem, the royal palace would not have been built for David either. Thus, both options for the meaning of "house" would be future to David's comments, and without any substantial textual evidence for either, both options become speculative. Thus, Bergen rightly notes that, because of this textual ambiguity, one could understand either the palace or the temple to be the object referred to as the house.[22] If the reference to the blind and the lame refers to the Jebusites, however, then whichever house is in mind would be forbidden to any Jebusite. In many ways, though, such a debate is immaterial. The message of the passage is that the blind and the lame would be prevented from certain benefits because they became a symbol of weakness. Blindness, as one of these representative disabilities, would become an especially important symbol for such.

---

20. Youngblood, "1, 2 Samuel," 856; Birch, "The First and Second Books of Samuel," 1236.

21. Birch, "The First and Second Books of Samuel," 1236.

22. Bergen, *1, 2 Samuel*, 321. See also Baldwin, *1 and 2 Samuel*, 198.

The Blind Seer, 1 Kings 14:4–6

Translation

The text

Three major passages discuss blindness in the books of Kings. The first passage is 1 Kgs 14:4–6, translated below.

וַתַּעַשׂ כֵּן אֵשֶׁת יָרָבְעָם וַתָּקָם וַתֵּלֶךְ שִׁלֹה וַתָּבֹא בֵּית אֲחִיָּה וַאֲחִיָּהוּ לֹא־יָכֹל לִרְאוֹת כִּי קָמוּ עֵינָיו מִשֵּׂיבוֹ:
וַיהוָה אָמַר אֶל־אֲחִיָּהוּ הִנֵּה אֵשֶׁת יָרָבְעָם בָּאָה לִדְרֹשׁ דָּבָר מֵעִמְּךָ אֶל־בְּנָהּ כִּי־חֹלֶה הוּא כָּזֹה וְכָזֶה תְּדַבֵּר אֵלֶיהָ וִיהִי כְבֹאָהּ וְהִיא מִתְנַכֵּרָה:
וַיְהִי כִשְׁמֹעַ אֲחִיָּהוּ אֶת־קוֹל רַגְלֶיהָ בָּאָה בַפֶּתַח וַיֹּאמֶר בֹּאִי אֵשֶׁת יָרָבְעָם לָמָּה זֶּה אַתְּ מִתְנַכֵּרָה וְאָנֹכִי שָׁלוּחַ אֵלַיִךְ קָשָׁה:

> 4. Jeroboam's wife did so; she set out and went to Shiloh, and came to the house of Ahijah. Now Ahijah could not see, for his eyes were dim because of his age.
> 5. But the LORD said to Ahijah, "The wife of Jeroboam is coming to inquire of you concerning her son; for he is sick. Thus and thus you shall say to her." When she came, she pretended to be another woman.
> 6. But when Ahijah heard the sound of her feet, as she came in at the door, he said, "Come in, wife of Jeroboam; why do you pretend to be another? For I am charged with heavy tidings for you." (NRSV)

Exegesis

Literary analysis

First, 1 Kgs 14:4 contains a wordplay concerning קום. The king's wife is said to have risen קום to go to the prophet. Then the same verse says the prophet's eyes were dim, or set, קום, so that he could not see. While her standing is an aspect of her strength, the prophet's failing eyesight is an aspect of his weakness. Nonetheless, in the end, the prophet is strengthened by God with insight about the woman, and the woman is weakened as she must face, powerlessly, the death of her child. In addition, while the prophet's setting of his eyes is involved with his lack of physical sight, the woman's rising to travel in deceit is associated with her lack of spiritual sight regarding God's power to control prophecy and the abilities of prophets.

Context

A number of similarities exist between this story and the deceiving of Isaac by Jacob in Gen 27. In both stories, someone who is blind due to age is visited by another who pretends not to be himself/herself. In 1 Kgs 14, though, the prophet knows of the deception and pronounces judgment on the lady's child. One does not know if the child would have been spared had Jeroboam's wife been honest about her identity. One may, though, recall Jacob's remarks to Rebekah about there being a curse on him and not a blessing should he be caught deceiving his father. A portion of the judgments pronounced against Jeroboam's wife might have been part of such a curse on a deceiver.

It must also be noted that the same word קום is used for the prophet's blindness in 1 Kgs 14 as was used for Eli's blindness in 1 Sam 4:15. Both these people's eyes were "set" due to old age. One may recall how with Eli it can be assumed that his vision was severely limited, not completely gone. Thus, Wiseman is correct to note that it may be more appropriate to understand Ahijah's eyesight as failing, not completely gone.[23]

General analysis

A number of insights regarding blindness in the Hebrew Scriptures can be gleaned from studying this passage. First, Paul R. House rightly notes that while the prophet is blind, God does not stop using him in service. God even helps accommodate for the prophet's blindness by telling him that Jeroboam's wife would come in disguise. Thus, God gave the prophet spiritual vision to compensate for his lack of physical vision.[24] The fact that Jeroboam's wife visited the prophet as requested by her husband shows that neither the king nor his wife thought the prophet's prophetic gift weakened because of his lack of sight.

One may also consider the nature of spiritual vision given to Ahijah. John M. Hull, a blind university professor, insightfully notes how, generally, a blind person would not be able to recognize a visitor by the sound of his/her footsteps. One may be able to recognize the sound of a family member's footsteps, since, among family members, at least, there are fewer possibilities from which to choose. If a visitor comes unexpectedly, though, it would be unlikely that his/her footsteps would be recognized among the myriad

---

23. Wiseman, *1 and 2 Kings*, 149.
24. House, *1, 2 Kings*, 191.

other footstep sounds of the other people who might visit.[25] Thus, the sound of the footsteps told the prophet only that *someone* was approaching, not *who*. God gave the prophet the insight concerning who was coming.

One might wonder, though, how much useful advice Jeroboam's wife would expect to receive from a prophet whom she assumed would not know who she was. It may be understood, then, that she did not assume such oracles as fixed and determined for one individual. She may have thought she could go to a prophet and, as long as she could manipulate the situation so he would give a favorable oracle, a favorable outcome would take place. The story of Balaam in Num 23–24, especially Num 23:10–12, describes a similar situation when a king desired a prophet to give a specific type of oracle. Whatever oracle the prophet uttered, the king would assume must come to pass. Balaam, though, could only utter the oracles God placed in his mouth. He could not choose whatever blessing or curse seemed appropriate. As with Balaam, so it was with Ahijah. Only the message God commanded must be uttered. God, then, is not to be understood as a force of magic that one can control. Thus, Ahijah must know who is speaking to him in order to give the oracle determined for that individual. In order for her to receive the right message, then, God needed to overcome both the prophet's disability and the woman's disguise, and he did.

Blinding the Syrians, 2 Kings 6:16–20

Translation

THE TEXT

The next passage to be considered is 2 Kgs 6:17–20. The passage appears below:

וַיִּתְפַּלֵּל אֱלִישָׁע וַיֹּאמַר יְהוָה פְּקַח־נָא אֶת־עֵינָיו וְיִרְאֶה וַיִּפְקַח יְהוָה אֶת־
עֵינֵי הַנַּעַר וַיַּרְא וְהִנֵּה הָהָר מָלֵא סוּסִים וְרֶכֶב אֵשׁ סְבִיבֹת אֱלִישָׁע:
וַיֵּרְדוּ אֵלָיו וַיִּתְפַּלֵּל אֱלִישָׁע אֶל־יְהוָה וַיֹּאמַר הַךְ־נָא אֶת־הַגּוֹי־הַזֶּה
בַּסַּנְוֵרִים וַיַּכֵּם בַּסַּנְוֵרִים כִּדְבַר אֱלִישָׁע:
וַיֹּאמֶר אֲלֵהֶם אֱלִישָׁע לֹא זֶה הַדֶּרֶךְ וְלֹא זֹה הָעִיר לְכוּ אַחֲרַי וְאוֹלִיכָה
אֶתְכֶם אֶל־הָאִישׁ אֲשֶׁר תְּבַקֵּשׁוּן וַיֹּלֶךְ אוֹתָם שֹׁמְרוֹנָה:
וַיְהִי כְּבֹאָם שֹׁמְרוֹן וַיֹּאמֶר אֱלִישָׁע יְהוָה פְּקַח אֶת־עֵינֵי־אֵלֶּה וְיִרְאוּ וַיִּפְקַח
יְהוָה אֶת־עֵינֵיהֶם וַיִּרְאוּ וְהִנֵּה בְּתוֹךְ שֹׁמְרוֹן:

---

25. Hull, *In the Beginning There Was Darkness*, 22.

17. Then Elisha prayed: "O LORD, please open his eyes that he may see." So the LORD opened the eyes of the servant, and he saw; the mountain was full of horses and chariots of fire all around Elisha.
18. When the Arameans came down against him, Elisha prayed to the LORD, and said, "Strike this people, please, with blindness." So he struck them with blindness as Elisha had asked.
19. Elisha said to them, "This is not the way, and this is not the city; follow me, and I will bring you to the man whom you seek." And he led them to Samaria.
20. As soon as they entered Samaria, Elisha said, "O LORD, open the eyes of these men so that they may see." The LORD opened their eyes, and they saw that they were inside Samaria. (NRSV)

Exegesis

Literary Analysis

One may observe the use of repetition in vv. 17, 20. In both verses, Elisha asks the Lord, by name, to open another party's eyes that that other party may see. The same words for "LORD, open, eyes," and "see," appear in those clauses. Then, in both verses, it is said that the Lord, by name, opened this other party's eyes, and that other party saw, with the same words for "LORD, open, eyes," and "saw." The next clause in both cases also begins with the same word for "behold." This provides literary flow to the passage and emphasizes how similar the two eye-openings were.

Context

A number of parallels exist between 2 Kgs 6:17–22 and Gen 19:11, the only other place in the Bible where this word for blindness, סַנְוֵרִים, occurs. First, both stories are set at night. In both stories, also, blindness is divinely placed on a crowd of enemies of people under God's protection. In Gen 19, the men of Sodom are blinded as they attempted to break into Lot's house to sexually assault the angelic visitors. In 2 Kgs 6, the enemy army of Syria is blinded as they attempt to harm Elisha and his servant. While different words are used in the Hebrew, in both stories, the enemy encompasses the lodging place of God's protected people (Gen 19:4; 2 Kgs 6:14). In both stories this blinding prevents the enemies from harming those under God's protection.

In addition, Num 22:31 says that Balaam's eyes are said to be opened so that he could see the angel with a drawn sword. In Num 22:31 and 2 Kgs 6:16–20, eyes are miraculously opened that one may see angelic beings. It must be noted, though, that Num 22:31 employs גלה (uncover) for open, while 2 Kgs 6 employs פקח, the usual word for opening the eyes of the blind. Nonetheless, Elisha's servant, like Balaam, received miraculous vision to behold a spiritual reality.

General Analysis

As with the men of Sodom, the blindness on the Syrians may also have involved a confused and dazed state of mental awareness. Iain W. Provan notes that the Syrians might simply have become disoriented enough to need one to lead them, but not so blind as to have no visual awareness of obstacles along the path.[26] It could be possible, though, that the blindness was more complete and Elisha had to lead them slowly in a line, single-file, so everyone in the army would be touching someone in order to keep the whole group together. Either way, the blinding resulted in the army's inability to ascertain the location of Elisha.

The elegant references to awareness and blindness in 2 Kgs 6:17–20 also bear relevance to this study. First, it must be noted that Elisha was aware of both the seen and the unseen throughout the story. He has knowledge of God's fiery army that his servant cannot see. Elisha also was aware of the secret plans of the enemy, which only the Syrians should have known. Elisha was aware of the path to Samaria while the Syrian army was blindly led there. Elisha also maintained the power to control, through prayer, the vision of those around him. Not only does Elisha have the eyes of his servant opened to see the fiery army, but he has the eyes of the Syrians both blinded and opened for the trip to Samaria. In fact, the same words for "open" and "eyes" occur with reference to both the servant and the Syrians. Clearly, then, God is to be understood as having given Elisha deep vision into reality along with power over others' vision in numerous aspects of reality, vision and power, which others less attached to God did not have. The only explanation in the text for why Elisha had such vision and power is that he prayed, making his requests for help known to God (2 Kgs 6:17, 20), and that he was attentive to God's voice (2 Kgs 6:8–9).

One may next consider Elisha's request to not slay the enemy army. While Elisha said that such action should be taken as the Syrians were to be compared with captives (v. 22), Elisha may also have been making the

26. Provan, *1 and 2 Kings*, 198.

strongest effort possible to observe the principle of Deut 27:18. One may recall how this verse says that one is cursed if he/she causes the blind to wander out of the path. Since the blinded Syrians were led against their knowledge, out of their intended path, into a trap in the capital city, it might have seemed necessary to treat them as kindly as possible once they were there and not take advantage of the blindness of the prisoners.

The Blinding of Zedekiah According to Kings, 2 Kings 25:7

Translation

THE TEXT

The final instance of blindness in the books of Kings is the blinding of Zedekiah in 2 Kgs 25:7. The text appears translated below:

וְאֶת־בְּנֵי צִדְקִיָּהוּ שָׁחֲטוּ לְעֵינָיו וְאֶת־עֵינֵי צִדְקִיָּהוּ עִוֵּר וַיַּאַסְרֵהוּ בַנְחֻשְׁתַּיִם וַיְבִאֵהוּ בָבֶל׃

> 7. They slaughtered the sons of Zedekiah before his eyes, then put out the eyes of Zedekiah; they bound him in fetters and took him to Babylon. (NRSV)[27]

NOTES

The Hebrew word order of this verse is noteworthy. Literally it is read, "And the sons of Zedekiah they slaughtered before his eyes, and the eyes of Zedekiah, they blinded . . . ." In both these first two clauses, the direct object is first followed by the verb. This emphasizes those first words, the sons of Zedekiah and the eyes of Zedekiah.

Exegesis

LITERARY ANALYSIS

Robert L. Cohn rightly notes the emphasis by repetition placed on the word עַיִן, "eye." This word occurs twice in this verse showing the importance

---

27. It should be noted here that in the parallel passage in 2 Chr 36:11–21, the blinding of Zedekiah is not mentioned.

placed on it.[28] One may develop this idea further, observing how the two references to "eyes" are in consecutive words. This may emphasize the idea that the eyes of Zedekiah that see the slaying of his sons are removed.

Context

Immediate biblical context

Analysis of 2 Kgs 24:19, to see how the word עַיִן is employed in wordplay, is used most elegantly in this passage. Second Kings 24:19 says that Zedekiah did evil in the Lord's eyes. Then, in 2 Kgs 25:7, Zedekiah's eyes, which would not see as God's did, would watch his sons being slain. Finally, those eyes would be removed. Such was the fate of the last king of Judah before the complete destruction of Jerusalem and the temple at the hands of Babylon.

Intertextual connections

A number of significant parallels exist between 2 Kgs 25 and Judg 16. First, the word עַיִן occurs in both Judg 16:21 and 2 Kgs 25:7. In addition, both Samson and Zedekiah were bound in bronze fetters and led away to captivity. In addition, both Samson and Zedekiah could be said to be resisting dominating foreign powers. For Samson, he was frequently fighting the Philistines (Judg 14–16). For Zedekiah, the action that prompted the siege, capture, and blinding, according to 2 Kgs 24:20, was the rebellion of Zedekiah against the king of Babylon who had previously made him a vassal. Zedekiah, then, received a similar punishment as Samson for an offense similar to Samson's.

Both Samson and Zedekiah were also in defiance against God. Samson was a Nazirite, forbidden to have his hair cut, but he knowingly placed himself in a situation where it would be cut (Judg 16:17–20). His strength subsequently left him. Second Kings 24:19 plainly says that Zedekiah did evil in the sight of the Lord. In addition, 2 Chr 36:13 says that Zedekiah violated an oath he made before God when he rebelled against the king of Babylon. Thus, both Zedekiah and Samson were blinded for the sin of rebelling against God and the crime of rebellion against a dominating power. This confirms the notion that blinding was seen as a punishment for rebellion.

---

28. Cohn, *1 Kings*, 168.

General Analysis

A number of observations may be made regarding this blinding, especially in the context of the blinding of Samson and other war captives discussed in that section of this study. It must first be noted that נקר is not used with reference to the blinding of Zedekiah as it is with the blinding of Samson. In 2 Kgs 25:7, the word עור is used. Literally, then, the text says that they "blinded" his eyes. This blinding occurred immediately after they killed the king's sons before his eyes. Thus, the last thing the king saw was the slaying of his sons. Zedekiah, who had rebelled against God and showed no spiritual vision, would lose his physical vision and maintain a most displeasing last image in his mind till the day he died.

Summary

Blindness is discussed a number of times in the Former Prophets. First, Samson's blinding is shown to take place as a result of his flagrant disregard of his vows to be a holy Nazirite. God, nonetheless, answers his prayers and strengthens the blind judge to perform one last great feat, the greatest of all his feats.

In the books of Samuel, blindness is discussed in three passages. First, in 1 Sam 3–4, Eli's progressively decreasing sight is followed in the text. As his vision fades, so does that of the people. Then, in 1 Sam 11:2, Nahash threatens to gouge out the right eye of the men of Jabesh Gilead. King Saul, though, leads a battle against Nahash, delivering the men of Jabesh Gilead, a deliverance those men remembered when Saul died. Finally, in 2 Sam 5:6–8, the Jebusites mock David by suggesting that even the blind and the lame could withstand them. When David commands that the blind and lame be slain in Jebus, he may have actually been referring to all the inhabitants of the city, labeling them all as blind and lame.

There are three blindness passages in the books of Kings. First, in 1 Kgs 14:4–7, blind Ahijah, under inspiration, correctly identifies Jeroboam's disguised wife so he could utter a message against her. Where such similar deception confused Isaac, this prophet was forewarned by God. Then, the concept of blindness and the opening of eyes is related a number of times in 2 Kgs 6:17–20. The prophet Elisha is said to have prayed and, according to such prayers, God would open eyes or bring about blindness. Finally, 2 Kgs 25:7 shows how the rebellious Zedekiah, who did evil in the eyes of the Lord, had his own eyes removed by the Babylonians. The last thing the king saw was the death of his sons at the hands of those Babylonians.

BLINDNESS IN ISAIAH

The next section of this study concerns the numerous blindness passages in Isaiah. First, the unusual command for Isaiah to shut the eyes of the people in Isa 6:9–10 is considered. Then, Isa 29:9–10, 18 is studied with reference to those who see being blind, and those who are blind, seeing. Then, one finds a discussion of the righteous king in Isa 32:3, 4 who would not dim the people's eyes. Next, Isa 35:5–6 is studied with reference to a great day when the eyes of the blind would be opened. Isaiah 42:7 is next analyzed with reference to how God's servant would open blind eyes and release people from prison. Next, Isa 42:16–20 is studied with reference to God's leading the blind along a new path and God's servant, himself, being blind. Isaiah 43:8 is next considered with reference to those who are blind but who have eyes. Then, Isa 44:9–18 is analyzed with reference to the blinding effects that idols have on those who build them. The blind and mute leaders in Isa 56:10 are considered next. Finally, the prophet's reference to his people's groping as the blind along a wall in Isa 59:10 is studied.

The Shutting of the People's Eyes, Isaiah 6:9–10

Translation

THE TEXT

The first reference to blindness in Isaiah is Isa 6:9, 10. This passage is translated below:

וַיֹּאמֶר לֵךְ וְאָמַרְתָּ לָעָם הַזֶּה שִׁמְעוּ שָׁמוֹעַ וְאַל־תָּבִינוּ וּרְאוּ רָאוֹ וְאַל־תֵּדָעוּ׃
הַשְׁמֵן לֵב־הָעָם הַזֶּה וְאָזְנָיו הַכְבֵּד וְעֵינָיו הָשַׁע פֶּן־יִרְאֶה בְעֵינָיו וּבְאָזְנָיו
יִשְׁמָע וּלְבָבוֹ יָבִין וָשָׁב וְרָפָא לוֹ׃

> 9. And he said, "Go and say to this people:
>   Keep listening, but do not comprehend;
>   keep looking, but do not understand.
> 10. Make the mind of this people dull,
>   and stop their ears,
>   and shut their eyes,
> so that they may not look with their eyes,
>   and listen with their ears,
> and comprehend with their minds,
>   and turn and be healed." (NRSV)

Notes

The translation of v. 9 as "keep listening" and "keep looking" is correct. Infinitive absolutes of the same verbal root follow their respective finite verb forms. Jeremiah 6:29 places the infinitive form of צרף after a perfect form, to suggest continuance.[29] This is a construction similar to Gen 8:7, which places the infinitive of יצא after the imperfect with reference to the raven's going out, thus, saying that the raven continued to move.

The word order in v. 10 in the Hebrew is noteworthy. Literally it begins, "fatten their heart, and their ears, make dull, and their eyes, shut up . . . ." This places the emphasis on the ideas of the ear and the eye. Those two powerful sensory organs, as opposed to other organs such as the nose and the hand, are what would be stricken with disability.

Exegesis

Context

Immediate biblical context

Isaiah 6:9–10 must be compared with Isa 6:1–8, the calling vision for Isaiah. There, the prophet sees the throne (Isa 6:1) and hears a voice (v. 8). It can be assumed that Isaiah understood both clearly as he was able to answer the invitation to be sent, and immediately, was sent with a message, Isa 6:9–13. The people, though, in their stubbornness and wickedness, would not understand no matter how well they saw or heard.

Immediately after the oracle of Isa 6:9–13, one finds the story of King Ahaz, in Isa 7, where after enemy armies threaten to conquer Judah, Isaiah is sent with a message to Ahaz regarding victory that God could give the king. In v. 11, the prophet asks the king to name any sign of his choosing, and God would give it. This would allow the king to behold the power of God clearly before taking the risk of trusting him for deliverance. In v. 12, the king replies that he would not test the Lord. Isaiah understands this as false piety in v. 13 and rebukes the king for wearying God. One may assume that it is not wrong to test God if he asked to be tested. While Isaiah attempted to help the king more clearly see God's power, the king rejected such sight, and so was blind to the truth and the path to deliverance. Not only are these passages connected by proximity and the previously mentioned thematic tie, but the idea of a remnant returning is common to both.

---

29. Kautzsch, ed., *Gesenius' Hebrew Grammar*, 343, 113.R.

In Isa 6:13, while the word "remnant" does not occur, it is said that a tenth of those scattered would return eventually. When Isaiah goes to visit Ahaz, God tells him to bring his son, whose name means "a remnant shall return" (Isa 7:3). The same word, שׁוּב, is used for "return" here as in Isa 6:13. Thus, one finds strong evidence for Isa 7 containing an illustration of the vision of Isa 6:9–13.

Intratextual connections

Deuteronomy 28:28, says that madness, blindness, and astonishment of heart would afflict the people who violate God's covenant. In Isa 6:9–10, both the eye and the heart are affected, though different words are used to refer to blindness. Nonetheless, one must consider Deut 28:28–29 when studying this and the following prophetic blindness passages to observe possible themes.

General analysis

The context of repenting suggests that a figurative interpretation for blinding and deafening is intended. In addition, as noted previously in this study, the mentioning of the eye at the center of a chiasm shows that such was the climax of the passage. Such blinding would continue until the land lay desolate (Isa 6:11).

One may wonder why a prophet would be commanded to make a people blind. One possibility, as set forth by Robert P. Carroll, is that it is not that Isaiah was commanded to make the people blind, but that he was reflecting back after a life of unsuccessful prophesying and attempting to explain why he was not heard. He, then, would be saying, after such a difficult life, that his prophecies were never intended to be obeyed anyway.[30] The problem with this theory is that it would require Isaiah to "put words in God's mouth." Isaiah, then, would have assumed what he thought God must have intended to say previously and presented such as God's words. The text, though, says that God, plainly and clearly, told Isaiah that his message would not be received positively.

One may, instead, consider Terry Briley's analysis of Isa 6:9–10 in the light of 1 Kgs 22:19–23. There, Micaiah tells of a conspiracy in heaven when a being says he would put a lying spirit into the prophets to confuse Ahab. If God's real intention were to deceive through such a conspiracy, he would

---

30. Carroll, *When Prophecy Failed*, 136.

not have made it known to Micaiah. Instead, a form of literary irony is used to show the king the foolishness of listening to those popular prophets around him. Similarly, it would not aid a mission of blinding a people if Isaiah was expected to announce that such was his intention. Rather, this use of irony would draw a small number of the people to realize their errors and repent. Isaiah, then, was not actually expected to make the people blind intentionally, but simply to tell the truth, knowing that the result would be that many people would choose blindness.[31]

While there are clearly no direct verbal parallels connecting Isa 6 and 1 Kgs 22, both do involve God's apparent announcing to a party his intent to keep the party in confusion and away from the right course of action. Briley insightfully notes that as one must conclude that a form of irony and satire is employed in the disclosing of such a conspiracy in 1 Kgs 22, a similar style is employed in the disclosing of such a similar conspiracy in Isa 6:9–10. Briley's analysis, then, provides a reasonable framework for understanding the intent behind God's command to make the people blind. While the people most likely would not heed the warning in Isa 6, as Ahab failed to heed the warning in 1 Kgs 22, it was hoped that the people would hear these words and, realizing the desperateness of their situation, repent before God, and maybe even learn again to see.

This continued refusal to heed God's warnings would have most devastating consequences. Gary V. Smith rightly notes that since the people see continually but do not change and understand, eventually, then, they would simply become blind so they would not see at all. As they repeatedly do not pay attention to the messages they hear, their hearts would grow fat and their ears heavy. As a result of rejecting God's Word, their eyes would become closed to the truth.[32] Alec Motyer rightly expresses this idea by saying that there is a point of no return when one rejects truth long enough after which hearing more truth has no effect.[33]

Finally, it was necessary for the people to understand, repent, and then, and only then, be healed. John M. Oswalt rightly notes that God could have chosen simply to allow the people to be healed without experiencing true repentance, but that would not solve the centuries-old problem of disobedience. Thus, the people must do what Isaiah did in vv. 1–8 and admit sin repentantly in order to receive their spiritual sight and healing. Isaiah must not water down the truth simply to help the people feel healed. He must be faithful, even if it reduces his popularity and results in deeper blindness

---

31. Briley, *Isaiah*, 101.
32. Gary V. Smith, *Isaiah 1–39*, 194.
33. Motyer, *Isaiah*, 73.

from those who repeatedly reject the truth.[34] Based on the comparisons with Isa 6:1–8 and Isa 7, blindness, then, refers to a state of spiritual dullness where one who refuses to obey loses the ability even to perceive what should be obeyed or why such obedience is important.

The Blind Who Understand and the Seeing Who Do Not, Isaiah 29:9–10, 18

Translation

THE TEXT

In Isa 29:9–19 an oracle is given that contains a number of significant references to blindness. Verses 9, 10, and 18 appear translated below:

הִתְמַהְמְהוּ וּתְמָהוּ הִשְׁתַּעַשְׁעוּ וָשֹׁעוּ שָׁכְרוּ וְלֹא־יַיִן נָעוּ וְלֹא שֵׁכָר:
כִּי־נָסַךְ עֲלֵיכֶם יְהוָה רוּחַ תַּרְדֵּמָה וַיְעַצֵּם אֶת־עֵינֵיכֶם אֶת־הַנְּבִיאִים וְאֶת־רָאשֵׁיכֶם הַחֹזִים כִּסָּה:

> 9. Stupefy yourselves and be in a stupor,
> blind yourselves and be blind!
> Be drunk, but not from wine;
> stagger, but not from strong drink!
> 10. For the LORD has poured out upon you
> a spirit of deep sleep;
> he has closed your eyes, you prophets,
> and covered your heads, you seers. (NRSV)

וְשָׁמְעוּ בַיּוֹם־הַהוּא הַחֵרְשִׁים דִּבְרֵי־סֵפֶר וּמֵאֹפֶל וּמֵחֹשֶׁךְ עֵינֵי עִוְרִים תִּרְאֶינָה:

> 18. On that day the deaf shall hear
> the words of a scroll,
> and out of their gloom and darkness
> the eyes of the blind shall see. (NRSV)

Notes

This text contains lists of consecutive imperatives, for example, "Blind yourselves, and be blind." *Gesenius Hebrew Grammar* explains how this

---

34. Oswalt, *The Book of Isaiah: Chapters 1–39*, 189.

frequently is to be understood as meaning that the second imperative is a consequence of the first. In Gen 42:18, for example, when Joseph says, "this do and live," using two consecutive imperatives, the living is to be understood as a result of the doing. This would make the second word in each pair in Isa 29:9 the consequence of the first. One would say, then, "close your eyes, and as a result, be blind."[35] This, of course, would be the natural result of eye-closing even without any linguistic direction toward that idea.

Exegesis

LITERARY ANALYSIS

The elegant wordplay in v. 9 may be analyzed here. The first two words, "הִתְמַהְמְהוּ," from מהה, and "וּתְמָהוּ," from תמה, have ה, מ, ת, and ו, in common, along with a number of vowels. The next word pair is simply two different forms of the verb שעע, and so wordplay would be expected. The author, then, wished to stress the ideas of astonishment and blindness.

CONTEXT

One must first note Deut 28:28–29 as was noted in the study of Isa 6:9–10. Deuteronomy 28:28 contains the word תִּמָּהוֹן, "astonishment," while Isa 29:9 contains the related verb, תמה. While Isa 29:9 does not use the same word for "blind" as Deut 28:28–29, the ideas of blindness and failing to observe God's teachings are common to both passages. One does find in Isa 29:18, though, with reference to healing, a related word for blind, עִוֵּר, which appears in Deut 28:29 and has already been shown to be derived from the same root as the word for "blindness" in Deut 28:28. Thus, one finds more evidence for keeping Deut 28:28–29 in mind when studying the blindness passages in Isaiah.

One must next recall Isa 6:9–10 when studying Isa 29:9–10. Both passages refer to shutting eyes using the rare word, שעע. The same disabling effect, then, would be in mind in Isa 29:9–10 as was in mind in Isa 6:9–10. Those who repeatedly refuse to gaze upon God's truth will have such ability to see taken away.

One may then consider the use of sarcastic language in Isa 6:9–10, as previously noted. John N. Oswalt also rightly notes the similar use of sarcastic language in Isa 29:9. The text could not possibly be understood

---

35. Kautzsch, *Gesenius' Hebrew Grammar*, 324, 110.F.

as literally and seriously commanding people to become drunk.[36] It is even less likely to understand this passage as seriously commanding people to become blind since just nine verses later, in Isa 29:18, the same text says that the eyes of the blind would one day be open to see a book. Such an inconsistency also suggests that Isa 29:9 should be understood as using sarcasm.

General analysis

Alec Motyer insightfully discusses a significance to the way Isa 29:9 says that the people were to blind themselves and be blind. The result of blinding oneself, then, is blindness.[37] Consistent with the message of Isa 6:9–10, Isa 29:9 suggests that one who shuts his/her eye to the truth, repeatedly, eventually becomes blind to the truth.

Next, in v. 10 it is said that the people's eyes would be shut and their seers covered. Then, in v. 18 it is said that while the deaf would hear, the blind, out of obscurity and darkness, would see. It has already been noted how blindness appears to be treated with more intense language literarily in passages such as Isa 29:18.

A number of significant insights emerge when one considers the passage as a whole. First, in vv. 11–12 it is said that the vision would be like a sealed book, which a learned man cannot read as it is sealed and an unlearned man cannot read because he is illiterate. This continues the theme of knowledge being hidden away from the eyes and hearts of the people, as discussed in v. 10. One may then note Gene M. Tucker's helpful analysis of v. 18. This verse refers to a book from which the deaf would hear words and how the blind would see. It is likely, then, that the eyes of the blind would be opened, literally or figuratively, so they could read the same book the deaf hear. The truth, then, would be made available by oral and written methods, to those thought unable to perceive it by those methods.[38] Thus, the blind see, and the deaf hear, the words of a book, but the seers and the learned are unable even to look upon the book. It would not be unreasonable to imagine the blind actually reading this book to the deaf.

Then, one may consider vv. 13–17. Verse 13 says that the people obey God with their lips but not their actions. Verse 15 adds how the people assume that God cannot see their wickedness, as if they are in the dark. Effectively, then, the people assume that God is blind, when, in reality, he sees and the people are blind. Then, v. 16 expresses how unusual it is for the clay

---

36. Oswalt, *The Book of Isaiah: Chapters 1–39*, 531.
37. Motyer, *Isaiah*, 191.
38. Tucker, "The Book of Isaiah, 1–39," 247.

to place itself above the potter and ask who made it. A theme of overturning is continued in v. 17 when God says that he would turn Lebanon into a fruitful field, and the fruitful field into a forest.

The theme of overturning, then, runs throughout this passage. First, the ones whom one would expect to see, the prophets, are unable. Then, the people assume that the all-seeing God is unable to see their wickedness, as if they can see better than the Almighty. The people believe that their deeds are in the "darkness," using the same root, חשך, for the word referring to "darkness" in v. 15 as in v. 18. In v. 16, the clay tries to assert itself above the potter. God then speaks again of his overturning with reference to fields and forests. Finally, the God who would blind the prophets would allow the deaf and the blind to hear and see his truths. Verse 19 continues the theme of overturning by naming blessings that would befall the meek.

Blindness, here, then becomes involved in this pattern of overturning. Those who think they can see are blind, and those who are blind will be given special insight from God. God is not in the darkness, or blind. He can control who sees what. One who is understood to be blind can be made to see whatever God wishes such a one to see, and one who is understood to have superior vision can be made blind.

This blindness apparently represents ignorance, as the context of v. 10 is that of a sealed vision. That which one's eyes are shut concerning is as if it were sealed. This ignorance, though, is directly involved with the concept of disobedience. Since the people do not truly obey God with their hearts, they would lose the gift of maintaining access to heaven's special knowledge. Since they assume God does not see them, God will make them no longer see him. The gift of truly seeing would be given to those thought too weak or lowly for such.

A Righteous King Not Making Eyes Dim, Isaiah 32:3

Translation

The text

One must next consider Isa 32:3, 4, translated here.

וְלֹא תִשְׁעֶינָה עֵינֵי רֹאִים וְאָזְנֵי שֹׁמְעִים תִּקְשַׁבְנָה׃
וּלְבַב נִמְהָרִים יָבִין לָדָעַת וּלְשׁוֹן עִלְּגִים תְּמַהֵר לְדַבֵּר צָחוֹת׃

    3. Then the eyes of those who have sight will not be closed,
       and the ears of those who have hearing will listen.
    4. The minds of the rash will have good judgment,

and the tongues of stammerers will speak readily and distinctly. (NRSV)

Notes

The Hebrew of v. 3 contains a syntactical chiasm, not clearly noticeable in translation. When referring to the seeing, the verb "close" appears first, but when referring to the hearing, the noun "ears" appears first. Hence, a parallel structure—verb, noun, noun, verb—is used in this verse.

Exegesis

Context

One may recall Isa 6:9–10 and Isa 29:9–10, which speak of the people's eyes being shut. Joseph Blenkinsopp rightly notes that while, in those former times, blindness would be the prevailing condition, in the presence of a righteous king, sight would not be dimmed. Such a righteous king would not act as the wicked who oppress the poor and hungry (Isa 32:6–7).[39] In addition, John N. Oswalt rightly observes that the problems of unrighteousness and blindness of the leaders, described in Isa 29:9–10, must be resolved before the sight of the people can be secure. The reformation, then, begins with the leaders and spreads to all the people.[40]

General analysis

Oswalt also notes that this case of sight not being dimmed is a result of the rule of a righteous, possibly Messianic, king. While more prose language appears in Isa 32 when compared with Messianic passages such as Isa 9 and 11, the grand, larger-than-human attributes of this extremely righteous and healing ruler set him apart as a possible Messianic figure.[41] This retaining of sight must be seen as figurative in the context of Isa 32:2. In this verse, it is said that a man would be a hiding place from a storm, a concept difficult to imagine literally. This righteous king, during the great Messianic era, then, would rule in such a way as to not hinder people's understanding about God

---

39. Blenkinsopp, *Isaiah 1–39*, 430.
40. Oswalt, *The Book of Isaiah: Chapters 40–66*, 581.
41. Oswalt, *Isaiah*, 362.

and his ways. Leupold rightly notes, then, that the people would be able to see clearly his truths.[42]

The Eyes of the Blind Shall Be Opened, Isaiah 35:5–6

Translation

THE TEXT

The next blindness text in Isaiah also carries a positive meaning. Isaiah 35:5–6 is translated below.

אָז תִּפָּקַחְנָה עֵינֵי עִוְרִים וְאָזְנֵי חֵרְשִׁים תִּפָּתַחְנָה׃
אָז יְדַלֵּג כָּאַיָּל פִּסֵּחַ וְתָרֹן לְשׁוֹן אִלֵּם
כִּי־נִבְקְעוּ בַמִּדְבָּר מַיִם וּנְחָלִים בָּעֲרָבָה׃

> 5. Then the eyes of the blind shall be opened,
>   and the ears of the deaf unstopped;
> 6. then the lame shall leap like a deer,
>   and the tongue of the speechless sing for joy.
> For waters shall break forth in the wilderness,
>   and streams in the desert. (NRSV)

Exegesis

LITERARY ANALYSIS

These two verses discuss restoration in a most orderly manner. First, blindness and deafness, two disabilities involving sensing, are said to be healed. Then, lameness and muteness, two disabilities involving doing and moving, are listed. (Whatever the cause of muteness, in the final analysis, speech still involves the movement of the tongue, as noted in v. 6.) Then, concerning the land, two types of desert conditions are said to be healed. Thus, an ingenious method of parallelism is employed to describe this great restoration. Blindness was deemed important enough to be placed at the head of the list.

---

42. Leupold, *Exposition of Isaiah*, 1:499.

Context

The context of this passage is the great promised restoration of the wilderness places for Israel (Isa 35:1). In fact, v. 6 adds that streams would flow in the deserts. Verse 10 adds the concept of pilgrimage in saying how the ransomed of the Lord would return to Zion. Motyer rightly observes that the ideas of desert and pilgrimage bring the Exodus into focus.[43] During the sojourn in the wilderness, in fact, it is said that God used Moses to bring water from a rock, a form of streams in the wilderness (Exod 17:6). The only possible verbal parallels between these two passages, though, are the references to desert, מִדְבָּר (Exod 17:1, Isa 35:6), and water, מַיִם (Exod 17:6, Isa 35:6). Nonetheless the common concepts of traveling (Isa 35:3-4, 10) and water flowing in the desert make a parallel likely. While restoration of sight to the blind is not mentioned directly in the book of Exodus, in Exod 15:26 God says he is the Israelites' Healer. Thus, these passages even have the theme of healing in common.

General Analysis

This passage places restoring sight to the blind as the first of a number of healings for the disabled, all of which would happen some day for Israel. Restoration of sight to the blind, then, was thought of clearly as a beautiful gift, comparable to flowing streams in the desert. One may wish to find a figurative explanation for Isa 35:5-6, but to do so, clear symbolic meanings for deafness, lameness, and muteness, as well as for blindness, would need to be discovered. For a literal interpretation, one would need to find a time in history when such healings happened and when the land literally became fruitful again or simply say that the fulfillment is future. In reality, though, as Gene M. Tucker observes, it may be difficult to separate physical from spiritual healing in the world to come, and so this passage may find its fulfillment in both spheres.[44]

---

43. Motyer, *Isaiah*, 217.
44. Tucker, "The Book of Isaiah, 1-39," 281.

The Servant Opening Blind Eyes, Isaiah 42:7

Translation

THE TEXT

Isaiah 42–43 contains a number of references to blindness that are necessary to this study. In this section, they are studied in the context of the servant poetry of Isa 41–53. Isaiah 42:7 is translated below:

לִפְקֹחַ עֵינַיִם עִוְרוֹת לְהוֹצִיא מִמַּסְגֵּר אַסִּיר מִבֵּית כֶּלֶא יֹשְׁבֵי חֹשֶׁךְ:

> 7. to open the eyes that are blind,
> to bring out the prisoners from the dungeon,
> from the prison those who sit in darkness.

Exegesis

LITERARY ANALYSIS

This verse is arranged using a style of simple block parallelism. First the verse lists, separately, the healing of blindness and the release of prisoners. Then, the two ideas are combined in the same order in the stating of the concept of those who sit in darkness in the house of bondage. This suggests a relationship between blindness and prison, examined further below.

In addition, the use of repetition of the word עִוֵּר in Isa 42 and 43, is discussed by Philip Stern. He insightfully observes how this word occurs seven times between Isa 42:7 and Isa 43:8. This is the most intense concentration of this word in the Hebrew Bible. This, then, suggests a great emphasis being placed on the idea of blindness.[45]

CONTEXT

The context of this verse contains a significant allusion to the creation story of Gen 1. Isaiah 42:5 refers to God as the One who creates the heavens, spreads out the earth, and sets breath in the peoples. Verse 6 says that the servant would be a light to the nations. The Hebrew words for "create, heaven, earth" (Isa 42:5; Gen 1:1), "light" (Isa 42:6; Gen 1:3), and "breath" (Isa 42:5; Gen 2:7) are in common between these two passages. God, the Creator, would set up the servant to be a light, creating light for the blind.

45. Stern, "The 'Blind Servant' Imagery of Deutero-Isaiah," 225.

The answer to the problem of blindness amid the nations, then, is the same answer to the blinding darkness of the primordial earth: God's new creation of light. The restoration of the blindness mentioned in Isa 42 would require a similar style of miraculous intervention. This is not, then, a blindness that can be cured by the methods of mortal humans.

General analysis

One must first discover the identity of the servant. One figure mentioned in Isa 40–66 who holds great prominence, according to Joseph Blenkinsopp, is Cyrus who did provide the way for Israel to return home. He, then, might be seen as the "servant."[46] While Cyrus was mentioned by name in Isa 44:28 and 45:1, and while he did do many great tasks for Israel (Ezra 1:1–3), it must also be noted that Cyrus is never directly named as God's servant, but, rather, as a shepherd (Isa 44:28) and as an anointed one (Isa 45:1). F. Duane Lindsey rightly notes that Cyrus, while he did facilitate the Jews' return to their homeland (Ezra 1:1–3), is not recorded as performing, himself, any great spiritual restoration or enlightenment for them.[47] Israel, though, is described directly as God's servant in Isa 41:8. Thus, Israel may be a more likely possibility for the identity of the servant in Isa 42 and 43.

One may also see a Messiah as the servant since such a great figure might be needed to do these mighty and spiritual tasks. H. H. Rowley notes how the interpretation of the servant may change throughout the book of Isaiah. While, as noted above, the servant is said directly to refer to Israel in Isa 41, the servant must be understood differently, for example, in Isa 53. There, it says that such would be bruised for our transgressions (v. 5) but in his mouth would be no deceit (v. 9). Nowhere in the other prophets is Israel described as being innocent in the context of its sufferings at the time of the exile. Thus, this servant here must refer to a messianic individual, however, the examination of such identity is beyond the scope of this study. This means, then, that while the servant may have referred to Israel in Isa 41, in places such as Isa 42 when such grand language is used to describe Israel's mission, a messianic figure may be understood as bringing about this great enlightenment.[48] Rowley, though, notes in addition that such a servant role in Isa 42 may be played by Messiah and Israel together. Messiah would lead Israel in its mission to enlighten the world.[49] While Rowley uses

46. Blenkinsopp, *Isaiah 40–55*, 212.
47. Lindsey, *The Servant Songs*, 52.
48. Rowley, *The Servant of the Lord and Other Essays on the Old Testament*, 51.
49. Rowley, *The Servant of the Lord and Other Essays on the Old Testament*, 56.

Jesus as the interpretation of Messiah and the church as the interpretation of Israel, two concepts whose defense reaches beyond the scope of this study, the essence of his statement is logical. This would be analogous to one's saying that Joshua defeated Ai (Josh 10:1) while, clearly, it can also be said that he led in the battle with all Israel supporting him (Josh 8). The servant, as described clearly as Israel as a whole, in Isa 41:8, would bear this light under the leadership of such a representative Jewish Messiah.

In addition, Richard M. Davidson insightfully analyzes the nature of the individual and corporate servant poetry in Isa 40–53 as the text oscillates between discussion of each. One similarity between both is that both are described as being a witness, or light, to the gentile (Isa 42:6–7; 43:8–10). Both are also referred to as chosen by God (Isa 42:1; 44:1). One difference is that while servant Israel commits sin, servant Messiah is innocent and suffers for servant Israel's sin (Isa 42:22–25; 53:5–7). In addition, servant Israel complains, while servant Messiah suffers silently (Isa 49:14; 53:7).[50] This suggests a clear relationship between the individual and corporate servants. While they are similar in a number of ways, servant Messiah is for servant Israel that which servant Israel lacks and most needs. The similarities between the individual and corporate servants, though, show how servant Messiah was closely associated with servant Israel, as a representative of servant Israel.

It may finally be noted that, whether or not Messiah performs the great actions of Isa 42:7, God is described as the originator, and people, the recipient. Whether Messiah, Israel, or Israel under Messiah do these tasks, the original cause and result would be the same: God would give sight to the blind.

One must now consider the connections between blindness and prison in Isa 42:7. Klaus Baltzer notes that those imprisoned in dark dungeons for long periods of time would naturally find their eyes weakened, maybe even blinded, by the lack of exposure to light.[51] Next, not only would dungeons have been dark and dreary, but, according to the evidence previously considered, a number of people in such facilities were blinded by the state. One need only recall Samson, Zedekiah, and the numerous accounts of blinded prisoners in Hittite culture for evidence of this. It may also be so that blindness is to be seen in Isa 42:7 as a form of prison, or, in the least, tantamount to prison. One would be bound up in a world without light, in a society and time when the blind would not be given the opportunities offered in twenty-first-century human culture.

50. Davidson, "The 'Servant,' ('Ebed) of Isaiah" 2.
51. Baltzer, *Deutero-Isaiah*, 146.

It is also noteworthy that both the opening of blind eyes and the releasing from prison would be performed by this "light," according to vv. 6–7. In reality, one who is blind needs more than simply light to see, but functioning eyes. In addition, the text does not say that Israel would be a light for the blind and a key for those imprisoned. Instead, the light would release both the blind and the prisoners. These ideas reinforce the notion that this passage is to be understood symbolically. The light of God's truths, to be understood in greater depth later in Isa 42, would aid those who cannot see it because of blindness and those who do not see it because of the darkness of prison.

God, then, tells his servant people that they would be a light to those in such blinding prisons. Those without knowledge of God's truths would be able to see and understand, being set free from the prison of ignorance.

The Servant's Blindness, Isaiah 42:16–20

Translation

The text

The next text is Isa 42:16–20, translated below:

וְהוֹלַכְתִּי עִוְרִים בְּדֶרֶךְ לֹא יָדָעוּ בִּנְתִיבוֹת לֹא־יָדְעוּ אַדְרִיכֵם אָשִׂים מַחְשָׁךְ
לִפְנֵיהֶם לָאוֹר וּמַעֲקַשִּׁים לְמִישׁוֹר אֵלֶּה הַדְּבָרִים עֲשִׂיתִם וְלֹא עֲזַבְתִּים:
נָסֹגוּ אָחוֹר יֵבֹשׁוּ בֹשֶׁת הַבֹּטְחִים בַּפָּסֶל הָאֹמְרִים לְמַסֵּכָה אַתֶּם אֱלֹהֵינוּ:
הַחֵרְשִׁים שְׁמָעוּ וְהַעִוְרִים הַבִּיטוּ לִרְאוֹת:
מִי עִוֵּר כִּי אִם־עַבְדִּי וְחֵרֵשׁ כְּמַלְאָכִי אֶשְׁלָח מִי עִוֵּר כִּמְשֻׁלָּם וְעִוֵּר כְּעֶבֶד
יְהוָה:
רָאִיתָ [רָאוֹת] רַבּוֹת וְלֹא תִשְׁמֹר פָּקוֹחַ אָזְנַיִם וְלֹא יִשְׁמָע:

16. I will lead the blind
    by a road they do not know,
by paths they have not known
    I will guide them.
I will turn the darkness before them into light,
    the rough places into level ground.
These are the things I will do,
    and I will not forsake them.
17. They shall be turned back and utterly put to shame—
    those who trust in carved images,
who say to cast images,
    "You are our gods."

> 18. Listen, you that are deaf;
> and you that are blind, look up and see!
> 19. Who is blind but my servant,
> or deaf like my messenger whom I send?
> Who is blind like my dedicated one,
> or blind like the servant of the LORD?
> 20. He sees many things, but does not observe them;
> his ears are open, but he does not hear.

Notes

First, the exact meaning of "Meshullam," translated as "My dedicated one," above, is difficult to determine. Possibilities, as noted by Blenkinsopp, are, "perfect one," "fully paid," or "submissive" (latter based on Arabic, from the root of the word, Muslim).[52] The exact meaning of this word, though, is immaterial to this study. Repeatedly, this verse refers to the disabled servant. Meshullam, who is also blind most likely, is this same servant, described repeatedly in parallelism. Other information regarding such word is not necessarily relevant to a study on blindness in the Hebrew Scriptures.

Exegesis

LITERARY ANALYSIS

First, Blenkinsopp insightfully notes parallels between Isa 42:1–9 and Isa 42:10–17. Isaiah 42:4 and Isa 42:10, 12 refer to the islands. Isaiah 42:7 and 42:16 concern assisting the blind. Isaiah 42:8 and 42:17 concern idols. Then, Isa 42:9 and 42:10 refer to something that is new. This would suggest, then, a literary connection between the two blindness verses. They, apparently, are to be seen as a unit.[53]

Next, as noted previously, blindness is strongly emphasized in vv. 18–19. In v. 18, the blind are said to be able to see one day, while fewer words are employed to describe the resolution of deafness. Blindness is mentioned three times while deafness is mentioned only once.

---

52. Blenkinsopp, *Isaiah 40–55*, 218.
53. Blenkinsopp, *Isaiah 40–55*, 214.

Context

Philip Stern insightfully connects Isa 42:19–20 with Isa 41:14, which says that Jacob is a worm. Worms are blind, and, so, do not see the light. Thus, God's servant, even in Isa 41, is said, in a way, to be blind.[54] When one considers Isa 41:14 with the blind worm and Isa 42:16, with the blind on the new way, a theme emerges of God's offering comfort and redemption to the blind.

General analysis

One must first note the contrast between the two halves of v. 16. First, it is stated that the blind would be led along paths they do not know. After this, it is said that the darkness would become light before them. Apparently, God would not only provide guidance for the blind in their spiritual disorientation, but work ultimately to reverse the blindness. Verse 17 gives further insight as to the nature of this blindness. Suddenly, the focus moves from sight and blindness to that of idolatry. This might suggest that idolatry generates a form of figurative blindness, blindness from the truth of the one, invisible God. In addition, Rebecca Raphael insightfully notes the irony presented here that those who worship visible idols are considered blind.[55]

Then, v. 19 refers to a blind servant and a deaf messenger. Klaus Baltzer rightly notes that one who is blind cannot function as a servant as effectively as one who is sighted, and one who is deaf might find it difficult to hear the message to bear.[56] Thus, it can be said that God is saying that this servant has been rendered incapable of performing the tasks such must perform.

One may next determine the identity of the servant. In Isa 42:24, it is said how Jacob and Israel have been made a spoil to the nations, and how the people have sinned, abandoning God's Torah. That would suggest that the servant here is Israel, who had been given the Torah. Israel here, though, is not described, as earlier, as giving sight or being under a Messiah who would give sight to the blind. This description shows the general blindness of idolatrous Israel. Here, then, it is God's servant Israel who is blind. It is Israel who is described once as being deaf and three times as being blind. This blindness is described in different words in v. 20. There, the people are said to see but not observe, have open ears, but not hear. This blindness, then, does not result from a lack of eyes, or the theoretical ability to receive light/truth,

---

54. Stern, "The 'Blind Servant' Imagery of Deutero-Isaiah," 226.
55. Raphael, *Biblical Corpora*, 123.
56. Baltzer, *Deutero-Isaiah*, 149.

but from the neglect of proper use of such eyes for recognizing and discerning light/truth. As Klaus Westerman rightly observes, they had seen the acts God performed and heard his words, but failed to apply the knowledge.[57]

Verse 24 even describes literal sins the people were said to have committed. They were said to have sinned, failed to walk in the Lord's ways, and neglected his Law. One must note, of course, that the opening verses of the Decalogue Law refer to the evils of idolatry, discussed in Isa 42:17. They had the Law, but did not follow it, just as one who has eyes could choose not to follow the guidance they provide. According to v. 25 this blindness extends beyond simply the concept of not understanding the law. The people are said also to have been punished with God's fiery wrath yet unaware of such. Apparently, then, as one who is blind is not aware of physical surroundings, these people were unaware of their punishments. Thus, Israel, who should be a light to the surrounding nations, must first be healed of blindness caused by idolatry and neglect of Torah.

The People Blind But with Eyes, Isaiah 43:8

Translation

THE TEXT

Next one must consider Isa 43:8, in translation below:

הוֹצִיא עַם־עִוֵּר וְעֵינַיִם יֵשׁ וְחֵרְשִׁים וְאָזְנַיִם לָמוֹ׃

> 8. Bring forth the people who are blind, yet have eyes,
> who are deaf, yet have ears! (NRSV)

Exegesis

The immediate preceding context is God's people, Jacob, who would be gathered from the nations (v. 5). This, of course, assumes that they would be scattered to the nations. Here, again, God refers to his people who have eyes but do not see, who have ears but do not hear. Klaus Baltzer rightly observes how the people, blind and deaf, should have been able to see and hear, since the organs of the eye and ear were present.[58]

---

57. Westermann, *Isaiah 40–66*, 111.
58. Baltzer, *Deutero-Isaiah*, 163.

To understand what is to be seen and heard, one must also note the judicial context of Isa 43:8. G. H. Grogan rightly notes how vv. 9 and 10 refer to witnesses and justifying, for example. In this court case, the nations are asked to bring witnesses, and Israel is called to be God's witness.[59] The issue for discussion in this court case is the validity of any god to rule (Isa 43:10). The true God calls for evidence for the nations' statements that their gods are mighty, and for the case of his might, he calls Israel, to stand as a witness concerning his might. Oswalt rightly comments that it is ironic that God's witness is blind and deaf, and so less able to testify about things seen and heard.[60] This must suggest, as Oswalt notes further, that the greatness of God would be so manifest that even the blind and deaf could testify about it.[61]

God's own past acts of saving the people (Isa 43:12), when no pagan gods were in Israel, should be evidence enough from former things that God is God. The people of Israel, though, who held such a history of witnessing God's wonders, would have had the spiritual eyes to consider, but chose to ignore the knowledge, effectively, then, becoming as blind. However much the people desire to see or hear, this evidence is so powerful that none could deny it. Even the blind and deaf who might even refuse to heed such a history would be useful witnesses for these wonders.

Idols Make One Blind, Isaiah 44:9, 18

Translation

THE TEXT

One may next consider Isa 44:9, 18, translated below:

יֹצְרֵי־פֶסֶל כֻּלָּם תֹּהוּ וַחֲמוּדֵיהֶם בַּל־יוֹעִילוּ וְעֵדֵיהֶם הֵמָּה בַּל־יִרְאוּ וּבַל־יֵדְעוּ לְמַעַן יֵבֹשׁוּ׃

> 9. All who make idols are nothing, and the things they delight in do not profit; their witnesses neither see nor know. And so they will be put to shame. (NRSV)

לֹא יָדְעוּ וְלֹא יָבִינוּ כִּי טַח מֵרְאוֹת עֵינֵיהֶם מֵהַשְׂכִּיל לִבֹּתָם׃

---

59. Grogan, "Isaiah," 260.
60. Oswalt, *The Book of Isaiah: Chapters 40–66*, 145.
61. Oswalt, *Isaiah*, 490.

18. They do not know, nor do they comprehend; for their eyes are shut, so that they cannot see, and their minds as well, so that they cannot understand. (NRSV)

NOTES

Literally v. 18 reads, "He has shut from seeing their eyes." This shows emphasis on the shutting and the keeping of them from seeing. In addition, the word translated "minds" in v. 18 is actually, לֵב, "hearts" in the Hebrew. This becomes significant when one wishes to compare this verse to other verses that discuss eyes and hearts together.

Exegesis

CONTEXT

First, Deut 4:28 refers to idols that, among a number of deficiencies, are lacking in the ability to see. These same blind idols, as discussed again in Isa 44:9–18, make their builders as blind and unintelligent, according to Isa 44:18. Next, in Num 15:39 the eye and the heart are what lead one to turn away from the commandments of God, one of which speaks against making graven images (Exod 20:4–6). Idolatry, in Isa 44:18, renders the heart and eye ineffective.

GENERAL ANALYSIS

Between Isa 44:9 and 44:18 is a story of one who uses wood for a number of tasks, the last of which is making an idol. Such a person, at one time, at least, had the vision to see the fire made from the wood (Isa 44:16). Then, in v. 18, as the builder makes an idol out of the wood, which cannot see (v. 9), this idolatry prevents the builder's eyes from seeing and the heart from understanding. The builder may physically be able to see a fire, but spiritually, all vision has left. In reality, Oswalt rightly notes that anyone who tries to set anything or anyone finite above the infinite God of the universe is clearly blind to the ridiculousness of such an idea.[62] Oswalt also insightfully notes that anyone who thinks an idol can save him/her must also be blind to spiritual reality (Isa 44:9, 17).[63] Such a person fails even to see and consider

62. Oswalt, *The Book of Isaiah: Chapters 40–66*, 185.
63. Oswalt, *Isaiah*, 503.

how he worships the idol he himself had recently formed from the fire (Isa 43:19). Something he/she, a finite individual, forms, himself/herself, could not possibly have the power of the infinite. In fact, such wooden idols would be vulnerable to the same fire that burns the similar pieces of wood used as fuel for the fire.

The Blind Watchmen, Isaiah 56:10

Translation

THE TEXT

Isaiah 56:10, the next blindness passage in Isaiah, appears below:

צָפוּ [צֹפָיו] עִוְרִים כֻּלָּם לֹא יָדָעוּ כֻּלָּם כְּלָבִים אִלְּמִים לֹא יוּכְלוּ לִנְבֹּחַ הֹזִים שֹׁכְבִים אֹהֲבֵי לָנוּם:

> 10. Israel's sentinels are blind,
>   they are all without knowledge;
>   they are all silent dogs
>   that cannot bark;
>   dreaming, lying down,
>   loving to slumber. (NRSV)

NOTES

It must first be noted that the word "Israel" does not actually appear in the Masoretic text of this verse. Rather, a pronominal suffix appears on "sentinels," to suggest that their owner is named in the previous verses. Such is named as Israel in v. 8. It must also be noted that the ketiv of the word for "sentinels" is actually צֹפוּ, "his sentinel," while the qere', which better agrees with the plural adjective, is צֹפָיו, "his sentinels."

Exegesis

LITERARY ANALYSIS

Motyer observantly notes the repetition of the particle, לֹא, and the word, ידע, "he knew," in analyzing the literary structure of Isa 56:10–11. Four times in Isa 56:10–11 is there a clause followed by a remark about something that does not happen. The first, third, and fourth times the reference to that which does not happen begins with לֹא יָדְעוּ, they do not know. The following chart summarizes Motyer's analysis:

- A. Blind watchmen.
    - B. They do not know.
- A. Mute dogs.
    - B. Cannot bark.
- A. Greedy dogs.
    - B. Do not know how to be satisfied.
- A. Shepherds
    - B. Do not know how to understand.[64]

Isaiah 56:10-11 is arranged chiasticly. The first and fourth entries mention more positive titles, watchmen and shepherds, while both the second and third entries mention dogs, using the same word, כֶּלֶב. The first and fourth entries simply concern lack of reasoning power. The second and third entries concern lack of competence at specific skills, barking and being satisfied. The blind watchmen, then, would be paralleled with the shepherds who have no understanding. While the dogs, in their muteness, lack certain specific skills, those with blindness lack knowledge altogether. This chiasm is shown below:

- A. Blind watchmen
    - B. Mute dogs.
    - B'. Greedy dogs.
- A'. Ignorant shepherds.

General analysis

Oswalt rightly discusses this idea of incompetent watchmen. He notes how,, according to Isa 21:1-12, watchmen would sit in towers where they could see approaching dangers. Possibly the watchmen in Isa 56:10 refer to seers and prophets who were to guide the people away from spiritual danger. They are blind, though, and so without knowledge. It is said, in fact, three times in vv. 10-11, that the watchmen lack knowledge. They are as mute dogs without ability to bark. Thus, even if they could perceive a danger approaching, they would not be able to respond. The next verse describes these people as being gluttonous and shepherds of irresponsible character. Verse 12, then, says they desire only to become drunk. Because of their blindness and incompetence, the watchmen would make the people blind also to any

---

64. Motyer, *The Prophecy of Isaiah*, 468.

dangers, as the people, too, would be uninformed.[65] Truly the repetition of "they do not know" emphasizes a central issue in these verses. These incompetent shepherds/watchmen are completely unable to do anything that a ruler is expected to do for the people. They are not only without knowledge, but also blind and mute, unable to perceive and to act on the perceptions.

Groping as the Blind, Isaiah 59:9–10

Translation

THE TEXT

The final blindness passage in Isaiah to be analyzed is Isa 59:10 where the prophet laments the corporate blindness of his own people. A translation follows:

נְגַשְׁשָׁה כַעְוְרִים קִיר וּכְאֵין עֵינַיִם נְגַשֵּׁשָׁה כָּשַׁלְנוּ בַצָּהֳרַיִם כַּנֶּשֶׁף בָּאַשְׁמַנִּים כַּמֵּתִים׃

> 10. We grope like the blind along a wall,
>   groping like those who have no eyes;
> we stumble at noon as in the twilight,
>   among the vigorous as though we were dead. (NRSV)

NOTES

The first two clauses in the Hebrew follow a chiastic arrangement of word order. The word order of the first clause, "We grope like the blind along a wall," is preserved adequately in the translation. In the second clause, in the Hebrew, however, the verb, "groping" appears after the noun, "like those who have no eyes." This means that the chiasm begins and ends with references to groping and has in its center references to matters of lack of sight.

Exegesis

LITERARY ANALYSIS

Isaiah 59 is chiastic. Verses 1 and 17–21 refer to salvation. Verses 2–9a and 11–16 concern types of sin, falsehood, and the reality, in identical words, of

---

65. Oswalt, *The Book of Isaiah: Chapters 40–66*, 468.

righteousness and justice being distant. In vv. 9b–10, the center and climax, the prophet says in the first person how his people have become blind and weakened. The following chiasm chart illustrates this:

    A. v. 1. Salvation.
        B. vv. 2–9a. sin and falsehood, justice and righteousness.
            C. vv. 9b–10. Blindness issues.
        B'. vv. 11–16. Sin and falsehood, justice and righteousness.
    A'. vv. 17–20. Salvation.

Watts, instead, suggests that one should structure the chiasm with the outer ends identical but to set vv. 4b–5b parallel with vv. 9b–11 and place vv. 8–9a as the center and climax.[66] There are no significant linguistic ties, though, between vv. 4b–5b and vv. 9b–11. In addition, vv. 8–9a parallel v. 14 so strongly with the same words used for "justice, righteousness," and "distant," רָחוֹק, that vv. 8–9a must be placed in a section parallel with the section containing v. 14. The unique and developed metaphor of blindness sets vv. 9b–10 apart as a central section. As a result, then, according to the chiastic arrangement of Isa 59 noted and recommended in this theology of blindness, one immediately notes blindness emphasized as a consequence of sin and turning away from God's established ways.

Context

Blenkinsopp insightfully compares Isa 59:9–11 with Deut 28:28–29. Deuteronomy 28, as one may recall, also contains a list of consequences for rejecting God's commandments. Deuteronomy 28:28–29 also mentions being as the blind, being in darkness, and the idea of such being at midday, with the same words for "blind, darkness," and "midday" used in the Hebrew, there as in Isa 59:9–10. While a different word for "grope" is used in Deut 28, the two words have essentially the same meaning and differ only in the first letter, מ, for Deuteronomy and ג, for Isaiah.[67] In addition, while a different word for "salvation" is used in Deut 28:29, both words come from the same root, ישׁע. This strongly suggests that Isa 59:9–11 alludes to Deut 28:28–29.

This finding adds considerable meaning to Isa 59. Not only is the prophet suggesting a connection between rebellion and blindness, but a covenantal relationship of cause and effect. This blindness experienced by the people in Isa 59 is a direct consequence of having to face the curses of the covenant pronounced against such rebels against God.

---

66. Watts, *Isaiah 34–66*, 282.
67. Blenkinsopp, *Isaiah 56–66*, 193.

Oswalt also insightfully compares Isa 59:9-11 with Isa 58:10. Both passages refer to light and darkness, using אוֹר for light in both passages, and both words, חֹשֶׁךְ and אֲפֵלָה, for darkness in both passages. The same word for "noonday" also appears in both passages. What is especially noteworthy is that in Isa 58:10 it is said that if the people would aid the less fortunate, their darkness would become light as noonday. In Isa 59:9-11, though, as justice is forsaken, that which should be light as noonday is dark and obscure.[68] This would mean that, just as performing justice and kindness leads to light, forsaking justice and kindness leads to a deepening of blindness.

General Analysis

Oswalt rightly notes that in Isa 59:9-11, Isaiah confesses the corporate sins of Israel. The sins named in Isa 59 are stated as his sins as well as the people's sins.[69] Their lack of justice results in a state of blindness as if they had no eyes. Most likely, this blindness in Isa 59 is figurative, a form of ignorance previously discussed. It would be difficult to imagine Isaiah's trying to write this down while he and all the people are made physically blind. Isaiah would be using symbolic language, interpreting figuratively the blindness discussed in Deut 28:28-29.

Summary

Blindness is mentioned a number of times in Isaiah. In Isa 6:9 10, Isaiah is commanded to make the people blind. This passage, though, must be employing literary irony as does 2 Kgs 22:19-23 to inspire repentance by appearing to disclose a conspiracy to prevent it. In Isa 29:9-18, it is noted that the seers would be as blind with reference to certain spiritual matters, but the blind would be able to see. In Isa 32:3-4, it is said that a righteous king, most likely Messianic, would not work to close people's spiritual eyes to the truth. Then, Isa 35:5-6 places the promise of a future opening of blind eyes in the context of healing a number of different disabilities and the turning of deserts into fountains. While it is difficult to determine exactly how literally or figuratively to understand this passage, it is clear that the healing of blindness is thought of in highly positive terms.

In Isa 42:7, it is said that God's servant would open blind eyes and release people from the darkness of prison. Israel, under the leadership of

---

68. Oswalt, *The Book of Isaiah: Chapters 40-66*, 520.
69. Oswalt, *Isaiah*, 630.

Messiah, would then work to do such an amazing feat. Then, after describing how God would lead the blind out of idolatry, Israel is described as being a blind servant, unable to function in the capacity of servant. Israel, in vv. 24–25, is described as forsaking God's Torah and even being unaware of the punishment. Then, in Isa 43:8, God notes that the case of his greatness is so strong that even the blind and deaf of his people, who have eyes and ears but do not use them, would be adequate witnesses to prove his case. Then, in Isa 44:9, 18, one finds another discourse concerning blind idols. Here, it is noted how ridiculous it is for one to trust his life and destiny to a formation of his/her hands. Then, Isa 56:10 describes Israel's rulers as blind and as mute dogs. This means that they are incapable of properly ruling. Finally, in Isa 59:10, at the heart of a chiasm of corporate confession, the prophet notes how sins such as neglecting justice and righteousness have brought upon the blindness discussed in Deut 28:28–29.

BLINDNESS IN THE REMAINING LATTER PROPHETS

The final section in this chapter concerns blindness in the remaining Latter Prophets. First, the four blindness passages in Jeremiah and the one in Ezekiel are considered. First, the discussion in Jer 5:21 concerning having eyes but not seeing is considered. Next, God's promise in Jer 31:8 to lead the blind, as well as those with child, back to Israel after the Babylonian Captivity is analyzed. After this, the references to the blinding of Zedekiah in Jer 39:6–7 and Jer 52:10–11 are analyzed together. Then, Ezek 12:1–13 is studied with reference to the people's having eyes but not seeing and a possible reference to the blinding of Zedekiah.

Next, this section examines blindness in the Minor Prophets. The blindness in the Day of the Lord in Zeph 1:17 is studied first. Then, three references to blindness in Zechariah are considered. First, the blinding of the right eyes of incompetent shepherds in Zech 11:17 is considered. Then, the blinding and maddening of horses in Zech 12:4 is studied. Next, one finds discussion of the wasting away of the eyes of those who attack Jerusalem in Zech 14:7. This section concludes with a study of the condemnation of offering blind and lame sacrifices in Mal 1:8.

Having Eyes But Not Seeing, Jeremiah 5:21

Translation

THE TEXT

The first blindness passage in Jeremiah, Jer 5:21, appears below:

שִׁמְעוּ־נָא זֹאת עַם סָכָל וְאֵין לֵב עֵינַיִם לָהֶם וְלֹא יִרְאוּ אָזְנַיִם לָהֶם וְלֹא יִשְׁמָעוּ׃

> 21. Hear this, O foolish and senseless people,
> who have eyes, but do not see,
> who have ears, but do not hear. (NRSV)

NOTES

One must first note that in the Hebrew, there is no word at all, such as a particle of apposition or a relative pronoun for "who," connecting the comments about the stupid hearts with those about having eyes that do not see and ears that do not hear. The halves of the verse, then, are not to be assumed as connected in such a manner. One may wish, then, to replace "who" with "they." Jack R. Lundbom, in the Anchor Bible Commentary, suggests one possible way to express this: "They have eyes but do not see, they have ears but do not hear."[70] This could open up the possibility that it is the strange gods (Jer 5:19) that are said to be blind and not the people.

In addition, the actual Hebrew word order of the final clauses of this verse is noteworthy. The words for "eyes" and "ears" begin each clause. Literally, then, based on the entirety of this information, the final clauses would read, "Eyes they have, but they do not see; ears they have, but they do not hear." Based on the word order, emphasis, then, is placed on the idea of the eyes and the ears.

Exegesis

LITERARY ANALYSIS

First, Patrick D. Miller rightly mentions a noteworthy word play that binds vv. 21 and 22. Verse 21 mentions those with eyes but who do not see, ראה. Verse 22 refers to those who do not fear, ירא, God. Those who do not see,

---

70. Lundbom, *Jeremiah 1–20*, 399.

then, also do not fear.[71] In fact, in the Hebrew, the forms of these words presented in Jer 5:21, 22 are nearly identical, both containing the same string of four consecutive consonants, א, ר, י, and ה.

Context

Charles L. Feinberg notes how Jer 5:21 bears striking similarities to two passages from the Psalms, Ps 115:5–6 and Ps 135:15–16. Both texts discuss how idols have eyes but do not see and ears but do not hear, using nearly identical words and word order. Psalm 115:5–6 is directly quoted while Ps 135:15–16 uses אזן rather than שמע with reference to the sense of hearing. Strange gods are in the context of Jer 5:21, being discussed as objects of the people's interest in v. 19. It could be suggested that, as with Pss 115 and 135, those who trust in these blind and deaf idols become as blind and deaf.[72] It must be noted that the statements about those trusting in idols becoming like them are found in the Psalms passages and not here in Jer 5. One must be careful not to import meaning from the Psalms passage to Jer 5 where it is not as directly suggested. Nonetheless, based on how these similar expressions appear in the Psalms, clearly referring to idols, a stronger case can be made that these similar expressions refer also to idols and not to the people in Jer 5:21. In addition, while Jer 5 does not actually describe the people directly as blind, the fact that they do not observe the hand of God in Creation, according to Jer 5:22, and his providence in the yearly harvest, according to Jer 5:24, renders them as good as blind and as blind as the idols they worship.

General analysis

One must, now, examine in depth who, or what, is described as having eyes but not seeing. Jeremiah 5:21 begins with a command for the stupid people to listen. Immediately after this command to listen is a description of those who have eyes but do not see. The person then starts with a second-person address, an imperative command to listen. The person, then, changes to a third-person description of a situation, those who have eyes but do not see. In Jeremiah, when the person changes after שמע, "hear," the text is not to be interpreted as beginning to talk about those called to hear in the third person. In Jer 6:19, for example, the earth is addressed with the command to

---

71. Miller, "The Book of Jeremiah," 621.
72. Feinberg, "Jeremiah," 417.

"hear." Then, there is a discussion of what would happen to the people. The earth is still addressed in the second person while the people are discussed in the third person. When the group called to hear is directly addressed regarding their own situations, as in Jer 2:4–5, second-person forms appear. Thus, even though no direct antecedent is immediately given for "them" in Jer 5:21, it can rightly be assumed that "them," does not refer to the people commanded to hear. The closest noun that might make any sense as such an antecedent, especially in the context of other passages dealing with those with eyes who do not see, is the strange gods in v. 19. It has already been noted how Deut 4:28 and Pss 115, 135 also discuss idols that have eyes and do not see.

Blindness, then, with reference to idols is not only spiritual but physical since their eyes do not function in any capacity. Those who follow them, though, lose the ability to recognize God's power and providence. Nonetheless, the most direct discussion of blindness in this passage is in the description of the idols, not the people.

Bringing the Blind from the North, Jeremiah 31:8

Translation

THE TEXT

The next passage to be considered in the book of Jeremiah is Jer 31:8. It appears in translation below:

הִנְנִי מֵבִיא אוֹתָם מֵאֶרֶץ צָפוֹן וְקִבַּצְתִּים מִיַּרְכְּתֵי־אָרֶץ בָּם עִוֵּר וּפִסֵּחַ הָרָה
וְיֹלֶדֶת יַחְדָּו קָהָל גָּדוֹל יָשׁוּבוּ הֵנָּה׃

> 8. See, I am going to bring them from the land of the north,
>   and gather them from the farthest parts of the earth,
>   among them the blind and the lame,
>   those with child and those in labor, together;
>   a great company, they shall return here. (NRSV)

Exegesis

LITERARY ANALYSIS

The second-fifth words in v. 8 contain a noteworthy pattern of alliteration, as noted by the Word Biblical Commentary. The last letter of one word begins the following word. מֵבִיא ends with an א, and אוֹתָם, the following word, begins with an א. Also, אוֹתָם ends with a מ, and מֵאֶרֶץ begins with a מ. The latter word ends with a ץ, while the word after it, צָפוֹן, begins with a צ. Such a pattern would force the reader to slow down to pronounce the words clearly, and also, then, to emphasize them.[73] This return from exile, then, introduced with language to encourage emphasis, would be momentous and awe-inspiring, but deliberately stated not to exclude or hinder the blind.

One may also note the pairs of words used to describe those assisted by God. First, one finds the blind and lame, two disability groups, then those with child and giving birth, two groups weakened by matters related to pregnancy. As, "with child" and "giving birth" can be understood as describing every aspect of pregnancy, so, "blind" and "lame" can be seen as representing all types of disabilities. This could be seen as another clear example where "blind" and "lame" are used as a merism.

In addition, it may also be noted that blindness and lameness are weakening conditions involving negative aspects of loss and doing without. Pregnancy and birth are weakening conditions involving the positive aspect of gaining, fulfilling the command to be fruitful and multiply (Gen 1:28). Thus, the structure of this verse suggests that every possible type of weakness, negative and positive, would be accommodated by God.

Context

One must first note parallels between Jer 31:8–9 and Lev 19:14. Jeremiah 31:8 and Lev 19:14 use the same word for "blind." Jeremiah 31:9 uses the verbal form, כשל, to which the noun, מִכְשׁוֹל, "stumbling block" (Lev 19:14) is related. God, then, would treat his people with the same dignity he commanded them to treat each other. As an Israelite should not cause the blind to stumble, according to Lev 19:14, God would not cause the weak, including the blind, to stumble, according to Jer 31:9.

One must next note the similarities between this passage and Isa 43:6–8. Both passages involve people's being brought from the north. The same words for "bring" and "north" appear in the Hebrew. One group, amid this multitude that is brought, is the blind, with the same word for "blind" being used in both places. This parallel reinforces the common meaning that God expressed intent toward returning these people in some latter day of favor.

---

73. Keown, Scalise, and Smothers, *Jeremiah 26–52*, 113.

General Analysis

J. A. Thompson rightly notes how Jer 31:8 appears to speak of the time of the return from the exile to Babylon, in the north. The people, especially the weakest, being brought back from Babylon would be led by God with special care and providence.[74] While Isa 43, though, appears to refer to figurative blindness, as previously noted, Jer 31:8 may refer more to physical blindness. There is no discussion made in Jer 31:8 of causing the people to see or hear anything in the domain of truth, a concept expressed in Isa 43:10. In addition, the groups mentioned in Jer 31:8 are difficult to place all symbolically. The verse mentions the blind, the lame, and those with child, the latter, extremely difficult to interpret exegetically with a clear spiritual meaning in the text. It has already been noted how the idiom "blind and lame" is often a merism referring to all disabilities. By including pregnant women in this group, the meaning expands to refer to all who are weak. Thus, this passage, mentioning blindness first, says that God would lead all who are weak back to their homeland by his special care.

The Blinding of Zedekiah, in Jeremiah, Jeremiah 39:6–7; 52:10–11

Translation

The text

Since Jer 39:6–7 and Jer 52:10 11 are nearly identical in nearly identical passages as they discuss this topic, both verses are considered together below in translation.

וַיִּשְׁחַט מֶלֶךְ בָּבֶל אֶת־בְּנֵי צִדְקִיָּהוּ בְּרִבְלָה לְעֵינָיו וְאֵת כָּל־חֹרֵי יְהוּדָה שָׁחַט מֶלֶךְ בָּבֶל:
וְאֶת־עֵינֵי צִדְקִיָּהוּ עִוֵּר וַיַּאַסְרֵהוּ בַנְחֻשְׁתַּיִם לָבִיא אֹתוֹ בָּבֶלָה:

> 6. The king of Babylon slaughtered the sons of Zedekiah at Riblah before his eyes; also the king of Babylon slaughtered all the nobles of Judah.
> 7. He put out the eyes of Zedekiah, and bound him in fetters to take him to Babylon. (NRSV)

וַיִּשְׁחַט מֶלֶךְ־בָּבֶל אֶת־בְּנֵי צִדְקִיָּהוּ לְעֵינָיו וְגַם אֶת־כָּל־שָׂרֵי יְהוּדָה שָׁחַט בְּרִבְלָתָה:

---

74. J. A. Thompson, *The Book of Jeremiah*, 570.

וְאֶת־עֵינֵי צִדְקִיָּהוּ עִוֵּר וַיַּאַסְרֵהוּ בַנְחֻשְׁתַּיִם וַיְבִאֵהוּ מֶלֶךְ־בָּבֶל בָּבֶלָה
וַיִּתְּנֵהוּ בְבֵית־[בֵית־]הַפְּקֻדֹּת עַד־יוֹם מוֹתוֹ׃

> 10. The king of Babylon killed the sons of Zedekiah before his eyes, and also killed all the officers of Judah at Riblah.
> 11. He put out the eyes of Zedekiah, and bound him in fetters, and the king of Babylon took him to Babylon, and put him in prison until the day of his death. (NRSV)

Notes

The Hebrew word order in these verses differs slightly when compared with the English above. In both clauses, when the killing of the officers is stated, the Hebrew text places the words for "officers" at the beginning of the respective clauses. When the eyes of Zedekiah are said to be put out, the Hebrew expression for "eyes of Zedekiah" appears first in both respective clauses. Lundbom rightly notes that this irregular word order places emphasis on the idea of the eyes of the king.[75] The same logic could be used to say that emphasis is placed on the officers, also mentioned irregularly first in their respective clauses.

Exegesis

Context

One may compare and contrast these passages in the context of 2 Kgs 25. In 2 Kgs 25, the slaughter of the other leaders at Riblah is not discussed until vv. 18–21, and then in significantly more detail. In addition, the Hebrew word order of 2 Kgs 25:7, as noted previously, suggests emphasis on the idea of the sons of Zedekiah rather than on the slaughtering. In both places in Jeremiah, the Hebrew word order is more standard with the verb "slaughter" mentioned first.

The situation is different, though, regarding the blinding of Zedekiah. As previously noted, in the Hebrew of both passages in Jeremiah, the direct object, the eyes of Zedekiah, is mentioned first. In 2 Kgs 25:7 the clause about the blinding of Zedekiah is exactly identical, with the word "eyes" also mentioned first. Such repetition of this exact clause with no difference among three passages further reinforces the extreme emphasis on this idea.

---

75. Lundbom, *Jeremiah 37–52*, 88.

General analysis

These two Jeremiah passages differ only slightly. First, while Jer 39 mentions the nobles of Judah, Jer 52 mentions the princes of Judah. Second, Jer 39 says that Zedekiah's eyes were put out in Riblah, while Jer 52 says that the princes were killed in Riblah.

Few additional exegetical concepts can be gained from this restatement of a story previously studied. This concept of the king's blinding, though, was deemed important enough for it to be mentioned twice in Jeremiah as well as once in 2 Kings. In addition, by listing the slaughter of the officials of Judah between that of Zedekiah's sons and the putting out of his eyes, one may get the literary sense that all these tragedies happened to the king, and then he was blinded. This sense would exist whether or not the killing of the officials actually happened before Zedekiah was blinded. The blinding of the king, then, would be a grim climax to all these disasters.

Finally, a thematic parallel exists between Jer 52:3 and Jer 5:23. Jeremiah 52:3 says that Zedekiah rebelled against the king of Babylon, an action that eventually resulted in his blinding. In Jer 5:23, the people of Judah, as noted previously to follow idols that have eyes but do not see, are said also to be rebellious against God. While different words for rebellion are used in both passages, one must note the similar concepts. In both cases rebellion and lack of sight are connected.

One, though, may find a poetic parallel in word sounds between these two passages. One of the words for "rebellious" in Jer 5:23 is, consonantally, מרה. The word for "rebelled" in Jer 52:3 is מרד. The difference is only one letter, and that one letter is only one letter different in the order of the Hebrew alphabet.[76]

Having Eyes But Not Seeing in Ezekiel, Ezekiel 12:2, 13

Translation

The text

The only significant references to blindness in the book of Ezekiel are found in Ezek 12:2, 13. These verses appear below:

---

76. On this phenomenon of letter permutation by alphabetic order, see Doukhan, *Hebrew for Theologians*, 64.

בֶּן־אָדָם בְּתוֹךְ בֵּית־הַמֶּרִי אַתָּה יֹשֵׁב אֲשֶׁר עֵינַיִם לָהֶם לִרְאוֹת וְלֹא רָאוּ אָזְנַיִם לָהֶם לִשְׁמֹעַ וְלֹא שָׁמֵעוּ כִּי בֵּית מְרִי הֵם:וַיִּתְּנֵהוּ בְּבֵית־[בֵית־] הַפְּקֻדֹּת עַד־יוֹם מוֹתוֹ:

2. Mortal, you are living in the midst of a rebellious house, who have eyes to see but do not see, who have ears to hear but do not hear. (NRSV)

וּפָרַשְׂתִּי אֶת־רִשְׁתִּי עָלָיו וְנִתְפַּשׂ בִּמְצוּדָתִי וְהֵבֵאתִי אֹתוֹ בָבֶלָה אֶרֶץ כַּשְׂדִּים וְאוֹתָהּ לֹא־יִרְאֶה וְשָׁם יָמוּת:

13. I will spread my net over him, and he shall be caught in my snare; and I will bring him to Babylon, the land of the Chaldeans, yet he shall not see it; and he shall die there. (NRSV)

Notes

A literal rendering of the first clause of v. 2, based on vocabulary and Hebrew word order, reads, "Son of humanity, amid a rebellious house you dwell." The expression translated "mortal" is "בֶּן־אָדָם," or "son of man/humanity." In addition, after saying that the people have ears and do not hear, the Hebrew continues to repeat the theme of the opening of the verse, saying, "for a rebellious house they are." In addition, in v. 13, when the text is translated to say, "yet he shall not see it," the opening particle in that clause is a vav consecutive, which can mean, "and, but, or yet."

Exegesis

Literary analysis

Verse 2 contains a chiastic structure. The verse begins and ends with a discussion of the people's rebelliousness. In the center and climax is a discussion of sensory organs that the people have but do not use.

Ezekiel 12:1–13 also employs a parallel structure. The passage can be divided as vv. 1–7 and 8–16. Each half contains references to lack of seeing, going to captivity, digging through the wall, carrying on one's shoulders, and covering the face to keep from seeing the ground. This, then, connects the different references to blindness, making them both part of a unified discourse.

Finally, Daniel I. Block observantly notes the repetition of certain relevant concepts relating to seeing. The term "in their sight," or "to their eyes," literally, from the Hebrew, appears seven times in Ezek 12:2–13. The word, ראה, also appears five times in this passage in different forms.[77] Clearly, then, issues relating to sight are central to this entire passage.

Context

Ezekiel 12:2 develops a theme set forth elsewhere in the Latter Prophets. One may recall Isa 6:9–10 and Isa 43:8, which both discuss people's having eyes and ears but not seeing. One may also compare Ezek 12:2 with Jer 5:21–23. Both passages mention the rebelliousness of the people of Judah. Related words for "rebellious" are even employed: מֹרֶה in Jer 5:23 and מְרִי in Ezek 12:2. Both passages also mention having eyes but not seeing and having ears but not hearing, even in that same order. It must be noted, though, that the statement in Jeremiah may refer more to the weakness of idols, and the statement in Ezekiel to the weakness of the people. Ezekiel 12 also does not mention the weakened condition of the people's hearts as does Jer 5:21. Finally, in contrast to the passages in both Isaiah and Jeremiah, Ezek 12:2 emphasizes most deeply how the people should see and hear but do not. While Isaiah and Jeremiah simply refer to having eyes and ears but not seeing and hearing, Ezekiel says that the people have "eyes to see" and "ears to hear" but neither see nor hear. The infinitive expressions "to see" and "to hear" appear only in Ezek 12:2. The contrast between what should happen with the eyes and ears and what does happen with the eyes and ears is further emphasized, then, in Ezek 12.

One may also compare Ezek 12:2 with Ezek 8:12 and Ezek 9:9. Iain M. Duguid rightly observes that while the people in Ezek 12 are said by God to not see, in Ezek 8:12 and Ezek 9:9 the people who are in wickedness say that God does not see and has forsaken them.[78] One must also note, though, that the judgment handed down in Ezek 9 shows that, in reality, God does see. In Ezek 12:2, then, God, who does see, says he would judge the people who should see but do not, and who previously said he does not see.

---

77. Block, *The Book of Ezekiel Chapters 1–24*, 365.
78. Duguid, *Ezekiel*, 160.

General Analysis

Ezekiel 12:3 gives a conclusive clue to the nature of this blindness. Ezekiel was to gather his things and remove himself as would happen to the people when taken into exile. God tells Ezekiel to perform both these actions in the people's sight, or literally, "to their eyes." If their literal eyes were unable to see, as v. 2 says, there would be no purpose in saying, twice, that actions would be done before such eyes. Therefore, the performing of Ezekiel's actions before the people's physical eyes was to guide them to see with their spiritual eyes that were able to see but not employed in such a task. They may have physically observed Ezekiel's unusual dramatics, but in their rebellion, they refused to see spiritually.

Regarding v. 13, one may note the cryptic reference to the prince who will go to captivity but never see it. Ralph H. Alexander insightfully notes that this, most likely, refers to Zedekiah who was blinded at Riblah on the way to prison in Babylon (2 Kgs 25:7).[79]

Daniel I. Block, though, argues that the reference to not seeing it does not concern the land of Babylon, but the land of Israel, since the vav consecutive does not necessarily mean "but," but could mean "and." Ezekiel 12:12 says how the prince would flee, covering his face so he would not see the land אֶרֶץ, as in v. 13, with his eyes. If Ezek 12:13 means that Zedekiah would no longer see his own native land, that would refer to permanent exile away from his home, not necessarily blinding.[80]

The first problem with this notion is that the most recent noun named before "it" in Ezek 12:13 is the land of the Chaldeans, Babylon. That would logically, then, be the likely default antecedent for "it." Thus, the "it" that would not be seen must be Babylon, or the land of the Chaldeans. The second problem with this notion is that immediately after saying he would not see "it," Ezek 12:13 says that he would die there. If the land that the king would not see is Judah, that land would most likely be the logical antecedent of "there," where he would die, and that appears immediately afterward. Jeremiah 52:11, though, says plainly that Zedekiah lived in Babylon in prison until the day of his death. Thus, "there," in Ezek 12:13, must refer to Babylon. If "there," which is Babylon or the land of the Chaldeans, refers the reader to the "it" that would not be seen, such an unseen place would necessarily also be Babylon. Zedekiah could not see Babylon as he, by then, did not have eyes any more to see it. The covering of his eyes so he would not see the land must refer to a different activity such as, possibly, the blinding

---

79. Alexander, "Ezekiel," 797.
80. Block, *The Book of Ezekiel Chapters 1–24*, 377, 378.

of Zedekiah on the way to Babylon, or the shame in fleeing the capital of his defeated land.

A reference to the blinding of Zedekiah in Ezek 12:13 completes a noteworthy play on the concept of blindness. First, the people had eyes but did not see spiritually. This would result in the king's losing his physical eyes and not seeing anything physically. Verse 12 also refers to the people's faces covered so they would not see the ground physically. Thus, their spiritual blindness would result in a form of physical blindness for them. Physical and spiritual blindness, then, are connected literarily here.

Blindness in the Day of the Lord, Zephaniah 1:17

Translation

The text

The first instance of blindness in the Minor Prophets occurs in Zeph 1:17 in the context of the Day of the Lord. The text appears below.

וַהֲצֵרֹתִי לָאָדָם וְהָלְכוּ כַּעִוְרִים כִּי לַיהוָה חָטָאוּ וְשֻׁפַּךְ דָּמָם כֶּעָפָר וּלְחֻמָם כַּגְּלָלִים׃

> 17. I will bring such distress upon people
> that they shall walk like the blind;
> because they have sinned against the LORD,
> their blood shall be poured out like dust,
> and their flesh like dung. (NRSV)

Notes

The Hebrew word order of the clause concerning the sinning would be literally translated, "For against the LORD they have sinned." This places emphasis on the One sinned against.

Exegesis

Context

Larry Lee Walker rightly notes that a number of parallels exist between Zeph 1:13–18 and Deut 28:28–30, which both discuss judgments for sin.[81] This analysis is correct since both passages contain references to the people being as the blind, with the same word for "blind" appearing in the Hebrew of both texts. Next, both Zeph 1:13 and Deut 28:30 refer to people's building of houses and not dwelling in them and their planting of vineyards and not enjoying the produce. While the word order is different between the passages, they have the Hebrew words for "build," "house," "not dwell," "plant," and "vineyard" in common. Thematically, both Deut 28:28 and Zeph 1:17 refer to troubled hearts, and Deut 28:29 and Zeph 1:18 refer to how nothing would save the people from their tragedies. Then, Zeph 1:17 says that this being as the blind is a result of the people's sins. This is, of course, similar to how the curses of Deut 28 have already been shown to be a result of the people's disobedience to God.

This clearly sets the blindness of the Day of the Lord in the context of the curses of the Covenant. The coming judgments would be a direct promised response by God to the people's sins.

General analysis

It is difficult to determine how literal or figurative one may take this passage since it is a prophecy, and one does not know exactly how prophecy is to be fulfilled until it is. No matter what, the mental blindness of confusion and terror might easily be associated with these judgments on such a day of darkness (Zeph 1:15–16) however literal the blindness is in the physical world. James Bruckner also rightly notes that such blindness may also involve a lack of orientation regarding God and his ways. Those suffering such, then, could not see God spiritually.[82]

---

81. Walker, "Zephania," 550.
82. Bruckner, *Jonah, Nahum, Habakkuk, Zephania*, 291.

Blinding the Shepherds, Zechariah 11:17

Translation

THE TEXT

One must now consider Zech 11:17 in the address to unfaithful shepherds. The translation follows:

הוֹי רֹעִי הָאֱלִיל עֹזְבִי הַצֹּאן חֶרֶב עַל־זְרוֹעוֹ וְעַל־עֵין יְמִינוֹ זְרֹעוֹ יָבוֹשׁ תִּיבָשׁ וְעֵין יְמִינוֹ כָּהֹה תִכְהֶה׃

17. Oh, my worthless shepherd,
   who deserts the flock!
May the sword strike his arm
   and his right eye!
Let his arm be completely withered,
   his right eye utterly blinded! (NRSV)

NOTES

Carol L. Meyers and Eric M. Meyers rightly note the use of infinitive absolutes for emphasis and intensification in this verse. The arm would not simply be dried up, but utterly dried up. The right eye would not simply grow slightly dim, but would grow utterly dim.[83]

Exegesis

CONTEXT

One may first recall the First Soldier's Oath, which, as noted previously, says that one who is an unfaithful warrior would face the divinely ordained penalty of blindness. In the Bible, one may recall Isa 56:10–11, which refers to blind watchmen and incompetent shepherds. In Isa 56, though, the incompetent leaders are already blind, while in Zech 11, it is threatened that they would become blind. This parallel, though, is useful because both Isa 56 and Zech 11 concern irresponsibility. That which struck the leaders in Isa 56 would, in some form, strike the irresponsible leaders described in Zech 11.

Then, Carol L. Meyers and Eric M. Meyers insightfully observe that 1 Sam 11:2, where the right eyes of fighting men were threatened to be

---

83. Meyers and Meyers, *Zechariah 9–14*, 292.

gouged out by a foreign king, the right eye represented the military might of the people of the city.[84] First Samuel 11:2, though, concerns a situation different from Zech 11 as the men of Jabesh-Gilead were not described as being incompetent leaders. Nonetheless, 1 Sam 11 provides useful information regarding the importance of the right eye.

Next, the context of the surrounding chapters of Zechariah provides insight regarding the identity of the flock. In Zechariah, the flock often refers to God's people, Judah. Zechariah 10:2–4 and 11:3–5 are examples.

General analysis

In Zech 11:17, God says that he would punish the shepherds who neglect the flock. Shepherds who would need a strong arm to handle a staff and a vigilant eye to see predators would lose these because of laziness and lack of taking responsibility. Often, as noted previously, when the word כהה is used with reference to the eye, it suggests a type of weakness associated with old age (Gen 27:1; Deut 34:7). While this may not be the only use for this idiom, the fact that the physical strength of these shepherds is said to soon weaken is consistent, at least, with some form of disabling condition. It is difficult to note how literal this verse is to be taken, especially as the reference to shepherds appears also to be figurative. Carol L. Meyers and Eric M. Meyers, though, are reasonable in suggesting that the worthless shepherds may refer specifically to false prophets who were originally to guide God's people with his wisdom.[85] However this would be fulfilled, H. C. Leupold rightly notes that the leaders who fail to use their eyes and arms for the tasks God gave them, such as aiding the weak and the broken (Zech 11:16), will find such members wasting away.[86]

Madness and Blindness of Horse and Rider, Zechariah 12:4

Translation

The text

The following is a translation of Zech 12:4.

---

84. Meyers and Meyers, *Zechariah 9–14*, 291.
85. Meyers and Meyers, *Zechariah 9–14*, 292.
86. Leupold, *Exposition of Zechariah*, 221.

בַּיּוֹם הַהוּא נְאֻם־יְהוָה אַכֶּה כָל־סוּס בַּתִּמָּהוֹן וְרֹכְבוֹ בַּשִּׁגָּעוֹן וְעַל־בֵּית יְהוּדָה אֶפְקַח אֶת־עֵינַי וְכֹל סוּס הָעַמִּים אַכֶּה בַּעִוָּרוֹן:

4. On that day, says the LORD, I will strike every horse with panic, and its rider with madness. But on the house of Judah I will keep a watchful eye, when I strike every horse of the peoples with blindness. (NRSV)

Exegesis

LITERARY ANALYSIS

Mark Allen Hahlen and Clay Alan Ham insightfully observe that the words for "panic, madness," and "blindness" in v. 4 all rhyme in the Hebrew, ending with the *-own* suffix.[87] This literary device would draw attention to those three words as a literary set, strengthening their intensity.

CONTEXT

Carol L. Meyers and Eric M. Meyers rightly note the parallels between this verse and Deut 28:28 in the curses of the covenant. Both verses mention God's smiting with astonishment, madness, and blindness, with the same words for "smite, madness, blindness," and "astonishment" used in the Hebrew, though the word order is different. Deuteronomy 28:28 and Zech 12:4, in fact, are the only two texts that use the Hebrew word תִּמָּהוֹן, "astonishment."[88] In both cases, the people of Israel are concerned, though Deut 28 discusses punishments placed on Israel, and Zech 12:4, judgments against those peoples who attack Jerusalem (Zech 12:3). Apparently plagues, often understood as curses of the covenant, fall on those outside Israel who interfere with God's plans for Israel.

In reality, this concept is not foreign to Deut 28. Verse 7 says that if Israel remained faithful to the covenant, its enemies would be smitten, approaching from one direction and fleeing in seven. According to v. 25, if Israel violated the covenant, the opposite would be true and Israel would be smitten, approaching the enemies from one direction and fleeing in seven. Even in Deut 28, then, those who invade righteous Israel would face at least

---

87. Hahlen and Ham, *Minor Prophets*, 461.
88. Meyers and Meyers, *Zechariah 9–14*, 319, 320.

some of the same penalties as Israel for interfering with the covenant God made with Israel.

General analysis

Again, it is difficult to know how literally to understand the blindness of Zech 12:4. The final result of such blindness, though, would be an inability to perceive and to fight properly.

Carol L. Meyers and Eric M. Meyers also insightfully note how the play of ideas regarding sight and blindness is also remarkable in this verse. It is said that God would open his eyes and smite with blindness. When God's eyes are opened for Judah so he can see, the judgment on the wicked is a smiting with blindness so they cannot see. God's vision results in the lack of vision for evildoers.[89]

Eyes Consuming Away in Sockets, Zechariah 14:12

Translation

The text

The focus now turns to those armies of surrounding nations that would eventually rise one last time against Jerusalem. The following is a translation of Zech 14:12:

> וְזֹאת תִּהְיֶה הַמַּגֵּפָה אֲשֶׁר יִגֹּף יְהוָה אֶת־כָּל־הָעַמִּים אֲשֶׁר צָבְאוּ עַל־יְרוּשָׁלָ͏ִם הָמֵק בְּשָׂרוֹ וְהוּא עֹמֵד עַל־רַגְלָיו וְעֵינָיו תִּמַּקְנָה בְחֹרֵיהֶן וּלְשׁוֹנוֹ תִּמַּק בְּפִיהֶם׃

> 12. This shall be the plague with which the LORD will strike all the peoples that wage war against Jerusalem: their flesh shall rot while they are still on their feet; their eyes shall rot in their sockets, and their tongues shall rot in their mouths. (NRSV)

---

89. Meyers and Meyers, *Zechariah 9–14*, 321.

Exegesis

LITERARY ANALYSIS

This verse contains a Hebrew repetition of the word מקק, consume away. Three things, flesh, eyes, and tongues, would consume away. The eye is the placed as the center item of the three in the list.

CONTEXT

One must first recall the ancient Near Eastern curses mentioned in chapter 2 in which a king proclaims blindness upon his foes in battle. In Zech 14, though, God would be placing blindness on his ultimate enemies as their eyes would waste away in their sockets. Such an army would be unable to offer physical resistance as their flesh would wither, unable to see to flee or aim correctly as their eyes would wither, and unable to speak out about these as their tongues would wither. As Carol L. Meyers and Eric M. Meyers rightly note, the socket, in which one would expect the eye to be protected, would provide no safety from this sudden debilitation, powerful enough to cause the army to consume away rapidly even while the soldiers yet stand.[90] Blindness acts as a significant judgment to further weaken the enemies of God and his people. This blindness is, then, not designed as a covenant curse, but more as a military defense strategy, somewhat similar in purpose to that which struck the men of Sodom (Gen 19:11) and the Syrians (2 Kgs 6:18).

The wasting away of the eye in Zech 14 is significant also because just a few verses prior is a discussion of how the city of Jerusalem in that day would be light all the time and extremely bright during the daytime. The blindness of Zech 14:12 would keep God's enemies, most directly, from beholding this wonder. They, because of their hatred, would be shut away from the marvels God would give.

Malachi and the Blind Sacrifices, Malachi 1:8

Translation

THE TEXT

The last occurrence of blindness in the Prophets is in the last book of the Prophets, Malachi. Malachi 1:8 appears translated below.

---

90. Meyers and Meyers, *Zechariah 9–14*, 454.

וְכִי־תַגִּשׁוּן עִוֵּר לִזְבֹּחַ אֵין רָע וְכִי תַגִּישׁוּ פִּסֵּחַ וְחֹלֶה אֵין רָע הַקְרִיבֵהוּ נָא לְפֶחָתֶךָ הֲיִרְצְךָ אוֹ הֲיִשָּׂא פָנֶיךָ אָמַר יְהוָה צְבָאוֹת:

8. When you offer blind animals in sacrifice, is that not wrong? And when you offer those that are lame or sick, is that not wrong? Try presenting that to your governor; will he be pleased with you or show you favor? says the LORD of hosts. (NRSV)

Exegesis

Context

One may first recall Deut 15:21, which lists two of the same three disabling conditions, blindness and lameness, that would invalidate an animal for cultic use as a first fruits offering. Both verses also use the word, רָע, evil—Deut 15:21 with reference to the evil blemish, and Mal 1:8 with reference to how one does not find evil in offering a blind sacrifice. While Deut 15:21, though, is concerned mainly with the first-fruits offerings, Andrew E. Hill insightfully notes how Mal 1:8 applies this list to all sacrifices. Any animal offered to God must be free from these conditions, according to Mal 1:8.[91] This is reasonable since Mal 1:8 lists no specific situation when this sacrifice would be offered, such as first fruits.

One must next note the context immediately before Mal 1:8. First, in Mal 1:2–5, God tells his people how much he loves them. In spite of this love, though, the people regard him with less respect than they would a governor. In Mal 1:6, God even says that he, as Father and Master to his people, does not receive the due respect. Verse 8 illustrated how one significant aspect of this disrespect is the offering of blind, lame, and sick sacrifices.

General analysis

Pieter A. Verhoef makes a number of insightful observations regarding the people's behavior based on the text of Mal 1:8. First, the people, apparently, are described as simply following the forms of a ritual without taking into consideration the importance of performing the ritual properly. They simply do the motions of the ritual regardless of the quality of the animal. In addition, these improper sacrifices were not simply offered by the people, but tolerated and accepted by the priests who could have refused them.

---

91. Hill, *Malachi*, 179.

In addition, the word, קרב, often a cultic term, is used for "present," when the people are invited to present their disabled offerings to the governor.[92] Clearly, then, God would have reason to be disappointed in his people's behavior. While the people would not be encouraged by God to worship the governor, using such a cultic word would draw their attention to their bringing of sacrifices before the true God. God, then, is comparing himself to an earthly governor whom all would understand deserves great respect.

Malachi 1:8 suggests that one significant reason for offering unblemished sacrifices is to show great respect to God. Since a governor would not accept a blemished offering, and since few people would consider bringing a governor a blemished gift, God, above all humans, would naturally deserve even more respect, as the highest Governor. Though the focus in Lev 22 and Deut 15 might center more around holiness, the interpretation offered by Mal 1:8 is valid. It would definitely be considered unholy to be disrespectful to God, and disrespectful to be unholy. Blindness, here, is one of the conditions listed in what is most likely a merism, discussing any blemish, as noted previously with reference to other uses of blindness and lameness in close proximity in the text.

Summary

A number of blindness passages in the remainder of the Latter Prophets are considered in this section. First, in Jer 5:21, it is noted that the idols that the people served had eyes but could not see. This showed the blindness of such false gods. Then, in Jer 31:8, God describes how he would assist all people of weakness, positive or negative, in the return trip from Babylon. Blindness represents a serious physical disability among these. Jeremiah 39:6–7 and Jer 52:10–11 describe the blinding of Zedekiah as a result of his rebellion. It is noteworthy that the eyes of Zedekiah consistently are emphasized throughout the various accounts of his demise. Next, Ezek 12:1–13 connects the spiritual blindness of those who have eyes to see but do not with the approaching physical blinding of Zedekiah, showing how spiritual blindness can lead to physical blindness in certain situations.

The remaining five references to blindness are in the Minor Prophets. Zephaniah 1:17 borrows language from the covenant curses in Deut 28:28–29 to describe the groping as the blind during the Day of the Lord. Then, Zech 11:17 expresses a theme similar to Isa 56:10 by describing how incompetent shepherd leaders would soon have their right eyes and right arms greatly weakened. The blindness then afflicts Israel's enemies, as in

---

92. Verhoef, *The Books of Haggai and Malachi*, 218.

Zech 12:4 when the horses of the enemies would be smitten with blindness. The curses that might strike unfaithful Israel based on Deut 28 would smite their enemies who interfere with God's plans. Then, in Zech 14:12, the eyes of those who would attack Jerusalem would be consumed. This is one aspect of a general wasting that would befall such enemies. Finally, Mal 1:8 discusses how the offering of blind sacrifices is a great sign of disrespect to God, as one would not even do such for an earthly governor.

THEOLOGICAL SYNTHESIS AND SUMMARY

The Cultus

One may recall the discussions in Torah concerning the prohibitions against offering blind sacrifices because such were blemished. Malachi 1:6–8 adds that an additional reason for not offering blind animals to the Lord is that offering such, which would be unthinkable before a governor, shows great disrespect to God who deserves only the best. This shows how the concept of offering perfect sacrifices was developed during the time of the prophets.

A number of allowances were given to the blind in the realm of Israelite religion. First, the story of Eli in 1 Sam 3–4 illustrates how a priest blinded by old age was not necessarily forbidden to function. Since Eli is not described as an עִוֵּר, and did not suffer from complete vision loss, he still could act as high priest. Blindness due to old age was also not a hindrance to the prophetic gift, this shown by the prophet's being given knowledge of the disguise of Jeroboam's wife in 1 Kgs 14.

One must, next, consider Samson, whose strong physical powers were taken away after he disregarded God's instructions regarding the proper keeping of his hair. God still used him in his weakened condition to perform his greatest feat (Judg 16). The total blindness of the judge did not make him unavailable to the miraculous power of God.

Causes of Blindness

Physical Causes

One cause of blindness in the prophets is old age. Eli and Ahijah are examples. Blindness is also described as being inflicted by other people. One may note the blindings of Samson and Zedekiah and the threatened gouging out of one eye by Nahash.

Spiritual Causes

One must next examine the cases when God directly brings about blindness. Second Kings 6:17–20 is the second example of the word סַנְוֵרִים in the Hebrew Bible. It has already been noted how, in both cases, this word appears: this blinding was performed to protect innocent servants of God from attacks by evil people. Then, in Zech 11:17, God says he would cause the right eyes of unfaithful shepherds to waste away. In Zech 12:4, God smites the horses of his enemies with blindness. Next, in Zech 14:12, God causes the eyes of those attacking Jerusalem to be consumed. Even the blindings inflicted by other people are often associated with spiritual causes. Samson's blinding came as a result of careless disregard of the duty to protect his Nazirite vows (Judg 13:5; 16:17–21). It has already been noted how Zedekiah's blinding came as a result of his disregard for God's authority and the oath he made to God to submit to Babylon as recorded in 2 Chronicles. It may also be noted that a number of individuals were delivered from blindness. The men of Jabesh Gilead were rescued from their undeserved blinding. After Elisha's prayer, his servant was healed of his blindness, which prevented him from seeing God's armies.

Social Justice

What one can observe about how the blind are to be treated, according to the Prophets, is found in passages that describe how God treats the blind. First, God used Samson, blinded by enemies because of disregard for God's commands, to perform his greatest feat. God also used Ahijah, blinded by age, to prophesy, even assisting him in outsmarting the visual disguise of Jeroboam's wife. Then, in Jer 31:8 God says that after the captivity to Babylon, he would personally lead, among many weakened groups, the blind. God would not simply make the blind to "fend for themselves" on such a difficult journey. Then, in a text studied more in depth in the next section, God, in Isa 35:5–6, promises that one day the eyes of the blind would be opened. Clearly, then, God, by his own actions, demonstrated a desire for the blind to occupy as useful and enjoyable positions as possible in society. God would even work miraculously to assist in this process, ultimately to reverse blindness itself and erase it from existence.

Reversal of Blindness

The Prophets contain few references to the prevention or healing of physical blindness. Some remarks on these passages and the topic in general in the Prophets follow. First, though, it must be noted that nowhere in the Prophets or in the Torah is there described a specific ritual or prayer for healing or preventing blindness. No instruction in any form is given regarding this matter. One must simply consider case examples where such happened and derive principles.

One must first consider the example of preventing blindness in 1 Sam 11 when the men of Jabesh Gilead were saved from such fate by an act of war by the Israelites, guided by God's Spirit (1 Sam 11:6, 7). In this case, as well as that of Moses' retaining his sight in old age, then, blindness is prevented by miraculous means, though, in completely different ways.

Next, two passages in the Prophets concern the healing of blindness. Elisha, in 2 Kgs 6:17–20, prays twice for eyes to be opened. The first time, his servant's eyes were opened to the reality of the heavenly army. The second instance involved Elisha's praying that the Syrian army's blinded eyes be opened. In both cases, the prayer of a man of God, or, holy man, קָדוֹשׁ, was enough to result in God's providing the miracle (2 Kgs 4:9). Thus, the prayer of one who is holy and righteous before God is all that is required, theoretically, for the reversal of blindness. Next, in Isa 35:5–6 it is predicted that, in the grand Messianic era, God would completely reverse blindness, opening the eyes of the blind. One day there would come a time when God would no longer seek to assist those who are blind or guide others in how to treat the blind. Rather, God would simply heal blindness. Clearly, then, it is God's desire that all should be done to prevent and heal blindness.

Meanings of Blindness

Meanings of Physical Blindness

Blindness in the physical realm was also often associated with weakness. In 2 Sam 5:6–8, the blind and the lame became symbols of weakest Jebusites, still able to defend against David's forces, as the city believed. Even if the Jebusites were attempting to invoke a curse, as in the First Soldier's Oath, blindness is still associated with the weakness with which David's forces would be smitten in the fulfillment of such a curse. According to Mal 1:6–8, such a blemish in an animal lowered the worthiness of such as an effective gift of value to show proper respect.

One may next recall how blindness was often connected with prison. Isaiah 42:7 places healing blindness in the context of release from prison. Samson and Zedekiah were both blinded before their imprisonment. The darkness of dungeons, most likely, played a significant role in this association. In a way, in addition, the lack of mobility often known by the blind could also be seen as imprisoning.

Finally, as noted previously, physical blindness was often associated with rebellion.

Meanings of Spiritual Blindness

The first meaning for spiritual blindness to be considered here is that of lack of perception. Isaiah 56:10 discusses this theme in noting how Israel's shepherds have become blind and like mute dogs. They, then, are said to have lost their effectiveness to lead. Their lack of vision would render them unable to perceive any evil that a shepherd should perceive to defend the sheep properly.

It has also been noted how, in addition to Zech 12:4, numerous passages in Isaiah such as Isa 42:16–20 and Isa 59:10 draw one's attention to blindness as an aspect of the covenant curses in Deut 28. Isaiah 6:9–10 and 29:9–10 and 18 show how blindness is connected with Israel's refusal to heed God's instruction. The blind servant poetry in Isa 42–43 also shows how a weakened spiritual state can be compared to disabilities such as blindness. Peter D. Quinn-Miscall rightly observes that salvation and restoration are described using the language of healing of such disability.[93] One need only consider Isa 42:6–7 for evidence of such.

Ezekiel 12:2, 13 illustrates how refusal to obey results in spiritual blindness, which, in Zedekiah's case, resulted further in physical blindness at the hands of the Babylonians. Such an imprisoning blindness, though, God would one day reverse, according to Isa 32:3–4.

The ultimate rebellion of idolatry is most deeply associated with blindness. Idolaters are said to worship idols that have eyes but do not see, according to Jer 5:21.

---

93. Quinn-Miascall, *Reading Isaiah*, 92.

VI

Blindness in the Writings

With an understanding of blindness in the Torah and Prophets, it is now necessary to consider the topic in the Writings. One finds the same methods employed in this chapter as the previous two, studying passage by passage all texts that concern blindness in the Writings. Each passage is considered with reference to issues of translation and exegesis. The chapter concludes with a theological summary and synthesis of the material previously discussed.

BLINDNESS IN THE PSALMS

The first passages to be considered in this chapter are in the Psalms. As a number of other passages studied in this chapter, these are prayers of individual people, showing deeper passion and emotion than one would find in simple historical accounts. These poetic passages, then, would show the attitudes people held toward the issue of blindness, and not simply the ideals that one is expected to hold.

Seven clear blindness passages are considered in the Psalms in this section. First, Ps 38:11 (10, English) with reference to the light having gone from the eyes is analyzed. Next, one finds an examination of Ps 40:13 (12, English) with reference to the effect of iniquity on the ability to see. Psalm 69:24 (23, English) is next considered with reference to the psalmist's prayer for the eyes of his enemies to be darkened. Psalm 94:7–9 is then examined, noting how the oppressors claim that God is blind. Then, Ps 115:5–7 and Ps 135:16, 17 are considered together because of their similarities. Finally, Ps 146:8 is considered with reference to God's being the One who opens blind eyes.

The Light Gone from the Eyes, Psalm 38:11 (10, English)

Translation

THE TEXT

The first blindness passage in the Psalms, Ps 38:11 (10, English), is presented below.

לִבִּי סְחַרְחַר עֲזָבַנִי כֹחִי וְאוֹר־עֵינַי גַּם־הֵם אֵין אִתִּי׃

> 11. My heart throbs, my strength fails me;
> as for the light of my eyes—it also has gone from me. (NRSV)

Exegesis

CONTEXT

One may recall the prayer to Enki written by Sin-Shamuh, the Scribe, discussed in chapter 2 of this study. There, the writer suffers also from conditions such as blindness, deafness, and the failing of his strength. In that case, as well as in Ps 38, the cause is thought to be related to the author's sins.

GENERAL ANALYSIS

It is first noteworthy that the reference to the light's no longer being with the eyes is part of a long litany of disabling conditions and situations. In the following verses, the psalmist describes himself as being as one who is deaf and mute as well as having numerous other ailments. Even his family and friends are said to have turned against him.

Peter C. Cragie suggests that this psalm could not be describing a real condition, present to the psalmist as one in such a situation would be too weak to write.[1] S. Edward Tesh and Walter D. Zorn discuss that such a complex and all-encompassing description could even be simply a symbolic way of portraying the sin of Israel as a whole and its consequences.[2]

While this passage could be figurative, the potential lack of ability to write it down during the illness is irrelevant to the discussion. It must be noted that Hezekiah wrote of his literal illness in detail after the healing (Isa 38:9–20). The psalmist could have composed this psalm after he recovered

---

1. Craigie, *Psalms 1–50*, 304.
2. Tesh and Zorn, *Psalms*, 295.

if he was too weak to write while sick. His thoughts during his illness would be processed and organized upon recovery and written or dictated then. Of course, if the psalm were dictated, no ability to write physically would be needed from the psalmist. Then, while this psalm may concern sins of Israel as a whole, it is still possible for one to suffer from a number of illnesses or for one to describe figuratively his/her suffering in the terms of a number of illnesses. Thus, one should not rule out the possibility that the psalmist is describing a real condition.

One may next consider directly the meaning of the light's being gone from the eyes. First, a possible figurative meaning has been considered above. H. C. Leupold logically notes that if the interpretation is literal, it may refer simply to blurred vision and not total blindness as the text does not say he is totally blind.[3] If the remarks are figurative, one may still find them relevant for understanding physical loss of vision because the description of a sad condition using these statements as symbols would be meaningless if the light's departing from the eyes conjured up no uncomfortable image in the physical world. Thus, insight may be gained regarding both literal and figurative blindness by analyzing this passage.

Rebecca Raphael suggests a parallel relationship between v. 11 and v. 12 (v. 10, 11 English). She suggests that the failing of the heart is to be seen as parallel with the abandonment by the loved ones and the disappearing of the light, with the setting afar off by the ones once near. This would mean that the weakening of the eyesight would mean distancing by friends and loved ones.[4] The weakness with this theory is that these two verses each seem to hold individually internal parallelism without needing to include surrounding verses. As loved ones who were no longer near parallel ones who were close being set afar off (two social traumas), the failing heart parallels the weakening eyesight (two bodily traumas). This is different from vv. 14–15 (13–14, English) which both begin with remarks about deafness and end with remarks about muteness, even using the same words to describe the conditions as the two verses discuss them. In that different case, the two verses might parallel each other with the remarks about deafness seen as a set and the remarks about muteness seen as a set. Such is not the case with vv. 11 and 12, which do not contain any verbal parallels binding the two verses together.

What one would next wish to analyze, then, is how his weakening of the eyes, however literal it is to be understood, is expressed. What is unique about his portrayal of his eye condition is how it is described as being a

---

3. Leupold, *Exposition of the Psalms*, 310.
4. Raphael, *Biblical Corpora*, 112.

situation of the light's no longer being with his eyes. That which is most important about his potential eyesight is being able to see the light, that which, as one recalls, was the first thing created, according to Gen 1:3–5. The psalmist, about deafness, simply notes that he is as a deaf man who cannot hear (Ps 38:14–15). With reference to the eye, though, the extra descriptive note is presented about a certain delight he cannot enjoy: the light.

It may also be noted that such an ailment is seen here as a consequence of sin. In vv. 4–5 (3–4, English) among a number of places in this Psalm, reference is made to the extent of the author's sin and iniquity. In v. 2 (1, English) God is implored not to punish the psalmist out of his anger. Thus, in the psalmist's view, the removal of light from the eyes is a result of sin, as is previously discussed with reference to the Torah and Prophets.

Iniquity Rendering One Unable to See, Psalm 40:13 (12, English)

Translation

THE TEXT

The next instance of blindness in the Psalms is Ps 40:13 (12, English). This is within another passage where the psalmist lists his woes. The verse appears below:

כִּי אָפְפוּ־עָלַי רָעוֹת עַד־אֵין מִסְפָּר הִשִּׂיגוּנִי עֲוֺנֹתַי וְלֹא־יָכֹלְתִּי לִרְאוֹת עָצְמוּ מִשַּׂעֲרוֹת רֹאשִׁי וְלִבִּי עֲזָבָנִי׃

> 12. For evils have encompassed me
> without number;
> my iniquities have overtaken me,
> until I cannot see;
> they are more than the hairs of my head,
> and my heart fails me. (NRSV)

Exegesis

CONTEXT

It must be noted how Ps 40 mentions matters of the heart and eye together as have a number of other passages such as Isa 6:9–10, and Ps 38:11, both of which use both words for "eye" and "heart" in the Hebrew. Numbers 15:39, in addition, says that the Israelites were to wear the tassels on their garments so they could see them and not go wandering after their hearts and eyes after which they would go a-whoring. Ezekiel 6:9, most likely alluding to Num 15:39, discusses how the people, in heart and eye, had gone a-whoring after idols. The first sin listed in the Bible, Gen 3:6, involved one making a judgment based on what the eye saw. While the verse does not directly mention the heart, the desirability to make one wise is close. Nonetheless, it may be worth noting how the two aspects of the being often associated with the origin of sin (the heart and the eye) are described as greatly troubled in Ps 40.

General analysis

The line in this verse which is of greatest interest in this study reads, according to the Hebrew, "My iniquities have overtaken me, and I am unable to see." Another connection between sin and a resultant lack of vision becomes apparent. While clearly, as Willem A. VanGemeren rightly observes, a lack of perspective is in mind,[5] one may ask, though, what is no longer visible. Most likely this text does not concern physical sight, as few other markers of physical sensory or motor damage are listed. His vision appears blocked as his sins overtake him. This presence of sin, most likely, is what is obstructing his vision. This verse may be suggesting that the psalmist is unable to see his spiritual condition, to see hope for relief, to see right from wrong, or to see the Presence of God because of his great number of iniquities that are in the way.

The Eyes of Enemies to Be Darkened, Psalm 69:24 (23, English)

Translation

The text

Twice, so far, a psalmist (Pss 38:1; 40:1) has made reference to his lack of sight as a result of sin. This time, a passage must be considered in which a psalmist (Ps 69:1) pleads that his enemies suffer similar fate. Psalm 69:24 (23, English) is translated below.

תֶּחְשַׁכְנָה עֵינֵיהֶם מֵרְאוֹת וּמָתְנֵיהֶם תָּמִיד הַמְעַד׃

> 23. Let their eyes be darkened so that they cannot see,
> and make their loins tremble continually. (NRSV)

---

5. VanGemeren, "Psalms," 323.

Exegesis

LITERARY ANALYSIS

This verse contains a merismic use of sensory and motor defects. The darkening of the eye and the weakening of the loins effect sensory and motor aspects respectively and act on opposite regions of the body. This may be analogous, then, to "blind and lame," previously discussed. It is also noteworthy, regarding the eye, how again the focus concerns light. The eyes of enemies are to become darkened so they cannot see. Darkness is the opposite of light in this context, and so the eyes would be stripped of their ability to see the gift of light, the first item made in creation week.

CONTEXT

Ancient Near Eastern context

One must first recall the numerous ancient Near Eastern texts regarding curses of blindness where one calls a judgment of blindness upon his enemies. Some curses of blindness would be proclaimed on one who damages a Mesopotamian king's stele, or on one who has someone with a disability do so to a boundary stone. One may recall other curses against those with the "evil eye" who would assail an Egyptian. The First Soldier's Oath in Hittite literature proclaimed the curses of blindness and lameness upon one who violated his oath to be a loyal soldier. Psalm 69:24 addresses both blindness of the eye and motor difficulties of the legs.

Angel Rodriguez, though, rightly notes how imprecatory psalms differ from what are often understood as texts of cursing. In the imprecatory psalms, one finds no magical or ritual acts and no direct curses. Instead such psalms simply contain prayers to God that he would use his divine power and authority to bring about justice.[6] While Rodriguez's arguments mainly concern other psalms such as Pss 5, 35, 58, 109, and 137, the principles may be applied to Ps 69. Psalm 69 contains no ritual, magical act. There is also no stated incantation named. The psalmist simply prays to God that these actions of blinding and weakening of the loins happen.

---

6. Rodriguez, "Inspiration and the Imprecatory Psalms," 40.

Immediate biblical context

One must consider the biblical context to gain an understanding of the justification of such a judgment. Verse 20 (19, English) says that the psalmist bore reproach and shame. Verse 22 (21, English) says that these evildoers gave him vinegar for drink, apparently in a negative context as it is followed by the psalmist's plea for judgment. These people are not, then, cursed for simply being a "bother" or minor irritation, but for committing great acts of evil and shame upon the psalmist.

In addition, as Marvin E. Tate insightfully notes, the judgments the psalmist requests against his enemies parallel his own situation. In v. 22 (21, English) it is said that the enemies gave the psalmist poison for food. In v. 23 (22, English) the psalmist prays that the enemies' table would become a snare. In vv. 3 and 4 (2, 3, English) the psalmist's eye is said to waste away and he is unable to stand. In v. 24 (23, English) the psalmist prays that the eyes of the enemies be darkened and their loins continually troubled, weakening their ability to stand.[7] The blindness, then, that the psalmist desires to smite his enemies would parallel his own troubled eyes.

Intertextual connection

Angel Rodriguez notes how this concept of seeking a form of divinely ordained *lex talionis* is common to imprecatory psalms. He notes, for example, how Ps 9:16 (15, English) says that the heathen are fallen into the pit they have dug and been caught in the snare they have laid.[8] Talion in the strictest sense, though, refers to doing to one what he/she actually did. In Ps 9, the act of the evildoers was not necessarily completed as the text does not say that the psalmist actually fell into the pit himself. While Ps 9, then, does not describe *lex talionis* in the strictest sense of repaying one with the act he/she did to another, the evildoers would still be punished in a way that fits the crime. This form of talion, though, would be similar to that described in Deut 19:20–21 where the malicious witness receives the penalty he/she intended to have performed against the one falsely accused.

Rodriguez also notes Ps 28:4, which literally contains a prayer that the wicked be rewarded according to the deeds they have done.[9] This is talion in the truest sense, as what was done to the psalmist would then be done to the evildoers according to the prayer. Psalm 69, then, continues this theme

---

7. Tate, *Psalms 51–100*, 199.
8. Rodriguez, "Inspiration and the Imprecatory Psalms," 47.
9. Rodriguez, "Inspiration and the Imprecatory Psalms," 45.

of talion, even as noted above, requesting a form of "eye for eye" justice. Since "eye for eye" is even named literally in the Torah three times, as an appropriate means of administering justice, the psalmist is not asking for a penalty that is unreasonable or unrighteous to request. He is simply pleading for divine justice. In addition, Rodriguez rightly discusses how the psalmist is setting his case before God, stepping out of the realm of personally settling vendettas, and simply leaving his struggles in God's hands. The psalmist is seeking ultimate deliverance, which would not take place unless justice is handed down against the evildoers. Thus, according to the biblical context, the psalmist is not seeking revenge, but justice against those perpetually set on evil.[10] Thus, the psalmist lets God, not himself, become angry and act (Ps 69:25 [24, English]), and as Gerald H. Wilson rightly notes, turns the task of darkening enemies' eyes over to God.[11]

It is also noted by Richard M. Davidson, in the *Handbook of Seventh-day Adventist Theology*, vol. 12, how imprecatory psalms such as 35, 58, and 69 employ language used in the curses of the covenant in Lev 26 and Deut 28. This makes passages such as Ps 69 not simply ramblings of one who feels oppressed, but claims before God that he would honor the covenant and the principles of the covenant by bringing justice.[12] In reality, Deut 28:29 refers to a plague of blindness and Deut 28:35 refers to a plague on the legs and knees, both plagues striking those who violate God's covenant. While different words are used, both the eye and the leg were named as objects to be smitten by the psalmist in the verse of interest in Ps 69. Thus, Ps 69 contains claims that God would simply be faithful to the covenant he had already established.

General analysis

It must be noted here that there is no evidence in the text that these curses ever actually came to pass. There is also no evidence concerning how literal or figurative the curses were intended to be. All one finds is a prayer by a troubled man for God to deliver him and give just judgment.

---

10. Rodriguez, "Inspiration and the Imprecatory Psalms," 63.
11. Wilson, *Psalms*, 955.
12. Davidson, "Biblical Interpretation," 81.

God Is Not Blind, Psalm 94:7–9

Translation

The text

In Ps 94, one finds an accusation that God is blind, stated by evildoers. The accusation and the results of such are translated below in Ps 94:7–9:

וַיֹּאמְרוּ לֹא יִרְאֶה־יָּהּ וְלֹא־יָבִין אֱלֹהֵי יַעֲקֹב׃
בִּינוּ בֹּעֲרִים בָּעָם וּכְסִילִים מָתַי תַּשְׂכִּילוּ׃
הֲנֹטַע אֹזֶן הֲלֹא יִשְׁמָע אִם־יֹצֵר עַיִן הֲלֹא יַבִּיט׃

> 7. "The LORD does not see;
>   the God of Jacob does not perceive."
> 8. Understand, O dullest of the people;
>   fools, when will you be wise?
> 9. He who planted the ear, does he not hear?
>   He who formed the eye, does he not see? (NRSV)

Exegesis

Context

One must note the context of these verses. In v. 5 it is said that these wicked people smite God's people and afflict his inheritance. Verse 6 says that these evildoers kill the widow, the stranger, and the orphan. This passage, then, most likely alludes to Exod 22:22–23, which says that if the widow and orphan are oppressed and cry out to God, he would hear and punish the oppressors. These passages have "widow," "orphan," and "hear" in common. The sense of hearing, the only sense mentioned in Exod 22:22–23, is the first sense mentioned in Ps 94:8. In Ps 94:7, then, the wicked incorrectly assume that God is unable to see these acts.

General analysis

It may be assumed, according to H. C. Leupold, that God's apparent lack of vision may be associated with his apparent failure to punish those committing wrongs. The crimes take place, and no punishment for such is said to have happened, according to the text. Then, the people say that God does not see.[13] This reasoning is logical: No one would really have evidence that God sees unless he also acts. Otherwise, God is simply a distant deity that may or may not even be watching. Thus, the evildoers continue in wickedness because it seems as if God is blind to the suffering.

In addition, the inability to see in vv. 6–7 is paralleled with the inability to understand. This would suggest that the purpose of seeing here is not simply visual perception, but a form of discerning vision that is able to make judgments.

God, though, in Ps 94, is not simply described in the language of one who closes his eyes, but of one who may or may not even have eyes. Verse 9 does not make reference to God as the One who sees as people see. Instead, it asks rhetorically if the One who formed the eye, himself, should be able to see. God, in Ps 94 as the Maker of the eye, must know everything there is to know about eyes and seeing. He should possess a much more powerful and perfect ability to see than any mortal. If the wicked were questioning God's choice to see rather than his ability to see, the verse might have appealed to a different action of God. The text might say, "Should not he who saw the light as good, and who saw the oppressive power of Egypt, see?" Instead, the justification for believing God is watching is based on his power in creating eyes. One mighty enough to create the eye could still choose to avert his gaze, but nonetheless, he still has great power to perceive visually; however, such is accomplished in the divine realm. Such extreme faculties of vision, then, would eventually be watching all that is good and evil. God is never blind to anything that happens. His eyes are even said to go to and fro upon the earth (Zech 4:10). The focus, then, is on the functioning of the eye itself, the actual potential to perceive visually, not merely the choice to turn one's gaze. God is powerful enough and wise enough to make an organ of seeing, so he is powerful enough to see everything, himself. Since God, who instructs nations, must rebuke (v. 10), this God who has the ability to see will use the knowledge he gains from his vision as a basis for righteous judgments and administering punishment on the wicked.

---

13. Leupold, *Exposition of the Psalms*, 670.

Idols Are Blind, Psalms 115:5–7; 135:16–17

Translation

THE TEXT

In the previous section it was discovered that it is ludicrous to say that God is blind. In the next two passages to be analyzed, Pss 115:5–7; 135:16, 17, idols are shown as blind. Since these two passages are nearly identical with the immediate context, they are translated together below.

פֶּה־לָהֶם וְלֹא יְדַבֵּרוּ עֵינַיִם לָהֶם וְלֹא יִרְאוּ׃
אָזְנַיִם לָהֶם וְלֹא יִשְׁמָעוּ אַף לָהֶם וְלֹא יְרִיחוּן׃
יְדֵיהֶם וְלֹא יְמִישׁוּן רַגְלֵיהֶם וְלֹא יְהַלֵּכוּ לֹא־יֶהְגּוּ בִּגְרוֹנָם׃

> 5. They have mouths, but do not speak;
>   eyes, but do not see.
> 6. They have ears, but do not hear;
>   noses, but do not smell.
> 7. They have hands, but do not feel;
>   feet, but do not walk;
>   they make no sound in their throats. (NRSV)

פֶּה־לָהֶם וְלֹא יְדַבֵּרוּ עֵינַיִם לָהֶם וְלֹא יִרְאוּ׃
אָזְנַיִם לָהֶם וְלֹא יַאֲזִינוּ אַף אֵין־יֶשׁ־רוּחַ בְּפִיהֶם׃

> 16. They have mouths, but they do not speak;
>   they have eyes, but they do not see;
> 17. they have ears, but they do not hear,
>   and there is no breath in their mouths. (NRSV)

Exegesis

CONTEXT

Immediate biblical context

Immediately preceding both these verses is the note that the idols of humankind are gold and silver, the works of their hands. Earlier still in both psalms, also, is a statement that God does whatever he desires to do (Pss 115:3; 135:6-8). As J. Clinton McCann rightly notes, the word for do, עשׂה, in the Hebrew is the same word used for "make," with reference to those who make idols. Whatever God desires to do, he does. Those who make idols, though, eventually lose any power they might have, as they would become like what they make (Pss 115:8; 135:18).[14]

Intertextual connection

Psalms 115 and 135 follow a nearly identical list of sensory and motor organs that idols possess but that also do not function. In a way, the idols in both these passages are similar to the people in Ezek 12 and the idols of Jer 5 that all have eyes but do not see. It is impossible to know which was written first, though. Nonetheless, as noted above, both Pss 115 and 135 join the ideas of idol blindness and human blindness by saying that those who trust in idols (which are blind) become like them. These passages also allude to Deut 4:28, which is the first passage in the Bible that discusses how idols do not see, or hear, or smell.

Rebecca Raphael insightfully notes how these passages in Pss 115 and 135 also bear parallels with Ps 94:9. As with Pss 115 and 135, Ps 94 refers to the ear and the eye. Psalm 115 even uses the same word for "hear" as Ps 94:9. She notes how the rare joining of all these concepts suggests an intertextual connection. While Ps 94:9 shows the sightedness of God, Pss 115 and 135 show the contrasting blindness of idols.[15] While it is impossible to determine which passage was written first, or if all these passages allude to a more ancient and general concept in Israelite culture, the message is not diminished. Psalm 94 says that God is not blind, and Pss 115 and 135 say that idols are blind.

General analysis

A number of similarities exist between these two passages. Leslie C. Allen observantly notes how both these passages in the Psalms are a satire against idols, showing how ridiculous it is to form an object and worship it.[16] Apparently such an idea was seen as so important that these verses of satire were placed in the Psalms twice.

In addition to the similarities named above, Pss 115:5–7 and 135:16, 17 are similar in a number of other ways. In both cases, the first, second, and third organs, in order, are the mouth, eye, and ear, though with reference to hearing, Ps 115:6 uses שמע while Ps 135:17 uses אזן. Idols, then, are

---

14. McCann, "The Book of Psalms," 1145, 1220.
15. Raphael, Biblical Corpora, 116.
16. Allen, *Psalms 101–150*, 148, 291.

described twice as having eyes but not seeing. They are blind, their eyes unable to function.

As noted above, immediately after these passages, it is said that those who make them and trust in them will be like them (Pss 115:8; 135:18), suggesting that the blindness of the idols would eventually spread to the makers. Derek Kidner insightfully notes that the verb for "be" could be either an imperfect or a jussive based on the form. Thus, these passages could say "Those who make them will be like them," or, "Let those who make them be like them."[17] As far as this study is concerned, the difference is minor. Either way, the blindness of idols is stated as a possible cause for possible future blindness of the people. Whether the people's blindness is predicted or merely desired, the blindness of the idols is still thought to be associated in some way with future blindness of the people.

In addition, Walter D. Zorn rightly notes how the idea of people becoming as their gods is not unique to these psalms. In 2 Kgs 17:15 and Jer 2:5, it is said that people became vanity after following vanities. One is always considered to be or become in the likeness of whom he/she worships.[18] In fact, Gen 1:26 even says humanity was made in God's image, thus, showing that God desired humanity to be as its Creator God. The idol-makers, though, are as blind as their idols, blind to the spiritual truths of God, as discussed in the study of Isa 44.

God, the Opener of Blind Eyes, Psalm 146:8

Translation

THE TEXT

The last occurrence of blindness in the Psalms is in Ps 146:8. It appears below:

יְהוָה פֹּקֵחַ עִוְרִים יְהוָה זֹקֵף כְּפוּפִים יְהוָה אֹהֵב צַדִּיקִים:

> 8. the LORD opens the eyes of the blind.
> The LORD lifts up those who are bowed down;
>   the LORD loves the righteous. (NRSV)

---

17. Kidner, *Psalm 73–150*, 405.
18. Zorn, *Psalms*, 352.

Notes

As mentioned previously, "eyes" does not appear in this verse. The concept, then, is assumed. When one as powerful as God opens something for the blind, using a word for "open," פקח, that has been shown nearly always to refer to eyes, that organ which is opened must necessarily be the eyes.

Exegesis

Context

While the meaning of this verse appears straightforward, one must understand the context. This psalm is a psalm of praise, the first of five psalms of praise, each starting with "Hallelujah," and that all comprise the end of the book of Psalms. Psalm 146:7 ends by saying that the Lord provides release for the prisoners. Verse 9 says that the Lord protects the stranger and aids the widow and the orphan. As Zorn rightly notes, the fact that the text of Ps 146 places God's name before each of five acts (releasing prisoners, opening eyes, strengthening the weak, loving the righteous, and protecting the stranger) emphasizes that it is God, and God only, who does these acts.[19] The blind, here, are also named within a list of a number of disadvantaged groups. In fact it is not uncommon for the blind to be mentioned along with the stranger, the widow, and the orphan, as all four of these groups are listed in close proximity in Lev 19:10–14.

General analysis

One may next determine how this blindness is to be understood. It can be said that, just as God is able and present to aid the literal widow and orphan, God is able and present to heal the literal eyes of those who are literally blind. Leupold, though, notes that since there is no evidence in the Hebrew Scriptures for God's opening the eyes of the physically blind, this verse must be understood figuratively.[20] One must recall, though, 2 Kgs 6:16–20 where the Syrian army, recently blinded (different word for blindness) by God, has their eyes opened (same word for "opened"). While this healing was of a sudden smiting of blindness by God and not of blindness caused by a birth defect or act of war, this is still an example of God's using his power to restore sight. In addition, according to Isa 35:5–6, a number of disabling

---

19. Zorn, *Psalms*, 521.
20. Leupold, *Exposition of the Psalms*, 986.

conditions are said to be healed. Thus, examples do exist in the Hebrew Scriptures of blindness being healed, or at least predicted to be healed. In addition, even if the Hebrew Scriptures do not mention a certain act as having taken place in the past, God is still theoretically able to do it since nothing is too hard for the Lord (Gen 18:14). Thus, simply saying that God has not performed a certain act literally in the past does not necessarily provide guidance as to whether or not he will perform that act literally in the future. Nonetheless, the brevity given to these concepts in Ps 146 leaves much open to interpretation, and so it may be fair to say also that God opens the eyes of the spiritually blind, an idea previously discussed in depth in this study.

In Ps 146:7–8, the opening of blind eyes is mentioned immediately after the releasing of prisoners. One may recall the connections, as previously noted, in Isaiah and in the stories of Samson and Zedekiah, between the blind and prisoners. One may even recall how a significant number of prisoners in the ancient Near East were blinded as part of their punishment. Psalm 146:7–8, though, provides further evidence for a connection between being blind and being a prisoner. Michael D. Goulder insightfully notes that since those in ancient prisons were often not allowed enough space to stand, they would become weak and would require strengthening, a strengthening possibly discussed in the subsequent statement, "The LORD lifts up those who are bowed down." Thus, these three statements may all relate to prisoners.[21] While the author of Ps 146 may have had prisoners in mind, one should not rule out the possibility that the blind, in general, are also to be considered. After all, Ps 146 also concerns widowhood and orphanhood, concepts not necessarily associated with prisoners.

It must also be noted that there is no reason to say that God opens the eyes of the blind, but cares nothing for the deaf or the crippled. As in previous cases, the reference to the blind must be seen as representative of all disabling conditions. Blindness, though, as a significant disability, perhaps even the most significant physical disability in ancient Hebrew thought, is listed as the example.

Summary

It is noted in this section how blindness occurs a number of times in the Psalms. First, Ps 38:11 (10, English) illustrates how sin could be understood to lead to the light departing from one's eyes. Psalm 40:13 (12, English) further develops this idea by connecting iniquity with losing the ability to see. Then, in Ps 69:24 (23, English) the psalmist prays that God will darken

---

21. Goulder, *The Psalms of the Return*, 285.

the eyes of his enemies. This is not simply a cry for vengeance, but a plea that God's system of justice, as described in the covenant, be upheld. In Ps 94:7–9 it is noted that, while the wicked may suggest that God is blind to their evil, God, who formed the eye, knows more about seeing than anyone. He would soon act, then, according to the text, providing deliverance for the oppressed. In Ps 115:5–7 and Ps 135:16–17, it is noted that the idols people form are blind, and that those who worship them become as blind. Finally, in Ps 146:8 it is said that God opens the eyes of the blind, both physically and spiritually. This blindness discussed here may even be as a result of being a prisoner.

BLINDNESS IN THE REST OF THE WRITINGS

This final section of this chapter concerns the remaining blindness passages in the Writings. After considering Job's dimming eyesight in Job 17:7, the discussion moves to Job's claims of being eyes to the blind in Job 29:15. Then, Prov 30:17 is analyzed with reference to the ravens plucking out the eye of one who mocks his/her parents. Next, the issue of the darkening of those gazing through the lattice in Eccl 12:3 is analyzed. Next, the matter of those wandering as the blind in Lam 4:14 is examined, followed by the remark about the darkening of the eyes in Lam 5:17. Finally, the last passage in the Hebrew Scriptures which discusses idols that do not see, Dan 5:23, is studied.

Job's Eye Dim, Job 17:7

Translation

THE TEXT

Job 17:7, the first of two blindness passages in the book of Job is translated below:

וַתֵּכַהּ מִכַּעַשׂ עֵינִי וִיצֻרַי כַּצֵּל כֻּלָּם׃

> 7. My eye has grown dim from grief,
> and all my members are like a shadow. (NRSV)

Exegesis

Context

Norman C. Habel notes how, in the context of this verse, one finds a number of other noteworthy references to blindness. In Job 16:16, Job says that his eyelids hold the shadow of death. Job 16:20 says that Job's eye, later to be darkened, pours out tears ("tears," not in the Hebrew) to God. Then, Job 17:2 says that Job's eye lodges amid his troublers.[22] In addition, in Job 17:12, he says that the light has been changed to darkness, and in v. 13, he says that he has made his bed in the darkness. Thus, the context of this passage strongly connects sorrow with difficulties of the eye.

General analysis

The simple understanding of the weakening of eyesight based on this verse is that such was due to sorrow and vexation on the part of Job. This word for "dim" is כהה, frequently seen to refer to the dimming of an eye due to old age. As noted, this does not necessarily refer to a complete loss of vision, though.

Most likely these references contain figurative meanings. Job 17:13 is clearly figurative, since it is common and not noteworthy for one to rest literally in his/her bed when it is literally dark at night. Job 17:13, then, connects the darkness with Job's state of extreme sorrow. Nonetheless, the shedding of tears does blur the vision, weakening the eyesight, especially when the tears are being shed. Job could have experienced weakening of eyesight that would have been a physical manifestation of the spiritual and emotional darkness that surrounded him. In addition, as Robert L. Alden rightly notes, it is impossible to rule out the possibility that Job's disease with which he was afflicted (Job 2:7) could have affected his literal eyesight. As a result, Job's dimming of eyesight could have been due to both physical and mental causes.[23]

---

22. Habel, *The Book of Job*, 277.
23. Alden, *Job*, 190.

Eyes to the Blind, Job 29:15

Translation

THE TEXT

A translation of Job 29:15 appears below:

עֵינַיִם הָיִיתִי לַעִוֵּר וְרַגְלַיִם לַפִּסֵּחַ אָנִי׃

> 15. I was eyes to the blind,
> and feet to the lame. (NRSV)

NOTES

The word order is irregular in the Hebrew of this verse. Literally, it reads, "Eyes was I to the blind, and feet to the lame was I." This shows the concepts of emphasis as the eye and the foot.

Exegesis

CONTEXT

Delitzsch insightfully draws the attention to Job 22:9. There, Job's visitors accuse him of not showing charity to the widow and fatherless. In Job 29:12–15, then, Job provides his defense against these allegations. He notes in vv. 13 and 16 how he has aided the widow, the fatherless, and the poor. Then, in v. 15, he explains how he even aided the disabled, a group not mentioned by Job's friends. Thus, Job shows himself as acting with extreme righteousness, aiding everyone in need and exceeding the demands of his friends.[24] One also sees in Job 29:12–15 another example of the blind being listed among widows and orphans, other disadvantaged segments of society.

GENERAL ANALYSIS

According to this verse, Job says that he was to the blind and the lame what the blind and the lame do not have. The emphasis on the eye and the foot shows emphasis on Job's being such for those people. One may see this, as previously noted, as a merism, and the references to the blind and lame

---

24. Delitzsch, *Biblical Commentary on the Book of Job*, 125.

being representative of all disabilities. Most likely, Job would have been ears to the deaf and a mouth to the mute.

The fact that Job mentioned assisting the disabled in his argumentation is significant. Carol A. Newsom rightly notes that for Job to name aiding the disabled as part of a defense of his righteousness, he believed it was a good action, not only in his mind, but according to his culture to help the disabled. Job, then, felt that it should be recognized by his hearers as a good action.[25]

Finally, actually being eyes and feet for those without such would have involved not simply trying to meet a small number of obvious physical needs, but in actually being for them that which they lack. Job would not have simply cast a morsel of bread to one who was blind and left the individual alone in his/her condition. Instead, to be eyes to such a one would have meant that Job would have helped the one who was blind come as close as he could to sightedness. Job might even have led a blind person and described scenery for such a one, for example. If the blind individual needed food, Job would have provided that in addition, but not in a humiliating or patronizing manner.

The Dishonoring Eye, Proverbs 30:17

Translation

THE TEXT

The one clear reference to blindness in the book of Proverbs is Prov 30:17, translated below:

עַיִן תִּלְעַג לְאָב וְתָבֻז לִיקֲּהַת־אֵם יִקְּרוּהָ עֹרְבֵי־נַחַל וְיֹאכְלוּהָ בְנֵי־נָשֶׁר׃

17. The eye that mocks a father
and scorns to obey a mother
will be pecked out by the ravens of the valley
and eaten by the vultures. (NRSV)

---

25. Newsom, "The Book of Job," 538.

Notes

The word translated "pecked," in the Hebrew, is נקר, used in Num 16:14, Judg 16:21, and 1 Sam 11:2 to mean "gouge." The connection between נקר and rebellion has already been noted.

Exegesis

Literary analysis

To understand this verse, one must consider the larger structure of the passage, Prov 30:8–33. Block parallelism is employed in this passage. Verses 8 and 9 consider satiety as the author, in v. 9, fears becoming too satisfied, שבע, with food. Verse 15 also concerns satiety with reference to that which is never satisfied, with שבא also used with reference to satiety. Following these two passages on each side of the parallelism, focus is on those who do evil to their fathers and mothers, with the same words used for "father" and "mother" in the Hebrew. Verse 11 concerns the generation that curses the father and does not bless the mother. Verse 17 says that one who mistreats father and mother would have his right eye plucked out by birds. Both sides next concern those who do what seems right to them. The generation in v. 12 wrongly sees itself pure in its own eyes, while the adulterous woman in v. 20 washes her mouth and says she is without wickedness. Verse 12, and vv. 18–20, then, make the next level. Verse 13, then, discusses a generation whose eyelids are lifted up with pride. At the end of the next section, vv. 21–32, v. 32 warns against being lifted up, with נשא used for "lift" in both verses. Finally, v. 14 and v. 33 concern strife. One may observe the following chart:

    A. vv. 8, 9. Satiety.
       B. v. 11, Dishonoring father and mother.
          C. v. 12, pure in own eyes.
             D. v. 13, lifted up.
    A. v. 15, Satiety.
       B. v. 17, Dishonoring father and mother.
          C. vv. 18–20, without wickedness.
             D. v. 32, lifted up.

According to this pattern, then, the mocking of the parents that leads to the removal of an eye parallels the cursing and failure to bless the parents. This further connects blindness with disobedience and the gouging out of an eye with outright rebellion. Even partial blinding, then, the removal of only one eye, may be associated interpretively with rebellion.

Context

Ancient Near Eastern context

One may recall Law 193 in the Code of Hammurabi, discussed in detail in chapter 2 of this study. There it is said that if the adopted child of a courtier leaves the ones with whom he/she lives and returns to his/her biological parents' home, the child's eye is to be removed. In Law 193, it is an adopted child punished with blinding, while in Prov 30:17 such is not necessarily the case. Proverbs 30:17 simply says that the eye that mocks father and mother shall be plucked out. In addition, the penalty in ancient Babylon was determined to be carried out by the state, while the penalty in Proverbs was said, however literally it is to be taken, to be carried out by wild animals.

Intertextual connection

Proverbs 30 also contains a number of strong allusions to the Decalogue. Verse 9 refers negatively to stealing and misusing God's name, with the same words for "steal" and "name" used that appear respectively in Exod 20:15, and v. 7. Prov 30:11, 17 refer to the mistreating of father and mother, with "father" and "mother" also appearing in Exod 20:12. Proverbs 30:20 refers to the adulterous woman's evil, the same root for "adulterous," נאף, occurring also in Exod 20:14. According to this parallel, the removal of the eye is as a direct result, not simply of mistreating parents, but of violating the Decalogue. The *Seventh-day Adventist Bible Commentary*, then, rightly notes how the removal of the mocking eye stands in sharp contrast to the long life that Exod 20:12 promises to those who honor father and mother and do not, then, mock them.[26]

In addition, Exod 21:15 says that one who smites his father or mother must be put to death. Exodus 21:17 says that one who curses his father or mother must also be put to death. This shows a strong tradition among Bible writers to place extreme dishonoring of parents as a most displeasing action, one worthy even of death, in some cases.

General analysis

Allen P. Ross rightly notes that the description of how rebellion against parents leads to the removal of an eye involves an application of the concept of

---

26. "Proverbs 30:17. Mocketh at His Father," 1050.

lex talionis. The eye that does the deep-rooted evil of mocking is removed.[27] This may be analogous to the case of the lazy shepherds of Zech 11:17 whose irresponsible right eyes and arms waste away. While this is not talion in the strictest sense, that is, eyes mocking the one who has a mocking eye, one still finds a sense of talion-style poetic justice.

In addition, Paul E. Koptak insightfully notes how birds such as vultures generally feed on bodies already dead. The removal and eating of the eye, then, could be done to one already dead somehow. The mocker, then, would die without proper burial, and that right eye so involved in the evil behavior would be eaten by birds. Koptak discusses further how, in ancient Israel, it was deemed extremely dishonoring for a dead body to be unburied. One may refer to 2 Sam 21:10 and 1 Kgs 14:11. The one who mocks, then, would die a dishonorable death and not be buried.[28] Even if the mocker is dead when the eye is removed, this passage is still relevant to a study on the theology of blindness since this text shows the fate of an eye that is involved in the doing of evil. It should be noted, though, that the text does not explicitly say the mocker is dead before the birds gouge out and eat his eye. It is conceivable that such would happen while the person is still alive. The consequence for mocking, then, would be partial blindness, and not death without proper burial. The fact that such an action is performed by birds that normally prey on the dead, though, suggests that however alive the person was physically, spiritually, and morally, he was as good as dead.

The Darkening to Come, Ecclesiastes 12:3

Translation

THE TEXT

The significant blindness passage in Ecclesiastes is found in Eccl 12:3, translated below:

בַּיּוֹם שֶׁיָּזֻעוּ שֹׁמְרֵי הַבַּיִת וְהִתְעַוְּתוּ אַנְשֵׁי הֶחָיִל וּבָטְלוּ הַטֹּחֲנוֹת כִּי מִעֵטוּ וְחָשְׁכוּ הָרֹאוֹת בָּאֲרֻבּוֹת׃

> 3. in the day when the guards of the house tremble, and the strong men are bent, and the women who grind cease working because they are few, and those who look through the windows see dimly; (NRSV)

---

27. Ross, "Proverbs," 1123.
28. Koptak, *Proverbs*, 660.

Exegesis

Context

The context of this passage aids greatly one's understanding of it. First, in Eccl 11:7, it is said that light is sweet, and that it is good for the eye to see the sun. The meaning of this light begins to become clearer in Eccl 11:8. There, one is encouraged to find joy in his/her many years, for darkness is said to be coming. Light, then, must refer to a joy present to the reader, while darkness represents some type of negative experience yet to come for one who lives many years. Ecclesiastes 11:9 addresses the youth directly, encouraging one to rejoice in his/her youth. After a note in v. 10 to avoid sorrow, Eccl 12:1 reminds one to remember his/her Creator in his/her youth. This remembering is recommended, according to the text, because days would come when one would say there is no joy. Verse 2 discusses light and darkness again, saying how the lights would be darkened in this time. Then, v. 7 concludes the discussion by noting how the dust eventually returns to the earth, and the spirit to him who gave it. This verse apparently alludes to Gen 2:7 where the breath of life, combined with the dust of the ground, produced a living soul. Ecclesiastes 12:7, then, speaks of the end of life. Thus, Eccl 11:7—12:8 appear to concern two time periods, the first, that of present joyful youth of the reader, and the second, that of darkness and lack of pleasure, yet to come, and climaxing with death.

General analysis

There are a number of ways one can interpret Eccl 12:3. One can understand every statement in this verse as part of a detailed allegory or take every statement in this verse completely literal. One may also interpret the text using both methods.

Roland E. C. Murphy notes that one wishing to interpret Eccl 12:3 as a detailed allegory may wish to understand the guardians as arms or trembling hands, the strong men as legs, the grinders as teeth, and the lookers through the lattice as eyes. Murphy notes, though, how these may seem arbitrary.[29] R. N. Whybray demonstrates another way to understand these terms by noting how the guardians, for example, could be hands, and the strong men, simply the bones. He says the grinders are teeth and the

---

29. Murphy, *Ecclesiastes*, 118.

lookers, eyes, as does Murphy.³⁰ More agreement can be observed regarding the teeth and eyes, then.

A more literal approach would see Eccl 12:3 describing a great disaster that would come. The grinders, then, would not refer to teeth, but to female servants who would retire indoors. Those looking through the lattice would not be eyes darkening through age, but women of leisure no longer able to gaze outside curiously.³¹

If one wishes to interpret Eccl 12:3 completely literally, certain logical problems arise, as noted by C. L. Seow. It seems illogical, for example, for the grinders at the mill to stop working altogether because they are few. One would either have them replaced with other workers, or simply accept a loss of productivity as the workers that are available do less work.³²

A third possibility must be considered. Robert Gordis observantly notes certain passages of Scripture which change metaphors and even change between the literal and the metaphorical. In Ps 127:4–5a, the metaphor is one of warfare, but in 5b, the metaphor is that of a trial before judges at the gates. In Ps 133:2–3, for example, the metaphor changes from that of sweet oil to that of dew.³³ In Ps 18, one even finds movement between the literal and the figurative. Psalm 18 begins with the psalmist literally saying how he loves the Lord, then, metaphorically calling the Lord his rock and fortress, then literally saying that he calls on the Lord and is saved from his enemies. Soon more metaphorical language of the snares of death is employed. Thus, it is not unreasonable to understand Eccl 12:3 as part of a passage dealing with aging but that does not follow one metaphorical or one literal scheme throughout it.

This could mean, then, that the grinders and the lookers through the lattice, which appear to be more clearly references to teeth and eyes, respectively, could refer to such, while the other statements in the verse and the chapter may need to be interpreted in ways beyond the scope of this study. This theme of interpreting Eccl 12:3 in a context of aging is logical in light of the rest of the portion, Eccl 11:7—12:7. If one is to rejoice in the light of his/her youth, and a dark time is coming that will climax in death, the time that is coming must refer to aging. One who is aging, as previously noted in the study on כהה, may experience a weakening of eyesight so those who look out to watch the world past the body would be dim.

30. Whybray, *Ecclesiastes*, 164.
31. Provan, *Ecclesiastes, Song of Songs*, 215.
32. Seow, *Ecclesiastes*, 356.
33. Gordis, *Koheleth*, 329.

While Eccl 12:3 may refer to aging, in a sense this passage may be considering a more cosmic issue. Seow insightfully notes, for example, how the idea of the sun, moon, and stars losing their abilities is described in Joel 3:4 (2:31, English) as events in the Great Day of the Lord at the end of the world. Zephaniah 1:14–15 also uses grand darkness as language of this great day.[34] Seow also notes that while Eccl 1:4–5 speaks of generations coming and going and the sun rising and setting to rise again, Eccl 12:2 speaks of the sun being darkened and not giving light again. This final setting may suggest a breaking of the cycle, a final setting of the sun at the end of the world. Thus, the language showing aging of a person may typify the aging of the world. The blindness, then, would not only be an aspect of personal aging, but a marker of the darkness coming at the end of the world.[35] One might also wish to consider Isa 51:6, which refers to the earth waxing old as a garment. In Eccl 12:2–3, then, the earth is described as waxing old as an elderly person.

The message of this passage, then, is that one must enjoy all the beauty of life as a gift of the Creator. Soon, a time of trouble will come when those pleasures will be taken away. One must enjoy seeing the richness of youth to the fullest, knowing that the darkness of growing old and the tribulations at the end of the world are coming. Blindness, then, refers to an aspect of discomfort associated with these times of personal and cosmic darkness.

Blind Murderers, Lamentations 4:14

Translation

THE TEXT

The book of Lamentations contains two references to blindness that are considered here. The first is Lam 4:14. It reads as follows:

נָעוּ עִוְרִים֙ בַּחוּצ֔וֹת נְגֹֽאֲל֖וּ בַּדָּ֑ם בְּלֹ֣א יֽוּכְל֔וּ יִגְּע֖וּ בִּלְבֻשֵׁיהֶֽם׃

> 14. Blindly they wandered through the streets,
>   so defiled with blood
>   that no one was able
>   to touch their garments. (NRSV)

---

34. Seow, *Ecclesiastes*, 354.
35. Seow, *Ecclesiastes*, 369.

Exegesis

Context

This passage connects blindness with blood and violence. The previous verse also refers to the sins of the prophets and priests who have shed the blood of the righteous in the midst of the city, Jerusalem, according to v. 13. One may recall Gen 9:6, which warns against the shedding of blood, with the same words for "shed" and "blood" used in the Hebrew. This sin is said, though, to result in blindness, according to this verse, not in the shedding of the murderers' blood by humanity as Gen 9:6 says. Blindness, often noted to be a covenant curse (Deut 28:28), is named in Lamentations as a result of violating the covenant God made with Noah. In addition, H. L. Ellison rightly notes that this passage also alludes to Gen 4 where Cain, who shed the blood of Abel (Gen 4:10), is made a wanderer (Gen 4:12) in the earth.[36] The idea of Cain's wandering, then, is joined to the idea of a blind man's wandering to create this intricate picture. It is not, then, for some minor mistake that such a consequence is endured; rather, for the sin of murder.

Finally, Delbert R. Hillers observantly notes parallels with the book of Leviticus. Lamentations 4:14–15 can be seen as alluding to Lev 13:45–46, the law concerning lepers. Both the defiled people in Lam 4:14–15 and the leper were to cry out "unclean, unclean," and both were not to be touched.[37] Kathleen M. O'Connor, then, rightly notes that as the lepers would be in exile, so the priests would wander in exile.[38] It must also be noted that these priests who should declare people clean or unclean would, themselves, be as unclean and wandering in exile. Wandering like the blind, then, is listed in the context of leprosy.

This verse also says that these prophets and priests wander blindly, or as the blind. According to Lev 21:16–24, previously noted in this study, a blind priest was forbidden from officiating. Since a leprous priest was also forbidden from functioning (Lev 22:4) these wicked people would be doubly barred from service before God. Blindness, then, in this context, gains the meaning of being one item in a list of disqualifiers for these priests.

With reference to the prophets being called blind, it is noteworthy that prophets were often called seers (1 Sam 9:9). Those who were to see, then, were blind. This may also be analogous to the blind watchmen of Isa 56:10, 11, previously discussed in this study.

---

36. Ellison, "Lamentations," 728.
37. Hillers, *Lamentations*, 143.
38. O'Connor, "The Book of Lamentations," 1063.

General analysis

One must determine whether this passage is discussing physical blindness, spiritual blindness, or a combination of both. The books of 2 Kings, 2 Chronicles, and Jeremiah are silent regarding a plague of literal blindness that smote the residents of Jerusalem. This reduces the likelihood that physical blindness is being discussed in this passage in Lamentations, though large numbers of the inhabitants of Judah could have been blinded by God or by the Babylonians who also blinded Zedekiah. These lamenting people, though, bearing so much guilt because of their rebellion against God, would have the spiritual blindness often discussed in Isaiah's writings.

Eyes Darkened from Sorrow, Lamentations 5:17

Translation

The text

The second reference to blindness in the book of Lamentations, Lam 5:17 appears translated below:

עַל־זֶ֤ה הָיָה֙ דָוֶ֣ה לִבֵּ֔נוּ עַל־אֵ֖לֶּה חָשְׁכ֥וּ עֵינֵֽינוּ׃

> 17. Because of this our hearts are sick,
> because of these things our eyes have grown dim. (NRSV)

Exegesis

Context

This sadness from sin and sorrow is similar to that described by Job in Job 17:7, though he employed the word "כהה" and not "חשׁך" to describe the weakening of his eyesight. Job also makes no mention of sin as a cause. Lamentations 5:17, though, declares the sorrow of sin as the cause of this form of blindness.

General analysis

The meaning of this verse is simple. The eye is darkened, חשׁך, and the heart is faint, because, according to the previous verse, the people are filled with sorrow as a result of their sins. Their sins, then, resulted in the desolations discussed in the book of Lamentations, and the sorrow from this weakened the eyes and hearts. Paul R. House, then, rightly notes that all these desolations made the people's eyes grow dim with tears.[39] Sorrow for sin, then, brings about a form of blindness. Certainly a tearful countenance would cloud the eyes from seeing the light as clearly. Inner depression would also darken the soul.

Gods Neither See, nor Hear, nor Know, Daniel 5:23

Translation

THE TEXT

The one blindness text in the book of Daniel, Dan 5:23 appears below.

וְעַל מָרֵא־שְׁמַיָּא הִתְרוֹמַמְתָּ וּלְמָאנַיָּא דִי־בַיְתֵהּ הַיְתִיו קָדָמָיךְ [קָדָמָךְ]
וְאַנְתְּה [וְ][אַנְתְּ] וְרַבְרְבָנַיִךְ [וְ][רַבְרְבָנָךְ] שֵׁגְלָתָךְ וּלְחֵנָתָךְ חַמְרָא שָׁתַיִן
בְּהוֹן וְלֵאלָהֵי כַסְפָּא־וְדַהֲבָא נְחָשָׁא פַרְזְלָא אָעָא וְאַבְנָא דִּי לָא־חָזַיִן וְלָא־
שָׁמְעִין וְלָא יָדְעִין שַׁבַּחְתָּ וְלֵאלָהָא דִי־נִשְׁמְתָךְ בִּידֵהּ וְכָל־אֹרְחָתָךְ לֵהּ לָא
הַדַּרְתָּ:

> 23. You have exalted yourself against the Lord of heaven! The vessels of his temple have been brought in before you, and you and your lords, your wives and your concubines have been drinking wine from them. You have praised the gods of silver and gold, of bronze, iron, wood, and stone, which do not see or hear or know; but the God in whose power is your very breath, and to whom belong all your ways, you have not honored. (NRSV)

Exegesis

CONTEXT

One must first note a contextual parallel within Dan 5, based on the Aramaic. Verse 5 says that the king saw, חזה, the writing. Both vv. 14 and 16 say that the king heard, שמע, of Daniel. In v. 22, Daniel says that the king persisted in his evil while he knew, ידי, the story of Nebuchadnezzar. Apparently, then, Belshazzar who could see, hear, and know, trusted gods who could do neither. The king's vision, though, only allowed him to see the

---

39. House, *Lamentations*, 468.

writing. Daniel needed to interpret it. It must be noted also that in both lists throughout Dan 5, references to seeing are made first.

In addition, Stephen R. Miller rightly draws the attention to Deut 4:28, Ps 115:4–8, and Ps 135:15–18 as parallels.[40] Deuteronomy 4:28 refers to idols of wood and stone, which neither see nor hear. Daniel 5:23 refers to gods of wood and stone, and, as previously noted, refers also to their inability to see or hear. Psalms 115 and 135 refer also to idols that do not see or hear, and these idols are said to be made of silver and gold (Pss 115:4; 135:15), two metals named in cognate form in Dan 5:23 as materials used in making idols. Daniel, then, draws the reader to various anti-idolatry passages in the Hebrew Scriptures to show, as Paul L. Redditt rightly notes, the blindness of Nebuchadnezzar's gods, gods as blind as the materials from which they are made.[41] Belshazzar even, according to Pss 115:8 and 135:18, became as those idols, blind, and so, unable to see clearly when watchfulness was most needed as an enemy army was rapidly approaching against him.

Summary

Blindness in Job 17:7 is shown to be associated with his deep sorrow and possibly, even, his unusual physical ailments. In Job 29:15, being eyes to the blind is understood by Job as a reputable enough act on his part to present in defense of his character. Being eyes to the blind, though, is more than simply assisting them now and then, but being for the blind what they lack. Then, Prov 30:17, in noting how ravens would pluck out the eye of one who mocks his/her parents, alludes to the Decalogue with reference to honoring father and mother. Such a great act of Commandment breaking as mocking and cursing parents would definitely carry such a judgment. In Eccl 12:3, the darkening of the ones looking through the lattice may not only refer to blindness in individual old age, but the darkening of the world in the Day of the Lord. In Lam 4:14, those priests and prophets who bear blood-guilt wander as the blind. The priests, as blind, and compared also with lepers, then, would be doubly disqualified from service. In Lam 5:17, the darkening of the eye is shown to be a result of the sorrow from sin and its consequences. Finally, Dan 5:23 contains the final reference to blind idols in the Hebrew Scriptures. Belshazzar, who trusted such blind idols, was unable to understand the writing on the wall.

---

40. Stephen R. Miller, *Daniel*, 164.
41. Redditt, *Daniel*, 97.

THEOLOGICAL SYNTHESIS AND SUMMARY

The Cultus

Little is said in the writings concerning blindness in Israelite cultus. The main text that addresses this issue is Lam 4:13. According to Lam 4:13-14, murderous behavior of the priests make them effectively blind, and, logically then, barred from ministry in the temple, which had ceased to exist by that time anyway.

Causes of Blindness

Physical Causes

As do the books of the Torah and the Prophets, the books of the Writings also mention old age as a cause of blindness, according to a likely interpretation of Eccl 12:2-3. Another cause of blindness named in the Writings is sorrow. Job 17:7 and Lam 5:17 are significant examples. Sickness can also be a cause of a form of blindness, according to Ps 38.

Spiritual Causes

A curse uttered by a human, but whose fulfillment lies within the domain of the divine, can be understood as a cause of blindness. In Ps 69, the psalmist prays that the eyes of his attackers would be darkened. These evildoers were not simply a minor inconvenience to the psalmist, but were causing great harm and distress. It has also been noted how a form of talionic justice is considered in this passage as the psalmist's eyes were troubled amid his trials. Thus, the psalmist is not simply seeking vengeance, but claiming that God would honor the covenant he had previously made.

Sin is also understood as a cause of blindness. Psalm 38, which discusses the light's having gone from the eyes, is set in a context of repenting from sin. One may even recall Ps 40, which associates inability to see with abundance of iniquity. The blinding sorrows of the Jews in Lam 5:17 were noted previously to be a result of their sins. Rebellion and disrespect of parental authority appear to be a cause of the gouging out of the eye in Prov 30.

God is also shown as allowing blinding conditions to befall the righteous. An adversary (the determination of whose identity reaches beyond the scope of this study) afflicted Job with conditions leading to his blinding sorrow (Job 2:1–7; 17:7). Nonetheless, God is shown as allowing this situation.

Social Justice

One must here consider Job 29:15. As noted previously, Job attempts to defend his claims to a righteous character by saying how he was eyes to the blind. He, then, would work to be for the blind what the blind cannot be for themselves. Job believed that such an action was righteous for him and would be perceived as righteous to those around him.

Reversal of Blindness

In Ps 146:8, God is shown to open the eyes of the blind. God is ultimately the One responsible for reversing blindness. In addition, as previously mentioned, Pss 38 and 40, and Lam 5 all mention sin as, at least involved in, the causation of blindness. It would stand to reason, then, that the removal of sin could have been involved in the removal of blindness.

Meanings of Blindness

Blindness in the Writings held the same meaning of weakness as it did elsewhere in the Hebrew Scriptures. As in Lev 19 and Deut 27, Job 29 lists the blind among other groups of disadvantaged, vulnerable people requiring assistance. Blindness may also have carried the meaning of being a result of sin as in Pss 38 and 40, and, as suggested by the curse of blindness, requested against the foes in Ps 69.

Spiritual Blindness

As in Jer 5, idolaters are said to worship idols that have eyes but do not see, according to Ps 115:5–8 and Ps 135:15–18. Psalms 115 and 135 continue by noting how those who trust in such idols eventually become like such idols, presumably blind also. Thus, rejection of God as the true object of worship can, then, be a cause of spiritual blindness, which makes idol worshippers as useless as the idols.

VII

Summary, Conclusions, and Implications

SUMMARY AND CONCLUSIONS

Until now, this study has considered, separately, blindness in the ancient Near East, Hebrew words for blindness, and blindness as it is understood in individual passages in the Hebrew Scriptures. One may now synthesize the knowledge gained from such analyses into a general theology of blindness in the Hebrew Scriptures. Such is the focus of this chapter. Respectively, this chapter concerns blindness in cultic and religious thought, causes of blindness as understood by the people, social justice issues relating to blindness, matters of healing of blindness, and finally, the meanings that blindness held in ancient Israelite thought and life.

Blindness in Cultic and Religious Thought

General Remarks about Blindness in Heaven and on Earth

In this section on blindness in cultic and religious thought, it is first necessary to note that nowhere in the Hebrew Scriptures are those described as living heavenly beings described as being blind. In the mythologies of Egypt and the Hittite empire, various deities are smitten with blindness. In the Bible, no angel is described as being blind, and all throughout the

Bible, God is described as seeing effectively. One may recall Gen 1, which frequently says how God saw creation that it was good. It is true that in Ps 94:6 the wicked suggest that God does not see, but God, according to v. 8, as the Maker of the eye, must logically possess perfect vision. It is the idols of the pagan nations, according to Deut 4:28; Ps 115:5–8; and Ps 135:15–18, that are blind. Thus, instead of a living deity losing his/her vision, the Bible states that God always sees and the idols never see.

It is next necessary to recall how God's original desire for humanity was that people see clearly (Gen 2:9; 3:6). In addition, even when blindness became a reality in this world, nowhere does the Bible say that the blind are given any special gifts or compensations from heaven. This is in contrast to Egyptian thought where the blind were often associated with the religious occupation of harper and ancient Sumerian thought where similarly the blind were given the task of being musicians. Thus, blindness, in the Hebrew Scriptures, is understood as a condition not designed originally by God, a deviation from the original order of creation. While the blind were to be treated with compassion, they possessed no special gifts to suggest that God would will them to have such a condition. Total blindness as a condition of damaged or missing eyes was even understood as a disqualifying blemish in Israelite cultus, demonstrating how such a condition was not to be seen as preferred by God.

Blindness in the Sanctuary System

As noted previously in this study, blindness was considered a blemish in a priest. A blind priest, while still a priest, was forbidden to officiate. One may compare this with the Babylonian prohibition concerning a blind person's being a diviner. In both cases, the reason appears to be simply that such a one was blemished. A significant difference, though, is that one could still be a priest in other ways in Israel if blind, but one could not function at all as a diviner if blind in Babylon. Eli's old age, though, did not disqualify him from performing the tasks he performed in the sanctuary at Shiloh. The murderous behavior of the priests, as described in Lam 4:13, 14, though, rendered them blind, or as good as blind. Such a blemish would necessarily bar them from priestly officiating if there were a temple in which to officiate.

Using similar language, blindness is also described as a disqualifying blemish in an animal. While blind animals are said to be forbidden because of their blemish in Leviticus, Mal 1:6–8 suggests that offering such would be a sign of grave disrespect. One would not even offer such to a governor.

Allowances for the Blind in Israelite Religion

It has already been noted how a blind priest was encouraged to eat of the holy food. A number of other allowances were given to the blind in Israelite religion. Felix Just rightly observes how the blind could occupy certain spiritual roles and still receive great respect. First, the story of Eli illustrates how a priest blinded by age could still function in at least a limited capacity. As shown by Isaac and Jacob, a father made blind by age was still understood to maintain authority to bless his children (Gen 27, 48). Blind Ahijah was still used by God to prophesy to the king's wife, the prophet even being given special insight from God to accommodate his disability.[1] When one recalls how Samson, though blinded by the Philistines, was still used by God to perform his greatest miraculous defeat of the Philistines, Just's argument is further strengthened.

Causes of Blindness

As discussed previously in this study, the causes of blindness below are divided into physical and spiritual domains. Such are considered in this order below. A number of the physical causes of blindness, though, according to the Bible, may have their roots in deeper spiritual causes.

Physical Causes

The first and most common physical cause of blindness in the Hebrew Scriptures is old age. The numerous parallels with other ancient Near Eastern texts have already been discussed in depth. One may recall Isaac, Jacob, Eli, and Ahijah as examples in the Hebrew Scriptures. One may also note Eccl 12:2–3, which probably describes blindness as one of many maladies faced by those growing old. Moses, though, according to Deut 34:6–7, miraculously avoided this struggle of growing old. Blindness due to age, as discussed in the study of Gen 48 and 1 Sam 3–4, is not necessarily complete as one may still maintain limited vision. One may next recall Job 17:7 and Lam 5:17 as examples of blindness caused by sorrow and Ps 38 as an example of blindness caused by sickness.

Blindness may also have been directly caused by another human agent. One may recall the talionic commands in Exod 21:23–25 and Lev 24:19–20 that prescribe "eye for eye" justice if one destroys the eye of another. Such

---

1. Just, "From Tobit to Bartimaeus, From Qumran to Siloam," 78–79.

a command also presupposes that one might destroy the eye of another wrongly to face this penalty. One need only falsely accuse another of a crime for which the penalty would be blinding to face blinding ordered by the courts, according to Deut 19:20–21. One may next recall the threat of blinding by Nahash and the actual blindings of Samson and Zedekiah. As noted previously, the gouging out of an eye by a human agent was often understood as a punishment for rebellion, though a master was not permitted to do so to a slave, according to Exod 21:26.

Spiritual Causes

In addition to considering how physical factors play a role in blindness, one must analyze how such are to be understood in the context of human character and God's involvement. One must first, then, note how in Exod 4:11 God says that he makes the blind and the seeing. Old age and a wrong act of a criminal, though, are also directly described as causing blindness. An analysis of how blindness first occurs in the Bible after Gen 3 suggests sin as a factor in allowing such conditions to exist. In reality, then, the message of Exod 4:11 is that God assumes responsibility for the condition of all people and will enable them to serve him as he sees fit. God does the creating. At times, though, imperfect clay is what he has with which to create.

In certain limited cases, God himself is shown to bring about blindness directly. One may recall Gen 19:11 and 2 Kgs 6:17–20 when God, to defend his vulnerable people, smote potential attackers with סַנְוֵרִים, blindness. In Zech 11:17, God says he would make the right eyes of unfaithful shepherds to waste away. In Zech 12:4, God smites his enemy's horses with blindness. Then, Zech 14:12 says that God would cause the eyes to rot of those attacking Jerusalem directly. Then, in Ps 69, it has been noted how the psalmist prays that a curse of darkening of the eyes would befall his attackers. In all these instances blindness is inflicted, predicted, and/or desired on those who directly oppose God and his character. It must be noted, though, that the Hebrew Scriptures list no formulas for how to curse another with blindness, and 2 Kgs 6 and Ps 69 are the only passages where a human seeks the blinding of another human. In both cases the blinding is simply requested to God with no complicated ritual or magical spell as texts from other ancient Near Eastern cultures describe their members doing.

Spiritual components may even exist in the previously mentioned cases of blindness listed as physically caused. Psalms 38 and 40 and Lam 5:17 all list blindness and/or weakening of eyesight in the context of the consequences of sin and iniquity. God is even seen as allowing the adversary to afflict Job with myriad trials including the weakening of eyesight due to sorrow (Job 2:1–7).

Even the blindings by other human agents may have had spiritual roots. Since God himself gave the *lex talionis* commands discussed three times in Torah, one who must receive such a punishment would be standing in violation of God's Law, making himself/herself subject to God-ordained penalties. Samson and Zedekiah had previously disregarded God's laws, and so, were vulnerable to whatever consequences might befall them.

Felix Just observes, though, that except for the talion laws, blinding is never described as a divinely ordained punishment. While Samson and Zedekiah were blinded after disobedience, the text nowhere states that such blindings were the punishment for such acts. These disobedient acts may have led to blinding by mortals as a consequence, but not as a punishment commanded by God. Nowhere else was Israel commanded to blind enemies, as was done by Israel's enemies to Samson and Zedekiah. The figuratively blind in Isa 42–43 are also never described as being punished, but rather, facing the possibility of redemption. In the talion laws, one would only be blinded for blinding another, and such punitive blinding was only to the extent of the original crime of blinding. One, then, must blind another in both eyes to face the possibility of total blinding from the state.[2]

Just's logic is sound. The text does not explicitly say that the acts of blinding were a punishment, even if going into exile is described as such. The blindings of Samson and Zedekiah, then, would be compared to a situation where a child would be struck by a car after playing in the street against the command of his/her parents. Being struck by a car is not a punishment for disobedience as would be a "time-out." Rather, being struck by a car is a consequence the parents wished to avoid by commanding the child not to play in the street. Even when God is said to smite people with blindness in Gen 19 and 2 Kgs 6, such is not described as a punishment, but as a means of protecting the innocent, as previously noted in this study. Psalms 38 and 40 also do not explicitly say that the weakening of the eyesight is a punishment for sin. Such failing of eyesight, however such is to be interpreted, may simply have been a natural consequence of iniquity. In Deut 28:29, however this blindness is to be understood, it is a corporate blindness against the whole people, and not a curse or punishment set to blind an individual, thus setting this passage in a different category. It must be noted, in addition, with the cases of blindness due to age, that such is not to be seen as a punishment befalling those without Moses' righteousness. Rather, one walking as close to God as Moses did might possibly receive special grace

---

2. Just, "From Tobit to Bartimaeus, From Qumran to Siloam," 158–59.

in this matter. God, though, is shown as working to reduce the probability of unfair instances of blindness and even proclaims eventual healing of all blindness in Isa 35:5–6.

Matters of Social Justice

In considering how the blind were to be treated in society, one may first analyze the example set by God in these matters, how he treated the blind in the context of society. Next, one can consider commands God gave regarding how human beings should treat the blind and issues relating to blindness. Finally, one may consider situations in the Bible where the blind were treated well or poorly and how the Bible shows whether or not this treatment was considered favorable.

God's Treatment of the Blind

God often used the blind and visually impaired in his service. God used Jacob and Ahijah, blinded by old age, to deliver prophetic messages concerning his people. Samson, though blind, was used by God to kill more enemies at his death than when he was alive. In Jer 31:8, God says that he, himself, would lead the blind, among other vulnerable people, back to Israel. Clearly, then, God, by his own actions, demonstrated a desire for the blind to occupy as useful and enjoyable positions as possible in society. God even provided miraculous power to ensure that his will in this matter would be accomplished.

God's Commands Concerning the Blind

The first command that God gave concerning the treatment of the blind is in Lev 19:14. One may recall how this verse says that one should not curse the deaf or cause the blind to stumble. Such a command, being placed in the context of charity and holiness, was binding, no matter how the blindness was caused or how intentionally the stumbling block was set. While Egyptian culture placed proper treatment of the disabled in wisdom literature, the God of Israel placed such in his codes of law and holiness. This would suggest that the God of Israel would directly hold his people accountable concerning their treatment of the disabled.

Then, Deut 27:18 says that one would be cursed if he/she misled the blind in the path. One may recall how on ancient Babylonian boundary stones curses are proclaimed against anyone who causes one who is blind to desecrate the stone. While the context of Deut 27:18 may include the protection of boundaries (Deut 27:17) v. 18 is a separate curse set in the broader context of Deut 27:15–26, that, as noted, involves a number of other issues associated with the Ten Commandments. Deuteronomy 27:17, in addition, contains a general command not to remove any boundary stone, not just one stone in particular as each Babylonian boundary stone did. Deuteronomy 27:18, then, reaches beyond ancient Babylonian boundary stones in commanding to not lead the blind astray in any situation, not simply that in which one would cause the blind to damage one specific boundary stone.

One may now note how God commanded the blind priest to be treated. First, such a one was still considered a priest, and though he was forbidden to officiate in the sanctuary, he was permitted to eat of the holy offerings and to provide food from such for his family. As previously noted, then, there is no reason a blind priest could not participate in non-officiating activities such as singing in a Levitical choir.

Next, God intended that the crime of unjust blinding never take place. The only time, according to Torah, when a human being was to be blinded was if such blinding was administered as talionic justice. If one blinded another, or worked to cause another to be unjustly blinded in the courts, the true offender would face blinding by the courts (Exod 21:23–25; Lev 24:19–20; Deut 19:20–21). One who was blinded, or, who might face unjust blinding from the state would be given respect and fair treatment in court. It is noteworthy that while other ancient Near Eastern law codes might prescribe talion for blinding, none of them prescribe it for attempting to trick the judicial system to blind another.

Then, Exod 21:26 describes the justice provided for a slave who was blinded by his/her master. While ancient Near Eastern law codes offered no means of compensation for a slave blinded by his/her master, a servant, male or female, in Israel, blinded by his/her master, would expect to be set free. Such a slave, then, would be removed from a potential abusive situation, and such an abusive master would be stripped of the easy object for repeated mistreatment.

The Actual Treatment of the Blind by People

In this section, one may first consider the stories of Isaac's and Jacob's blessing of their children. Both fathers were blind at the time, and while Jacob worked to deceive his father, Joseph sought to ensure that not even an accidental misunderstanding took place regarding which son was which. While

Joseph's sons appear to live in peace together, Jacob and Esau remained enemies for several years as a result of Jacob's deception (Gen 28–33). The negative consequences of taking advantage of the disabled are also shown in how Jacob faced a similar blind-style deception at the hands of his uncle.

One may next recall how Job saw it as an appropriate strategy to discuss his fair treatment of the disabled as an example of his righteousness. He would be eyes for the blind, being for them, as previously noted, what they did not have. Thus, even the stories in the Hebrew Scriptures illustrate proper treatment of the blind.

Reversal of Blindness

The Hebrew Scriptures contain few references to the prevention or healing of physical blindness. Some remarks on these passages and the topic in general in the Hebrew Scriptures follow. First, though, it must be noted that, contrary to other ancient Near Eastern writings, nowhere in the Hebrew Scriptures is there described a specific ritual or prayer for healing or preventing blindness. No instruction in any form is given regarding this matter. One must simply consider case examples where such happened and derive principles.

One must first consider the examples of preventing blindness. One must first note Deut 34:7 and righteous Moses' remarkable retaining of clear eyesight till the day he died. One, then, can consider 1 Sam 11 when the men of Jabesh Gilead, who were to be blinded in one eye by Nahash, were delivered by the Israelites under Saul as he was strengthened by God's Spirit (1 Sam 11:6–7). In both cases, then, blindness is prevented by miraculous means.

Next, one may consider passages that actually discuss the healing of blindness. One, of course, can recall how God is the supreme agent who opens, פָּקַח, the eyes, as noted in Gen 21:19, for example. One may next consider the story of Elisha and the Syrian army in 2 Kgs 6:17–21. Both times when Elisha prays for eyes to be opened, God responds by doing so, the first time, so Elisha's servant could see God's army, and the second time, so the Syrians could see that they were led to Samaria. In this latter story, the prayer of a holy man resulted in this miraculous opening of eyes. Even the psalmist in Ps 38, when discussing the light having departed from his eyes, lists such in a context of sin and its results. As noted previously, he freely confesses his condition of sin in this text, especially at the beginning of the psalm. Then, in Ps 40 as previously noted, the failure of sight is listed even in the same verse as a discussion of the abundance of iniquity. Thus, it can be assumed that, in these cases, blindness appeared to be a result of sin, and in the case of Elisha, the prayer of a holy man, presumably dwelling in less sin, could reverse blindness.

Next, Isa 35:5–6 predicts the opening of the eyes of the blind in the great Messianic era. Truly this fits the character of God who opens the eyes of the blind, according to Ps 146:8. One day, blindness, as all disabilities, would be erased from existence. God would no more need to empower the blind to succeed or work to defend them since their sight would be restored. Clearly, then, it is God's desire that all should be done to prevent and heal blindness. It is reasonable to assume that for a human seeking healing from blindness, such a one should pray for such, desiring holiness and forgiveness from sin. Nonetheless, if it is possible for a priest, one who is to be holy before God, still to be blind, holiness may not always be enough to save one from blindness.

Meanings of Blindness

Meanings of Physical Blindness

In understanding the meanings to ancient Israel of physical blindness, one must first understand the intensity and gravity associated with the condition. One may recall how based on frequency counts of the common, specific words for disabilities, words often found in disability lists, there are significantly more references to total and permanent blindness in the Hebrew Scriptures than there are to any other physical disability. The language associated with blindness is often more intense than that associated with other disabilities. When disabilities are listed, blindness is often at or near the beginning of the list. Finally, blindness is most frequently singled out as a representative disability when making a merism to show reference to all disabilities. Thus, blindness held a special intensity in Israelite thought as a most profound and troubling condition.

Blindness was also associated with weakness. In Genesis, as barrenness weakened the matriarchs, blindness weakened the patriarchs. One may note also the curses described in the conclusion of the law collection by the unknown Sumerian king discussed in chapter 2 of this study. Blindness of males is placed immediately before barrenness of females.

The blind, as representative of other disability groups, as discussed in 2 Sam 5:6–8 may be considered here. Whether the blind were presented because ones as weak as they could defend such a mighty city, or whether a curse of debilitating blindness was pronounced against invaders, blindness carries a meaning of weakness and vulnerability. The lack of blindness in old age is seen as a mark of strength in Moses. Finally, the blind are often mentioned along with other groups of vulnerable people such as widows and orphans in texts that concern charitable treatment of the blind (Lev 19:14; Deut 27:18; and Job 29:15).

Blindness held a unique meaning in the sanctuary system. There, blindness, as a blemish, held the meaning of imperfection, or a deviation from God's ideal, for both priest and animal sacrifice. (One may recall how blindness was not part of God's design at Creation.) Neither a blind priest nor a blind animal was permitted to approach the Lord.

Blindness may also be associated with prison. One may recall how both Samson and Zedekiah were blinded immediately before their imprisonment. Isaiah 42:7 and Ps 146:8 set the healing of blindness in the context of release from the captivity of prison. The darkness of dungeons and the binding lack of mobility experienced by the blind, no doubt, gave justification for such a connection.

Finally, one must not neglect the association between blindness and rebellion. One may recall that all passages in the Hebrew Scriptures that concern the gouging out of eyes, even Num 16:14, are set in the context of rebellion. The references to blinding as a penalty for defiance in other ancient Near Eastern cultures strengthen such an association.

What is not found in the Hebrew Scriptures are parallels to the omen texts of the Babylonian and Hittite cultures. Nowhere in the Hebrew Scriptures, for example, is it said that certain misfortune would befall a city or individual if a certain number of blind individuals are seen or if one is born with a certain unusual eye defect. It is true that a blind person was barred from officiating as a priest, but such was not considered a sign of bad fortune against the sanctuary. Blind Israelites, even blind priests, would then be free of the stigmas attached to the blind in other cultures. No blind Israelite was to be made to feel as if he/she was "bad luck" to his/her family or community.

Meanings of Spiritual Blindness

Blindness, as a spiritual symbol, often referred to a lack of perception. Both Exod 23:8 and Deut 16:19 say that a bribe blinds the eyes of those who should be expected to perceive clearly. Isaiah 56:10 explores this theme further in saying that Israel's shepherds have become blind and as mute dogs, no longer competent to lead.

Then, in Gen 3, the serpent declares that Adam and Eve were blind, unable to perceive certain aspects of knowledge concerning evil. As noted previously, though, humanity's power to perceive God face to face was lost when Adam's and Eve's eyes were opened.

Such loss of spiritual perception is often connected with spiritual rebellion against God. According to Deut 28:28-29, blindness was a consequence of Israel's violating God's covenant (Deut 28:15). It has been noted how numerous texts in Isaiah such as Isa 42:16-20 and Isa 59:10 draw one's attention to the concept of blindness as part of the covenant curses in Deut 28. Isaiah 6:9-10 and 29:9-10 and 18 show how blindness is connected with Israel's refusal to heed God's instruction. Then, in Ezek 12:2, 13 it is said that such rebellion leads to spiritual blindness, and, ultimately, physical blindness, for Zedekiah.

Blindness is also involved in discussions concerning idolatry. Idolaters are said to worship idols that do not see, according to Deut 4:28 and Dan 5:23, and have eyes but do not see, according to Jer 5:21, Ps 115:5-8, and Ps 135:15-18. Psalms 115 and 135 even go as far as to say that those who trust in idols become like such idols: blind also. This fate, apparently, meets the idol-builder in Isa 44:9, 18.

Stigma

One must next consider the concept of stigma as it relates to blindness in the Hebrew Scriptures. Saul M. Olyan discusses the intensity of the stigmas attached to a number of disabilities discussed in the Hebrew Bible, one of which was blindness. He notes, for example, that listing the blind with the widow and orphan in Job 28 associates them with such marginalized groups. Even Ps 146:6-8, which shows how God gives sight to the blind as he helps the widow, still stigmatizes the blind by listing them with other such marginalized, weakened groups.[3] The blind would have been stigmatized in the sanctuary system since such could not officiate as priests, and so were disqualified on the grounds of a disability.[4] Olyan also discusses the talion laws as in Exod 21:23-25. One who was naturally or accidentally blinded might be mistakenly assumed to be one bearing the mark of one who committed the crime of blinding another.[5] Olyan notes how the blind are further stigmatized in the curses of Deut 28:28 by having their disability

---

3. Olyan, *Disability in the Hebrew Bible*, 6-7.
4. Olyan, *Disability in the Hebrew Bible*, 32.
5. Olyan, *Disability in the Hebrew Bible*, 42.

listed as a consequence for the community's violating the covenant.[6] Exodus 23:8, with reference to the blinding effect of a bribe, stigmatizes the blind by associating such condition with faulty judgment.[7] Passages such as Isa 56:10 associate blindness with ignorance and incompetence to be watchmen, stigmatizing the blind by connecting their disability with such negative traits.[8]

One may respond to this by saying that such stigmatizing in the Bible should not be seen as a blemish in the character of God. First, it is a fact that the blind cannot do certain tasks that the sighted can, and thus are weaker in certain ways. Since God commanded mercy to be shown to widows and orphans by allowing them to glean in the fields (Deut 24:19–22) such other types of marginalized people were to be shown compassion. By grouping the blind with those other marginalized groups, one would expect compassion toward the blind also to be recommended, and it clearly was, since Job thought such compassion was an example of a good character. It must also be noted that fewer employment opportunities existed in ancient Israel for the blind than exist in twenty-first-century America, where the blind may use computers and other assistive devices to function independently. The blind would have been similar to the widow and the orphan in how, for all such groups, there were few opportunities for independent means of livelihood. Such people must be given charity, then, lest they starve.

While one who was blinded by the state could cast a stigma on all blind people, statistically, there would necessarily be more people not blinded as a punishment for bad character than those who were. This is because for everyone blinded for blinding another, there would be that "other" who was first blinded in addition to all the people accidentally blinded or blinded from birth. Thus, most blind people encountered in ancient Israel would not have been blinded as a penalty for committing a crime. One must also recall that, since Lev 19:14 and Deut 27:18 make no distinction between those naturally blinded and those blinded as a punishment, all blind people, however their condition was caused, were to be shown mercy. Clearly, then, God is shown as working to minimize the stigma on the blind. Finally, at least, the blind in ancient Israel would not bear the stigma borne by the blind in surrounding cultures that believed in omens. One who was blind in such a culture as ancient Babylon would be made to feel at fault for a military defeat if such defeat was predicted to come on a city with blind people living in it. A blind person in ancient Israel, however the blindness was caused, would never be made to feel responsible for any tragedy since

---

6. Olyan, *Disability in the Hebrew Bible*, 34.
7. Olyan, *Disability in the Hebrew Bible*, 35.
8. Olyan, *Disability in the Hebrew Bible*, 7.

no such omen texts appear in the Hebrew Bible. Even if the blindness was caused by a curse or act of judgment from God, such a blindness would not directly cause tragedies to fall on others.

It is true that blindness was used in Hebrew literature as a symbol for ignorance and bad judgment. This is a convenient symbol, the meaning of which was not so powerful as to remove the validity of Lev 19:14 or Deut 27:18. In addition, not all such negative comparisons must be seen as stigmatizing. One, for example, may speak of a person as being childish without stigmatizing or devaluing children. Such a childish person simply behaves in ways often associated with small children. Similarly, one who shows lack of spiritual insight can be described as blind without those who are physically blind suddenly being seen as of lesser value.

The barring of a blind priest from officiating does appear to be a serious case of stigmatizing. Nonetheless, one may contrast this with the Arua Institution when the blind were forced to become slaves of the temple. At least in ancient Israel, the blind associated with the sanctuary were to be fed. Even their families were to be fed from the holy offerings. Apparently the meaning of the symbol of being blemish-free was powerful enough for God to see it appropriate to make such a command. Nonetheless, such blind people were to be shown compassion as they were to be fed and not mistreated, according to Lev 19:14. Thus, the blind author of this dissertation takes no offense when reading the various blindness passages in the Bible. God shows compassion to the blind, even working miracles through them as in the case of Samson. That is enough to show the goodness of God as described by the Bible writers concerning the blind.

IMPLICATIONS OF THIS RESEARCH

Academic Implications

In considering the implications of this research and points for further research, one must consider both academic and practical realms. In the academic realm, each of the Scriptural passages considered in this study could be analyzed at a scholarly level to determine meanings connected with blindness more unique to the individual passages. One could also compare and contrast individual passages in the Hebrew Scriptures. Additional work, for example, could be done comparing and contrasting the various passages discussing prohibitions concerning blemished animals. Additional work could also be done comparing and contrasting how the topic of blindness is discussed in the Hebrew Scriptures with how it is discussed elsewhere in the ancient Near East as new manuscripts are constantly being discovered and translated. One may even wish to compare and contrast how blindness is treated in the Hebrew Scriptures with how it is treated in rabbinic literature and the writings of the church fathers. Academic studies at the dissertation level should also be done on other disabilities, such as deafness, lameness, muteness, or infertility.

Practical Implications

With reference to practical implications of this study, it is useful first to consider what Thomas E. Reynolds describes as the "cult of normalcy." He notes how society has standardized understandings of what a normal, able-bodied human being should be, and that what deviates from that norm is excluded or treated as outside the normal group. Those with disabilities, then, are often treated as abnormal, not following the guidelines of such cult of normalcy.[9] One who is blind, then, is not "normal" since he/she does not see as most other people do, and so such a one would experience mistreatment, either consciously or unconsciously, as one who is not a member of the accepted group. The author of this dissertation understands firsthand how, in elementary and high school, other children may mistreat one who is blind by placing obstacles in his/her path or by calling names.

While the Bible recognizes that the blind are different, a more balanced approach is presented. It is true that the blind were barred from officiating as priests, but they were not removed from the priesthood altogether and were expected to eat of the holy food. While blindness appears to be a trait seen only after the onset of sin and that deviates from the original design of creation, the blind were to be treated with respect, not tripped by stumbling blocks (see above paragraph and Lev 19:14). Thus, the biblical principle is that the blind are loved by God, and so must be treated with compassion and dignity, and allowed to function as freely as physically possible while recognizing their limitations.

It is then the task for further research to determine how the blind in twenty-first-century human society must be treated. Since the Hebrew Bible is recognized as canonical by Jews and Christians, emphasis should be placed first on the treatment and roles of the blind and visually impaired in the synagogue and church. Then, the followers of such Scriptures can further apply such principles in their dealings with the rest of society.

---

9. Reynolds, *Vulnerable Communion*, 60.

The Blind in the Religious Community

With reference to the blind themselves, it appears, based on the research in this study, that the blind must recognize that there may be impassible limitations placed upon them by their religious community. Just as a blind priest was not permitted to officiate, a Jew who is blind may not be permitted to perform rituals that require vision such as reading from the Torah scroll or lighting candles for Sabbath services.[10] Similarly, if a Christian denomination does not permit the blind to perform certain tasks based on religious reasons, the blind in that denomination may seek other ways to serve the Lord. A blind individual must understand that whether or not he/she agrees that such tasks should be forbidden, God does not force one to act contrary to his/her conscience (Ezek 4:12–15). Thus, if it violates the conscience of the community for a blind person to perform such a task, the blind individual must seek opportunities to serve elsewhere. In Judaism, for example, a blind individual may be permitted to read from the Haftara in Braille if such materials are provided.[11] Blind individuals in the Christian community should feel comfortable performing any task they are permitted to perform, from taking communion, to leading in worship services. As the blind priest was still to be sustained as a priest, and as blind prophets and judges were still blessed with the power of God, the blind in religious communities should be allowed to function as much as possible.

One way the blind can serve in their religious communities is by willingly choosing to allow themselves to function as living illustrations regarding the texts in the Hebrew Scriptures concerning figurative blindness. One who is blind could preach a sermon about what it is like to dwell in darkness and to need one to lead him/her (Isa 42:7–18). Such a sermon need not stigmatize the blind, as it can be clearly understood that spiritual blindness is concerned with physical blindness only as a convenient illustration. The blind might have special insights concerning such passages, which the sighted would not consider. Thus, it may even be true that certain aspects of further academic research concerning blindness in the Hebrew Scriptures may be best done by the blind.

---

10. Ruconich and Schneider, "Religions and Their Views of Blindness and Visual Impairment," 214.

11. Ruconich and Schneider, "Religions and Their Views of Blindness and Visual Impairment," 214.

The Religious Community

With reference to the religious community to which the blind or visually impaired may belong, certain principles may be applied. First, if there are limitations that must be placed on the blind, for conscientious/religious or practical reasons, one could suggest that such limitations should be as few as possible and should be well-communicated and understood. The principle of not leading the blind astray on the path (Deut 27:18) may apply here. One who is blind in a religion where the blind generally do not become religious leaders should be warned of such a situation as he/she considers seminary. Such a person may still seek a degree, but he/she might also choose to learn a practical trade in case there is no work available for him/her in his/her denomination.

The principle of not placing a stumbling block before the blind may be applied with reference to accessibility issues. It is often recommended that doors such as those for restrooms and elevators be marked with Braille labels for the blind.[12] It might be said that failing to post these simple signs might cause the blind to stumble because of the inconvenience and potential embarrassment that would ensue from stepping into the wrong room, especially if such is the wrong restroom. If a youth group constantly plays picture games, a blind participant may feel alienated, and such alienation might be seen as a stumbling. Finally, the most obvious application of this verse, the direct placing of stumbling blocks to trip the blind, must be addressed. Children who mock or directly mistreat the blind should be firmly guided away from such activities, being shown how the Bible condemns such behaviors.

Job 29:15, regarding being eyes to the blind, may be applied in a number of ways. The principle is that one who is righteous is one who does all that is possible to remove the disabling effects and consequences of blindness. To do this, though, one must understand the situation of the blind.

A number of obstacles are faced by the blind with reference to religious services. Often the blind are unable to have access to the printed materials in the institution, such as hymnals or bulletins. It can be said that the greatest obstacle faced by the blind and visually impaired with reference to attending religious services is transportation. Since many such people are unable to drive, they must rely on others to drive them to and from church. This problem is especially true among the elderly, who suddenly find themselves unable to attend church, and so, socially isolated from a community they no longer know would care about them.[13]

---

12. Bishop, "Blindness and Visual Impairment and the Religious Community," 240.
13. Bishop, "Blindness and Visual Impairment and the Religious Community," 240.

Sighted members of religious communities may be admonished, based on Job 29:15, to provide services designed to ease these discomforts for the blind. Vans could be provided to offer rides for the blind and those with other disabilities. Bulletins could be provided electronically to the blind who have computers. The Seventh-day Adventist church hymnal has been made available by the author of this dissertation as a text file for computers distributed by Christian Record Services, a Seventh-day Adventist organization dedicated to serving the blind Christian community.[14] Using this text-based computer file, a blind computer user may read along with the hymns at whatever speed is necessary. This was done because Braille is often slow to read, and Braille books are significantly larger and more bulky than printed books. The existence of such services, though, may not be satisfactory without dissemination of the knowledge of such systems. Thus, the blind must be made aware of all resources available to them within their religious communities.

Jews and Christians, then, could use these same principles when interacting with the blind in general society. Following simple rules of courtesy can keep the blind from being misled or made to stumble. Much embarrassment and confusion, for example, can be avoided by a sighted person introducing himself/herself to a blind person at the start of a conversation rather than expecting the blind individual to guess who is speaking.[15] As noted previously in this study, the blind at times struggle with recognizing voices. What is seen as a game to the sighted becomes an irritation to the blind who must play this "game" with so many people who all think the blind can quickly guess voices.

In the Hebrew Scriptures, blindness, both physical and spiritual, is shown to be a most serious condition. Though it was not God's original intention for blindness to exist, he is described as working in powerful ways to provide for the needs of the blind. The proper treatment of the blind by other people is even considered a matter of holiness in a number of passages. Those who seek to follow the teachings of the Hebrew Scriptures, then, must continue to find new applications of such biblical principles that what is described as God's desire for the eyes of the blind to be opened may be best realized.

---

14. The Jewish Braille Institute of America provides Braille resources for the Jewish community. Ruconich and Schneider, 205.

15. Bishop, "Blindness and Visual Impairment and the Religious Community," 244.

Bibliography

Abrams, Judith Z. *Judaism and Disability*. Washington, DC: Gallaudet University, 1998.
Agus, Aharon R. E., and Jan Assmann, eds. *Ocular Desire: Yearbook for Religious Anthropology*. Berlin: Akademie Verlag, 1994.
Alden, Robert L. *Job*. New American Commentary, vol. 11. Nashville, TN: Broadman and Holman, 1993.
———. "Malachi." *The Expositor's Bible Commentary* 7:701–25. Grand Rapids: Zondervan, 1988.
Alexander, Ralph H. "Ezekiel." *The Expositor's Bible Commentary* 6:737–996. Grand Rapids: Zondervan, 1988.
Allen, James P. "From the Berlin 'Hymn to Ptah.'" In *Context of Scripture*, edited by William W. Hallo, 1:20–21. Leiden: Brill, 1997. <http://dx.doi.org/10.1163/2211-436X_cos_aCOSB_1_14>
———. "A Ramesside Stela." In *Context of Scripture*, edited by William W. Hallo, 1:20–21. Leiden: Brill, 1997. <http://dx.doi.org/10.1163/2211-436X_cos_aCOSB_1_13>
Allen, Leslie C. *Psalms 101–150*. Word Biblical Commentary, 21. Rev. ed. Nashville, TN: Thomas Nelson, 2002.
Allen, Ronald B. "Numbers." *The Expositor's Bible Commentary*, 2:657–1008. Grand Rapids: Regency Reference Library, 1990.
Alter, Robert. *Genesis*. New York: Norton, 1996.
Ancient Egyptian Literature. Translated by John L. Foster. Austin, TX: University of Texas, 2001.
Andersen, Francis I. *Job*. Tyndale Old Testament Commentaries. Downers Grove, IL: InterVarsity, 1976.
Anderson, A. A. *The Book of Psalms*. 2 vols. New Century Bible Commentary. Grand Rapids: Eerdmans, 1972.
———. *2 Samuel*. Word Biblical Commentary, vol. 11. Dallas, TX: Word, 1989.
Archer, Gleason L., Jr. "Daniel." *The Expositor's Bible Commentary*, 7:3–157. Grand Rapids: Zondervan, 1988.
Arnold, Bill T. *1 & 2 Samuel*. The NIV Application Commentary Series. Grand Rapids: Zondervan, 2003.
———. "עשׁו." In *New International Dictionary of Old Testament Theology & Exegesis*, edited by Willem A. VanGemeren, 4:204. Grand Rapids: Zondervan, 1997.
Ashby, Godfrey. *Go Out and Meet God: A Commentary on the Book of Exodus*. International Theological Commentary. Grand Rapids: Eerdmans, 1998.

Ashley, Timothy R. *The Book of Numbers*. New International Commentary on the Old Testament. Grand Rapids: Eerdmans, 1993.

Assmann, Jan. "Occular Desire in a Time of Darkness: Urban Festivals and Divine Visibility in Ancient Egypt." In *Ocular Desire: Yearbook for Religious Anthropology*, edited by Aharon R. E. Agus and Jan Assmann, 13-29. Berlin: Akademie Verlag, 1994.

Assyrian Dictionary. Edited by A. Leo Oppenheim. Chicago: The Oriental Institute of Chicago, 1956-61. S.v. "uppudu," "Nātilu in La Nātilu," and "Zaqtu."

Avalos, Hector. *Illness and Health Care in the Ancient Near East*. Atlanta: Scholars, 1995.

Avalos, Hector, Sarah J. Melcher, and Jeremy Schipper, eds. *This Abled Body: Rethinking Disabilities in Biblical Studies*. Atlanta: Society of Biblical Literature, 2007.

Bailey, Randall C. *Exodus*. The College Press NIV Commentary. Joplin, MO: College, 2007.

Baker, David W. *Joel, Obadiah, Malachi*. The NIV Application Commentary Series. Grand Rapids: Zondervan, 2006.

———. *Nahum, Habakkuk, and Zephania*. Tyndale Old Testament Commentaries. Downers Grove, IL: InterVarsity, 1988.

Baldwin, Joyce G. *1 and 2 Samuel*. Tyndale Old Testament Commentaries. Downers Grove, IL: InterVarsity, 1988.

———. *Daniel*. Tyndale Old Testament Commentaries. Downers Grove, IL: InterVarsity, 1978.

———. *Haggai, Zecharia, Malachi*. Tyndale Old Testament Commentaries. Downers Grove, IL: InterVarsity, 1972.

Baltzer, Klaus. *Deutero-Isaiah*. Hermeneia. Minneapolis: Augsburg Fortress, 2001.

Barker, Kenneth L. "Zechariah." *The Expositor's Bible Commentary*, 7:595-697. Grand Rapids: Zondervan, 1988.

Barker, Kenneth L., and Waylon Bailey. *Micah, Nahum, Habakkuk, Zephania*. New American Commentary, vol. 20. Nashville, TN: Broadman and Holman, 1998.

Barton, George Aaron. *A Critical and Exegetical Commentary on the Book of Ecclesiastes*. International Critical Commentary. Edinburgh: T. & T. Clark, 1959.

Barucq, André, and François Daumas. *Hymnes et Prières de L'Egypte Ancienne*. Paris: Cerf, 1980.

Beckman, Gary. *Hittite Diplomatic Texts*. Writings from the Ancient World, vol. 7. Atlanta: Scholars, 1996.

———. "The Storm-God and the Serpent (Illuyanka)." In *Context of Scripture*, edited by William W. Hallo, 1:150, 151. Leiden: Brill, 1997.

Bellinger, W. H., Jr. *Leviticus and Numbers*. New International Biblical Commentary, vol. 3. Peabody, MA: Hendrickson, 2001.

Bennett, Robert A. "The Book of Zephaniah." *The New Interpreter's Bible*, 7:659-704. Nashville, TN: Abingdon, 1996.

Bergen, Robert D. *1, 2 Samuel*. New American Commentary, vol. 7. Nashville, TN: Broadman and Holman, 1996.

Berlin, Adele. *Lamentations: A Commentary*. Old Testament Library. Louisville, KY: Westminster/John Knox Press, 2002.

Birch, Bruce C. "The First and Second Books of Samuel." *The New Interpreter's Bible*, 2:949-1383. Nashville, TN: Abingdon, 1994.

Bishop, Virginia. "Blindness and Visual Impairment and the Religious Community." In *Diversity and Visual Impairment: The Influence of Race, Gender, Religion, and*

Ethnicity on the Individual, edited by Madeline Milian and Jane N. Erin, 223-49. New York: American Foundation for the Blind Press, 2001.

Bland, Dave. *Proverbs, Ecclesiastes, & Song of Songs*. The College Press NIV Commentary. Joplin, MO: College, 2002.

Blenkinsopp, Joseph. *Isaiah 1-39*. Anchor Bible, vol. 19. New York: Doubleday, 2000.

———. *Isaiah 40-55*. Anchor Bible, vol. 19A. New York: Doubleday, 2002.

———. *Isaiah 56-66*. Anchor Bible, vol. 19B. New York: Doubleday, 2000.

Block, Daniel I. *The Book of Ezekiel Chapters 1-24*. New International Commentary on the Old Testament. Grand Rapids: Eerdmans, 1997.

———. *Judges, Ruth*. New American Commentary, vol. 6. Nashville, TN: Broadman and Holman, 1999.

Boda, Mark J. *Haggai, Zechariah*. The NIV Application Commentary Series. Grand Rapids: Zondervan, 2004.

Boling, Robert G. *Judges*. Anchor Bible, vol. 6A. Garden City, NY: Doubleday, 1975.

Bottero, Jean. *Mesopotamia: Writing, Reasoning, and the Gods*. Chicago: University of Chicago, 1992.

Briggs, Charles Augustus, and Emilie Grace Briggs. *A Critical and Exegetical Commentary on the Book of Psalms*. International Critical Commentary, vol. 1. Edinburgh: T. & T. Clark, 1952.

Briley, Terry. *Isaiah*. The College Press NIV Commentary, vol. 1. Joplin, MO: College, 2000.

Brown, Francis, S. R. Driver, and Charles A. Briggs. *The Brown-Driver-Briggs Hebrew and English Lexicon*. Peabody, MA: Hendrickson, 1999.

Brownlee, William H. *Ezekiel 1-19*. Word Biblical Commentary, vol. 28. Waco, TX: Word, 1986.

Broyles, Craig C. *Psalms*. New International Biblical Commentary, vol. 1. Peabody, MA: Hendrickson, 1999.

Bruckner, James K. *Exodus*. New International Biblical Commentary, vol. 2. Peabody, MA: Hendrickson, 2008.

———. *Jonah, Nahum, Habakkuk, Zephania*. The NIV Application Commentary Series. Grand Rapids: Zondervan, 2004.

Brueggemann, Walter. "The Book of Exodus." *The New Interpreter's Bible*, 1:677-981. Nashville, TN: Abingdon, 1994.

Bryan, Cyril P. *Ancient Egyptian Medicine: The Papyrus Ebers*. Chicago: Ares, 1930.

Budd, Philip J. *Leviticus*. New Century Bible Commentary. Grand Rapids: Eerdmans, 1996.

———. *Numbers*. Word Biblical Commentary, vol. 5. Waco, TX: Word, 1984.

Carpenter, Eugene, and Michael A. Grisanti. "רקנ." *New International Dictionary of Old Testament Theology & Exegesis*, edited by Willem A. VanGemeren, 3:158-59. Grand Rapids: Zondervan, 1997.

Carroll, Robert P. *Jeremiah: A Commentary*. Old Testament Library. Philadelphia: Westminster, 1986.

———. *When Prophecy Failed: Cognitive Dissonance in the Prophetic Traditions of the Old Testament*. New York: Seabury, 1979.

Childs, Brevard S. *Exodus: A Commentary*. Old Testament Library. Philadelphia: Westminster, 1974.

Christensen, Duane L. *Deuteronomy 1-11*. Word Biblical Commentary, vol. 6A. Dallas: Word, 1991.

———. *Deuteronomy 21:10—34:12*. Word Biblical Commentary, vol. 6B. Nashville, TN: Thomas Nelson, 2002.
Clements, Ronald E. "The Book of Deuteronomy." *The New Interpreter's Bible*, 2:271–538. Nashville, TN: Abingdon, 1994.
———. *Ezekiel*. Westminster Bible Companions. Louisville, KY: Westminster John Knox, 1996.
———. *Isaiah 1–39*. New Century Bible Commentary. Grand Rapids: Eerdmans, 1980.
Clifford, Richard J. *Proverbs: A Commentary*. Old Testament Library. Philadelphia: Westminster, 1999.
Clines, David J. A. *Job 1–20*. Word Biblical Commentary, vol. 17. Dallas, TX: Word, 1989.
———. *Job 21–37*. Word Biblical Commentary, vol. 18A. Nashville, TN: Thomas Nelson, 2006.
Cogan, Mordechai, Jr. *I Kings*. Anchor Bible, vol. 10. Garden City, NY: Doubleday, 2001.
Cogan, Mordechai, and Hayim Tadmor, Jr. *II Kings*. Anchor Bible, vol. 8. Garden City, NY: Doubleday, 1988.
Cohn, Robert L. *1 Kings*. Berit Olam, vol. 1. Collegeville, MN: Liturgical, 2000.
Cole, R. Alan. *Exodus*. Tyndale Old Testament Commentaries. Downers Grove, IL: InterVarsity, 1973.
Cole, R. Dennis. *Numbers*. New American Commentary, vol. 3B. Nashville, TN: Broadman and Holman, 2000.
Collins, Billie Jean. "The First Soldiers' Oath." In *Context of Scripture*, edited by William W. Hallo, 1:165–67. Leiden: Brill, 1997.
Collins, John J. *Hermeneia—A Critical and Historical Commentary on the Bible*. Minneapolis: Augsburg Fortress, 1993.
Cook, F. C., ed. *The Bible Commentary: Exodus–Ruth*. Grand Rapids: Baker, 1953.
Cooke, G. A. *A Critical and Exegetical Commentary on the Book of Ezekiel*. International Critical Commentary, vol. 1. Edinburgh: T. & T. Clark, 1951.
Cooper, Lamar Eugene, Sr. *Ezekiel*. New American Commentary, vol. 17. Nashville, TN: Broadman and Holman, 1994.
Cotter, David W. *Genesis*. Berit Olam 1. Collegeville, MN: Liturgical, 2003.
Craigie, Peter C. *The Book of Deuteronomy*. New International Commentary on the Old Testament. Grand Rapids: Eerdmans, 1976.
———. *Psalms 1–50*. Word Biblical Commentary, vol. 19. Waco, TX: Word, 1983.
Craigie, Peter C., Page H. Kelley, and Joel F. Drinkard. *Jeremiah 1–25*. Word Biblical Commentary, vol. 26. Dallas, TX: Word, 1991.
Creamer, Deborah B. "Including All Bodies in the Body of God: Disability and the Theology of Sallie McFague." *Journal of Religion, Disability & Health* 9, no. 4 (2005) 55–70.
Crenshaw, James L. *Ecclesiastes: A Commentary*. Old Testament Library. Philadelphia: Westminster, 1987.
Dahood, Mitchell. *Psalms I: 1–50*. Anchor Bible, vol. 16. Garden City, NY: Doubleday, 1966.
———. *Psalms II: 51–100*. Anchor Bible, vol. 17. Garden City, NY: Doubleday, 1968.
———. *Psalms III: 101–150*. Anchor Bible, vol. 17A. Garden City, NY: Doubleday, 1970.
Dalley, Stephanie. "The Descent of Ishtar to the Underworld." In *Context of Scripture*, edited by William W. Hallo, 1:381–84. Leiden: Brill, 1997.
Darr, Katheryn Pfisterer. "The Book of Ezekiel." *The New Interpreter's Bible*, 6:1075–1607. Nashville, TN: Abingdon, 2001.

Daube, David. *Studies in Biblical Law*. New York: Ktav, 1969.
Davidson, Richard M. "Biblical Interpretation." *Handbook of Seventh-day Adventist Theology*. Commentary Reference Series, vol. 12. Hagerstown, MD: Review and Herald, 2000.
―――. *Flame of Yahweh: Sexuality in the Old Testament*. Peabody, MA: Hendrickson, 2007.
―――. "Revelation/Inspiration in the Old Testament: A Critique of Alden Thompson's 'Incarnational Model." In *Issues in Revelation and Inspiration*, edited by Frank Holbrook and Leo Van Dolson, 105-35. Berrien Springs, MI: Adventist Theological Society Publications, 1992.
―――. "The 'Servant,' ('Ebed) of Isaiah." Class handout, Old Testament Department, Andrews University, 2006.
Davies, Andrew. *Double Standards in Isaiah: Re-evaluating Prophetic Ethics and Divine Justice*. Biblical Interpretation Series, vol. 46. Leiden: Brill, 2000.
Dearman, J. Andrew. *Jeremiah and Lamentations*. The NIV Application Commentary Series. Grand Rapids: Zondervan, 2002.
Delitzsch, Franz. *Biblical Commentary on the Book of Job*. 2 vols. Biblical Commentary on the Old Testament. Grand Rapids: Eerdmans, 1949.
―――. *The Biblical Commentary on the Prophecies of Isaiah*. 2 vols. Biblical Commentary on the Old Testament. Grand Rapids: Eerdmans, 1960.
―――. *Biblical Commentary on the Proverbs of Solomon*. Biblical Commentary on the Old Testament, vol. 2. Grand Rapids: Eerdmans, 1952.
―――. *Biblical Commentary on the Psalms*. Biblical Commentary on the Old Testament, vols. 2, 3. Grand Rapids: Eerdmans, 1959.
―――. *Commentary on the Song of Songs and Ecclesiastes*. Biblical Commentary on the Old Testament. Grand Rapids: Eerdmans, 1952.
DeVries, Simon J. *1 Kings*. Word Biblical Commentary, vol. 12. Nashville, TN: Thomas Nelson, 2003.
Diamond, A. S. "An Eye for an Eye (Part 2)." *Iraq* 19 (Autumn 1957) 151-55.
Diodorus of Sicily. *Diodorus of Sicily*. Translated by C. H. Oldfather. 10 vols. London: Heinemann, 1933.
Dosch, Gudrun. "Non-Slave Labor in Nuzi." In *Labor in the Ancient Near East*, edited by Marvin A. Powell, 223-35. The American Oriental Series 68. New Haven, CT: American Oriental Society, 1987.
Doukhan, Jacques. *Hebrew for Theologians*. Lanham, MD: University Press of America, 1993.
Dozeman, Thomas B. "The Book of Numbers." *The New Interpreter's Bible*, 2:3-268. Nashville, TN: Abingdon, 1994.
Driver, Samuel Rolles. *The Book of Genesis*. Westminster Commentary. London: Methuen, 1943.
―――. *A Critical and Exegetical Commentary on Deuteronomy*. International Critical Commentary. Edinburgh: T. & T. Clark, 1951.
Driver, Samuel Rolles, and George Buchanan Gray. *A Critical and Exegetical Commentary on Job*. International Critical Commentary. Edinburgh: T. & T. Clark, 1958.
Duguid, Iain M. *Ezekiel*. The NIV Application Commentary Series. Grand Rapids: Zondervan, 1999.
Durham, John I. *Exodus*. Word Biblical Commentary, vol. 3. Waco, TX: Word, 1987.

Eaton, Michael A. *Ecclesiastes*. Tyndale Old Testament Commentaries. Downers Grove, IL: InterVarsity, 1983.
Eichrodt, Walther, and Adele Berlin. *Ezekiel: A Commentary*. Old Testament Library. Philadelphia: Westminster, 1970.
Ellison, H. L. "Lamentations." *The Expositor's Bible Commentary*, 6:695–733. Grand Rapid: Zondervan, 1988.
Encyclopaedia Judaica. 1971 ed. S.v. "Blindness."
Engelhard, David Herman. "Hittite Magical Practices: An Analysis." Ph.D. dissertation, Brandeis University, Dept. of Mediterranean Studies, 1970.
Enns, Peter. *Exodus*. The NIV Application Commentary Series. Grand Rapids: Zondervan, 2000.
Estes, J. Worth. *The Medical Skills of Ancient Egypt*. Canton, MA: Science History, 1993.
Evans, Mary J. *1 and 2 Samuel*. New International Biblical Commentary, vol. 1. Peabody, MA: Hendrickson, 2000.
Feinberg, Charles L. "Jeremiah." *The Expositor's Bible Commentary*, 6:357–691. Grand Rapids: Zondervan, 1988.
Fitzmyer, Joseph A. S. J. "The Inscriptions of Bar-Ga'yah and Mati'el from Sefire." In *Context of Scripture*, edited by William W. Hallo, 2:213–17. Leiden: Brill, 1997.
Foster, Benjamin R. "Diurnal Prayers of Diviners." In *Context of Scripture*, edited by William W. Hallo, 1:417–18. Leiden: Brill, 1997.
Fredenburg, Brandon L. *Ezekiel*. The College Press NIV Commentary. Joplin, MO: College, 2002.
Fretheim, Terence E. "The Book of Genesis." *The New Interpreter's Bible*, 1:321–674. Nashville, TN: Abingdon, 1994.
Fuhs, H. F. "Rā'ā." In *Theological Dictionary of the Old Testament*, edited by G. Johannes Botterweck and Helmer Ringgren, 13:208–42. Grand Rapids: Eerdmans, 1999.
———. "Yārē." In *Theological Dictionary of the Old Testament*, edited by G. Johannes Botterweck and Helmer Ringgren, 6:290–315. Grand Rapids: Eerdmans, 1999.
Gane, Roy. *Leviticus, Numbers*. The NIV Application Commentary Series. Grand Rapids: Zondervan, 2004.
Gane, Roy, and Jacob Milgrom. "קרב." *Theological Dictionary of the Old Testament*. Edited by G. Johannes Botterweck and Helmer Ringgren, 13:135–48. Grand Rapids: Eerdmans, 1999.
Garrett, Duane A. *Proverbs, Ecclesiastes, and Song of Songs*. New American Commentary, vol. 14. Nashville, TN: Broadman and Holman, 1993.
Gelb, I. J. "The Arua Institution." *Revue d'Assyriologie et d'Archéologie Orientale* 66 (1972) 1–32.
———. "Prisoners of War in Early Mesopotamia." *Journal of Near Eastern Studies* 32 (1973) 70–98.
"Gen 3:5. Your Eyes Shall Be Opened." In *Seventh-day Adventist Bible Commentary*, edited by Francis D. Nichol, 1:230. Washington, DC: Review and Herald, 1978.
Gerstenberger, Erhard S. *Leviticus: A Commentary*. Old Testament Library. Louisville, KY: Westminster John Knox, 1996.
Goldingay, John E. *Daniel*. Word Biblical Commentary, vol. 30. Dallas, TX: Word, 1989.
———. *Isaiah*. New International Biblical Commentary, vol. 1. Peabody, MA: Hendrickson, 2001.

Goldingay, John, and David Payne. *A Critical and Exegetical Commentary on the Book of Isaiah 40–55*. International Critical Commentary, vol. 1. Edinburgh: T. & T. Clark, 2006.

Gordis, Robert. *Koheleth: The Man and His World*. Text and Studies of the Jewish Theological Seminary of America, vol. 19. New York: The Jewish Theological Seminary of America, 1951.

Gordon, Robert P. *I and II Samuel: A Commentary*. Grand Rapids: Regency Reference Library, 1986.

Gorman, Frank H., Jr. *Divine Presence and Community: A Commentary on the Book of Leviticus*. International Theological Commentary. Grand Rapids: Eerdmans, 1997.

Goulder, Michael D. *The Psalms of the Return: Book V, Psalms 107–150*. Sheffield, UK: Sheffield Academic, 1998.

Gray, George Buchanan. *A Critical and Exegetical Commentary on the Book of Isaiah I–XXVII*. International Critical Commentary, vol. 1. Edinburgh: T. & T. Clark, 1956.

———. *A Critical and Exegetical Commentary on Numbers*. International Critical Commentary. Edinburgh: T. & T. Clark, 1956.

Greenberg, Moshe. *Ezekiel 1–20*. Anchor Bible, vol. 22. New York: Doubleday, 1983.

———. *Understanding Exodus*. Melton Research Center Series. New York: Behrman House, 1969.

Grogan, G. W. "Isaiah." *The Expositor's Bible Commentary*, 6:3–354. Grand Rapids: Zondervan, 1988.

Grueggmann, Walter. *Deuteronomy*. Abingdon Old Testament Commentaries. Nashville, TN: Abingdon, 2001.

Guinan, Ann K. "Divination." In *Context of Scripture*, edited by William W. Hallo, 1:421–26. Leiden: Brill, 1997.

Güterbock, Hans G. "An Initiation Rite for a Hittite Prince." In *American Oriental Society, Middle West Branch, Semi-Centennial Volume*, edited by Denis Sinor, 99–103. Bloomington, IN: Indiana University Press, 1969.

Habel, Norman C. *The Book of Job: A Commentary*. Old Testament Library. Philadelphia: Westminster, 1985.

Hahlen, Mark Allen, and Clay Alan Ham. *Minor Prophets*. The College Press NIV Commentary, vol. 2. Joplin, MO: College, 2006.

Hall, Gary H. *Deuteronomy*. The College Press NIV Commentary. Joplin, MO: College, 2000.

Hallo, William W., ed. *Context of Scripture*. 3 vols. Leiden: Brill, 1997.

Hamilton, Victor P. *The Book of Genesis: Chapters 1–17*. New International Commentary on the Old Testament. Grand Rapids: Eerdmans, 1990.

———. *The Book of Genesis: Chapters 18–50*. New International Commentary on the Old Testament. Grand Rapids: Eerdmans, 1995.

———. "פקח." In *New International Dictionary of Old Testament Theology & Exegesis*, edited by Willem A. VanGemeren, 3:665–66. Grand Rapids: Zondervan, 1997.

Harman, Allan M. "'Ayin." In *New International Dictionary of Old Testament Theology & Exegesis*, edited by Willem. A. VanGemeren, 3:385–90. Grand Rapids: Zondervan, 1997.

Harris, J. Gordon, Cheryl A. Brown, and Michael S. Moore. *Joshua, Judges, Ruth*. New International Biblical Commentary, vol. 1. Peabody, MA: Hendrickson, 2000.

Harris, R. Laird. "Leviticus." *The Expositor's Bible Commentary*, 2:501–654. Grand Rapids: Regency Reference Library, 1990.

Harrison, R. K. "Blindness." In *Interpreter's Dictionary of the Bible*, edited by G. A. Buttrick et al., 1:449. Nashville: Abingdon, 1962.

———. *Jeremiah and Lamentations*. Tyndale Old Testament Commentaries. Downers Grove, IL: InterVarsity, 1973.

———. *Leviticus*. Tyndale Old Testament Commentaries. Downers Grove, IL: InterVarsity, 1980.

Harrison, R. K., and E. H. Merrill. "עוּר" *New International Dictionary of Old Testament Theology & Exegesis*, edited by Willem A. VanGemeren, 3:356–57. Grand Rapids: Zondervan, 1997.

Hartley, John E. *The Book of Job*. New International Commentary on the Old Testament. Grand Rapids: Eerdmans, 1988.

———. *Genesis*. New International Biblical Commentary, vol. 1. Peabody, MA: Hendrickson, 2000.

———. *Leviticus*. Word Biblical Commentary, vol. 4. Dallas, TX: Word, 1992.

Hartman, Louis F., and Alexander A. Di Lella. *The Book of Daniel*. The Anchor Bible, vol. 23. Garden City, NY: Doubleday, 1978.

Herodotus. *The History*. Translated by David Greene. Chicago: University of Chicago Press, 1987.

Hill, Andrew E. "הכה." *New International Dictionary of Old Testament Theology & Exegesis*, edited by Willem A. VanGemeren, 2:598–99. Grand Rapids: Zondervan, 1997.

———. *Malachi*. Anchor Bible, vol. 25D. New York: Doubleday, 1998.

Hillers, Delbert R. "Bĕrît 'Ām: 'Emancipation of the People.'" *Journal of Biblical Literature* 97 (1978) 175–82.

———. *Lamentations*. Anchor Bible, vol. 7A. New York: Doubleday, 1982.

Hobbs, T. R. *2 Kings*. Word Biblical Commentary, vol. 13. Waco, TX: Word, 1985.

Hoffner, Harry A., Jr. "The Disabled and Infirm in Hittite Society." In *Eretz-Israel: Archaeological, Historical, and Geographical Studies*, edited by Hayim Tadmor and Miriam Tadmor, 27:84–90. Jerusalem: Israel Exploration Society, 2003.

———. "Hittite Laws." In *Context of Scripture*, edited by William W. Hallo, 2:106–19. Leiden: Brill, 1997.

———. "Middle Hittite Period (ca. 1450–1350 BCE) The King to Kaššū in Tapikka 13." In *Context of Scripture*, edited by William W. Hallo, 3:49. Leiden: Brill, 1997.

———. "The Treatment and Long-Term Use of Persons Captured in Battle According to the Maşat Texts." In *Recent Developments in Hittite Archaeology and History*, edited by K. Aslihan Yener and Harry A. Hoffner Jr., 61–72. Winona Lake, IN: Eisenbrauns, 2002.

Holbrook, Frank, and Leo Van Dolson, eds. *Issues in Revelation and Inspiration*. Berrien Springs, MI: Adventist Theological Society Publications, 1992.

Holladay, William L. *Jeremiah 1*. Hermeneia—A Critical and Historical Commentary on the Bible. Minneapolis: Augsburg Fortress, 1986.

Hooks, Stephen M. *Job*. The College Press NIV Commentary. Joplin, MO: College, 2006.

Hossfeld, Frank-Lothar, and Erich Zenger. *Psalms 2*. Hermeneia—A Critical and Historical Commentary on the Bible. Minneapolis: Augsburg Fortress, 2005.

House, Paul R. *1, 2 Kings*. New American Commentary, vol. 8. Nashville, TN: Broadman and Holman, 1995.

———. *Lamentations*. Word Biblical Commentary, vol. 23B. Nashville, TN: Word, 2004.

Houtman, Cornelis. *Exodus*. Historical Commentary on the Old Testament. Leuven: Peeters, 2000.
Huey, F. B., Jr. *Jeremiah, Lamentations*. New American Commentary, vol. 16. Nashville, TN: Broadman and Holman, 1993.
Hull, John M. *In the Beginning There Was Darkness*. Harrisburg, PA: Trinity, 2001.
Jacob, Benno. *The Second Book of the Bible: Exodus*. Hoboken, NJ: Ktav, 1992.
Janzen, J. Gerald. *Abraham and All the Families of the Earth: A Commentary on the Book of Genesis*. International Theological Commentary. Grand Rapids: Eerdmans, 1993.
Jenni, E., and D. Vetter. "Ayin." In *Theological Lexicon of the Old Testament*, edited by Ernst Jenni and Claus Westermann, 2:874–80. Peabody, MA: Hendrickson, 1997.
Johnston, Gordon H. "שׁגג." In *New International Dictionary of Old Testament Theology & Exegesis*, edited by Willem A. VanGemeren, 1:902–3. Grand Rapids: Zondervan, 1997.
———. "שׁמם." In *New International Dictionary of Old Testament Theology & Exegesis*, edited by Willem A. VanGemeren, 2:1145–47. Grand Rapids: Zondervan, 1997.
Jones, Douglas Rawlinson. *Jeremiah*. New Century Bible Commentary. London: Marshall Pickering, 1992.
Jones, Gwilym H. *1 and 2 Kings*. 2 vols. New Century Bible Commentary. Grand Rapids: Eerdmans, 1984.
Just, Felix N. W. "From Tobit to Bartimaeus, From Qumran to Siloam: The Social Role of Blind People and Attitudes toward the Blind in New Testament Times." Ph.D. diss., Yale University, 1997.
Kaiser, Otto. *Isaiah 1–12: A Commentary*. Old Testament Library. Philadelphia: Westminster, 1983.
———. *Isaiah 13–39: A Commentary*. Old Testament Library. Philadelphia: Westminster, 1974.
Kaiser, Walter C., Jr. "Exodus." *The Expositor's Bible Commentary*, 2:287–498. Grand Rapids: Regency Reference Library, 1990.
———. "The Book of Leviticus." *The New Interpreter's Bible*. Nashville, TN: Abingdon, 1994. 1:985–1191.
Kalland, Earl S. "Deuteronomy." *The Expositor's Bible Commentary*, 3:3–235. Grand Rapids: Zondervan, 1992.
Kautzsch, E., ed. *Gesenius' Hebrew Grammar*. 2nd English ed. New York: Oxford University Press, 1910.
Keil, Carl Friedrich. *Biblical Commentary on the Book of Daniel*. Biblical Commentary on the Old Testament. Grand Rapids: Eerdmans, 1959.
———. *The Books of the Kings*. Biblical Commentary on the Old Testament. Grand Rapids: Eerdmans, 1952.
———. *The Prophecies of Jeremiah*. 2 vols. Biblical Commentary on the Old Testament. Grand Rapids: Eerdmans, 1960.
Keil, Carl Friedrich, and Franz Delitzsch. *Biblical Commentary on the Books of Samuel*. Grand Rapids: Eerdmans, 1950.
———. *Biblical Commentary on the Old Testament: The Pentateuch*. Biblical Commentary on the Old Testament. Grand Rapids: Eerdmans, 1959.
———. *Biblical Commentary on the Prophecies of Ezekiel*. Biblical Commentary on the Old Testament, vol. 1. Grand Rapids: Eerdmans, 1952.
Keown, Gerald L., Pamela J. Scalise, and Thomas G. Smothers. *Jeremiah 26–52*. Word Biblical Commentary, vol. 27. Dallas, TX: Word, 1995.

Kidner, Derek. *Genesis*. Tyndale Old Testament Commentaries. Downers Grove, IL: InterVarsity, 1967.
———. *The Proverbs*. Tyndale Old Testament Commentaries. London: Tyndale, 1964.
———. *Psalm 1–72*. Tyndale Old Testament Commentaries. Downers Grove, IL: InterVarsity, 1973.
———. *Psalm 73–150*. Tyndale Old Testament Commentaries. Downers Grove, IL: InterVarsity, 1975.
———. *A Time to Mourn and a Time to Dance: Ecclesiastes and the Way of the World*. Downers Grove, IL: InterVarsity, 1976.
King, L. W., ed. *Babylonian Boundary-Stones and Memorial-Tablets in the British Museum*. London: Oxford University, 1912.
Kissling, Paul. *Genesis*. The College Press NIV Commentary, vol. 1. Joplin, MO: College, 2004.
Kiuchi, Nobuyoshi. *Leviticus*. Apollos Old Testament Commentary, vol. 3. Downers Grove, IL: InterVarsity, 2007.
Klein, Jacob. "Enki and Ninmaḫ." In *Context of Scripture*, edited by William W. Hallo, 1:516–18. Leiden: Brill, 1997.
Kleinig, John W. *Leviticus*. Concordia Commentary. St. Louis: Concordia, 2003.
Koehler, Ludwig, and Walter Baumgartner. *The Hebrew and Aramaic Lexicon of the Old Testament*. 5 vols. Leiden: Brill, 1994–95.
Konkel, August H., Jr. *1 & 2 Kings*. The NIV Application Commentary Series. Grand Rapids: Zondervan, 2006.
Koptak, Paul E. *Proverbs*. The NIV Application Commentary Series. Grand Rapids: Zondervan, 2003.
Kramer, Samuel Noah, and John Maier. *Myths of Enki: The Crafty God*. New York: Oxford University Press, 1989.
Leichty, Erle. *The Omen Series Summa Izbu*. Texts from Cuneiform Sources 4. Locust Valley, NY: Augustin, 1970.
Leupold, H. C. *Exposition of Ecclesiastes*. Grand Rapids: Baker, 1952.
———. *Exposition of Genesis*. 2 vols. Grand Rapids: Baker, 1953.
———. *Exposition of Isaiah*. 2 vols. Grand Rapids: Baker, 1968.
———. *Exposition of the Psalms*. Grand Columbus, OH: Wartburg, 1959.
———. *Exposition of Zechariah*. Grand Rapids: Baker, 1971.
Levine, Baruch A. *Leviticus*. The JPS Torah Commentary. Philadelphia: The Jewish Publication Society, 1989.
———. *Numbers 1–20*. Anchor Bible, vol. 4A. Garden City, NY: Doubleday, 1993.
Lichtheim, Miriam. "Dua-Khety or the Satire on the Trades." In *Context of Scripture*, edited by William W. Hallo, 1:122–25. Leiden: Brill, 1997.
———. "Harpers' Songs." In *Context of Scripture*, edited by William W. Hallo, 1:48–50. Leiden: Brill, 1997.
———. "Instruction of Amenemope." In *Context of Scripture*, edited by William W. Hallo, 1:115–22. Leiden: Brill, 1997.
Lindsey, F. Duane. *The Servant Songs: A Study in Isaiah*. Chicago: Moody, 1985.
Livingstone, Alasdair. "Dialogue of Pessimism or the Obliging Slave." In *Context of Scripture*, edited by William W. Hallo, 1:495–96. Leiden: Brill, 1997.
Lohfink, Norbert. *Qoheleth*. Minneapolis: Fortress, 2003.
Long, Jesse C., Jr. *1 & 2 Kings*. The College Press NIV Commentary. Joplin, MO: College, 2002.

Longman, Tremper, III. *The Book of Ecclesiastes.* New International Commentary on the Old Testament. Grand Rapids: Eerdmans, 1998.

———. *Daniel.* NIV Application Commentary. Grand Rapids: Zondervan, 1999.

———. *Jeremiah, Lamentations.* New International Biblical Commentary. Peabody, MA: Hendrickson, 2008.

Lundbom, Jack R. *Jeremiah 1-20.* Anchor Bible, vol. 21A. New York: Doubleday, 1999.

———. *Jeremiah 21-36.* Anchor Bible, vol. 21B. New York: Doubleday, 2004.

———. *Jeremiah 37-52.* Anchor Bible, vol. 21C. New York: Doubleday, 2004.

Machinist, Peter. "Provincial Governance in Middle Assyria and Some New Texts from Yale." *Assur* 3, no. 2 (1982) 1-37.

Maclaren, Alexander. *Genesis-Numbers.* Expositions of Holy Scripture, vol. 1. Grand Rapids: Baker, 1974.

Maekawa, Kazuya. "Collective Labor Service in Girsu-Lagash: The Pre-Sargonic and Ur III Periods." In *Labor in the Ancient Near East,* edited by Marvin A. Powell, 49-71. The American Oriental Series 68. New Haven, CT: The American Oriental Society, 1987.

Manniche, Lise. *Music and Musicians in Ancient Egypt.* London: British Museum, 1991.

———. "Symbolic Blindness." *Chronique d'Egypte* 53, no. 105 (1978) 13-21.

Mangano, Mark. *Esther & Daniel.* The College Press NIV Commentary. Joplin, MO: College, 2001.

Mathews, Kenneth A. *Genesis 1—11:26.* New American Commentary, vol. 1A. Nashville, TN: Broadman and Holman, 1996.

———. *Genesis 11:27—50:26.* New American Commentary, vol. 1B. Nashville, TN: Broadman and Holman, 2005.

Mauchline, John, ed. *1 and 2 Samuel.* New Century Bible Commentary. London: Oliphants, 1971.

Mayes, A. D. H. *Deuteronomy.* New Century Bible Commentary. Grand Rapids: Eerdmans, 1979.

McCann, J. Clinton, Jr. "The Book of Psalms." *The New Interpreter's Bible,* 4:641-1280. Nashville, TN: Abingdon, 1996.

McCarter, P. Kyle, Jr. *I Samuel.* Anchor Bible, vol. 8. Garden City, NY: Doubleday, 1980.

———. *II Samuel.* Anchor Bible, vol. 9. Garden City, NY: Doubleday, 1984.

McComiskey, Thomas E., ed. *Zephaniah, Haggai, Zechariah, Malachi.* The Minor Prophets, vol. 3. Grand Rapids: Baker, 1998.

McConville, J. G. *Deuteronomy.* Apollos Old Testament Commentary, vol. 5. Downers Grove, IL: InterVarsity, 2002.

McKane, William. *A Critical and Exegetical Commentary on Jeremiah.* 2 vols. International Critical Commentary. Edinburgh: T. & T. Clark, 1986.

Merrill, Eugene H. *Deuteronomy.* New American Commentary, vol. 4. Nashville, TN: Broadman and Holman, 1994.

Meyers, Carol L., and Eric M. Meyers. *Zechariah 9-14.* Anchor Bible, vol. 25C. New York: Doubleday, 1993.

Mikliszanski, J. K. "The Law of Retaliation and the Pentateuch." *Journal of Biblical Literature* 66 (1947) 295-303.

Milgrom, Jacob. *Leviticus 17-22.* Anchor Bible, vol. 3A. Garden City, NY: Doubleday, 2000.

———. *Leviticus 23-27.* Anchor Bible, vol. 3B. Garden City, NY: Doubleday, 2001.

———. "Lex Talionis and the Rabbis." *Bible Review* 12 (April 1996) 16-48.

———. *Numbers.* The JPS Torah Commentary. Philadelphia: The Jewish Publication Society, 1990.

———. *Studies in Levitical Terminology.* Berkeley, CA: University of California, 1970.

Milian, Madeline, and Jane N. Erin, eds. *Diversity and Visual Impairment: The Influence of Race, Gender, Religion, and Ethnicity on the Individual.* New York: American Foundation for the Blind Press, 2001.

Miller, Patrick D. "The Book of Jeremiah." *The New Interpreter's Bible,.* 6:555–926. Nashville, TN: Abingdon, 2001.

Miller, Stephen R. *Daniel.* New American Commentary, vol. 18. Nashville, TN: Broadman and Holman, 1994.

Mitchell, Hinkley G., John Merlin Powis Smith, and Julius A. Bewer. *A Critical and Exegetical Commentary on Haggai, Zechariah, Malachi, and Jonah.* International Critical Commentary. Edinburgh: T. & T. Clark, 1951.

Montgomery, James A. *A Critical and Exegetical Commentary on the Book of Daniel.* International Critical Commentary. Edinburgh: T. & T. Clark, 1950.

———. *A Critical and Exegetical Commentary on the Books of Kings.* International Critical Commentary. Edinburgh: T. & T. Clark, 1951.

Moore, George F. *A Critical and Exegetical Commentary on Judges.* International Critical Commentary. Edinburgh: T. & T. Clark, 1958.

Motyer, J. Alec. *Isaiah.* Tyndale Old Testament Commentaries. Downers Grove, IL: InterVarsity, 1999.

———. *The Prophecy of Isaiah.* Downers Grove, IL: InterVarsity, 1993.

Murphy, Roland E. *Ecclesiastes.* Word Biblical Commentary, vol. 23A. Dallas, TX: Word, 1992.

———. *Proverbs.* Word Biblical Commentary, vol. 22. Nashville, TN: Thomas Nelson, 1998.

Murphy, Roland E., and Elizabeth Huwiler. *Proverbs, Ecclesiastes, Song of Songs.* New International Biblical Commentary, vol. 1. Peabody, MA: Hendrickson, 1999.

Naude, Jackie A. "Ra'ah." *New International Dictionary of Old Testament Theology & Exegesis,* edited by Willem A. VanGemeren, 3:1007–15. Grand Rapids: Zondervan, 1997.

Nelson, Richard D. *Deuteronomy: A Commentary.* Old Testament Library. Louisville, KY: Westminster John Knox, 2002.

Newsom, Carol A. "The Book of Job." *The New Interpreter's Bible,* 4:319–637. Nashville, TN: Abingdon, 1996.

Nissinen, Martti. With contributions by C. L. Seow and Robert K. Ritner. *Prophets and Prophecy in the Ancient Near East: Writings from the Ancient World.* Atlanta: Society of Biblical Literature, 2003.

Nunn, John F. *Ancient Egyptian Medicine.* Norman, OK: University of Oklahoma, 1996.

O'Connor, Kathleen M. "The Book of Lamentations." *The New Interpreter's Bible,* 6:1013–72. Nashville, TN: Abingdon, 2001.

Ollenburger, Ben C. "The Book of Zechariah." *The New Interpreter's Bible,* 7:735–840. Nashville, TN: Abingdon, 1996.

Olson, Dennis T. "The Book of Judges." *The New Interpreter's Bible,* 2:723–888. Nashville, TN: Abingdon, 1994.

Olyan, Saul M. *Disability in the Hebrew Bible.* New York: Cambridge University, 2008.

Oswalt, John N. *Isaiah.* The NIV Application Commentary Series. Grand Rapids: Zondervan, 2003.

———. *The Book of Isaiah: Chapters 1–39*. New International Commentary on the Old Testament. Grand Rapids: Eerdmans, 1986.

———. *The Book of Isaiah: Chapters 40–66*. New International Commentary on the Old Testament. Grand Rapids: Eerdmans, 1998.

Pardee, Dennis. "Divination." In *Context of Scripture*, edited by William W. Hallo, 1:287–94. Leiden: Brill, 1997.

Patterson, Richard D. *Nahum, Habakkuk, Zephaniah*. Wycliffe Exegetical Commentary. Chicago: Moody, 1991.

Patterson, Richard D., and Hermann J. Austel. "1, 2 Kings." *The Expositor's Bible Commentary*, 4:3–300. Grand Rapids: Zondervan, 1988.

Paul, Shalom. *Studies in the Book of the Covenant in the Light of Cuneiform and Biblical Law*. Supplements to Vetus Testamentum, vol. 18. Leiden: Brill, 1970.

Petersen, David L. *Zechariah 9–14 and Malachi: A Commentary*. Old Testament Library. Louisville, KY: The Westminster/John Knox Press, 1995.

Pope, Marvin H. *Job*. Anchor Bible, vol. 15. Garden City, NY: Doubleday, 1965.

Powell, Marvin A., ed. *Labor in the Ancient Near East*. The American Oriental Series 68. New Haven, CT: The American Oriental Society, 1987.

Price, James D. "לפא (ōpel)." In *New International Dictionary of Old Testament Theology & Exegesis*, edited by Willem A. VanGemeren, 1:479–81. Grand Rapids: Zondervan, 1997.

———. "דשח." In *New International Dictionary of Old Testament Theology & Exegesis*, edited by Willem A. VanGemeren, 2:312. Grand Rapids: Zondervan, 1997.

Propp, William H. C. *Exodus 1–18*. Anchor Bible, vol. 2. Garden City, NY: Doubleday, 1999.

———. *Exodus 19–40*. Anchor Bible, vol. 2A. Garden City, NY: Doubleday, 2006.

Provan, Iain. *1 and 2 Kings*. New International Biblical Commentary, vol. 1. Peabody, MA: Hendrickson, 1995.

———. *Ecclesiastes, Song of Songs*. The NIV Application Commentary Series. Grand Rapids: Zondervan, 2001.

———. *Lamentations*. New Century Bible Commentary. Grand Rapids: Eerdmans, 1991.

"Proverbs 30:17. Mocketh at His Father." In *Seventh-day Adventist Bible Commentary*, edited by Francis D. Nichol, 3:1050. Washington, DC: Review and Herald, 1977.

Quinn-Miascall, Peter D. *Reading Isaiah*. Louisville, KY: Westminster John Knox, 2001.

Raphael, Rebecca. *Biblical Corpora: Representations of Disability in Hebrew Biblical Literature*. London: T. & T. Clark International, 2008.

Redditt, Paul L. *Daniel*. New Century Bible Commentary. Sheffield, UK: Sheffield Academic, 1999.

———. *Haggai, Zechariah, and Malachi*. New Century Bible Commentary. Grand Rapids: Eerdmans, 1995.

Reyburn, William D., and Euan McG Fry. *A Handbook on Genesis*. UBS Handbook Series. New York: United Bible Societies, 1997.

Reynolds, Thomas E. *Vulnerable Communion: A Theology of Disability and Hospitality*. Grand Rapids: Brazos, 2008.

Ringgren, Mitchel. "דשח, *hāšak*." In *Theological Dictionary of the Old Testament*, 5:245–59. Grand Rapids: Eerdmans, 1999.

Ritner, Robert K. "Coffin Text 157, 'Cultic Abomination of the Pig.'" In *Context of Scripture*, edited by William W. Hallo, 1:30–31. Leiden: Brill, 1997.

———. "Daily Ritual of the Temple of Amun-Re at Karnak." In *Context of Scripture*, edited by William W. Hallo, 1:55–57. Leiden: Brill, 1997.

———. "The Turin Judicial Papyrus (The Harem Conspiracy against Ramses III)." In *Context of Scripture*, edited by William W. Hallo, 3:27–30. Leiden: Brill, 1997.

Roberts, J. J. M. *Nahum, Habakkuk, and Zephaniah: A Commentary*. Old Testament Library. Louisville, KY: Westminster/John Knox, 1991.

Robertson, O. Palmer. *The Books of Nahum, Habakkuk, and Zephaniah*. New International Commentary on the Old Testament. Grand Rapids: Eerdmans, 1990.

Rodriguez, Angel M. "Inspiration and the Imprecatory Psalms." *Journal of the Adventist Theological Society* 5, no. 1 (1994) 40–67.

Rooker, Mark F. *Leviticus*. New American Commentary, vol. 3A. Nashville, TN: Broadman and Holman, 2000.

Ross, Allen P. "Proverbs." *The Expositor's Bible Commentary*, 5:883–1134. Grand Rapids: Zondervan, 1988.

Roth, Martha. *Law Collections from Mesopotamia and Asia Minor*. Atlanta: Scholars, 1995.

———. "The Laws of Eshnunna." In *Context of Scripture*, edited by William W. Hallo, 2:332–35. Leiden: Brill, 1997.

———. "The Laws of Hammurabi." In *Context of Scripture*, edited by William W. Hallo, 2:335–53. Leiden: Brill, 1997.

Rowley, H. H. *The Book of Job*. New Century Bible Commentary. Grand Rapids: Eerdmans, 1980.

———. *The Servant of the Lord and Other Essays on the Old Testament*. London: Lutterworth, 1952.

Ruconich, Sandra, and Katherine Standish Schneider. "Religions and Their Views of Blindness and Visual Impairment." In *Diversity and Visual Impairment: The Influence of Race, Gender, Religion, and Ethnicity on the Individual*, edited by Madeline Milian and Jane N. Erin, 193–222. New York: American Foundation for the Blind Press, 2001.

Rylaarsdam, J. Koert, and J. Edgar Part. "The Book of Exodus." *The Interpreter's Bible*, 1:832–1099. Nashville, TN: Abingdon, 1980.

Sailhamer, John H. "Genesis." *The Expositor's Bible Commentary*, 2:3–284. Grand Rapids: Regency Reference Library, 1990.

Saoggin, J. Alberto. *Judges: A Commentary*. Old Testament Library. Philadelphia: Westminster, 1981.

Sarna, Nahum. *Exodus*. The JPS Torah Commentary. Philadelphia: Jewish Publication Society, 1991.

———. *Genesis*. The JPS Torah Commentary, vol. 1. Philadelphia: Jewish Publication Society, 1989.

Schneider, Tammi J. *Judges*. Berit Olam, vol. 1. Collegeville, MN: Liturgical, 2000.

Schuller, Eileen M. "The Book of Malachi." *The New Interpreter's Bible*, 7:843–77. Nashville, TN: Abingdon, 1996.

Schunck, K. D. "Kāhâ." *Theological Dictionary of the Old Testament*, edited by G. Johannes Botterweck and Helmer Ringgren, 7:58–59. Grand Rapids: Eerdmans, 1999.

Scott, R. B. Y. *Proverbs, Ecclesiastes*. Anchor Bible, vol. 18. Garden City, NY: Doubleday, 1965.

Seitz, Christopher R. "The Book of Isaiah 40–66." *The New Interpreter's Bible*. Nashville, TN: Abingdon, 2001. 6:309–552.

Seow, C. L. *Ecclesiastes*. Anchor Bible, vol. 18C. New York: Doubleday, 1997.

Seow, Choon-leong. "The First and Second Books of Kings." *The New Interpreter's Bible*. Nashville, TN: Abingdon, 1999. 3:3–295.

The Shamash Religious Texts. Translated by Clifton Daggett Gray. Chicago: University of Chicago, 1901.

Sherwood, Stephen K. *Leviticus, Numbers, Deuteronomy*. Berit Olam. Collegeville, MN: Liturgical Press, 2002.

Shupak, Nili. "The Eloquent Peasant." In *Context of Scripture*, edited by William W. Hallo, 1:98–104. Leiden: Brill, 1997.

Simpson, Cuthbert A. "The Book of Genesis." *The Interpreter's Bible*. Nashville, TN: Abingdon, 1980. 1:39–829.

Sinor, Denis, ed. *American Oriental Society, Middle West Branch, Semi-Centennial Volume*. Bloomington, IN: Indiana University Press, 1969.

Smick, Elmer B. "Job." *The Expositor's Bible Commentary*. Grand Rapids: Zondervan, 1988. 4:843–1060.

Smith, Gary V. *Isaiah 1–39*. New American Commentary, vol. 15A. Nashville, TN: Broadman and Holman, 2007.

Smith, Henry Preserved. *A Critical and Exegetical Commentary on the Books of Samuel*. International Critical Commentary. Edinburgh: T. & T. Clark, 1951.

Smith, James E. *1 & 2 Samuel*. The College Press NIV Commentary. Joplin, MO: College, 2000.

Smith, John Merlin Powis, William Hayes Ward, and Julius A. Bewer. *A Critical and Exegetical Commentary on Micah, Zephaniah, Nahum, Habakkuk, Obadiah, and Joel*. International Critical Commentary, vol. 1. Edinburgh: T. & T. Clark, 1911.

Smith-Christopher, Daniel L. "The Book of Daniel." *The New Interpreter's Bible*. Nashville, TN: Abingdon, 1996. 7:19–152.

Sparks, Kenton L. *Ancient Texts for the Study of the Hebrew Bible*. Peabody, MA: Hendrickson, 2005.

Speiser, E. A. *Genesis*. Anchor Bible, vol. 1. Garden City, NY: Doubleday, 1982.

Sprinkle, Joe M. *The Book of the Covenant: A Literary Approach*. Journal for the Study of the Old Testament Supplement Series 174. Sheffield, England: Sheffield Academic Press, 1994.

Stendebach, F. J. "'Ayin." *Theological Dictionary of the Old Testament*. Edited by G. Johannes Botterweck and Helmer Ringgren. Grand Rapids: Eerdmans, 1999. 11:28–44.

Stern, Philip. "The 'Blind Servant' Imagery of Deutero-Isaiah and Its Implications." *Biblica* 75, Fasc. 2 (1994) 224–232.

Stetter, Cornelius. *The Secret Medicine of the Pharaohs*. Carol Stream, IL: Quintessence, 1993.

Stewart, David Tabb. "Deaf and Blind in Leviticus 19:14 and the Emergence of Disability Law." Unpublished paper presented to the Biblical Scholarship and Disabilities Group. Society of Biblical Literature, Philadelphia, PA, November 19, 2005.

Stol, Marten. "Blindness and Night-Blindness in Akkadian." *Journal of Near Eastern Studies* 45 (1986) 295–299.

Stuart, Douglas K. *Exodus*. New American Commentary, vol. 2. Nashville, TN: Broadman and Holman, 2006.

Szpakowska, Kasia. *Behind Closed Eyes*. Swansea, UK: Classical Press of Wales, 2003.

Tadmor, Hayim, and Miriam Tadmor, eds. *Eretz-Israel: Archaeological, Historical, and Geographical Studies*. 28 vols. Jerusalem: Israel Exploration Society, 2003.

Tate, Marvin E. *Psalms 51–100*. Word Biblical Commentary, vol. 20. Dallas, TX: Word, 1990.

Taylor, John B. *Ezekiel*. Tyndale Old Testament Commentaries. Downers Grove, IL: InterVarsity, 1969.

Taylor, Richard A., and E. Ray Clendenen. *Malachi*. New American Commentary, vol. 21A. Nashville, TN: Broadman and Holman, 2004.

Tesh, S. Edward, and Walter D. Zorn. *Psalms*. The College Press NIV Commentary, vol. 1. Joplin, MO: College, 1999.

Thompson, J. A. *Deuteronomy*. Tyndale Old Testament Commentaries. Downers Grove, IL: InterVarsity, 1974.

———. *The Book of Jeremiah*. New International Commentary on the Old Testament. Grand Rapids: Eerdmans, 1980.

Thompson, R. Campbell. "Assyrian Medical Texts." *Proceedings of the Royal Society of Medicine (Sect Hist Med)* 17 (1924) 1–34.

———. "Assyrian Medical Texts: II." *Proceedings of the Royal Society of Medicine (Sect Hist Med)* 19 (1926) 29–78.

Tigay, Jeffrey H. *Deuteronomy*. The JPS Torah Commentary. Philadelphia: The Jewish Publication Society, 1996.

Towner, W. Sibley. "The Book of Ecclesiastes." *The New Interpreter's Bible*, 5:267–360. Nashville, TN: Abingdon, 1997.

Toy, Crawford H. *A Critical and Exegetical Commentary on the Book of Proverbs*. International Critical Commentary. Edinburgh: T. & T. Clark, 1948.

Tsumura, David Toshio. *The First Book of Samuel*. New International Commentary on the Old Testament. Grand Rapids: Eerdmans, 2007.

Tucker, Gene M. "The Book of Isaiah, 1–39." *The New Interpreter's Bible*, 6:27–305. Nashville, TN: Abingdon, 2001.

VanGemeren, Willem A. "Psalms." *The Expositor's Bible Commentary*, 5:3–880. Grand Rapids: Zondervan, 1991.

Van Leeuwen, Raymond C. "The Book of Proverbs." *The New Interpreter's Bible*, 5:19–264. Nashville, TN: Abingdon, 1997.

Vanstiphout, H. L. J. "The Dialogue between a Supervisor and a Scribe." In *Context of Scripture*, edited by William W. Hallo, 1:590–92. Leiden: Brill, 1997.

Van Voss, M. S. H. G. Heerma, D. J. Hoens, et al., eds. *Ancient Egyptian Magical Texts*. Religious Text Translation Series, NISABA. Translated by J. F. Borghouts. Leiden: Brill, 1978.

Verhoef, Pieter A. *The Books of Haggai and Malachi*. New International Commentary on the Old Testament. Grand Rapids: Eerdmans, 1987.

Vetter, D. "Ra'ah." *Theological Lexicon of the Old Testament*, edited by Ernst Jenni and Claus Westermann, 3:1176–83. Peabody, MA: Hendrickson, 1997.

Von Rod, Gerhard. *Genesis: A Commentary*. Old Testament Library, vol. 1. Philadelphia: Westminster, 1972.

von Soden, W. "'Iwwēr." In *Theological Dictionary of the Old Testament*, edited by G. Johannes Botterweck and Helmer Ringgren, 10:575. Grand Rapids: Eerdmans, 1999.

Wächter, L. "'Iwwēr: Etymology." In *Theological Dictionary of the Old Testament*, edited by G. Johannes Botterweck and Helmer Ringgren, 10:575. Grand Rapids: Eerdmans, 1999.

Walker, Larry Lee., Jr. "Zephania." *The Expositor's Bible Commentary*, 7:537–65. Grand Rapids: Zondervan, 1988.

Waltke, Bruce K. *The Book of Proverbs Chapters 15–31*. New International Commentary on the Old Testament. Grand Rapids: Eerdmans, 2005.

Watts, John D. W. *Isaiah 1–33*. Word Biblical Commentary, vol. 24. Waco, TX: Word, 1985.

———. *Isaiah 34–66*. Word Biblical Commentary, vol. 25. Waco, TX: Word, 1987.

Weinfeld, Moshe. *Deuteronomy and the Deuteronomic School*. New York: Oxford University, 1972.

———. *Deuteronomy 1–11*. Anchor Bible, vol. 5. New York: Doubleday, 1991.

Weiser, Artur. *The Psalms: A Commentary*. Old Testament Library. Philadelphia: Westminster, 1962.

Wenham, Gordon J. *The Book of Leviticus*. New International Commentary on the Old Testament. Grand Rapids: Eerdmans, 1979.

———. *Genesis 1–15*. Word Biblical Commentary, vol. 1. Waco, TX: Word, 1987.

———. *Genesis 16–50*. Word Biblical Commentary, vol. 2. Dallas, TX: Word, 1994.

———. *Numbers*. Tyndale Old Testament Commentaries. Downers Grove, IL: InterVarsity, 1981.

Westbrook, Raymond, ed. *A History of Ancient Near Eastern Law*. Handbook of Oriental Studies, Section 1, The Near and Middle East, vol. 72, no. 1. Leiden: Brill, 2003.

———. "Lex Talionis and Ex 21:22–25." *Revue Biblique* 93 (1986) 52–69.

———. "Mesopotamia: Old Babylonian Period." In *A History of Ancient Near Eastern Law*, edited by Raymond Westbrook, Handbook of Oriental Studies, Section 1, The Near and Middle East, vol. 72, no. 1, 1:377. Leiden: Brill, 2003.

Westermann, Claus. *Isaiah 40–66: A Commentary*. Old Testament Library. Philadelphia: Westminster, 1969.

Wevers, John W. *Ezekiel*. New Century Bible Commentary. Grand Rapids: Eerdmans, 1982.

Whybray, R. N. *Ecclesiastes*. New Century Bible Commentary. Grand Rapids: Eerdmans, 1989.

———. *Isaiah 40–66*. New Century Bible Commentary. London: Oliphants, 1975.

———. *Proverbs*. New Century Bible Commentary. Grand Rapids: Eerdmans, 1994.

Willis, Tim. *Jeremiah-Lamentations*. The College Press NIV Commentary. Joplin, MO: College, 2002.

Wilson, Gerald H. *Job*. New International Biblical Commentary, vol. 1. Peabody, MA: Hendrickson, 2007.

Wilson, Gerald H. *Psalms*. The NIV Application Commentary Series, vol. 1. Grand Rapids: Zondervan, 2002.

Wiseman, Donald J. *1 and 2 Kings*. Tyndale Old Testament Commentaries. Downers Grove, IL: InterVarsity, 1993.

———. *The Vassal-Treaties of Esarhaddon*. London: British School of Archaeology in Iraq, 1958.

Wolf, Herbert. "Judges." *The Expositor's Bible Commentary*, 3:375–506. Grand Rapids: Zondervan, 1992.

Woods, Clyde M., and Justin M. Rogers. *Leviticus-Numbers*. The College Press NIV Commentary. Joplin, MO: College, 2006.
Wright, Christopher, J. H. *Deuteronomy*. New International Biblical Commentary, vol. 4. Peabody, MA: Hendrickson, 1996.
Wright, J. Stafford. "Ecclesiastes." *The Expositor's Bible Commentary*, 5:1137–97. Grand Rapids: Zondervan, 1988.
Wyatt, Nicolas. *Religious Texts from Ugarit: The Words of Ilimiilku and His Colleagues*. Sheffield, UK: Sheffield Academic, 1998.
Wynn, Kerry H. "The Normate Hermeneutic and Interpretations of Disability within the Yahwistic Narratives." In *This Abled Body: Rethinking Disabilities in Biblical Studies*, edited by Hector Avalos, Sarah J. Melcher, and Jeremy Schipper, 91–101. Atlanta: Society of Biblical Literature, 2007.
Yadin, Yigael. *The Art of Warfare in Biblical Lands: In Light of Archaeological Study*. 2 vols. New York: McGraw-Hill, 1963.
Yener, K. Aslihan, and Harry A. Hoffner Jr., eds. *Recent Developments in Hittite Archaeology and History*. Winona Lake, IN: Eisenbrauns, 2002.
Yong, Amos. *Theology and Down Syndrome*. Waco, TX: Baylor University, 2007.
Youngblood, Ronald F. "1, 2 Samuel." *The Expositor's Bible Commentary*, 3:553–1104. Grand Rapids: Zondervan, 1992.
———. *The Book of Isaiah*. Grand Rapids: Baker, 1993.
Younger, K. Lawson, Jr. *Judges and Ruth*. The NIV Application Commentary Series. Grand Rapids: Zondervan, 2002.
———. "Saba'a Stela." In *Context of Scripture*, edited by William W. Hallo, 2:274–75. Leiden: Brill, 1997.
Zimmerli, Walther. *Ezekiel 1*. Hermeneia—A Critical and Historical Commentary on the Bible. Minneapolis: Augsburg Fortress, 1979.
Zorn, Walter D. *Psalms*. The College Press NIV Commentary, vol. 2. Joplin, MO: College, 2004.

www.ingramcontent.com/pod-product-compliance
Lightning Source LLC
Chambersburg PA
CBHW071236230426
43668CB00011B/1456